THE RISE OF
POLITICAL
ANTI-SEMITISM
IN GERMANY
& AUSTRIA

Peter Pulzer

Revised Edition

Harvard University Press
Cambridge, Massachusetts
1988

LIBRARY OF CONGRESS
Library of Congress Cataloging-in-Publication Data

Pulzer, Peter G. J.
    The rise of political anti-semitism in Germany and Austria/
P. G. J. Pulzer, —Rev. ed.
        p.   cm.
    Bibliography: p.
    Includes index.
    ISBN 0-674-77166-4 (alk. paper)
    1. Antisemitism—Germany. 2.   Antisemitism—Austria. 3. Germany—
Politics and government—1871–1933. 4. Germany—Ethnic relations.
5. Austria—Politics and government—1867–1918. 6. Austria—Ethnic
relations.   I.   Title.
DS146.G4P8 1988
323.1´1924´043—dc19   88-15062
                                                              CIP

REFERENCES

Full bibliographical details are given the first time any book is mentioned. An abbreviated title is given at the first reference to a book in any one chapter. The following abbreviations are used:

ADB	*Alldeutsche Blätter*
ATZ	*Akademische Turnzeitung*
AZJ	*Allgemeine Zeitung des Judentums*
AZ	*Arbeiter-Zeitung*
DVB	*Deutsches Volksblatt*
DW	*Deutsche Worte*
DZ	*Deutsche Zeitung*
JCEA	*Journal of Central European Affairs*
KZ	*Kreuzzeitung*
MDS	*Mitteilungen des deutschen Schulvereins*
MIU	*Monatsschrift der Österreichisch-Israelitischen Union*
MVA	*Mitteilungen aus dem Verein zur Abwehr des Antisemitismus*
NDAZ	*Norddeutsche Allgemeine Zeitung*
NFP	*Neue Freie Presse*
NG	*Nachlass Gross*
NP	*Nachlass Pichl*
ODR	*Ostdeutsche Rundschau*
ÖSA	*Österreichisches Haus, Hof-, und Staatsarchiv*
ÖStH	*Österreichisches Statistisches Handbuch*
ÖV	*Österreichischer Volksfreund*
ÖVA	*Österreichisches Verwaltungsarchiv*
ÖW	*Österreichische Wochenschrift*
PAR	*Politisch-Anthropologische Revue*
StBR	*Stenographische Berichte des Reichstages*
StPA	*Stenographische Protokolle über die Sitzungen des Hauses der Abgeordneten des österreichischen Reichsrates*
StPrA	*Stenographische Berichte des Preussichen Abgeordnetenhauses*
UDW	*Unverfälscht Deutsche Worte*
ZDSJ	*Zeitschrift für Demographie und Statistik des Judentums*

CONTENTS

List of Illustrations

PREFACE

~~1988~~
1964

I have tried to show in this book that modern political anti-Semitism is different from any earlier, sporadic outbreaks of Jew-baiting. It was brought about by conditions which had not existed before the last third of the nineteenth century; only then was it possible to organize political movements wholly or partly on the basis of anti-Semitism, and to make anti-Semitism part of a coherent set of ideas. Indeed, the word anti-Semitism itself— with its attempt to draw on the support of science—made its first appearance in 1879.

To achieve this, I have used two approaches. In the first place I have traced its theoretical and doctrinal background in the second half of the nineteenth century, especially in Germany and German Austria. In choosing my illustrative examples I have necessarily had to be selective: if I have devoted more space to Dühring or Langbehn than to Hegel or Schopenhauer, this is not because I consider them better or more important thinkers, but simply because they had a more immediately measurable impact on anti-Semitic politics. In addition, where an illustration from the experience of some other country has seemed apposite, I have not hesitated to use it.

Second I have tried to trace the impact of anti-Semitic ideas on the everyday politics of the two Empires. Viewed from 1914 this history must seem dismal and unimportant, certainly less noteworthy than that of Russia or France. If the anti-Semitism of those years had been nothing more than the last convulsions of an ancient prejudice—as Marxist critics interpreted it—my research might have been at best of mild antiquarian interest. Viewed from the present day, this choice of countries needs no defence, for we know that within a decade of 1914 these mildewed controversies were resurrected as the prophecies of a new civilization. The period of 1867–1914 becomes important

ix

because during it the movements and ideologies developed which matured after 1918. Side by side with the lack of outward success we must observe the extent to which anti-Semitism penetrated the general stock of political thinking and undermined the acceptance of the liberal values of the nineteenth century. The Age of Reason laid many old ghosts, the twentieth-century Age of Unreason has conjured many new ones. The period of our studies is that of hibernation and underground survival. For this reason I have added an Epilogue showing the course of this revival, and how dependent it was on developments before the First World War. For the same reason I have deliberately not attempted to write a general history of anti-Semitism, or of such special topics as the Ritual Murder Controversy, the Protocols of the Elders of Zion, or the Dreyfus Case, which—fascinating stories on their own merits—have been written about elsewhere.

I have had access to the papers of Eduard Pichl in the *Verwaltungsarchiv* of Vienna, containing a mass of letters, posters, manifestoes, minutes, and clippings which relate not only to Schönerer (whose friend Pichl was) but to the Austrian anti-Semitic movement in general. I have also seen the papers of the Austrian Liberal leaders, Ignaz Plener and Gustav Grosz, in the *Haus- Hof- und Staatsarchiv* of Vienna. Where I have had to rely on secondary sources, this is indicated. All translations are my own, unless otherwise indicated.

I have been helped by the only other works which, to my knowledge, refer directly to my subject: Paul Massing's *Rehearsal for Destruction*, published in America in 1949; Dr. Kurt Wawrzinek's paper in *Historische Studien* (1927), a scholarly and detailed chronology of the first phase of German anti-Semitism; Dr. Martin Broszat's unpublished Cologne dissertation *Die antisemitische Bewegung im wilhelminischen Deutschland*; and Dr. Eva Richmann's stimulating attempt to analyze in general terms the failure of the "German-Jewish symbiosis," *Hostages of Civilization*, published in 1950. I am also most grateful to Professor G. L. Mosse, of the University of Wisconsin, for permission to read the manuscript of his paper, *The German Right and the Jewish Question, 1918–1933*. All these works have been helpful to me. They refer to Germany only, however; no comparable books exist on Austria. For this reason the Austrian chapters go into rather more detail than the German ones, while the German chapters concentrate on filling the gaps left by existing literature, which lie mainly after 1890.

When I began my study almost no serious work existed on the intellectual and cultural roots of modern German anti-Semitism, but in the meantime a number of good studies have appeared, notably Fritz Stern's *The Politics of Cultural Despair* and Professor Rotenstreich's *The Recurring Pattern*.

The origin of this book is in a Ph.D. thesis which I wrote under the supervision of Professor Hugh Seton-Watson while I was a research student at King's College, Cambridge, and which was accepted by the University of Cambridge in 1960. I wish to record my thanks to the successive Provosts and Fellows of King's College, Cambridge, for enabling me to undertake most of the research necessary for this book. Inevitably I owe a great debt to the staff and resources of the Wiener Library, London, as well as of the Viennese Archives and the *Hauptarchiv* in Berlin. I should also record my debt to the many friends, too numerous to list, who have read some or all of the manuscript (but cannot, of course, be held responsible for any errors or misjudgments which remain) and who have given me advice or encouragement at various states of writing.

I acknowledge with gratitude permission from the following publishers to quote their books: Tavistock Publications (London) to quote from *Working-Class Anti-Semite* by J. H. Robb; Columbia University Press (New York) to quote from *Pietism as a Factor in German Nationalism* by K. S. Pinson; Harper & Row, Inc. (New York) to quote from *Rehearsal from Destruction* by P. Massing and *Dynamics of Prejudice* by B. Bettelheim and M. Janowitz; George Allen & Unwin Ltd. (London) and Harcourt, Brace & World, Inc. (New York) to quote from *The Origins of Totalitarianism* by Hannah Arendt; and the Macmillan Company (New York) to quote from *The Idea of Nationalism* by H. Kohn.

PETER G. J. PULZER

Oxford, June, 1964

INTRODUCTION
TO REVISED EDITION
1988

When this book first appeared in 1964 it was something of a pioneering work and suffered from some of the defects of that genre. It was not, of course, the first historical work on German anti-Semitism and my research would have been much more difficult without that of my predecessors, such as Kurt Wawrzinek, Paul Massing and Eva Reichmann.[1] It was an attempt both to show the interconnection between the relevant ideologies and organizations in Imperial Germany and the Austro-Hungarian Empire and to discuss the question of continuity between the Imperial epoch and the rise of National Socialism after 1918.

It appeared near the beginning of a deluge of works, both monographic and synoptic, that re-assessed the path of modern German history and, in particular, the role of the *Kaiserreich* in determining its direction. In this respect the names of Fritz Fischer, Helmut Böhme, Hans-Ulrich Wehler and John Roehl[2] particularly spring to mind, though this selective list scarcely does justice to the scale of what has been achieved. In addition a vast amount of work has been done on German-Jewish social history, the legal and political status of German Jews and the anti-Semitic movements themselves, both pre- and post-1918. The names of Jacob Toury, Jacob Katz, Uriel Tal, Avraham Barkai and Shulamit Volkov in Israel, Reinhard Rürup, Hermann Greive and Werner Jochmann in Germany, Werner Mosse and Arnold Paucker in Britain, and Ismar Schorsch, Ernest Hamburger and Marjorie Lamberti in America[3]—to cite yet another incomplete list—illustrate the variety and scope of this research. On Austria the volume of research is rather smaller, though here, too, the advances have been notable. Nothing illustrates this growth of interest better than the proliferation of institutes devoted to the study of one aspect or another anti-Semitism, racialism or the modern Jewish experience. Some of these, like the Wiener Library in London (and now Tel-Aviv), are old-established and the earlier books, including mine, could not have been written without them. Others, like Yad Vashem in Jerusalem, are primarily interested in documenting the Holocaust, but this cannot be done to the exclusion of pre-1933 anti-Semitism. But even more significant is the creation of institutes and teaching and research posts dealing directly with the problem of anti-Semitism. Of these the most notable is the *Zentrum für Antisemitismusforschung* at the Technical University of Berlin, founded in 1982.[4] Special sessions devoted to aspects of Jewish-Gentile relations have become normal at meetings of the American Historical Association or at West German *Historikertage*; the subject, it could be argued, has entered the mainstream of historical enquiry.

In view of that the question therefore naturally arises how much of the argument in my book still stands up after the passage of twenty-four years, and how much of what I wrote then I should now want to modify. Two assumptions must underlie any serious book on this subject. The first is that political anti-Semitism before 1918 arose in the context and the conditions of that period; its causes should therefore not be analysed with ahistorical or anachronistic references to later events. The years 1867 to 1918 form a period in its own right that deserves to be studied on its own terms. The second is that it is idle to pretend that we should be as interested as we are in the anti-Semitism of the Imperial era if it had not been for Hitler, the Third Reich and the Holocaust. An essential part of our knowledge of that era is what came afterwards.

Hence I would defend myself against the mild and courteous reproof in Richard Levy's excellent history of anti-Semitic parties for biasing my book towards the "forerunners of Nazism" rather than the main-stream anti-Semites who can scarcely be lumped together as proto-Nazis.[5] There is much to be said for Professor Levy's division of the anti-Semitic movement into "parliamentary" and "revolutionary" wings,[6] rather than into the Christian–conservative and racialist as I do, though there is no doubt room for both and the two cleavages overlap to a considerable degree. Nor would I dispute that in the *Kaiserreich* the parliamentary wing—that is, those anti-Semites who aimed, by forming parties and fighting elections, to bring in discriminatory legislation—outnumbered those who despaired of constructing their racial utopia through the existing institutions. I would claim, however, that the parliamentarians, for reasons of personal inadequacy and political failure, left less of an imprint on German politics, and are therefore, in a historically valid sense, less important. The anti-Semitism that mattered in the German Empire and the Weimar Republic was not that of a handful of parliamentary demagogues, nor even of vandalism, physical violence and terrorism, but the pervasive non-acceptance, within significant sectors of German society, of the Jew as a truly equal fellow-citizen.[7] The evidence for that assertion has to be retrospective. It consists of the relative smoothness with which Jews were eased out of one profession or economic sector after another after 1933, the lack of protest against the principle of discrimination, as opposed to specific instances of it. All this suggests that there had always been a widespread right-wing anti-Semitic consensus that would enable much of German society to adapt painlessly to "a system of 'post-liberal' *apartheid*."[8]

In this context it is impossible to escape the issue of "continuity" in German history. Much of the recent interest in Imperial Germany stems from the realization that the rise of Nazism cannot be explained solely in terms of the Crash of 1929, the defects of the Weimar Republic and the resentments evoked by the Paris Peace Settlement. Instead, it sought the causes of Weimar failure in the structural faults of the pre-1914 system; extreme versions of this thesis talked of a German *Sonderweg* (special path) and *Fehlentwicklung* (faulty development).[9] In so far as one of my theses is that "the period of 1867–1914 becomes important because during it the movements and ideologies developed which matured after 1918" and that the revival of anti-Semitism in the 1920's "was dependent on developments before the First World War" (p. ix–x), I must count myself a member of that school, at any rate of its non-extreme tendency.

It has always seemed evident to me that a force as elemental as National Socialism, with anti-Semitism as an essential, though not its sole, ingredient must have deep roots in the political culture in which it flourished. That is not, of course, the same as saying that all German history is the history of the origins of the Third Reich: this particular nail was hit on the head by Francis Carsten when he said

> I do not believe that National Socialism was an "accident" in the course of German history, or a "strange aberration"... The roots of National Socialism reach far back into the nineteenth century, but not into the dim Germanic or mediaeval past.[10]

One's interim conclusion, then, is that there could have been no Third Reich without the pre-1918 Empire and no "final solution" without the anti-Semitism of that epoch; but equally that the anti-Semitism of the Empire did not lead inexorably to the Holocaust. It was a necessary condition for it, but not a sufficient one. *NB*

The most recent research into the Empire has, indeed, tended to emphasise the distinctions between the pre- and post-World War I years and to analyse the evolving political forms of the later Empire with fewer value judgments about the "failure" to develop in a liberal–parliamentary direction. A number of relevant points emerge from such interpretations. The first is that though much of the ideological agenda that constituted the Nazis' appeal had been formulated by 1914, the majority of even the most extreme anti-Semites and racialists of the period were still restrained by the morality of traditional Western civilization, whether Christian or secular. Some of the survivors of that period did embrace Nazism, such as Theedor Fritsch, compiler of the best-selling *Handbuch der Judenfrage*, and Heinrich Class, president of the Pan-German League,[11] though the Nazis did not thank him. But equally characteristic were figures like Houston Stewart Chamberlain, author of the influential *The Foundations of the Nineteenth Century*, of whom his widow claimed that he would not have approved of the *Kristallnacht*.[12] What repelled many of the older *völklisch* propagandists about the Nazis was their limitless vulgarity and their violence: they roused the masses, they fought parliamentary elections and were therefore, however paradoxically, tainted with democracy. I therefore feel little need to modify my question-and-answer in the Epilogue "What, then, was special about the Nazis? To put it bluntly, they had the courage of their convictions" (p. 315) or the assertion that ideologically "the arsenal was fully assembled by 1918. It was merely a question of waiting for the order to fire" (p. 292). Courage is perhaps an awkward word, since it commonly suggests virtue. What did characterize the Nazis at all stages was the willingness, indeed eagerness, to drive to new extremes the abuse, vandalism and physical violence of their anti-Semitic predecessors and contemporaries. Two factors contributed more than any others to the change. The first was the polarizing and disintegrative effect on German society of defeat and attempted social revolution. The second was the presence of a major political figure whose guiding principle was racial manichaenism. But for Hitler, German history would have been different, before as well as after 1933. But to attribute the century's cataclysm to one man is to over-simplify. There is no audience without a prior willingness to listen.

A second point is that during the Wilhelmine period the essentially paternalist tone of German politics, the domination of at any rate liberal and conservative politics by local notables, gave way to a more autonomous and insubordinate style of participation, especially among the peasant and lower middle-class population. On the Left this was characterized by the growth of the Social Democratic Party, on the Right by a whole clutch of agrarian, artisan, nationalist and imperialist pressure groups, founded in the 1890's and gradually expanding up to the outbreak of the First World War. In some instances the leadership remained in the hands of older elites, e.g. in the aristocratic domination of the Agrarian League, but in all instances the effect was potentially subversive: it amounted to a greater insistence by hitherto subordinate groups on the right to influence policy-making. This process has been graphically illuminated by Geoff Eley and David Blackbourn for Germany and, with all due regard for the different environment, by John Boyer and Gavin Lewis for Austria.[13]

Their findings are of considerable relevance to the historian of modern anti-Semitism. The question has often arisen whether anti-Semitism, nationalism, imperialism or xenophobia owe their strength to deliberate manipulation by politicians of the *status quo*, who seek by these means to export domestic conflicts or divert demands harmful to their interests; or whether, on the contrary, such movements are themselves the spontaneous expression of discontent and have to be considered as authentic, autonomous popular phenomena. The "social imperialism" school, which favors the first interpretation, has been influential in the past ten or fifteen years, as the works of Wehler, Berghahn and indeed the whole Fischer school demonstrate.[14]

They have been countered by a number of more recent monographs, such as those of Eley and Blackbourn, emphasizing the relative immunity from manipulation of the various German popular movements and showing that these had a will and interests of their own. The work of Boyer and Lewis show the same for Austria, though here the popular character of anti-Semitism has in any case been generally accepted by historians. I find myself more convinced by the "autonomy" than the "manipulation" explanation, my own researches having led me to the conclusion that

> Anti-Semitism was a "spontaneous" product, arising out of a particular situation, not a creed foisted on a public from above by an unscrupulous ruling class (p. 321)

This does not mean that there were no manipulators, merely that they do not account for the appeal of what Eley has called the "anti-democratic, populist offensive organized around a radical–nationalist counter-utopia."[15]

The emphasis of this discussion has so far been on Germany and in particular on Germany before 1918. In this it simply reflects the weight of scholarly research. But there has also been a revival, if on a more modest scale, of interest in Austrian and, in particular, Viennese Jewry, of which the journal *Studia Judaica Austriaca* is the most prominent symptom. The current fascination with the culture of *fin-de-siècle* Vienna does not deal primarily with politics in general or anti-Semitism in particular. But it has replaced a largely anecdotal and impressionistic view of the role of Jews in modern culture and the rise of the bourgeoisie with a much more meticulously documented one[16]. In doing so it has not conclusively accounted for anti-Semitism, or the particularly vigorous popular form it took in Vienna, whether in 1895 or 1938, but has given a much clearer account of the conditions that made it possible. The identification of German and Austrian Jews with liberalism, as the protector not only of their social and economic but of their political interests, made both them and it more vulnerable. The much greater prominence, both absolute and relative, of Jews among the intellectual, professional, commercial and industrial middle-class of German-speaking Austria added to the tensions between the various social and linguistic groups in which Jews were clearly associated with one side. Here, even more than in Germany, anti-Semitism, though exploited by opportunists and demagogues, was the product of genuine conflicts of interest. To say that is not to excuse or justify. It is simply to recognize that anti-Semitism is a phenomenon to be explained, not explained away. This point is particularly pressed by Ivar Oxaal in his excellent article, where he argues that I should have made more of it, at least in the Austrian context.[17]

Lest this defense of my original arguments should seem too complacent in the light of so much scholarly addition to my subject, let me suggest five topics on which I should present my conclusions with somewhat different emphases if I were writing the book now.

1. The first concerns the contrast between the predominantly conservative anti-Semitism of the Stöcker phase (1877–90) and the predominantly radical anti-Semitism of the Böckel-Ahlwardt phase (1890 onwards). While I emphasise the novel character of the Böckel-Ahlwardt agitation (pp. 102–9) and would not wish to lose sight of the continuing influence of conservative anti-Semites, as defined by Professor Levy, I should now want to lay greater stress on the general change in the political style of Imperial Germany as the 1890's progressed. I might not wish to go as far as one recent historian in talking of "a re-definition of the political nation" in this period[18]; it nevertheless seems more evident to me now than in 1964 that the new anti-Semites were part of a wider radicalization of politics that included the aristocratically-led Agrarian League, the middle-class nationalist lobbies and the growth of Jewish activism in response to the anti-Semitic assault through such bodies as the *Centralverein deutscher Staatsbürger jüdischen Glaubens* and the *Verband der deutschen Juden*. The research on Jewish activism has also thrown new light on the varieties of anti-Semitism in Germany, in particular in sections of the Imperial and state administrations.[19]

2. Given these new findings, and given that the proclaimed objective of all anti-Semites was to reverse the legal emancipation of the Jews, as enshrined in the Law of 3 July 1869, I should

now wish to move the whole question of Jewish legal rights, and of Jewish access to the public service and to political careers much further into the center of the stage, rather than to relegate it to the status of background information, as in Chapter I. My reasons for this are the following. In the first place the 1869 law did not settle the question of the legal rights of Jews. The constitutions of many of the states of the Empire continued to discriminate aginst them; for instance, Article 14 of the Prussian constitution, in force until 1918, declared state schools to be Christian institutions. Secondly, the battle for securing the emancipation of Jews had been long drawn-out and bitter. It is therefore difficult to dissent from Reinhard Rürup's contention that "the process of emancipation, lasting for the best part of a century, militated by its very duration against a satisfactory solution of the 'Jewish Question'."[20] Indeed I would go further and argue not, as Rürup does, that the rise of anti-Semitism revived a Jewish Question quiescent in the Liberal epoch, but that the permanent prominence of the Jewish Question facilitated the revival of anti-Jewish feelings once the economic down-turn had begun.[21] Thirdly, governments widely evaded the obligation to treat Jews as equal citizens, as the endemic debates about appointments to the officer corps, the judiciary and university posts showed. The same applied to the increasing difficulties Jews experienced in entering politics, except under the aegis of the Social Democratic Party. These topics have indeed been the main objects of my most recent research.[22]

3. The points raised under the last two headings lead to one of the central questions in the elucidation of political anti-Semitism. It is widely assumed in the literature, and was widely assumed at the time, that the principal impetus towards anti-Semitism came from those who were—or thought they were— the victims of the rapid economic transformations of the late nineteenth century. That much of the anti-Semitism of this period was indeed anti-modernist in its inspiration, seeing its target not merely in capitalism and urbanization but in the intellectual and cultural trends of the day is undeniable and well-documented. A number of important books that have come out since mine amplify this convincingly, in particular those of Hans-Jürgen Puhle, Robert Gellately and Shulamit Volkov.[23]

However, for a number of reasons it will not do simply to

equate the surges and decline of anti-Semitism with the cycles of economic activity, even though they coincide closely; nor to assert, without further argument, that anti-Semitism was merely an epiphenomenon of economic depression, as does Hans Rosenberg in his influential essay.[24] One reason is that this argument does not explain why the Jew should have been such an attractive target for venting the discontents and frustrations of the economically threatened. Part of the answer must be the very contentiousness of the Jews' recent emancipation, as argued above, another part the strength of religious belief, with all its anti-Jewish implications, in a population still at an early stage of urbanization.

In any case, as the period progressed anti-Semitism did not necessarily or even predominantly come from these declining strata. I would argue that in the two decades before the outbreak of the World War the most aggressive and strident anti-Semitism came from ultra-nationalist and ultra-imperialist groups, preaching racially-based integral nationalism and a Social Darwinist view of the world. The proponents of such views in Austria–Hungary—the followers of Schönerer and the readers of Guido von List and Jörg Lanz von Liebenfels—in many ways qualify as a threatened social group, if only by virtue of being a German minority in a multi-national empire. But this cannot be said of the businessmen, professional men and intellectuals who supported the Pan-German League, the Navy League and the more extreme student fraternities or youth and gymnastic organizations, or such fads and fancies as social anthropology.

Many of them were prosperous and successful and, if socially mobile, then in an upward direction. Indeed, for this very reason many of these extreme nationalists favored such modernizing reforms as the furthering of technical education and the inheritance tax schemes of Chancellor Bülow—proposals that were anathema to the agrarian-based Right—precisely because they regarded them as essential to the success of an expansionist foreign policy. For the same reason the bigger nationalist leagues were not explicitly anti-Semitic before 1918, even while containing within their ranks some of the most rabid racialists (cf. Heinrich Class' position in the Pan-German League). Such men saw the Jew as a scapegoat not for the bankruptcy of the village cobbler but for the imperfections in the German national spirit and Germany's under-achievement on the world stage.

I devote considerable space to these bodies in my book (ch. 23 to 26) and emphasize that "nationalism had, by the beginning of the twentieth century, become the main driving force behind anti-Semitism" (p. 221). Nationalism was not a homogeneous force and also played a part in peasant-artisan anti-modernism, but I should now want to <u>place greater emphasis than before on</u> the contrast between the anti-Semitism of those who were, in <u>effect, a disappointed second generation of the National Liber</u>al <u>bourgeoisie and the more tradition-bound opponents of a secu</u>lar liberal society.

The considerations lead to the two final points, the attitudes towards anti-Semitism on the part of political Catholicism and Social Democracy respectively.

4. In dealing with the religious roots of anti-Semitism I drew a distinction between the attitudes of Austrian and German popular Catholicism (pp. 266–70), at any rate once the *Kulturkampf* had subsided. There is much validity in this: above all the *Zentrum*—at least in the Reichstag and in Prussia, less so in Bavaria—consistently opposed any discriminatory legislation. For instance, *Zentrum* politicians were always ready to oppose anti-Semitically inspired attacks on ritual slaughter. After 1918, as the *Zentrum* became more committed to the defense of parliamentary democracy, some of its members were prominent in the *Verein zur Abwehr des Antisemitismus*.[25] Nevertheless relations between the Jewish and Catholic communities in Germany were never easy. The latent anti-clericalism of many Jews, their instinctive liberalism, their identification with urban, commercial and secular interests contrasted with the predominantly rural, provincial, defensive and protectionist mental universe of the Catholics. This contrast grew rather than diminished as the Church and the *Zentrum* lost their grip on those who migrated to the towns and the *Zentrum* became more than ever dependent on a peasant-artisan electoral base and an alliance with the Conservatives. In local agitation and in the Catholic press, including the leading newspapers, *Germania* and *Kölnische Volkszeitung*, an anti-Jewish undertone was rarely absent. I should therefore be inclined to agree with David Blackbourn's judgment that is the *Zentrum* "anti-Semitism did not appear as a set of formal demands and policies, but its assumptions had been

tacitly incorporated in to the party's policies."[26]

Religious roots were not only Catholic; indeed in Germany active and aggressive anti-Semitism was commoner among Protestants. However, it is worth asking whether the fairly clear-cut distinction between Christian-conservative and *völkisch-racialist* anti-Semitic propaganda tells us much about the relative appeals of these two messages. I am more strongly convinced than I was when I wrote the book that a tradition of religiously-inspired Jew-hatred—or at least of unfavorable stereotyping—was a necessary condition for the success of anti-Semitic propaganda, even when expressed in non-religious terms and absorbed by those no longer religiously observant. That, at any rate, is persuasively argued by Hermann Greive, whose recent book is one of the most important contributions to the debate.[27]

5. The German and Austrian Social Democratic labor movements also consistently opposed any proposals smacking of discrimination and frequently denounced anti-Semitism as an atavistic barbarity. In so far as middle-class Jews in both Empires were beginning to vote Social Democrat by 1914 it was primarily on the grounds of the party's stand against anti-Semitism. The situation was not, however, quite straightforward. There was a tendency, which I deal with in chapter 27, to regard anti-Semitic agitation as quite useful in so far as it exposed "capitalist corruption", and a temptation to regard organs specifically devoted to fighting anti-Semitism, such as the *Verein zur Abwehr des Antisemitismus* and the liberal press of Berlin and Vienna, as being apologists for capitalism. The more popular forms of Social Democratic propaganda, especially the humorous papers such as *Der Wahre Jakob* quite often made use of Jewish stereotypes. Such barbs were generally fairly mild, but their frequency must have done something to neutralize the effect of the party' s official anti-anti-Semitic stand.[28]

The prominence of Jewish intellectuals in the labor movement also caused considerable tensions. These intellectuals rarely took up Jewish grievances, so they did not affect the party's response to the anti-Semitic movement. But their sometimes patronizing attitudes towards humbler party officials and their identification with heteredox ideological positions (e.g. Rosa Luxemburg and Rudolf Hilferding among the Radicals) earned them resentments that were on occasion expressed in anti-Semitic terms.[29] Moreover the dogmatic insistence of almost all Social Democrats that the Jews were not a nation and that the Jewish Question was a symptom of backward political conditions which would be solved when Socialism made total assimilation possible and inevitable, contributed little to the easing of group relations in the everyday politics of pre-1914 or inter-war Central Europe.[30]

If, given all the above *caveats*, I still think a reprint of my book worthwhile it is because I am convinced that its main arguments have stood the test of time and that some of them have been reinforced by the research of others. Though the Liberal parties, and individual Liberals, in Central Europe often wavered in their resistance to anti-Semitism, the fate of Jews was tied to the fortunes of Liberalism. There were, as I suggest, many reasons for the weakness of Liberalism in Central Europe, but one of them was the close association of a *parvenu* Jewish middle class with it. The less developed an indigenous liberal bourgeoisie was, the more it depended on exogenous entrepreneurs for the impetus to capitalist transformation. In Germany these were disproportionately Jews, in Austria predominantly, in Hungary overwhelmingly so. The more exposed the position of Jews in the industrial, commercial and professional middle class, the more dependent they were on political Liberalism. The more Liberalism was identified in the popular mind with Jews, the less successful its general appeal: "a study of the theoretical content of anti-Semitism will show us that it represents in the first place a reaction against this ideology. It flourished when it did because to many people Liberalism seemed undesirable and harmful" (p. 29). This weakness in the forces of Liberalism made it very much easier for National Socialism to triumph, and the immunization of large sectors of the population to racial tolerance made it easier for them to support, or at least not oppose, the racialist propaganda and actions of the Nazis.[31] The Imperial epoch is not, in some mechanistic way, the prelude to the Third Reich, but an understanding of it is essential to understanding what followed. In so far as I have tried to contribute to this understanding, I hope my book will continue to be useful to scholars and students.

Introduction

REFERENCES

1 Kurt Wawrzinek, *Die Entstehung der deutschen Antisemitenparteien*. (*Historische Studien* 168. Berlin, 1927); Paul W. Massing, *Rehearsal for Destruction: A Study of Political Anti-Semitism in Imperial Germany* (New York, 1949); Eva G. Reichmann, *Hostages of Civilisation: The Social Sources of National Socialist Anti-Semitism* (London, 1949).

2 Fritz Fischer, *Griff nach der Weltmacht: Die Kriegszielpolitik des Kaiserlichen Deutschland 1914–1918* (Düsseldorf, 1961) (*Germany's Aims in the First World War*, 1967); ibid., *Krieg der Illusionen: Die deutsche Politik von 1911 bis 1914* (Düsseldorf, 1969) (*War of Illusions*, 1975); Helmut Böhme, *Deutschlands Weg zur Grossmacht: Studien zum Verhältnis von Wirtschaft und Staat während der Reichsgründungszeit 1848–1881*, Cologne, 1966; Hans-Ulrich Wehler, *Bismarck und der Imperialismus* (Cologne, 1969) and his popular text-book, *Das deutsche Kaiserreich 1871–1918* (Göttingen, 1973), (*The German Empire*, Leamington Spa, 1985); John C. Roehl, *Germany Without Bismarck: The Crisis of Government in the Second Reich, 1890–1900* (London, 1967).

3 Jacob Toury, *Soziale und politische Geschichte der Juden in Deutschland 1847–1871: Zwischen Revolution, Reaktion und Emanzipation* (Düsseldorf, 1977); Jacob Katz, *Out of the Ghetto: The Social Background of Jewish Emancipation, 1770 to 1870* (Cambridge, Mass., 1973); Uriel Tal, *Christians and Jews in Germany Religion, Politics and Ideology in the Second Reich, 1870–1914* (Ithaca, 1975); Avraham Barkai, "The German Jews at the Start of Industrialisation—Structural Change and Mobility, 1835–1860" in: Werner E. Mosse et al., *Revolution and Evolution. 1848 in Jewish History* (Tübingen, 1981); Shulamit Volkov, *The Rise of Popular Antimodernism in Germany. The Urban Master Artisans, 1873–1896* (Princeton, 1978); Reinhard Rürup, *Emanzipation und Antisemitismus: Studien zur "Judenfrage" in der bürgerlichen Gesellschaft* (Göttingen, 1975); Hermann Greive, *Geschichte des modernen Antisemitismus in Deutschland* (Darmstadt, 1983); Werner Jochmann, Werner Mosse and Arnold Paucker, contributions to symposia of the Leo Baeck Institute, detailed in the Bibliographical Note; Ismar Schorsch, *Jewish Reactions to German Anti-Semitism, 1870–1914* (New York, 1972); Ernest Hamburger, *Juden im öffentlichen Leben Deutschlands. Regierungsmitglieder, Beamte und Parlamentarier in der monarchischen Zeit, 1848–1918* (Tübingen, 1968); Marjorie Lamberti, *Jewish Activism in Imperial Germany. The Struggle for Civil Equality* (New Haven, 1978).

4 See Reinhard Rürup, "Emanzipationsgeschichte und Antisemitismusforschung. Zur Überwindung antisemitischer Vorurteile" in Rainer Erb and Michael Schmidt (eds.) *Antisemitismus und Jüdische Geschichte. Studien zu Ehren von Herbert A. Strauss* (Berlin, 1987).

5 Richard S. Levy, *The Downfall of the Anti-Semitic Political Parties in Imperial Germany* (New Haven, 1975), p. 2.

6 *Op. cit.*, p. 32 and *passim*.

7 See the contributions of Peter Pulzer, Werner E. Mosse and Reinhard Rürup in Arnold Paucker (ed.) *The Jews in Nazi Germany, 1933–1945* (Tübingen, 1986), esp. pp. 24, 49–50, 100–1; Shulamit Volkov, "Kontinuität und Diskontinuität in deutschen Antisemitismus, 1878–

1948," *Vierteljahrshefte für Zeitgeschichte* 33 (1985).

8 The phrase is Werner E. Mosse's in Paucker, *op. cit.*, p. 52.

9 For a sophisticated, influential version of this thesis, see Ralf Dahrendorf's *Democracy and Society in Germany* (London, 1967). It pervades most of the works cited in note 2.

10 F. L. Carsten, "The Historical Roots of National Socialism" in E. J. Feuchtwanger (ed.), *Upheaval and Continuity. A Century of German History* (London, 1973), p. 131.

11 See below, p. 51.

12 Geoffrey C. Field, *Evangelist of Race: The Germanic Vision of Houston Stewart Chamberlain* (New York, 1981), p. 12.

13 Geoff Eley, *Reshaping the German Right. Radical Nationalism and Political Change after Bismarck* (New Haven, 1980); David Blackbourn, *Class, Religion and Local Politics in Wilhelmine Germany. The Centre Party in Württemberg before 1914* (New Haven, 1980); John Boyer, *Political Radicalism in Late Imperial Vienna. Origins of the Christian Social Movement, 1848–1897* (Chicago, 1981); Gavin Lewis, *Kirche und Partei im politischen Katholizismus. Klerus und Christlichsoziale in Niederösterreich* (Salzburg, 1977).

14 Volker R. Berghahn, *Der Tirpitz-Plan. Genesis und Verfall einer innerpolitischen Krisenstrategie unter Wilhelm II.*

15 Eley, *op. cit.*, p. 358.

16 See the works listed in para.9 of the Bibliography.

17 Ivar Oxaal, "The Jews of Young Hitler's Vienna" in Ivar Oxaal, Michael Pollak and Gerhard Botz (eds.) *Jews, Antisemitism and Culture in Vienna* (London, 1987), p. 33.

18 Blackbourn, *op. cit.*, p. 10.

19 See the works of Lamberti and Paucker, cited in note 3; also Evyatar Friesel, "The Political and Ideological Development of the Centralverein", *Year Book XXIX of the Leo Baeck Institute* (London, 1986) and Part I of Jack Wertheimer, *Unwelcome Strangers. East European Jews in Imperial Germany* (New York, 1987).

20 Reinhard Rürup, "Kontinuität und Diskontinuität der 'Judenfrage' im 19. Jahrhundert. Zur Entstehung des modernen Antisemitismus", in Hans-Ulrich Wehler (ed.) *Sozialgeschichte Heute. Festschrift für Hans Rosenberg zum 70. Geburtstag* (Göttingen, 1974), p. 398.

21 *Ibid.*, p. 403; Peter Pulzer, "Why was there a Jewish Question in Imperial Germany?", *Year Book XXV of the Leo Baeck Institute* (London, 1980), p. 139.

22 See note 16 above and Peter Pulzer, "Die jüdische Beteiligung an der Politik", in Werner Mosse and Arnold Paucker (eds.) *Juden im Wilhelminischen Deutschland 1890–1914* (Tübingen, 1976), pp. 143–239; *ibid.*, "Religion and Judicial Appointments in Imperial Germany" *Year Book XXVIII of the Leo Baeck Institute* (London, 1983); see also Norbert Kampe, "Jüdische Professoren im Deutschen Kaiserreich" in Erb & Schmidt, *op. cit.* (note 4) and the pioneering works of Ernest Hamburger (note 3) and Jakob Toury, *Die politischen Orientierungen der Juden in Deutschland* (Tübingen, 1966).

23 Hans-Jürgen Puhle, *Agrarische Interessenpolitik und preussischer Konservatismus im Wilhelminischen Reich, 1893–1914* (2nd edn., Bonn, 1975); Robert

Gellately, *The Politics of Economic Despair. Shopkeepers and German Politics 1890–1914* (London, 1974); for Shulamit Volkov, see note 3 above.

24 Hans Rosenberg, *Grosse Depression und Bismarckzeit. Wirtschaftsablauf, Gesellschaft und Politik in Mitteleuropa* (Berlin, 1967), pp. 88–117.

25 Barbara Suchy, "The Verein zur Abwehr des Antisemitismus (II)—From the First World War to Its Dissolution in 1933", *Year Book XXX of The Leo Baeck Institute* (London, 1985), pp. 90–1.

26 David Blackbourn, "Roman Catholics, Anti-Semitism and the Centre Party in Imperial Germany" in Paul Kennedy and Anthony Nicholls (eds.), *Nationalist and Racialist Movements in Imperial Germany Before 1914* (London, 1981), p. 123.

27 Greive, *op. cit.* See note 3.

28 See the documentation in Rosemarie Leuschen-Seppel, *Sozialdemokratie und Antisemitismus im Kaiserreich. Die Auseinandersetzung der Partei mit den Konservativen und völkischen Strömungen des Antisemitismus 1871–1914*, (Bonn, 1978).

29 The most complete recent discussion of this topic is by Robert S. Wistrich, *Socialism and the Jews. The Dilemmas of Assimilation in Germany and Austria–Hungary* (London, 1982).

30 See Donald L. Niewyk's sensitive and balanced *Socialist, Anti-Semite and Jew. German Social Democracy Confronts the Problem of Anti-Semitism, 1918–1933* (Baton Rouge, 1971).

31 Peter Merkl's analysis of the autobiographical essays of Nazi veterans show that those with the strongest anti-Semitic views had grown up in an ultra-nationalist home environment before 1914. *Political Violence under the Swastika. 581 Early Nazis* (Princeton, 1975), pp. 447–457.

THE JEWS AND THEIR ENVIRONMENT

I

The Jews

A study of anti-Semitism must be preceded by a study, however brief, of those whom it intended as its victims. The Jews, it is frequently alleged, predominate in certain trades and professions, have a predilection for intermediary and nonproductive occupations, and, in artistic life, have a genius that is interpretative and critical rather than creative. It is said that they dominate politics, the press, finance; that they like to rule, influence, exploit, to earn their bread by the sweat of other men's brows.

We cannot understand the reasons for the peculiar position which Jews occupy in the social structure of most countries, or why this maldistribution reached such extreme forms in Germany and Austria, in contrast with Great Britain or the United States, without glancing at the social history of the Jews since the destruction of Jerusalem. In its outline it is well known. As a dispersed nation acting as an international commercial class, the Jews are in the same category as the Syrians in the Roman Empire, the Chinese in Southeast Asia, the Indians in East and South Africa, or the Armenians in the Ottoman Empire. But they were, in addition, peculiar in being the only tolerated religious minority in medieval Europe; they were useful to princes, lay and ecclesiastical, in an age which forbade usury to Christians; they were not allowed to own land and were excluded from the practice of guild crafts. Thus, throughout the period when Europe was predominantly agricultural, they were an almost exclusively town people, and those of them who lived in villages plied urban trades.

The Jews establish themselves as an exclusively commercial class only when they enter a country less developed economically than they are themselves. When they crossed the Alps and the Rhine into Germany, they came into territory much more

3

backward than the Mediterranean. Later, during the fourteenth and fifteenth centuries the kings of Poland invited them in order to supply their kingdom with a middle class. Similarly in nineteenth-century Hungary, where a rigid social structure prevented peasants and craftsmen from expanding in business and forbade aristocrats to soil themselves with money, Jews, experienced in seizing opportunities not already monopolized by Gentiles, inevitably rushed into the vacuum. They did the same, though to a lesser extent, in Germany and Austria.

No doubt, too, their natural concentration in commerce and towns sharpened those intellectual accomplishments which are generally said to accompany urban existence—greater perspicacity, the elaboration of theoretical thought, an inclination to radicalism—and sharpened also their alleged revulsion from agricultural work. A drift from country to town is observable at many periods of history; the opposite is rarer. Even highly organized "back to the land" movements in recent decades have met with little success. It is ironical, in fact, that one of the most spectacular voluntary enterprises of land reclamation in this century took place in Israel.

Jewish aversion to manual work was probably no greater than among the rest of mankind, but pressure to take it up could not always be resisted. Especially in the "Russian Pale"* Jews were too numerous and their freedom of movement too restricted to enable all of them to subsist in nonproductive occupations. They were forced to turn to handicraft and, later, industrial labor. Emaciated by having for generations lived in towns, they took, in the main, to industries and manufactures which required skill and concentration, in particular tailoring, rather than energy. According to the Russian census of 1897, more Jews than non-Jews in the Pale were engaged in the clothing industry, which occupied 16.5% of all gainfully employed Jews.[1] Factory work was also inescapable for Jews who migrated from backward into highly developed countries, and most of the Jews who left Russia and Poland for the United States or Great Britain became wage earners.

---

* Those regions of the Russian Empire, comprising in the main Lithuania, Poland, White Russia, and the Western Ukraine, to which Jews were by law restricted.

4

Thus, for different reasons, absorption into the industrial proletariat became inescapable in both Russia and America; in Central Europe, and particularly in Germany and German Austria, Jews succeeded in staving off this fate. Their main motive was fear of becoming submerged in a mass-organized Gentile world. Often independence brought no economic benefit; shirt making or umbrella mending in a slum attic meant a low income and long hours, but it enabled the Jew to observe his religious festivals and dietary practices in peace, and to perpetuate voluntarily his own little ghetto.

It was the same tradition of being one's own master that led so many Jews into the liberal professions. The religious factor is less directly at work here, because most educated Jews broke with orthodoxy, but the long tradition of "being independent," ultimately traceable to religious causes, combined with the difficulties of entering the public service, were jointly responsible.*

It is in the light of this exceptional Jewish concentration in the bourgeoisie of Germany and Austria that we must study the link between the fate of the Jews and that of Liberalism. They contributed to its establishment, benefited from its institutions, and were under fire when it was attacked. It was not merely from legal emancipation that Jews hoped to gain. Their political ambitions went beyond the satisfaction of their own particular grievances and became those of the bourgeoisie in general: the abrogation of aristocratic privileges, the sweeping away of particularism, the repeal of paternalistic commercial legislation, and a unified legal system. Thus Gentiles could see their interests served by supporting Jewish emancipation.

To trace the extent of Jewish participation in public life is more difficult than might at first seem. The only official statistics are religious, yet there was, in addition to those who continued officially to acknowledge Judaism, a growing number who went over to Christianity for reasons of varying validity and a growing number of children of mixed marriages. In absolute numbers these did not amount to much, before 1914 at any rate.

* Schmerling, the Austrian Liberal leader, favored opening the Civil Service to Jews in 1861, since "it would be desirable to make other careers than commerce and journalism available to educated Jews" (Franz, *Liberalismus*, p. 196).

Ruppin's statement that "in Central Europe one Jew in 800 leaves the community every year"[2] relates to the post-war period. Between 1890 and 1914 the annual average of baptisms in Hungary was about 300; in Vienna the annual number of resignations from the Jewish community averaged about 500, or just over 3%—an exceptionally high percentage.[3] In Bohemia, Rauchberg estimates that "there can hardly have been more than 1000 resignations" between 1890 and 1900, out of a population of nearly 100,000.[4] Most German Jews who embraced Christianity became Protestants; between 1889 and 1910 there were 12,375 such conversions.[5]

Are such persons still to be considered "Jews"? Much ink has been spilt on this question to which, in the last analysis, no satisfactory answer can be given. But to the man in the street they remained part of that fearsome and mysterious entity, "the Jews"; and if a Jewish or semi-Jewish family environment is considered to exert as strong an influence on character and outlook as any comparable environment, we must certainly include them in the Jewish category. Both Marx and Disraeli were baptized in infancy, yet most anti-Semites would claim them as Jews. So would most Jews.

If it is difficult to establish the total number of "Jews," it is still more difficult to achieve certainty in individual cases. Statements by anti-Semitic authors, the most numerous source, are notoriously unreliable. Houston Stewart Chamberlain calls Karl Kautsky "that highly gifted Jew."[6] Kautsky not only appears on posters depicting Jewish left-wing rogues[7] but is assumed to be Jewish by several scholars who are certainly not anti-Semitic.[8] At one time or another some anti-Semitic author has labeled as racially undesirable anyone whom he happens to disapprove of—Dr. Adenauer,[9] Lord Beaverbrook,"[10] Napoleon,[11] Pius IX,[12] Goethe,[13] Bismarck,[14] Jack the Ripper,[15] Gavrilo Princip,[16] Picasso,* and, most common of all, some rival anti-Semite with whom he has just quarreled.

Even more embarrassing could be the belated discovery of Jewish blood in some dignitary of an anti-Semitic body, as

---

* Picasso's paintings express "the Levantine race-soul" (Günther, *Rassenkunde des judischen Volkes*, p. 311).

happened in the cases of Anna Gierke* and Colonel Düsterberg who, as one of the leaders of the *Stahlhelm* and a German National candidate in the 1932 presidential election, turned out to have had a Jewish grandfather.

However, a brief attempt to sketch the role of the Jews in Germany and Austria during the nineteenth century must be made.

Final emancipation in both empires dates from 1867. Jews had already enjoyed a brief period of equality in 1848, and the repeal of their civic rights which followed the collapse of the revolution could last only as long as the general reaction.

Jews were prominent in the revolution of 1848 from the beginning. Two of them were among the insurgents killed in Vienna on March 13;[17] in Berlin, out of 230 casualties, twenty were Jewish.[18] In both cities the victims of all faiths were buried in common graves. Altogether five Jews were members of the Frankfurt Parliament—including Gabriel Riesser, the vice-president—which in the *Grundrechte* proclaimed complete civil equality and freedom of conscience and association.[19] Within a year all German states except Bavaria had granted legal equality. Five Jews also sat in the Prussian National Assembly, and they were represented in at least seven of the smaller states.[20] In Vienna Adolf Fischhof was elected president of the Security Committee after the flight of the Emperor (May 17). After the capture of the city by Windischgratz many Jews were among the revolutionary leaders put on trial. Two journalists, Hermann Jellinek and Alfred Becher,[21] were executed; a third succeeded in escaping to America. Fischhof was imprisoned.

The revocation of the Austrian constitution in 1851 made it possible to re-impose many of the old restrictions. In Prussia emancipation was not rescinded but widely evaded by administrative means; all branches of the public service were virtually closed to Jews. The events of 1866 and 1867, which helped Liberalism into power in both countries, renewed the mutually beneficial alliance between Liberals and Jews.

The Jews could be counted on for loyalty to the new idea of

* She was the daughter of Otto Gierke who had married a Jewess. She was elected as a German National deputy in 1919 but not readopted in 1920 as a candidate.

7

the German Empire. As members of the commercial classes they had everything to gain from national unity and the sweeping away of internal legal and economic barriers. Similarly in Austria the Jews associated themselves culturally with the German community of which the Liberals were mainly representative. They sympathized with the Liberals' anti-clericalism and naturally wished for the repeal of the 1855 Concordat which had given the Church considerable privileges in matters of education, matrimony and property, as well as granting the Papacy the right to influence the status of other religious denominations.

So emancipation was but one of the spate of liberalizing measures passed by the Parliament of the North German Confederation, the Reichstag of the Second Empire, and the Reichsrat of the Cisleithan Monarchy.* The North German Parliament declared in 1867 that

> rights of residence, settlement, vocational pursuit or acquisition of property [were not to be refused] on grounds of religious belief or lack of local citizenship.[22]

Although the constitutional propriety of forcing the hand of the individual states was doubtful, they adjusted their legal codes in accordance with this resolution. Emancipation became law in Prussia on July 3, 1869. It was extended to Bavaria when the three southern states joined the North German Confederation. (The other two had anticipated the action of the Confederation in this matter: Baden in 1862, Württemberg in 1864.)

Notwithstanding the prominence which individual Jews had succeeded in gaining in trade, finance, politics, and literature during the earlier decades of the century, it is from this brief Liberal summer of the 'sixties and 'seventies that we must date their rise to the astonishing part they played in public life until the coming of Hitler.

In Germany, at least, this rise was not due to numerical increase.[23] In 1871 the Jews of the German Empire numbered 512,000 (or 1.25% of the population) ; in 1910 they numbered 615,000 (or 0.95%). Outside Berlin and Hamburg they were concentrated in the East, in the provinces bordering Poland

* The frontier between the two halves of the empire ran along the River Leitha; the Hungarian part was therefore known as the transleithan, the other as the cisleithan.

The Jews

(Poznania, Silesia, West Prussia), and in the Southwest, along the Rhine–Main artery (Baden, Alsace, Palatinate, Hesse, Franconia). But for immigration the Jewish community would have declined even more markedly compared with the rapidly increasing population of Germany, for the Jewish birth-rate was perceptibly lower.*

TABLE I. JEWISH AND TOTAL BIRTH RATES IN GERMANY, 1875–1910[24]

| Years (mean) | Births per 1000 of Population | |
	Total	Jews Only
1875–1880	41	32
1885–1890	39	25
1895–1900	36	22
1905–1910	33	17

More interesting and more significant, however, than these vital statistics is the evidence of internal migration by Jews, in particular the trek to the capitals. In 1816 42% of the Prussian Jews lived in Poznania and 2.7% in Berlin; in 1910, 6.4% lived in Poznania and 21.6% in Berlin.[25] In 1816 Berlin was third in size among Prussian Jewish communities, after Breslau and Poznán. In part, the rush to Berlin coincided with the general swelling of the capital, but the Jewish contribution was relatively much larger.

The figures were even more striking for Austria. Except for a small number of "tolerated" wealthy Jews—who in 1847 numbered 197 families[27]—access to Vienna was barred altogether. After that, fed first from the Czech lands and then from the inexhaustible reservoir of Galicia, the Jewish community grew to one of the world's most important.

* For example, of the 2531 Jews living in Leipzig in 1875, only 527 (or 20.2%) were natives of the city; 237 were immigrants from Russia, 241 from Galicia, and 92 from Bohemia (Andree, *Zur Volkskunde der Juden*, Bielefeld, 1881, p. 260). By 1910, 78,700 (or 12.8%) of the Jews living in Germany were first-generation East Europeans; 21,7000 of them were resident in Greater Berlin (Adler-Rudel, *Ostjuden in Deutschland*, Tübingen, 1959, p. 164).
† Figure for 1860.

9

TABLE 2. GROWTH OF JEWISH POPULATION OF BERLIN[26]

Year	Total Population	Jews	Jews as Percentage of Total Population
1816	197,717	3,373	1.7
1849	412,154	9,595	2.3
1867	702,437	27,602	3.9
1880	1,122,330	53,949	4.8
1895	1,677,304	86,152	5.1
1910	2,071,257	90,013	4.4
1910 (Greater Berlin)	3,734,258	144,007	3.6

TABLE 3. GROWTH OF JEWISH POPULATION OF VIENNA[28]

Year	Total Population	Jews	Jews as Percentage of Total Population
1857	476,220	6,217*	1.3
1869	607,510	40,227	6.1
1890	817,300	99,444	12.0
1890 (enlarged)	1,341,190	118,495	8.7
1910	2,031,420	175,294	8.6

In Budapest, which in the nineteenth century grew faster than any other European capital, the Jews in 1910 numbered 203,687 or nearly one-quarter of the population.[29] So prominent was the Jewish element in the Hungarian capital that it was colloquially known as "Judapest."

This mass migration helps to explain why Jews were held to be so influential; and since the anti-Semitic movement in both empires began in the capitals one can perhaps understand why the earliest publicists were haunted by the vision of Jewish inundation. Thus Otto Böckel could, in 1886, harrow his Berlin audience with the thought that if the Jews were to continue to increase at the same rate, there would be 923,000 of them in Berlin by 1980, and Cologne would show 1,200,000 compared with 700,000 Germans.[30]

* Figure for 1860.

Of Jewish predominance in finance much has been written and little need be added here. Since the eighteenth century the dynasty of Rothschild had risen to a pre-eminent place in four countries; of the two leading banking houses of Berlin, Bleichröder and the *Disconto-Gesellschaft* of Hansemann, the first was Jewish. In Vienna all the major houses were Jewish except that of the Greek Sina.[31] Beside them were the numerous smaller bankers and brokers of Berlin, Frankfurt, Hamburg, and Vienna. A newer development, for the moneyed Jew was after all a familiar phenomenon, was the crowding of the liberal professions by Jews, especially in the capitals.

The first of these professions to attract Jews was medicine, which at one time was the only one open to them. The next profession to attract them was journalism, and finally the law and academic callings. What was particularly interesting was that the intelligentsia, which was ultimately the most hated section of the secularized Jewish bourgeoisie, was overwhelmingly recruited from those who had succeeded in business. This applied *a fortiori* to the great banking dynasties. In our day the Rothschilds, the Warburgs, the Sassoons, and the Cassirers are more famous for the books they write than the money they make. This recruitment of the intellectual professions from the sons of businessmen is not an exclusively Jewish phenomenon; it is common enough among Gentiles. In part it is a question of absorbing the surplus intelligence produced by the commercial classes; in part a question of social status. The businessman is never quite sure of being accepted, the professional man is safe from the suspicion of being a parvenu or a climber. We may spurn the millionaire for having once been a ragpicker, even while we drink his martinis. No one spurns the surgeon for being the son of a ragpicker. Thus stepping up socially might seem preferable, even at the expense of stepping down economically.

I do not suggest that this is the whole explanation for the Jewish quest of the intellectual; it is undoubtedly a trait which Jews betray more markedly than the average person, and one for the satisfaction of which a poor Jew will be prepared to make greater sacrifices than a non-Jew.

There is no doubt that Jews were "over-represented" (if one accepts such a concept) in the educated classes and the professions.

The figures of children attending the grammar schools (*gymnasia*) of Berlin in 1887 were:[32]

	Boys	Girls
Protestants	6904	3446
Catholics	278	63
Jews	1898	1693
Others	26	12

For every 100,000 males of each denomination in Prussia, there studied at Prussian universities (as an average for the period 1887–1897) 33 Catholics, 58 Protestants, and 519 Jews.[33] Part of the explanation may be that the Jewish community as a whole was more prosperous than either of the other two;[34] but that is unlikely to be the whole explanation.

In the major Austrian universities, Jews were even more generously represented.

TABLE 4. PERCENTAGE OF JEWS AMONG STUDENTS IN AUSTRIA, 1890

Universities[35]	
Vienna	33.6%
Prague (German section)	31.6
Czernowitz	22.3
Technical Universities[36]	
Vienna	23.7%
Prague (German section)	21.0
Brno	16.0

As early as 1880, of the students in the medical faculty in Vienna 38.6% were Jews, in the legal faculty 23.3%.[37]

The farther East we go, the more strikingly do we find that the bourgeois is also a Jew. In Bukovina, in the period before 1914, Jews owned the three biggest breweries, all six oil refineries, 28 out of 34 major sawmills, and all the hotels in Czernowitz. The glazing and plumbing trades were Jewish monopolies.[38] In 1914, 86% of practicing lawyers were Jews.[39]

In Hungary figures for 1920 show that while 0.1% of the agricultural laborers, 0.4% of the dwarf-holders, and 7.3% of the industrial workers were Jewish, they constituted 23% of the actors and musicians, 34% of the authors, 51% of the lawyers, 60% of the doctors in private practice, and the overwhelming majority of the self-employed in commerce and finance (but not manufacturing industry) .[40] Figures for the post-1918 Polish Republic tell the same tale.[41]

There was no profession which was more completely dominated by Jews than journalism. Most of the leading organs of opinion, the *National-Zeitung* of Berlin, the *Frankfurter Zeitung,* the *Neue Freie Presse* of Vienna, were owned and edited by Jews. The same applied to the independent weeklies such as Karl Kraus' *Die Fackel* and Maxilian Harden's *Zukunft.* Of the twenty-one dailies published in Berlin during the 1870's, thirteen were owned by Jews, four had important Jewish contributors, and only four had no connection with Jews. In the three humorous papers—*Ulk, Kladderadatsch,* and *Berliner Wespe*—Jews had a monopoly on political satire.[42] It can be said that only in the specifically clerical or conservative press were no Jews to be found. The "Liberal" press, which grew up with industry and parliamentarism and flourished by advertising and sensational reporting, owed its origins almost entirely to Jews.

But the economic and political influence of the Jews during these decades paled beside their complete domination of Viennese cultural life in the generation before 1914. It is not merely that the Jews provided the patronage, the audience, and by press criticism the canons of taste, they provided also the creators: Arthur Schnitzler, Stefan Zweig, Franz Werfel. Gustav Mahler was appointed Director of the Opera in 1898, which made him musical dictator of the city. Lewinsky and Sonnenthal scintillated on the boards of the *Burgtheater.* Heinrich Friedjung was the doyen of historians. Beside them were others, like Sigmund Freud and Arnold Schönberg, whose genius was not established beyond controversy. "In the invigorating air of this remarkable cosmopolis," says Julius Braunthal in his autobiography,[43] "Jewish talent blossomed as vigorously as it did in Granada under Moslem rule." This was the nursery of anti-Semitism.

Yet there was another side to the medal. Because most of the people in certain wealthy and influential classes were Jews, it did not follow that most Jews were either wealthy or influential. Only 10 to 15% of the Austrian Jews lived in Vienna; the great bulk led an indescribably miserable existence in Galicia and Bukovina. It is estimated that toward the end of the century some 5000 to 6000 died of starvation annually.[44] And as the number of Galician Jews increased in Vienna, the Jewish *haute bourgeoisie* became less and less representative of Viennese Jewry as a whole, while the peddler, the old-clothes dealer, and the *Lumpenproletarier,* scraping an irregular existence on the periphery of the economic system, became typical. Ironically, though it was against the Jewish capitalist that anti-Semitism was ostensibly aimed, the banker, the stockbroker, and the financier got away lightly. Lueger, the anti-Semitic Lord Mayor of Vienna, did not scruple to dine in their mansions.

In any case, how important was Jewish concentration in particular occupations or cities? Are we not, in our search for exact statistics, taking the anti-Semitic case too much at its own valuation? The number of Jewish cornbrokers is no doubt fascinating to the student of sociology, but does it illuminate the causes of anti-Semitism? Are these statistics, which are the stock-in-trade of standard anti-Semitic literature, anything more than rationalizations by and for the already converted? Rather is it not true that the anti-Semitic image of the Jew bears little relation to the objective Jew; that the Jew of the anti-Semites is simply a handy target for fears, hatreds, and prejudices the origins of which must be sought within the anti-Semites themselves; and that he is a "scapegoat" for disasters which cry out for simple explanations?

To argue thus is to underrate the complexities of political paranoia. Most political plot-mongering, whether directed against Jews or Freemasons, Jesuits or Trotskyites, commits the error of attributing to a single cause events or developments which have many interacting causes, and to the voluntary, coordinated initiative of a few evil men events or developments which result from technical change or widely and honestly held convictions. But the plot-monger's explanations would not be nearly so persuasive if they did not bear some relation to ascertainable fact and to a hard core of genuine evidence. The charges against the chosen villain may be embellished by the most lurid fantasy, vast invalid conclusions may be drawn from trivial or isolated facts—but if there were *no* Jewish international bankers, if the Masons were *not* a secret society, if there had been *no*

Communist sympathizers in the United States Foreign Service, the myths about them would lose their point. The "big lie," that propaganda technique about which Hitler was so disarmingly frank, would have the most minimal appeal if it were pure invention, if it were a fabrication from beginning to end. To succeed it needs to be a half-truth, difficult to refute without elaborate logical arguments and a vast apparatus of evidence.

Statistics about the Jewish social structure show how heavily Jews were involved in occupations which were in any case objects of suspicion and distrust; they show whether Jews were powerful competitors in certain overcrowded or influential professions. This exposed situation of the Jewish community in Germany and Austria, and its political and social vulnerability, will be better understood if we take a closer look at the structure of these two states.

REFERENCES

1 235,993 as against 222,764: K. Kautsky, *Rasse und Judentum* (2nd ed., Stuttgart, 1921), p. 77.
2 A. Ruppin, *Die Soziologie der Juden* (Berlin, 1930), Vol. I, p. 312.
3 *Ibid.*, Vol. I, p. 306.
4 H. Rauchenberg, *Der nationale Besitzstand in Böhmen* (Leipzig, 1905), Vol. I, p. 382.
5 Ruppin, *op. cit.*, Vol. I, p. 299.
6 H. S. Chamberlain, *The Foundations of the Nineteenth Century* (London, 1912), Vol. II, p. 361.
7 E. Fuchs, *Die Juden in der Karikatur* (Munich, 1921), p. 285.
8 For example, A. Leschnitzer, *The Magic Background of Modern Anti-Semitism* (New York, 1956), p. 67. A. G. Whiteside, *Austrian National Socialism before 1918* (The Hague, 1962), p. 19.
9 J. von Leers, *Juden sehen dich an* (Berlin, 1933), p. 10.
10 T. Fritsch, *Handbuch der Judenfrage* (37th ed., Leipzig, 1934), p. 287.
11 H. Scharff von Scharffenstein, *Das geheime Treiben, der Einfluss und die Macht des Judentums in Frankreich seit hundert Jahren, 1771–1871* (Stuttgart, 1872), pp. 12–13.
12 *Ibid.*, p. 100; also C. Paasch, *Eine deutsch-jüdische Gesandtschaft und ihre Helfer* (Leipzig, 1981), Vol. III, p. 116.
13 Quoted by O. Jöhlinger, *Bismarck und die Juden* (Berlin, 1921), p. 118.
14 Paasch, *op. cit.*, Vol. III, p.130
15 Quoted by *MVA*, Oct. 27, 1894, p. 336, and July 4, 1896, p. 215.
16 E. Ludendorff, *Wie der Weltkrieg 1914 "gemacht" wurde* (Munich, 1935), p. 29.
17 H. Tietze, *Die Juden Wiens. Geschichte, Wirtschaft, Kultur* (Leipzig–Vienna, 1933), p. 184. The two victims were Karl Heinrich Spitzer, a technical

student, and Bernard Herschmann, a weaver's mate.

18 S. M. Dubnow, *Die neueste Geschichte des jüdischen Volkes* (Berlin, 1920–23), Vol. II, p. 309.

19 A. Kober, "Jews in the Revolution of 1848 in Germany," *Jewish Social Studies*, Vol. X, No. 2 (1948), pp. 142–3.

20 *Ibid.*, pp. 144–7.

21 Dubnow, *op. cit.*, Vol. II, p. 357; K. F. Eder, *Der Liberalismus in Alt-Österreich, Geisteshaltung, Politik und Kultur* (Munich, 1955), p. 115.

22 Dubnow, *op. cit.*, Vol. II, p. 329.

23 The relevant statistical material for the section which follows is buried in the volumes of the *Statistisches Jahrbuch für das deutsche Reich* and *Preussiche Statistik*. I am indebted to the valuable abstracts made by H. Silbergleit, *Die Bevölkerungs- und Berufsverhältnisse der Juden im Deutschen Reich* (Berlin, 1930), and H. Krose, S.J., *Konfessionsstatistik Deutschlands* (Freiburg, 1904).

24 Silbergleit, *op. cit.*, p. 17.

25 *Ibid.*, p. 9.

26 *Ibid.*, pp. 2, 25.

27 Dubnow, *op. cit.*, Vol. II, p. 121.

28 *Statistische Jahrbücher der Stadt Wien*; Dubnow, *op. cit.*, Vol. II, p. 327.

29 *Annuaire Statistique Hongrois*, Vol. XIX, pp. 18, 20.

30 O. Böckel, *Die Juden—die Könige unserer Zeit* (8th ed., Berlin, 1887), p. 10.

31 Tietze, *op. cit.*, p. 231.

32 Speech by Stöcker in the Prussian Diet, *StPrA*, XVII, Leg-Per., 2. Sess., March 20, 1890, Vol. 349, p. 871.

33 W. Lossen, *Der Anteil der Katholiken am akademischen Lehrante in Preussen. Nach statistischen Untersuchungen* (Cologne, 1901), pp. 114–15. Figures exclude theological faculties.

34 A. Ruppin, "Die sozialen Verhältnisse der Juden in Preussen und Deutschland," *Jahrbücher fur Nationalökonomie und Statistik*, Series III, Vol. XXIII (1902), pp. 769, 776.

35 *Öst H*, Vol. XI, pp. 56–7.

36 *Öst H*, Vol. XI, pp. 65–6.

37 B. Windt, "Die Juden an den Mittel- und Hochschulen Österreichs seit 1850," *Statistische Monatsschrift*, Vol. VII (1881), pp. 442–57.

38 H. Sternberg, *Zur Geschichte der Juden in Czernowitz* (Tel Aviv, 1962), pp. 34–7.

39 *Ibid.*, p. 76.

40 C. A. Macartney, *October Fifteenth, A History of Modern Hungary* (Edinburgh, 1956), Vol. I, p. 19.

41 G. Gliksman, *L'Aspet Economique de la Question Juive en Pologne* (Paris, 1929), pp. 100–102.

42 F. P. G. Malbeck, *Der Einfluss des Judentums auf die Berliner Presse von 1800–1879* (Dresden, 1935), pp. 24–6. Although the purpose of this Nazi historian is to justify Stöcker's anti-Semitic campaign, he is scrupulous about giving chapter and verse. See also E. Kahn, "The Frankfurter Zeitung," *Leo Baeck Year Book II* (London, 1957), pp. 223–35.

43 J. Braunthal, *In Search of the Millenium* (London, 1945), p. 17.

44 S. R. Landau, *Unter jüdischen Proletariern* (Vienna, 1898), p. 14.

2

The Structure of Germany and Austria

The events of 1866 and 1867—the expulsion of Austria from the German Confederation, the battle of Sadowa, the establishment of the North German Confederation—transformed the internal politics of both Germany and Austria. Liberalism came to power in both countries, although for different reasons.

In Germany Liberalism triumphed because the Liberals stood for national unity and, now that their most cherished dream had been attained, they were prepared to forgive Bismarck for raising the Prussian army in breach of the constitution. Indeed, without a strong dose of political and economic Liberalism the newly united country could not have survived, a fact which Bismarck, who had no sympathy with Liberal ideals, realized. Parliamentarism, the collapse of commercial barriers, the unification of the legal system, the abolition of the hundred-and-one privileges and liberties which had accumulated for centuries, these were the conditions of a strong, centralized administration, and they were exactly what the Liberals had been hungering for.

The unification of Germany was not the mere transference of the Prussian Junker system to a larger area. In the negotiations to secure national unity, Bismarck was forced, and prepared, to make considerable sacrifices at the expense of the class to which he belonged. Bismarck was an opportunist and a tactician; in particular he acknowledged at this time no consistent economic doctrine. The Conservatives, the party of the Junkers, formed an embittered and obstructive minority, so that government without the Liberals was impossible.

While his conversion to universal suffrage had been originally inspired by anti-Liberalism, by a desire to exploit the exaltation of victory in order to punish the Prussian opposition,[1] it could also serve constructive nationalist aims and might reassure the

Catholic minority, Liberals outside Prussia (especially in the southern states), and particularists in the newly annexed provinces.

Thus from 1867 onward, the lower house of the German parliament* was elected by universal manhood suffrage. The powers of the Reichstag under the Imperial Constitution, however, were not very wide. Its assent was needed for all legislation (subject to a veto of the Bundestag, the Second Chamber representing the governments of the individual states), but it could not initiate legislation, many sources of revenue were outside its scope, and over foreign affairs it had no control at all. There was no ministerial responsibility. The German Empire had a democratic suffrage but not parliamentary government.

Bismarck, occupied with diplomacy, took little part in the many economic reforms. The work was chiefly that of two of his ministers, Rudolf Delbrück, president of the Federal Chancellery, and Otto von Camphausen, deputy president of the Prussian ministry. Both were confirmed "Manchester men," believers in free trade and *laissez-faire*.

Between 1867 and 1871 the North German Diet, and later the Reichstag repealed the usury and debt laws, unified the weights and measures by adopting the metric system, transferred postal communications to the competence of the Reich,† and made the gold mark the unit of currency. It proclaimed *Freizügigkeit*, complete freedom of movement for individuals and merchandise, and *Gewerbefreiheit*, abolishing the remaining privileges of the guilds. The *Aktiennovelle* facilitated the formation of limited liability joint-stock companies.[2] Import duties on corn and manufactures were progressively lowered, and in 1877 all duties on iron and steel goods were abolished, although this was the last victory of economic liberalism.

Favorable circumstances had combined to speed Germany's industrial expansion. The beginnings of large-scale industry coincided with the building of railways and the facilitation of company formation. One has only to consider that in Britain sixty years separated the application of steam to textile

---

* It was the parliament of the North German Federation until 1871, of the Empire thereafter.
† Except, as philatelists will know, for Bavaria and Württemberg.

manufacture and the first railway, nearly a century elapsed between the beginnings of industrialization and the Companies Act of 1862. Moreover, by entering the field late, Germany was able to take advantage of improvements in machine design which made the exploitation of mines and factories easier and more profitable than in Britain. To this must be added the French indemnity of five thousand million gold francs, which was paid more quickly than the German government had expected (and rather more quickly than the German economy could safely absorb).

The years following 1867 were marked by wild speculation and expansion. It was the *Gründerzeit*. The typical figure of the period was the *Gründer* (promoter), hawking the shares of any kind of company, safe, risky, or downright fraudulent, to a population seized with a mania for reckless investment. In 1872, forty-nine new banks and sixty-one chemical plants were founded in Prussia; in all twice as many companies were promoted in that year as in the years 1790–1867.[3] Railways represented the best opportunity for plausible jobbers; of all the "bubbles" the most notorious was the Rumanian railway company of Dr. Hirsch Strousberg, a Russian Jew, but the only difference between his and other men's frauds was that his fraud was more impudent and involved more money.*

A boom of such proportions could not last; and free trade was not in the short-run interests of Germany. Cheaper English iron flooded the German market, as did cheaper Russian grain. The German textile industry found it difficult to compete with the more highly mechanized mills of Lorraine. In May, 1873, came the Viennese bank crash, fourteen days after the Emperor Francis Joseph had opened Parliament with the words:

> The impetus of national economic life and the steady augmentation of state credit give us well-founded hopes for a complete balancing of the budget in the near future.

In October, 1873, came the crash in Berlin. Although some industries, particularly iron and steel, were badly hit,[4] not even the recession could halt the feverish growth of investment. In

---

* Detailed but by no means exhaustive accounts of these enterprises are to be found in the works of Otto Glagau and Rudolf Meyer (see Chapter 9).

1874, there were 857 new companies founded with a total capital of 3307 million marks—300 million more than the total joint-stock capital of Prussia in 1870.[5]

In Austria the political and economic situation was in some respects similar. Defeat, the desire for reform, and the need to come to terms with Hungary helped the *Bürgerministerium* ("bourgeois ministry") into power. With one short break, the Liberals were in power from 1867 to 1879, and for the last eight of those years Prince Adolf Auersperg was prime minister. They established the Dual Monarchy with Vienna and Budapest as joint capitals, repealed, with the *leges infandae et abominabiles*,[6] the Concordat, and granted complete legal equality to all nationalities and religions.

In practice, the establishment of the Dual Monarchy created as many new problems as it solved old ones. In a decade in which the foundations of the Catholic Church were being shattered in Italy, France, and Spain, Austria seemed the last stronghold,* and the Church party was determined to maintain the federal, historic, and Catholic character of the monarchy.

The Liberals who had largely created the system of 1867 had traditionally combined constitutionalism with German nationalism. When it became clear in 1866 that Bismarck had ruled out the "greater German" solution on which they had based their hopes, they concentrated on securing the position of the Germans in Austria, a proceeding which the constitution, for all its proclamations to the contrary, favored.

The Imperial party, realizing that nationalism would mean the end of the empire, had to pursue a policy of strengthening the traditional and supranational institutions of the empire; equally, it was anti-Magyar, and it regarded the *Ausgleich* as a blow at the authority of the crown, and the Hungarian policy of discrimination against minorities as running counter to its federalist principles. The Archduke Francis Ferdinand, assassinated in 1914, advocated devolution for the different nationalities of the empire on principles which, in the Austrian context, were ultraconservative rather than liberal.

So, too, the Right had to oppose, as long as it could,

---

* "Casca il Mondo (the world is tumbling)," Cardinal Antonelli, the Papal Secretary of State, exclaimed on hearing the news of Sadowa.

secularism and constitutionalism. Until 1873, partially until 1879, they boycotted the new Reichsrat.

> Why am I against attending Parliament? [wrote Karlon, a Styrian Conservative]. That has its reasons not merely in the juridical shortcomings of the present constitution but in its revolutionary character, which signifies atheism in religion, and popular sovereignty in political matters; whoever stands on this incline . . . will ultimately fall into the abyss which the ideas of the year 1789 opened.[7]

And the *Katholikentag* of 1877 declared:

> The Austrian monarchy can maintain the struggle only in the same moral alliance with the Church in which it had its origins, foundations and growth.[8]

Austria, like Germany, went through its *Gründer* period under Liberal auspices, smaller in extent than that of her northern neighbor, but every whit as hectic and fraudulent. The guilds had already lost their privileges in 1860; 682 new companies, between 1867 and May, 1874, were founded, including 443 new banks; the new flotations of the years from 1871 to 1873 alone had a capital value of 4000 florins.[9] It was in Vienna (and not for the last time in history) that the crash came when the boom had outrun its course.

Notwithstanding the depressed conditions which followed the crash, industrialization, aided by a rapid growth of population, went on apace in both empires. Especially in Germany progress was astounding, as comparison with Britain, easily the world's leading industrial power in 1870, will show.

Economic historians have in recent times disputed whether the protracted and far from uniform industrialization of Great Britain could be called a "revolution." In Germany, on the basis of the above statistics, a much better case could be made for describing the changes as revolutionary. Although the "industrial revolution" in Germany happened much more quickly and appeared to achieve greater results, it was, in another important sense, less complete. Precisely because the industrialization of Britain was drawn out so long, because it started experimentally and continued tentatively, it was in the end more thorough; and the middle class which emerged from it was larger, and better able to impose its moral and political ideas and its standards of behavior. Whole economic classes which had existed before the middle of the eighteenth century (the peasants and the independent craftsmen) had by 1914 either disappeared or become economically insignificant. For a century or more it was true that any man possessing the right combination of energy and luck could make his fortune by building a business.

TABLE 5. INDUSTRIAL EXPANSION IN
BRITAIN AND GERMANY, 1870-1919[10]

		Germany	Great Britain
Coal Production	1871	38	113
(metric tons, in millions)	1913	278	292
	Increase	637%	147%
Pig Iron Production	1875	2,029	6,469
(metric tons, in millions)	1910	14,793	10,380
	Increase	629%	60%
Steel Production	1875	370	723
(metric tons, in millions)	1910	13,698	7,613
	Increase	3,602%	953%

This never applied to Germany. Within a generation of the beginnings of industrialization combines and cartels had concentrated the ownership and control of industry in a remarkably small number of hands. "By 1900," writes Clapham, "there was hardly a trade which had not its cartel, strong or weak."[11] This early ossification in the structure of industry meant that industrialization had much less effect on the social structure of the country. The industrial revolution, in so far as this term implies a general change in a country's way of life as opposed merely to the substitution of techniques, was, in Germany, far from complete.

The guilds did not disappear. Although they had been shorn of their privileges in 1811 and completely deprived of them in 1869, and although the master craftsmen whom they represented

were particularly hard pressed by the impact of factory production, they succeeded in staging a counterattack. As late as the
1850's, there were seventy trades in which guild membership or a
craftsman's certificate was compulsory.[12] Between 1878 and
1886 laws were passed to limit again the unconditional *Gewerbefreiheit* of 1869. In 1904, the last pre-war year for which such
statistics are available, there were over 3000 guilds, half of them
compulsory. Their membership was half a million, representing
an estimated 35 to 40% of the master craftsmen of Germany.[13] To
the student of anti-Semitism this early inhibition of social
mobility and large-scale survival of "pre-capitalist" classes is of
great importance. There is not a single anti-Semitic "Reform
Party" which does not include in its program items for the
strengthening of artisans and peasants, often claiming outright
the re-establishment of compulsory corporations.

In cisleithan Austria preindustrial conditions survived to an
even greater extent. Industrialization was slower and more
localized; it penetrated only to Vienna and its suburbs, Upper
Styria, and Northern Bohemia. Slovenia, Galicia, and the Alpine
provinces were no more than touched by industry. In 1914, there
were only seven cities of 100,000 inhabitants* in a country of 28
million, compared with forty-one such cities in Germany and
thirty-nine in Great Britain.

As in Germany, the period of genuinely competitive
enterprise was short, and the contrast between a market economy
and the large-scale survival of independent producers quite
unable to adapt themselves to it was even more striking. In
agriculture, the producer was a peasant just emerging from
feudalism. (Serfdom had been abolished in 1848.) In industrial
production the artisans continued to survive and were strong
enough to achieve a partial reversal of unqualified freedom of
enterprise in 1883. An interesting sidelight on the uneasy
relationship between the old and the new is shown by the
uncertain dividing line separating guilds and trade unions. The
Webbs' well-known judgment that the modern trade union is
not the successor of the medieval guild[14] applies to Britain, not
to Germany or Austria. An outstanding example of this

* Vienna, Prague, Brno, Lvov, Cracow, Trieste, and Graz. Hungary with a
population of 20,000,000 had only two, Budapest and Szeged.

interrelationship is the Austrian guild of tanners and leather workers, which became a union about 1870, reformed itself into a guild, and finally became a trade union in 1896. In 1899 a guild in Maribor which had existed since the sixteenth century became a union.[15] And it has been pointed out that most of the German or Austrian Socialist leaders who claimed "proletarian" origins in fact began their careers as journeymen, not as factory workers.[16]

Liberalism never really struck root in either Germany or Austria. It came to power in 1867; by 1879 Bismarck had turned to the Conservatives, and the Auersperg administration had disintegrated over the Balkan question. During those twelve years it had shown some of its best and some of its worst characteristics. It had undoubtedly rid both states of many hoary abuses and anachronistic institutions; to adapt a phrase of Adlai Stevenson's, it had "dragged these countries, kicking and screaming into the nineteenth century." But there is no doubt that the unsavory speculations, the uncompromising gospel of commercialism, and the often unreflecting repetition of Voltairean clichés discredited it in the minds of many, even of those who had not suffered losses themselves. The impact of those years was all the more shattering because the social structure of the two empires was comparatively rigid; if (as Marx said) the French bourgeoisie executed its aristocracy while the British married its daughters, the German and Austrian bourgeoisie achieved neither. The triumph of money, though an indisputable economic fact, was not acknowledged socially.

In the parliaments, the salons, and the boulevards men and women were seen who five or ten years earlier had been of little consequence; in the theatres the worthy German classics had to make room for the licentious plots and vulgar tunes of Offenbach; parks, resorts, and spas were no longer restricted. Conspicuous among the new regiment of *parvenus* were men like Trollope's Sebastian Melmotte who "at a moment . . . burst out into sudden splendour. There was an hotel, with carriages and horses almost unnumbered; there came into their rooms a crowd of dark, swarthy, greasy men, who were entertained sumptuously." Not all were Jews, and they were not the first Jews to rank with the nobility, but the changes which society had undergone were the result of usages with which Jews were particularly associated and which were popularly supposed to

24

benefit Jews more than anyone else. One pamphleteer complained:

> In their business and in their social gatherings, which take place out of doors and where they can be observed, they are so engrossed by their own circle that they see and hear only their own affairs and conversation; but if they were to listen and to look to their left and right, their ears and eyes would perceive much that was not pleasant. Christians, who happen to observe different manners, self-control and formalities outwardly as well, must be amazed and pained by the behaviour of Jewish families. There is no exhaustive expression to describe the unseemliness, the offensiveness and the noise, as if they were entirely amongst themselves, which are to be observed in public gardens, especially in bathing places, in the streets, on tramways and railway stations, in every province and town. They might well refrain from this bumptiousness if they had any idea that there is an invisible boundary which distinguishes and separates the genuinely refined from the parvenu. It is really to be marvelled at that their behaviour does not provoke more objections than is the case. The sensitive among them are ashamed, but even they are too much involved and do not succeed in securing an improvement.[17]

In the social, economic, and political spheres, the revolution was equally sudden, equally unmistakable in its impact, and equally incomplete. Liberalism was never the creed of the multitude. Too many people had suffered and too many had been disillusioned during the brief Liberal triumph to be consoled with the slogans of Samuel Smiles, which were all the Liberals could offer them. Liberalism remained the possession of a minority, which from the 1870's onward was steadily diminishing, but holding out longest, perhaps, in the press and the universities. Because neither the economy nor the society of the German and Austrian Empires was ever thoroughly liberalized, the alliance between the ruling class and the lower middle class—officials, humbler professional men, tradespeople, artisans—could come about. It was this strange alliance that formed the basis of political anti-Semitism. It was a coalition of extremes against the common enemy.

REFERENCES

1 W. Gagel, *Die Wahlrechtsfrage in der Geschichte der deutschen liberalen Parteien* (Düsseldorf, 1958), pp. 38–45.
2 G. Stoltenberg, *Der deutsche Reichstag, 1871–73* (Düsseldorf, 1955), for details of the debates.
3 P. W. Massing, *Rehearsal for Destruction* (New York, 1949), p. 5.
4 Sir J. H. Clapham, *The Economic Development of France and Germany, 1815–1914.* (4th ed., Cambridge, 1936), p. 284; G. Stolper, *The German Economy, 1870–1914. Issues and Trends* (New York, 1940), p. 34.
5 Stolper, *op. cit.*, p. 36.
6 Papal Allocution of June 22, 1868, Eder, *Liberalismus in Alt-Österreich*, p. 171.
7 Letter to Franz Graf, Nov. 25, 1873, P. Molisch, *Briefe zur deutschen Politik in Österreich von 1848 bis 1918* (Vienna–Leipzig, 1934), p. 29.
8 W. Klopp, *Leben und Wirken des Sozialpolitikers Karl Freiherr von Vogelsang* (Vienna, 1930), p. 187.
9 R. Charmatz, *Österreichs innere Geschichte von 1848–1907* (3rd ed., Leipzig, 1918), Vol. II, p. 10.
10 Figures from Stolper, *op. cit.*, pp. 41–2; Clapham, *op. cit.*, pp. 281, 235, 339; S. B. Clough and C. W. Cole, *Economic History of Europe* (3rd ed., Boston, 1952), p. 358. German coal production includes lignite.
11 Clapham, *op. cit.*, p. 314.
12 *Ibid.*, p. 324.
13 *Ibid.*, p. 335.
14 S. and B. Webb, *A History of Trade Unionism* (2nd ed., London, 1892), pp. 13–14.
15 C. A. Gulick, *Austria from Habsburg to Hitler* (Berkeley–Los Angeles, 1948), Vol. I, p. 15.
16 Whiteside, *Austrian National Socialism*, p. 29.
17 Anon., *Wer trägt die Schuld an der Antisemiten-Bewegung?* (Berlin, 1886), p. 17.

THE REJECTION OF LIBERALISM

"Elle nait," said Georges de Lagarde of the Reformation, *"d'une collaboration des idées et des faits."*[1] That this applies to any movement in history ought to be a truism, but it is frequently ignored. The Reformation was a theological movement and Luther was a theologian; he was neither the first nor the last of a long line of critics of the organization and teachings of the Catholic Church. The Reformation was also a political movement; it was welcomed by princes who resented the pretension of the Church to rule them and who were anxious to make religion a more pliable servant. It was also an economic movement; the peasants of Germany thought it meant the end of feudal obligations, and the Anabaptists of Münster thought it heralded a new age of anarcho-communism. While the exact causal relationship between the Reformation and capitalism is an open question, it is true that the Reformation had a greater appeal in merchant communities than elsewhere. Luther's *Theses* and Calvin's *Institutes* were not regarded by their authors as political or economic manifestoes, yet their ideas succeeded, where those of Wyclif and Hus had failed, at least in part because purely secular conditions were more favorable to their acceptance.

This moral the historian of political anti-Semitism should keep constantly in mind. His first task should be to strike an intelligent balance between a historical description of the evolution of ideas and an analysis of the objective conditions which make those ideas acceptable. H. Stuart Hughes, in discussing the problems of writing intellectual history, distinguishes between three "manageable" approaches:

> that which deals with popular ideas and practices — "folklore and community sentiments"; that which deals with the activities of ruling minorities and the aspirations of rival minorities; that which deals with ideas which will eventualy inspire governing

élites, "ideas which have still to win their way".[2]

We shall have relatively little to do with the second; but we shall be concerned with both the first and the third. At the beginning of our period anti-Semitism, whether political, social, or religious, was discredited, and it was accepted by only a small minority of the politically dominant groups. In the course of the next thirty years it was tirelessly preached by an increasing number of self-appointed prophets, until it re-established itself. However, it succeeded not only among the élite but also among the masses; that is to say, it progressed along both what Mr. Hughes calls the "higher" and the "lower" levels of thought—at the level of "intellectually clear and significant statements" and at the level of "popular effusions in the nature of slogans."[3]

The years up to the outbreak of the First World War are those in which the ideology of anti-Semitism was being elaborated, attended by overt political success in Austria, but not in Germany. The triumph of anti-Semitism twenty years after that was due to a breakthrough at both levels, to a consensus of the élite, who were accessible to ideas, and to the masses, who were responsive to slogans. In both cases, we must remember that the amalgam of notions with which anti-Semitism is associated was never dead, that there was at best a period of latency and underground survival, providing continuity. For this reason alone we shall also have to consider briefly the ideologies and items of popular wisdom inherited in the 1860's.

In examining the theoretical corpus on which anti-Semites have drawn, the historian is interested in the ideas themselves rather than the individual devotee. But it is of course also possible to examine anti-Semitism in a different way, as that of the psychologist. He tries to find out why some individuals are susceptible to anti-Semitism and not others, and what types of personality are likely to go with anti-Semitic views. Those two approaches are complementary rather than contradictory; between them they enable us to ask questions the answers to which should go a long way toward clearing our minds. These are:

1. What are the personal characteristics which cause certain people to respond to the political factors that encourage anti-Semitism?

2. What are the political situations which cause people to give

28

vent to the anti-Semitism latent in their personalities?

We should try always to bear both questions in mind, since people respond unevenly to similar political stimuli, and even when anti-Semitism is particularly strongly represented in certain classes or regions, there will always be numerous exceptions within the class or region concerned. The scientific law that like causes have like effects must be applied with the greatest caution to politics.

Very few men are trained historians, sociologists, and psychologists at the same time, and the present author is not one of them. Moreover, the techniques for investigating the political motivations of individuals have been elaborated only recently, so that there is little or no material for the period before 1914. Though such inquiries are illuminating, they cannot be regarded as being, by the strictest canons, directly relevant. For the period from 1871 to 1918 we must content ourselves with a more traditional presentation.

The dominant ideology of this period, as we have seen, was Liberalism; a study of the theoretical content of anti-Semitism will show us that it represented, in the first place, a reaction against this ideology. It flourished when it did because to many people Liberalism seemed undesirable and harmful. Not all anti-Liberalism was necessarily anti-Semitic. Our present task is to isolate and examine those elements of anti-Liberalism which were. We ought to begin by looking at the general themes. The views of a few typical ideologues, which are relevant to various stages in the development of anti-Semitism, will appear in their context in later chapters.

The main tenets of nineteenth-century European Liberalism may be summarized as parliamentary government, the rule of law, the absence of legally established class privileges, a laissez-faire economy, and freedom of speech and association. Against almost all of these anti-Semites took a stand. In addition to these, its institutional aspects, Liberalism had a far wider meaning. It was a set of moral qualities, those of rationalism, humanism, and—to give it its German context— Aufklärung. To be "liberal" means, in German even more than in English, to be just, broadminded and generous. The anti-Semites opposed not only the institutions of Liberalism, they fought its whole moral system, and its whole concept of human existence.

REFERENCES

1 G. de Lagarde, *Récherches sur l'Esprit de la Réforme* (Paris, 1926), p. 13.
2 H. S. Hughes, *Consciousness and Society. The Re-Orientation of European Social Thought, 1890–1930* (London, 1959), pp. 9–10.
3 *Ibid.*, p. 9.

3

Romantic Conservatism

To write the history of anti-Semitism in nineteenth and twentieth-century Germany is to write the history of the German Right. This is true even though some anti-Semitism, especially in the 1880's, used a strong leftist vocabulary. The reason for this correlation we have to seek in the circumstance that gave birth to the German Right, namely the Wars of Liberation against Napoleon. This means that German nationalism had to seek its inspiration defensively in the past, which was politically illiberal, and it had to proclaim its opposition to the ideals that Napoleon's armies were supposed to be carrying through Europe, namely those of the French Revolution. Romantic German nationalism was therefore cultural and opposed to the idea of the nation-state; it was authoritarian, opposed to constitutionalism, but also to Caesarism; it was pluralist and corporatist, opposed to individualism, egalitarianism, and Roman law. It proclaimed the primacy of the "national community," so that virtue lay merely in being consciously a German. It was therefore not merely anti-parliamentary or anti-Semitic, it was anti-Western. It rejected the political and moral tradition of the Anglo-Saxon world, of Switzerland and the Netherlands, of France, and, some would say, Italy. Ranke, writing about the Restorations of 1815, calls them "a reaction of the nordic-Germanic world against the revolutionary Latin nations."[1]

There was therefore nothing surprising about the Conservatives' attitude toward the emancipation of the Jews in the 1860's. Since the struggle for emancipation was so closely connected with the struggle for Liberalism, those who opposed the one opposed the other also, hoping to kill both birds with the same stone. The nationalism which created the Second German Empire, implying the doctrine of popular self-determination and resulting in a constitutional nation-state, was very different from that of Fichte, Arnim, and Herder. That had been *grossdeutsch* not *kleindeutsch,* looking back to the days of German greatness in the heyday of the Holy Roman Empire. Romantic, conservative nationalism recoiled from Bismarck's cavalier treatment of dynasties and the privileges of legitimacy, and from the proclamation of written constitutions creating new sovereignties.

In the 1870's German nationalism was Liberal, and to be anti-Liberal was to be anti-Nationalist. It was only in the 1890's that Conservatives and anti-Semites joined the National Liberals in promoting Imperialism, with which anti-Semitism soon became inextricably connected. But during the Liberal period, in both Germany and Austria, the anti-Semites were not merely conservative, they were reactionary, refusing to accept the triumph of the ideas of the 1848—or for that matter of 1789.

Had these Conservatives read Marx, they might well have agreed with his analysis of those events:

> The revolutions of 1648 and 1789 . . . were the proclamations of the political order for the new European society. The bourgeoisie was victorious . . . a victory of bourgeois over feudal property, of nationality over provincialism, of competition over guilds, of the division of estates over primogeniture, of the domination of the land by the owner over the domination of the owner by the land, of enlightenment over superstition, of the family over the family name, of industry over heroic indolence, of civil law over mediaeval privileges.[2]

That the Conservatives of both empires were able to make their peace so quickly with the new order showed how much less "victorious" the revolution was than Marx had supposed: but at this stage they had not yet awoken to this fact. For the present the backwoodsmen of Pomerania and the eastern marches were no more content with the new dispensation than were their predecessors under Kleist, Arnim, and von der Marwitz who, in opposition to Hardenberg's reforms and his emancipation of the Jews,* formed the *christlich-germanische Tischgesellschaft* from

---

* This was a partial emancipation only. It was not extended to the Polish territories annexed after 1814 and therefore excluded the majority of Prussian Jews after that date.

which "Jews, Frenchmen, and philistines" were excluded.[3] Anti-Semitism, then as later, was a conscious part of conservative medievalism.*

Hence, in the 1870's, conservative anti-Semitism was closely linked with the *Antikanzlerliga,* led by Rudolf Meyer and Joachim Gehlsen, the purpose of which was to drive Bismarck from office by a determined press campaign. In both empires it struck not only at the theory behind the new political structure but at the practical consequences. The economic disasters of 1873 gave a considerable fillip to this propaganda, but they did not start it off, for capitalism was as undesirable when successful as it was when bankrupt.

The Catholic Church could not be expected to welcome either the creation of a powerful new national state with a Protestant majority, or the new sway which secular and materialist ideas seemed to have gained over men's minds in both empires. As we shall see later, the Catholic Church in Germany had good reasons to eschew anti-Semitism, but in Austria conditions were different and there it succeeded in overcoming its inhibitions.

But there is yet another direct and permanent connection to be traced between Romanticism and anti-Semitism. This is illustrated by the dichotomy in all German thought in the past 150 years, between the Rationalist tradition of Lessing, Klopstock, and Kant and the Romantic reaction to it—between, in fact, the pro- and anti-Western movements.

In contrast with the first generation of English, French, and German Romantics, children of the eighteenth century who welcomed the French Revolution, the later Romantic despised Rationalism and the Enlightenment. He detected the sin of intellectual arrogance in it. He championed intuition against analysis, imagination against empiricism, faith against the intellect, and history against science. He rejected the individualism and cosmopolitanism of the preceding generation which seemed to overemphasize the happiness of the individual.[4] It would be facile to "blame" the Romantics for anti-Semitism; it nevertheless

---

* Cf. Oelsner's letter to Varnhagen: "The hatred against the Jews brings us increasingly nearer the Middle Ages, of which our sentimental age is so tenderly fond" (Aris, *op. cit.*, p. 402.).

remains true that anti-Semitism is a part of the Romantic answer to the Western Rationalism of the Liberals.

REFERENCES

1 Quoted by R. Aris, *A History of Political Thought in Germany from 1789 to 1815* (London, 1936), p. 405.
2 *Neue Rheinische Zeitung*, Dec. 15, 1848.
3 Aris, *op. cit.*, p. 405.
4 See H. S. Reiss, *The Political Thought of the German Romantics* (Oxford, 1955), pp. 2, 7.

4

Constitutionalism and the Rule of Law

The political and the economic individualism of the post-1867 period were equally repugnant to the romantic, anti-Semitic conservatives. With equal vehemence they opposed the supremacy of law and contract over custom and status, and any constitutional theories based on popular sovereignty.

Here Catholic theorists were on much firmer grounds than Protestants. Karl von Vogelsang, the intellectual mentor of the Austrian conservatives,* firmly basing himself on the medieval world order as the political and social ideal, and reinforced by the Syllabus of Errors and the encyclical *Quod Apostolici Muneris,* condemned root and branch liberalism, modernism, and the primacy of positive law. Natural as well as divine law rejects the sovereignty of contract; it implies the autonomy of the individual as preached by the serpent in the Garden of Eden.[1]

> Not natural law, which God created with the first man, not the laws of Christendom, not even the precepts of natural religion were henceforth to be the limits for the omnipotence of the state over its citizens; the blasphemy that "law is the public conscience" was declared to be the axiom of Liberalism.[2]
>
> The Christian state of ethical and natural law is suspended and in its place is put the sovereign state . . . in which the economically strongest create the majority which makes laws for the weak.[3]

His German contemporary Konstatin Frantz,† too, lamented that the "natural order" had been put upside down. Above all the neglect of agriculture and the contempt for country life were the chief causes of the moral, material, and intellectual decline of conditions in Germany.[4] The Bismarckian revolution had

---

* For a full analysis of his ideas, see Chapter 18.
† For a full analysis of his ideas, see Chapter 9.

saddled Germany with an unstable party system, an accentuation of social differences, and the growth of Socialism, with popular confusion caused by the wholesale breaches with tradition in 1866, with a revival of religious disunity.[5] To talk (as Ludwig Loewe, a Jewish Progressive deputy had done) of "our modern nationality" was nonsense; nationality was traditional or it was nothing.[6]

And who has benefited from all the new-fangled institutions?

> What does the peasant care whether they have the same laws a day's journey from his village as at his home? But he must desire all the more to keep to his traditional law with which all the habits of his life are entwined. Similarly, what does the petty burgher, whose business transactions do not extend beyond his immediate neighbourhood, care? So that exactly those elements who form the stable basis of a nation, not only have no interest in a general and uniform civil code, they are decidedly harmed by being required to fit themselves into the new legal provisions. Only the mobile section of the population is at all interested in it, i.e., those who have no fixed abode, or who travel frequently, or whose business activities result in far-flung connections. Hence it is at merchants and manufacturers and most of all pure speculators, that opportunity will henceforth smile: to start from one point and everywhere set up business, everywhere speculate in land and buy up estates, because the legal forms and conditions of such transactions are everywhere the same. So it is for the purpose of providing elbow-room for this mobile element that we have shaken the solid foundations.[7]

By the same token, who has gained most from this new elevation of legal forms to a principle of universal and exclusive validity, this reduction of all relationships to a question of contract?

> It need hardly be said that nothing suits the Jewish point of view better than the idea of the so-called constitutional state, in which no more regard is paid to men's religion than to their real conditions of life and to the historical facts on which the character and political position of individual states is founded. Instead, all institutions and laws are measured entirely by abstract concepts of law; consequently the constitutional state recognises neither Jews nor Christians, only citizens.[8]

It is the system within which Shylock is able to insist on his bond.[9]

Perhaps the greatest enemy of all is Roman law, and here the nationalist ideology of resistance to the French Revolution is especially influential. Though the earliest Prussian reactionaries, such as von der Marwitz, already thundered against Roman law, legal nationalism as a school of thought derives from Savigny. Transmitted by Hegel and Lorenz von Stein, German historical jurisprudence found its greatest expression in Gierke's works.[10] According to him, the compilation of the reformed civil code must "come forth from the very own spirit of our people."[11]

Gierke was no anti-Semite, but nothing was easier than to draw a racial moral from the Germanic concept of creative toil and the Semitic one of exploitation and profit, especially when this was needed to bolster some special pleading on behalf of a particular class.

The agrarian reformer Ottoman Beta, contrasting the legacy of Frederick the Great with that of Bleichröder (the Jewish banker who was Bismarck's financial adviser) wrote that anti-Semitism was the new scourge of the soulless *jus:*

> The anti-Semites . . . demand what is called German or national law, such as has maintained itself in rudiments in Mosaic law, where we read: The earth is the Lord's! They demand that the periwigs learned in *jus* should also bow before the word of God.[12]

The anti-Semites

> recognise in Roman law and its defenders the chief enemies of the people's welfare and of national development.[13]

Needless to say, the Agrarian League, the anti-Semitic landowners' association,* also hankered after the *Landrecht* of Frederick the Great, calling in their manifesto for "homestead legislation on the basis of German consciousness of law" *(deutsches Rechtsbewusstsein).*[14]

The specter of Roman law was not yet laid at the beginning of the twentieth century, when the *Deutscher Rechtsbund,* founded in 1901, resolved:

> to fight against the legalism ('Juristentum') which all but

* See Chapter 13.

37

exclusively dominates the government, and for laws suitable to the nation in our legislation . . . .

We have a lawyers' code, parts of which are totally incomprehensible to the people. The German people has, to its own detriment, far too exclusively entrusted its law to a caste of learned judges, who are insufficiently familiar with its conditions of life. Thus an alienation has arisen between the people and its legal system . . . . If your lawyers lack the comprehension to achieve a thorough reform on their own initiative and to lead us to social justice, then the people must take the renewal of law into its own hands and gird its loins for a great national deed.[15]

Nationalist opposition to Roman law was not confined to Germans. The Hungarian anti-Semitic leader Simonyí denounced the "legalistic hair-splitting of the un-national Roman law."[16] That favorite butt, the lawyer, was often the victim of attacks on the *Rechtsstaat*. The spirit of Jack Cade breathes through this editorial in the anti-Semitic *Deutsches Tagblatt* in 1889:

The activity of defending counsel as a rule consists mainly in misleading the judges and, in so far as laymen are involved, the jurymen; in dragging in errors and confusion and fishing in muddy waters; in slandering and abusing honest witnesses and casting suspicion on them; in instructing their clients beforehand in what they should say, in impeding, during the proceedings, the ascertainment of truth by means of cross-questioning and interruptions, in tempting the presiding magistrate, who is perhaps insufficiently versed in routine, to commit legal errors so as to be able to appeal later on against the verdict on the strength of these.[17]

The modern legal system, one gathers from all these criticisms, if not actually a Jewish racket, at least favors the views and interests of those classes with which the Jews are associated; no wonder the legal profession should be so attractive to Jews. Anti-Semitic programs frequently contain proposed measures for reducing legal costs and simplifying legal procedure.[18]

The rule of law is closely connected with legislation by parliament, a wide, though not necessarily universal, suffrage and a party system. All these institutions imply the principle of human equality before the law, and in determining what the law should be.

The "unreality" of party politics, and the manipulations of cliques are frequently assailed, especially as these appeal to specifically Jewish talents:

> If it is a question of social and political ideas [writes Konstantin Frantz] then the commercial talent innate in the Jews becomes the talent for agitation, and just as they have proved their superiority in big deals, they do so no less in our party life.[19]

Nor did the leaders of an Austrian peasant movement doubt who was behind the constitution-mongering of 1867:

> It was primarily the capitalists and the Jews who set forth the cry for a constitution of the kind we now have.[20]

The journal of international anti-Semitism, equating parliamentarism with plutocracy, lamented that "the national labour of the peoples should henceforth benefit this international guild of money-makers, just as today's judaised democracy *(verjudete Demokratie)* desires it."[21] The sentiment was echoed by the League of the Russian People (the "Black Hundreds") at the time of the 1905 Revolution:

> The cry of "Down with the autocracy!" comes from the blood-suckers who are commonly known as Jews, Armenians and Poles. Beware of the Jews! They are the root of all evil, the sole cause of our misfortunes . . . . Down with the traitors, down with constitutions![22]

Vampires

Some "radical" anti-Semites in the 1880's—Böckel in Germany, Schönerer in Austria, and Drumont in France, for instance—supported universal suffrage and even the payment of parliamentary deputies, hoping to rally "the people" against the oligarchs. But the majority was as hostile to it then as it has been in the twentieth century. Frequently the dislike of parliamentary government combined with that of capitalism in the advocacy of a corporate state:

> There is no doubt [wrote Vogelsang] that a people which has lost its corporate institutions can be governed only in the Byzantine manner, by a centralised and bureaucratised state apparatus.[23]

For Catholic anti-Semitic social reformers, under the influence of neo-Thomism and *Rerum Novarum,* corporatism was especially attractive, but the predilection was equally great among German Protestant conservatives. Here the inspiration was often national- ist. For the earlier generation the Loi Le Chapelier of 1791 which abolished the guilds in France was the symbolic enemy. Admittedly by the 1870's "Manchester" had become the standard dirty word.

Pastor Stöcker, the founder of the Berlin Christian-social movement, personally advocated corporations[24] in both the official programs (1878 and 1895) of his party.[25] Many later anti-Semites followed suit, including Simonyí and Theodor Fritsch,[26] and corporatism also made an appearance in point 25 of the Nazi Party's 1920 program.[27]

Even the more democratic anti-Semites, such as Jules Lemaitre and Paul Déroulède, were soon disillusioned; they tended, after the turn of the century, to favor plebiscitary and other "direct" forms of democracy, by-passing parliaments and parties. At any rate there are sufficient premonitions here of Charles Maurras' classic distinction between *le pays légal* and *le pays réel*.

REFERENCES

1 *Vaterland*, March 28, 1877.
2 W. Klopp (ed.), *Die sozialen Lehren des Freiherrn Karl von Vogelsang. Grundsätze einer christlichen Gesellschafts- und Volkswirtschaftslehre* (St. Pölten, 1894), p. 25.
3 *Ibid.*, p. 34.
4 K. Frantz, *Der Untergang der alten Parteien und die Parteien der Zukunft* (Berlin, 1878), p. 82.
5 K. Frantz, *Die Religion des Nationalliberalismus* (Leipzig, 1872), pp. 229–43.
6 *Ibid.*, p. 225.
7 K. Frantz, *Der Nationalliberalismus und die Judenherrschaft* (Munich, 1874), pp. 34–5.
8 *Ibid.*, p. 13.
9 *Ibid.*, p. 13.
10 The clearest statement is to be found in his *Das deutsche Genossenschaftsrecht* (Berlin, 1868).
11 O. von Gierke, *Der Entwurf eines bürgerlichen Gesetzbuches und das deutsche Recht* (Leipzig, 1889), pp. 1–2.
12 O. Beta (i.e., O. H. Bettziech), *Der Geist Bleichröders und der Geist Friedrichs des Grossen* (Berlin, n.d. [1890]), p. 7.
13 *Ibid.*, p. 8.
14 F. Salomon, *Die deutschen Parteiprogramme*, Vol. II (Berlin, 1907), p. 78.
15 *PAR*, Vol. I, No. 2 (1902), pp. 145–6.

16 I. Simonyí, *Der Judaismus und die parlamentarische Komödie* (Bratislava, 1883), p. 73.

17 *Deutsche Antisemitenchronik, 1888–1894* (Zurich, 1894), p. 25. The sentiment was not restricted to Germany. See E. Drumont, *La France Juive devant l'Opinion* (Paris, 1886), pp. 264–70.

18 For example, Böckel's Erfurt Programme, para. XII (Appendix II, p. 329; Schönerer's Linz Programme, Point 27 (ch. 17, p. 145), Programme of the United Christians, Point 6 (ch. 19, p. 167).

19 Frantz, *Der Untergang der alten Parteien*, p. 54.

20 *Mittelstrasse*, Sept. 1, 1881.

21 *Schmeitzners Internationale Monatsschrift*, Vol. II, No. 12 (1883), p. 759.

22 H. Valentin, *Anti-Semitism Historically and Critically Examined* (London, 1936), p. 86.

23 Klopp, *Die sozialen Lehren* (2nd ed.), p. 248.

24 Speech in Berlin, Dec. 12, 1881. A. Stöcker, *Christlichsozial. Reden und Aufsätze* (Bielefeld–Leipzig, 1885), p. 121. Also, *ibid.*, p. 365.

25 F. Salomon, *Die deutschen Parteiprogramme*, Vol. I (Berlin, 1907), pp. 47–8.

26 Simonyí, *op. cit.*, p. 83; T. Fritsch, *Der demokratische Gedanke* (1917); in P. Lehmann (ed.), *Neue Wege* (Leipzig, 1922), pp. 40–4.

27 M. Oakeshott, *Social and Political Doctrines of Contemporary Europe* (Cambridge, 1939), p. 193.

5
Capitalism and Social Mobility

Dissatisfaction with the practical consequences of Liberalism was even stronger in economic than in political matters; anti-capitalism was, after all, one of the oldest and most natural forms of anti-Semitism. Liberal society was characterized by a high degree of social mobility with a premium on individual worth and ability. Perhaps this pill was the hardest to swallow. All those who had an assured place in an ordered hierarchy, even if it was a comparatively lowly one, looked with distaste on an order which allowed others to rise to positions of eminence and influence by means which were not always admirable and certainly harmful to such traditional classes as artisans, peasants, and landowners.

Paul de Lagarde affirmed in 1886:

> It is a lie when Germans are reproached with intolerance . . . .
> What does exist . . . is the consciousness that the Jews, by using means which we consider dishonourable, know how to acquire as much money and real property as possible, so that, in consequence of the riches which have flown into their hands, they push into positions which we should not grudge them if they showed the tact which in most cases they lack, if they could make us forget, through outstanding achievements, the ways in which the wealth of their nation has often been gained.[1]

Some years earlier a pseudonymous Conservative member of the Reichstag pointed out the speed with which Jews were monopolizing business, banking, and the more lucrative professions, such as the law. He similarly complained that Jews acquired their disproportionate wealth to insure for themselves the most comfortable careers and the least laborious work.[2] This might indeed be so; it is a process welcomed by a Liberal society

42

for Jews and non-Jews alike. The anti-Semite, however, sees that it enables the previously unemancipated Jew to rise faster than anyone else, and that it is part of a system from which Jews stand to gain more than others, even if they are not its sole beneficiaries.

By the same token anti-Semitism is anti-capitalist since capitalism is one of the causes of social mobility. It is not, of course, opposed to private property. Indeed its complaints against capitalism are that it destroys traditional and far worthier forms of property. It draws the distinction between "*schaffendes*" (creative) and "*raffendes*" (grasping) capital—the artisan's or the agriculturist's, compared with the banker's, the broker's, or middleman's. In the earlier period even large-scale manufacture —which succeeds, by using sweated labor, in underselling the honest subsistence manufacturer; or whose interests influence government policy at the expense of agriculture—came into this category.

> We show the people that the roots of their plight are in the power of money, in the mercenary spirit of the stock exchange,

Stöcker explained.[3] Indeed it was a constant complaint among anti-Semites that the Marxists refused to regard stock exchanges or banks as more wicked than other capitalist institutions. Liebermann von Sonnenberg, another anti-Semitic deputy, explained the difference:

> Only *that* capital is dangerous which multiplies itself without labour, which grows to limitless proportions through stock-exchange gambling and financial operations; *that* capital is not dangerous, whose turnover is made possible only by labour . . . as with large industrial undertakings, and which provides a livelihood for large numbers of people, that capital which consists of landed property, which nourishes a great many people and whose owners receive but a modest rent . . . . Only bourse capital, usurious capital, *that* is the capital you must combat.[4]

"It is certainly no fault of ours," he amplified on a later occasion, "that this capital is mainly in Jewish hands."[5]

Indeed it would be hard to find the anti-Semitic program which did not contain items for the protection of "honest" property and the control and taxation, if not abolition, of the stock exchange and other strongholds of "mobile" capital. This was in the course of time reinforced with the argument that capitalism was un-German. The German Social Reform Party, in its 1895 program, demanded:

> Thorough organisation of German labour on a national basis and reformation of our legal system by displacing the capitalist excesses of the present laws through German national legal principles *(deutsch- nationale Rechtsanschauungen)*.[6]

Fifteen years earlier the court preacher Adolf Stöcker had already called for "a return to a more Germanic and Christian economic life."[7]

Such was the enmity toward capitalism that we find in anti-Semitic programs proposals which look very much like pure Socialism—for instance, the nationalization of railways, insurance, banking, or advertising. Indeed a great many anti-Semites proclaimed themselves Socialists, and this becomes more comprehensible when we remember that, especially in Germany, many eminently conservative thinkers, inspired by a tradition of bureaucracy and mercantilism, were grouped in the school of *Kathedersozialisten.* (By no means all of these were anti-Semitic.) Adolf Wagner, the editor of the *Staatssozialist,* was particularly anxious to deny the Marxists' claim to a monopoly of Socialism, in the leading article of the journal's first issue:

> In my opinion it is urgently necessary that the possessing classes, and the conservative as well as liberal elements in the state, Church and society, should summon the courage to devote to Socialism an objective study, uncoloured by political, ecclesiastical or social spectacles, and that we should get to know it above all else. Socialism is nowadays summarily identified with Social Democracy, with political, religious and philosophical radicalism, especially with materialism, or is at least considered indissolubly linked with it . . . . Whoever, as a Social Democrat, for instance, asserts that a Socialist necessarily has to be a Social Democrat, Republican and materialist, deliberately confuses Socialism with other things . . . . Socialism is the economic system which is decidedly opposed to economic individualism, i.e., the teachings of the Physiocrats and of Adam Smith and his school, which has gained such wide influence in our legislation.
>
> For Socialism deals, by definition, with a fundamental

re-shaping of certain aspects of our law of property, especially of the private ownership of land and capital, and the law of contract, particularly with the removal of the present law of labour contracts.[8]

There were of course a number of men who were primarily Socialists and secondarily anti-Semitic. Fourier and Dühring are perhaps the most outstanding.* But a number of leftist anti-Semites occasionally liked to be considered Socialists also. Wilhelm Marr claimed that "anti-Semitism is a Socialist movement, only in nobler and purer forms than Social Democracy;"[9] Ernst Schneider, the Viennese anti-Semitic leader described himself as "a Socialist and an anti-Semite,"[10] and Drumont contested a municipal seat in 1890 and a parliamentary seat in 1893 as a self-styled Socialist.[11]

Yet this nomenclature is misleading. Much of this anti-capitalism was inspired by a hostility to industrialism as such—indeed to urban civilization—and was aimed at organized labor as much as at organized capital. As time went on and big business was more closely associated with the political Right, the emphasis changed slightly and captains of industry, such as Stumm, Krupp and Siemens became folk-heroes, embodying "creative" capital. This was true even of the much-vaunted "Socialists" in the Nazi Party. Gottfried Feder, the author of their first economic program, was obsessed with "loan capital" and "the breaking of interest slavery," but he was not opposed to the private ownership of the means of production as such.[12] And Otto Strasser, who broke with Hitler in 1932 on the issue of economic policy,† was more interested in reviving the peasantry than in reconstructing industry. Indeed, in view of its idealization of agriculture, this trend of thought is better described as populist. It is very similar to prairie radicalism, except that anti-Semitism was a much less important component of the North American movements.[13] William Jennings Bryan, with his "cross of gold" oratory and his fundamentalist rejection of modern knowledge, would fit very easily into the sort of European movement we are considering. American populism

---

* The relation between Socialism and anti-Semitism is discussed in Chapter 28.
† "The Socialists leave the party" was the title of his manifesto, justifying the split.

also achieved some "socialist" successes, such as the erection of state-owned silos by the Non-Partisan League in North Dakota.

REFERENCES

1 P. de Lagarde, *Lipman Zunz und seine Verehrer (1877); Mitteilungen* (Göttingen, 1884–1891), Vol. II, pp. 160–1.
2 "Hilarius Bankberger" (i.e. F. F. Perrot?) *Die sogenannte deutsche "Reichsbank"* (2nd ed., Berlin, 1877), p. 16.
3 W. Frank, *Hofprediger Adolf Stöcker und die christlichsoziale Bewegung* (2nd ed., Hamburg, 1935), p. 77.
4 Speech in Leipzig, Jan. 23, 1885. M. Liebermann von Sonnenberg, *Beiträge zur Geschichte der antisemitischen Bewegung, vom Jahre 1880–1895* (Berlin, 1885), p. 297.
5 Speech in Reichstag, Dec. 7, 1892. *StBR*, IX, Leg., 2 Sess., p. 322.
6 F. Specht and P. Schwabe, *Die Reichstagswahlen von 1867 bis 1903* (2nd ed., Berlin, 1904), p. 418.
7 Stöcker, *Christlich-Sozial*, p. 366.
8 Quoted, *ibid.*, p. xiv.
9 *ÖV*, Feb. 15, 1891.
10 Letter to Vogelsang, Feb. 10, 1883. J. Allmayer-Beck, *Vogelsang. Vom Feudalismus zur Volksbewegung* (Vienna, 1952), p. 82.
11 R. F. Byrnes, *Anti-Semitism in Modern France* (New Brunswick, New Jersey, 1950), p. 164.
12 G. Feder, *Der deutsche Staat auf nationaler und sozialer Grundlage. Neue Wege in Staat, Finanz und Wirtschaft* (Munich, 1923), *passim*.
13 See R. Hofstadter, *The Age of Reform* (New York, 1955), pp. 77–81.

6

Racialism

Racialism is not, of course, restricted to the particular period we are studying; racial anti-Semitism had appeared in 1848 and even earlier.[1] An early classic on the supremacy of the Nordic–Aryan race was Count Arthur de Gobineau's essay,[2] and even it had its predecessors.[3] It evoked no immediate response, but its elements were all to reappear in the work of Houston Stewart Chamberlain, Alfred Rosenberg, and all the imitators' imitators in the four corners of German-speaking Europe.

It was a point of view which, in the first anti-Semitic reaction against the system of 1867, was represented by only one writer, Wilhelm Marr, who, it is generally believed, invented the word "anti-Semitism." Little is known about him personally; his origins are obscure, but he may have been the baptized son of the Jewish actor Heinrich Marr.[4] What little he reveals about himself shows that he was a journalist who was dismissed from his job to suit the requirements of the *"Judenpresse."*[5] His grievance, genuine or not, made him determined to return to a subject which he had already attempted—unsuccessfully—ten years earlier.[6] But economic conditions and the political climate in 1873 were very different from those of 1863. There were many Germans who now felt, rightly or wrongly, that they had been elbowed out of their place in the sun by the ubiquitous and universally successful Jew. So *Der Sieg des Judentums über das Germanentum* went through twelve editions in six years. Its real significance lay in its title: "The victory of Judaism over Germandom, regarded from the nondenominational point of view." In other words, Jew was contrasted not with Christian, but with German, along a line of division which was not accidental and remediable but eternal and indelible.

The work is one of unqualified pessimism. The Germans have

lost the battle without knowing it was on. From there he develops an argument which, though deliberately disowning many of the traditional clichés about the Jews, succeeds in frightening his reader with the specter of this cunning, rootless, worldly wise race, condemned to wander, destined to conquer, where it can.

The decision to move the fight against the Jews from the religious to the racial field was a clever one. Emancipation had been justified on the ground of religious tolerance; any anti-Semitism, therefore, had to face the damaging criticism of religious prejudice. Moreover, in view of the growing indifference of the middle and working classes to religion, a call to rally to the defense of Christianity was unlikely to evoke an enthusiastic response. The element of the pseudoscientific, the up-to-date, the apparently objective, and the dialectical in this six penny version of Darwin made it attractive to those who considered themselves as having "grown out of" traditional Christianity. Marr was careful to disown any motives of religious intolerance:

> There must be no question here of parading religious prejudices when it is a question of race and when the difference lies in the "blood,"

he wrote in 1880,[7] and the theme recurs in all his pamphlets.

Marr acknowledges that during the Middle Ages Jews were used as scapegoats and whipping boys by princes[8] and that they have undoubtedly aided industrial expansion.[9] It is neither surprising that Jews welcolmed the revolutions of 1789 and 1848,[10] nor that, having gained supremacy, they show no mercy to their former oppressors.[11] The Jews have beaten the Germans in an open fight;[12] German stupidity, by the adoption of Jewish economic doctrines, has helped the Jews to power.[13]

> We Germans, have, with the year 1848, completed our official abdication in favour of Judaism . . . . The Thirty Years' War which Jewry has officially waged against us since 1848 . . . does not even leave open the hope of sorne rotten Peace of Westphalia.[14]

There were no signs so far of a Jewish *Götterdämmerung;* on the

contrary, England is ruled by Disraeli and France by Gambetta.*
The 1800-year struggle with Judaism is nearing its end; life and
the future belong to Judaism, death and the past to Germandom.[15] *Finis Germaniae! Vae Victis!*

Although the natural conclusion of such an argument was that
the end had irremediably come for Germany, Marr was in fact
persuaded to enter the fray. He became editor of a shortlived
periodical, *Die Deutsche Wacht,* published a pamphlet urging
Germans not to vote for Jews,[16] and in 1879 founded the
Antisemiten-Liga, the first organization anywhere to bear such a
title. The following is the purpose of the league, according to the
statutes:

I. *Purpose of the Association*

1. The purpose of the association formed under the name of
'League of Anti-Semites" is to bring together non-Jewish
Germans of all denominations, all parties and all walks of life into
a common, fervent union which will strive, by setting aside all
special interests and all political differences, and with the greatest
energy, earnestness and industry, towards the one aim of saving
our German fatherland from complete Judaisation and to make
life tolerable there for the descendants of the original inhabitants.

2. It strives towards this goal by strictly legal methods, by
opposing, with all lawful means, the further displacement of
Germanism by Judaism, by making it its task to force the Semites
back into a position corresponding with their numerical strength
by liberating Germanism from the oppressive weight of Jewish
influence in social, political and ecclesiastical matters, and by
securing for the children of Teutons their full rights to office and
dignity in the German fatherland.[17]

Membership was divided into two classes, the *"Berufene"* and the
"Erwählte" (the called and the chosen) ; after six months'
membership a *"Berufener"* could become an *"Erwählter,"* but in
cases of exceptional merit, promotion could be accelerated.
Already the hierarchic leadership principle, later to be so closely
associated with anti-Semitism, is in evidence.

Marr never became prominent in anti-Semitic politics. He
retired from agitation after only a few years, although he
contributed from time to time to the *Österreichischer Volksfreund,*

* *Der Sieg*, pp. 28–9. The evidence for Gambetta's being even partly Jewish is
far from conclusive.

the Viennese weekly, under a pseudonym. His importance, however, must be accurately assessed. He was the first to appreciate the possibilities opened by propaganda on racial lines and the advantage of using extreme and unscrupulous rather than polite and respectable methods in a matter which appealed, in essence, to extreme and unscrupulous sentiments.

The men who followed him (Eugen Dühring was the most important) made much greater pretensions than he to intellectual stature. Their teachings bore full fruition only after the First World War; before that the details of their doctrinal corpus interested few people outside small bands of enthusiastic devotees, but they were not without indirect influence. If the peasants and innkeepers who voted, in the 1880's and 1890's, for Böckel and Ahlwardt were fundamentally not interested in ethnology, they were roused by a campaign of agitation which, in radicalism, scurrility, and irresponsibility, the Christian–conservative wing of the movement simply could not compete with.

The arguments rehearsed by the theorists of racial anti-Semitism are by now familiar. The Aryan races are as superior to the Semitic in morals as in corporal stature and health; the Aryan is simple and pious, the Semite a sensuous scoundrel; the Aryan lives by honest labor, the Semite by management, jobbing, and exploitation; the Aryans are the true creators in philosophy, religion, and science, the Semites the imitators and plagiarists.

Dühring entered the field in 1881 with *Die Judenfrage als Racen- Sitten- und Kulturfrage*. This in itself announced that the Jewish question was to be discussed on a new level: it had become one of race, morals, and (happy inspiration) *Kultur*.

Dühring, a blind lecturer in economics and philosophy at Berlin University, was a philosophic anarchist. In the years of confusion after the anti-Socialist law (1878) his views gained such a following in the Social Democratic Party as to occasion a refutation from Engels.[18] Dühring's was the sort of "national" Socialism which later became increasingly associated with anti-Semitism everywhere, looking upon the individualism of *"Juden-liberalismus"* as undesirable both politically and economically.

Dühring preached national self-sufficiency in a controlled economy.[19] In this he was the disciple of Right-wing traditions; but, unlike the *Kathedersozialisten,* he also wanted this limited Socialism to be based on the enthusiasm of the masses and a sort of general will. This was a concept which at any rate began as the property of the Left. While anti-Semitism does not inexorably follow from such a theory, it is quite consistent with it. Some of the argument in *Die Judenfrage* is familiar anti-Liberal stock-in-trade:

> The doctrine of egalitarian free economics and of corresponding human rights in economics, as they were formulated in a humanely well-meaning way by the Scotsmen Hume and Smith, were used by the Jews in order to derive from them their monopoly.[20]

but it goes further in suggesting the fundamental reason for this:

> The Jewish skull is no thinker's skull—all the time the Lord God and business affairs have claimed all the space in it.[21]

It was a question of "racial honor" to rid all public offices, business, and finance of this "incomparably inferior race."[22]

Dühring so far represented the *ne plus ultra* of anti-Semitic extremism and gained a following in a number of the *Reformvereine* then springing up. He inspired one of their main organs, the *Westfälische Reform,* and he was above all influential in the student movement. Through the students he influenced Georg von Schönerer.

This new point of view, that of the irredeemable depravity of the Jews, was taken up in the 1890's by Theodor Fritsch, an engineer of Leipzig, who had been active in the first stirrings of the anti-Semitic movement in Saxony. He made up for his mediocre intellect by the assiduity and profusion of his propaganda which for nearly half a century made him probably the most tireless of anti-Semitic publicists. His writings cover a bewildering variety of topics from the advocacy of garden cities to a refutation of the Theory of Relativity.[23] He was one of the few anti-Semites of his generation who continued their public activities into the 1920's and became a Nazi Reichstag deputy.

His death in September, 1933 evoked a fulsome tribute from Julius Streicher.[24] For him "the dawn of the racial question" was "one of the greatest steps forward in human knowledge,"[25] and with books, pamphlets, and periodicals his *Hammer* publishing house enlightened the German people about progress in this field of science.

51

Racialism obviously implied a different attitude to religion from that of Christian-conservative anti-Semitism. This derived from two sources. The first was the growing tendency to explain religion in positive terms, i.e., that men create their own gods rather than that God creates men; hence the racialist, as we have already seen, regarded all religion and morality as the product of race. There was, secondly, the Romantic movement, and the rediscovery and popularization of Nordic myths and folktales which had begun with Herder.

In this striving for a Germanic religious synthesis several schools are discernible, though all are to a varying degree anti-Christian. The Jewish religion is of course *ipso facto* out of court; but Christianity also contains too many Semitic elements; it is too humane in promising salvation to the weak and degenerate. This was the Nietzschean attitude adopted by the extreme nihilistic wing. Frank paganism appears with Gobineau who, for instance, writes to his sister that he was thinking of making himself a high priest of Odin, Thor, and Frey,[26] and with some of Schönerer's followers.[27] Wagner cannot quite make up his mind between it and purified Christianity, so he divides his admiration equally between the undefiled Germanic hero and the Knight of the Holy Grail. Dühring attempted the theme in *Der Ersatz der Religion durch Vollkommeneres und die Ausscheidung alles Judentums durch modernen Völkergeist* (the substitution of religion by The More Complete and the exclusion of Judaism by the modern folk-spirit). "Religion" became cults resting on outward observances and stagnant morality, the Asiatic legacy to the West.

> We Germans have little cause [he wrote elsewhere] to mislead, through the affectations of a Hebraic orientalism, the sensibilities which our Nordic heavens and our Nordic world have been stimulating for millenia.[28]
> Those who wish to cling to the entire Christian tradition are in no position to turn against Judaism with sufficient force.[29]

Dühring, as an atheist, went farther than most. A more orthodox statement will be found in Fritsch's contributions to the *Antisemitische Correspondenz*.[30] Germans must reject the Old Testament, which is nothing more than a *Judenverherrlichungsgeschichte* (a story to glorify the Jews) and with it the fallacy that the Jews were the people of God from whose ranks the Redeemer had come.

Christ was clearly an Aryan and an anti-Semite. He despised the Jewish spirit of Pharisaism and was hated and rejected by the Jews. In any case, none but an anti-Semite could ever have become the Ideal. Christianity arose in Palestine because it was there that Semitic oppression of the Aryan was at its worst; it was the revolt of the Aryan consciousness of morality *(arisches Sittenbewusstsein)*. In the religious life of the people, Judaism must be regarded as the enemy of German life, of truth, and of *Vernunft*. Hence the need for a new and ideal Germanized Christianity, purged of all Hebrew elements. Ultimately, racial anti-Semitism would show the way to a new *Weltanschauung,* to which Christianity would be in the same relationship as the child to the man.[31] More widely read than either Dühring or Fritsch as a propagandist of the "non-Jewish Christ" was Houston Stewart Chamberlain. His vast apparatus of ill-digested secondary works enabled him to declare,

> the probability that Christ was no Jew, that he had not a drop of genuinely Jewish blood in him, is so great that it is almost equivalent to certainty.[32]

Christ's teaching was "not the perfecting of the Jewish religion, but its negation," a reaction against the Jews' "formalism and hard-headed rationalism."[33] This view of religion became of doctrinal importance to racial anti-Semitism, inescapable if the only permitted basis of any thought, any characteristic, was to be "the blood."

Liberalism, as we defined it earlier, was more than an economic or constitutional theory; it was a set of values, based on what are nowadays vaguely termed "human rights." The racialists showed how swift was the transformation of anti-Semitic doctrines once the revival of the 1870's was under way. In the dislike of individualism, *laissez-faire,* and legal equality there is much that is basic and consistent. But the racialists went further. Any universal morality, the whole "banal and myopic pretext of toleration"[34] is, by definition, fundamentally *anathema* to anti-Semitism, culminating in the "master-race" theory and in a Nietzschean contempt for the "slave morality" which gives the weak as much right to live as the strong.

Although German anti-Semitic publicists often quoted unkind remarks made about Jews by Kant—anthologies of anti-Semitism among the great, such as Luther, Goethe, and Voltaire, were a favorite device—they could not approve of Kant's general moral philosophy, and attacks on it, either direct or indirect, were not lacking. Especially the extreme racialist wing could have no patience with

> All this chatter about fundanental moral laws in every human breast, about the categorical imperative of conscience, of a so-called independent morality common to all men.[35]
>
> It is not morality that makes Jews bad, but the Jews make bad morality.[36]

The spread to Germany of the Ethical Movement, a colorless, well-meaning organization with the aim of disseminating general good will, was subjected to fierce attack in a series of pamphlets published by the (Dühringite) *Westfälische Reform*. Such a body for all its high-mindedness, could be nothing but a *Judenschutz-truppe*,* created to undermine belief in the racial basis of morality.

> But there is one point, which is as a matter of fact the main point, about which our *Moralkolporteure* are particularly evasive; they do not want to know that morals and religion are the products of race.'[37]

Similarly attacked was "the false humanitarianism which lies behind the notions of equal rights for all." The mistake of those who voted for Jewish emancipation was:

> in the assumption that all men and all people were equally endowed in spirit and sensibility and with the same urge in their hearts to do good and spread joy and happiness around them. Exceptions were believed to have arisen through oppression, ill-treatment . . . on the part of more powerful elements. It was from such causes that people believed the bad qualities of Jews had to be explained.[38]

Since Kant was a recognized "great German," attacks had to be circumspect, though Dühring attributed his shortcomings to his "bigoted Scots origins."[39] For non-Germans the task was easier. Maurice Barrès refers to those French intellectuals who

---

* A "squad for the protection of Jews."

had been *Dreyfusards* during the Affair as "drunk with unwholesome Kantism."[40] Replying to the statement of a "distinguished
professeur"* that "Kant's philosophy, more or less modified, is the
basis of almost all the courses of moral philosophy given,
particularly in France," he says:

> This Kantism in our classrooms claims to classify the universal
> man, man in the abstract, taking no account of individual
> differences. Its tendency is to make our young Lorrainers,
> Provençaux, Bretons and Parisians of this year into an abstract
> ideal man, everywhere identical with himself, while our need is
> for men firmly rooted in our soil, in our history, in our national
> conscience, and adapted to the French necessities of this day and
> date. The philosophy taught by the state is in the first instance
> responsible if people consider it intellectual to despise the
> National Unconscious . . . . A verbalism which removes the
> child from all reality, a Kantism which uproots from the soil of
> the dead . . . this is our reproach against the University, this is
> what makes its product, "the intellectual," an enemy of society.[41]

The attitude of the conservative propagandists we have
considered is an essentially pre-liberal one. It represents the regrets
for the Christian-monarchic-agrarian age; it is clearly a rearguard
action fought by a generation which had lost the battle. With the
discovery of racial theories and the substitution of universal
morality by horde morality, we are in a decidedly post-liberal
atmosphere—post-liberal because this second school has accepted
certain of the liberal concepts, in particular the positivist attitudes
to law and religion and the notion of mass participation in politics.

The tone of the new appeal is more violent, more prophetic,
more apocalyptic; it derives from, and generates, sadism, persecution mania, and hysteria. It is ultimately nihilistic, no more
respectful of Junkers and cardinals than it is of Jews and Liberals.
It is atheist without being rationalist. Unable either to ignore or
destroy Christianity, it tries to adapt and transform it. It is based
upon the "myth," a conflation of ancient tribal paganism and
fin-de-siècle mysticism. It is anti-Semitic not as a means to an end,
not for the purpose of winning a move in the political game, but
as an end in itself. It stands for tribal purification through a
perpetual cathartic riot of intolerance.

* Bouteiller?

REFERENCES

1 See, for example, S. W. Baron, "The Impact of the Revolution of 1848 on Jewish Emanicpation," *Jewish Social Studies*, Vol. XI, No. 3 (1949), p. 211.
2 A. de Gobineau, *Essai sur l'Inégalité des Races* (Paris, 1853–5).
3 For example, G. Klemm, *Allgemeine Kulturgeschichte der Menschheit* (1845); E. von Wintersheim, *Vorgeschichte der deutschen Nation* (1852); and the works of the Hellenist J. K. Fallmereyer.
4 Dubnow, *Die neueste Geschichte*, Vol. III, p. 10.
5 W. Marr, *Der Sieg des Judentums über das Germanentum vom nicht konfessionellen Standpunkt aus betrachtet* (6th ed., Berne, 1879), pp. 24–5.
6 W. Marr, *Der Judenspiegel* (Hamburg, 1862).
7 W. Marr, *Vom jüdischen Kriegsschauplatz. Eine Streitschrift* (Berne, 1879), p. 19.
8 W. Marr, *Der Sieg*, p. 13.
9 *Ibid.*, p. 20.
10 *Ibid.*, p. 20.
11 *Ibid.*, p. 9.
12 *Ibid.*, p. 37.
13 *Ibid.*, p. 44.
14 *Ibid.*, p. 27.
15 *Ibid.*, p. 38.
16 W. Marr, *Wählet Keinen Juden! Der Weg zum Siege des Germanentums uber das Judentum* (Berlin, 1879).
17 *Statuten des Vereins der Antisemiten-Liga.*
18 A useful summary of Dühring's Socialism may be found in P. Gay, *The Dilemma of Democratic Socialism* (New York, 1952), pp. 94–104.
19 E. C. Dühring, *Kritische Geschichte der Nationalökonomie und des Sozialismus* (Berlin, 1871).
20 E. C. Dühring, *Die Judenfrage als Rassen-, Sitten- und Kulturfrage. Mit einer weltgeschichtlichen Antwort* (2nd ed., Karlsruhe-Leipzig), p. 18.
21 *Ibid.*, p. 61.
22 *Ibid.*, p. 140.
23 T. Fritsch, *Die Stadt der Zukunft* (Leipzig, 1896); *Einsteins Truglehre. Allgemeinverständlich dargestellt und widerlegt* (Leipzig, 1921).
24 R. H. Phelps, "Theodor Fritsch und der Antisemitismus," *Deutsche Rundschau*, Vol. LXXXVII, No. 5 (1961), p. 449.
25 J. Müller, "Die Entwicklung des Rassenantisemitismus in den letzten Jahrzehnten des 19. Jahrhunderts," *Historische Studien*, 372 (Berlin, 1940), p. 36.
26 R. D'O. Butler, *The Roots of National Socialism, 1783–1933* (London, 1941), p. 140.
27 For example, E. Wachler, *Kann de Edda Religionsbuch der Deutschen werden?* (Eger, 1905).
28 Dühring, *Die Judenfrage*, p. 25.
29 *Ibid.*, p. 27.
30 Unfortunately complete files of this very valuable publication are not available, and I have therefore had to make use of the summary by Müller,

op. cit. In Dec. 1888, Fritsch was sentenced to seven days' imprisonment for publishing blasphemy.

31 *Antisemitische Correspondenz*, Nos. 4, 10, 137, 139, 170, 174, 224. See Müller, *op. cit.*, pp. 70–91.

32 Chamberlain, *Foundations of the Nineteenth Century*, Vol. I, pp. 211–12.

33 *Ibid.*, p. 221.

34 Dühring, *Die Judenfrage*, p. 116.

35 Anon. (E.C. Dühring?), *Der Antisemitismus und die ethische Bewegung* (Berlin, 1893), p. 19.

36 *Ibid.*, p. 26.

37 *Ibid.*, p. 15–16.

38 Anon. *Der Antisemitismus, Berechtigung und Notwendigkeit, sowie Zwecke und Ziele desselben* (Dortmund, 1889), pp. 105–6.

39 E. Döll, *Dühringwahrheiten* (Leipzig, 1908), p. 116.

40 M. Barrès, *Scènes et Doctrines du Nationalisme* (Paris, 1899), Vol. I, p. 37.

41 *Ibid.*, pp. 49–51.

7
Sadism and Nihilism

Anti-Semitism, it should be evident by now, is the outlet for all those who feel that Liberalism, with its moral obligations, inhibits desires or personalities—or that Liberalism, with its equality of opportunity, leaves the sufferer at an unfair disadvantage. It is a revolt, not of the sentimental idealist or the hardheaded reformer, but of the dionysiac element in man, a hunger for precivilized standards of conduct. Unlike the Socialist or Communist, who believes in a blueprint for reorganizing society on a basis of equality and universal rights,* the anti-Semite merely wishes to remove obstacles that block the path to his own power and prosperity; it is not a question of "comrades in the struggle" but of "sauve-qui-peut." Hence we have the strong elements of sex envy and sadism. For the first we need go no further than Adolf Hitler.

The black-haired Jewish youth lies in wait for hours on end, satanically glaring at and spying on the unsuspicious girl whom he plans to seduce, adulterating her blood and removing her from the bosom of her own people. The Jew uses every means to undermine the racial foundations of a subjugated people. In his systematic efforts to ruin girls and women he strives to break down the last barriers of discrimination between himself and other peoples. The Jews were responsible for bringing Negroes into the Rhineland with the ultimate idea of bastardising the whole white race.[1]

This pestilential adulteration of the blood, of which hundreds of thousands of our people take no account, is being systematically practised by the Jew today. Systematically these negroid parasites in our national body corrupt our innocent fair-haired girls and thus destroy something which can no longer be replaced in this world.[2]

This was not a new point. The earliest historian of Stöcker's

* Communist *practice*, in states governed by them, is a different matter.

Christian–Social movement noted, in the 1880's,

> the observation made by many others beside myself . . . that there
> were in Berlin, at the beginning of the eighties, establishments
> where the only sight was that of young Jewish men in the
> intimate company of beautiful girls of Christian descent.[3]

The theme may not recur in quite these terms in the writings
and thoughts of other anti-Semites, but the great fears of
miscegenation, and the constant references to Jewish sensuality
and to purity of blood strike even the most casual of observers. In
this respect anti-Semitism is but one expression of generalized
xenophobia, for in countries where other racial problems steal
the limelight from the Jewish one, for instance in the United
States or the Union of South Africa, it is Negro sensuality and
the danger of Negro and white blood pollution that is stressed
most often. According to a study on "Anti-Semitism Within
American Labor," made by the Institute of Social Research in
America during the war:

> The charge of debauchery was relatively rare in the long list of
> alleged Jewish individual and social misdemeanours. On the
> whole, allusions to Jewish lewdness play a much smaller part in
> American anti-Semitic literature than they did in the writings of
> German anti-Semites. In America Negroes tend to be the objects
> of unconscious sex envy [4]

Even in Britain, where xenophobia assumes milder forms, it is
often at the back of such hostility as exists against the United
States armed forces, Italian miners, or Carribean immigrants.

We do not need to say much of sadism. We know from the
events of our own times that the worship of toughness, the
sanctity of violence, the delight of jackboots and in beating and
torturing are not only integral features of anti-Semitism, but in
many cases its attraction and driving force. If this appears less
prominently in earlier anti-Semitic movements, then we must
remember that in organized violence, as in so much else,
standards have risen during the last three generations. But it is
there all right. Hannah Arendt lists some of the extraordinary
sadistic fantasies which accompanied the donations to the appeal
in memory of Colonel Henry (who had committed suicide
when his part in forging the Dreyfus *bordereau* came to light).[5]

The cloistered, scholarly Lagarde exclaimed that "this usurious vermin" should be exterminated "like trichinae and bacilli";[6] and the Jesuit preacher of the 1890's, Father Abel, prided himself on the possession of a stick with which his father had once assaulted a Jew in a railway carriage. Later he presented it to a fellow anti-Semite as a token of friendship.[7]

The pogrom, after all, is as old as the Diaspora.

For a refined example of literary anti-Semitic sadism we must go to a French author's description of the public degradation of Captain Dreyfus:

> Another minute's respite still . . . . As nine o'clock struck, the general drew his sword, the commands rang out, the infantry presented arms and the cavalry flashed their sabres, the little platoon detached itself from the angle of an immense square. Four men, in their midst the traitor, marching stiffly, on one side the executioner, a veritable giant. The five or six thousand people who were present and moved by the tragic waiting period had only one thought: "Judas is marching too well."
>
> A spectacle more exciting than the guillotine, set up on the cobblestones, early in the morning, on the Place de la Roquette. He was one of the happy men of this world, despised, abandoned by all: "I am alone in the universe," he might have cried.
>
> In this desert, he marched firmly, his jaw kept high, his body well held, his left hand on the grip of his sword, his right hand swinging. Could his dog have licked those hands? Taking a diagonal line, the sinister group arrived four paces from the general astride his horse and halted brusquely. The four artillery —men retired, the clerk of the court spoke, the rigid silhouette did nothing, except to raise an arm and let go a cry of innocence, while the Guards Adjutant, terrible in his size and magnificent in his bearing, tore off so quickly and so slowly the buttons, the chevrons, the epaulettes, the red bands, terrible moment came when he broke the sword on his knee.
>
> After some seconds, when he had been left disgraced and disarmed, the instinctive cries of the crowd insisted, with a fury that outdid itself, that this homunculus in gold, who had become a homunculus in black, should be killed.
>
> But the law protected him in order to subject him to the prescribed humiliations.
>
> Judas up to that time had been a little immobile speck, beaten by all these winds of hatred. Now, like a marching pillory, he had to meet the looks of all.

He marches off.

The military wall round which he marches represses its rage, but seems ready to burst with fury. At every moment I imagine that a sword will be lifted. The crowd on the railings and on the rooftops is still calling for his death.

As he came towards us, his cap pressed on to his brow, his pince-nez on his ethnic nose, his eye furious and dry, his whole face hard and defiant, he shouted—what do I say?—he ordered, in an intolerable voice: "You will tell the whole of France that I am innocent!"

"Judas!" "Traitor!" It was a storm. Through the fatal potency which he bears, or the potency of the ideas associated with him, the unfortunate forced from us all a discharge of antipathy. That countenance of a strange race, that impassive rigidity, his whole mien revolted the most self-possessed spectator. When I saw Emile Henry his feet tied, his hands tied, being dragged to the guillotine, all I had in my heart was a sincere sympathy for an unfortunate of my race. But what had I to do with him who was called Dreyfus?

"In three years," someone said, "he will be a captain of Uhlans." Oh no! surely there is not a group of men in the world who would accept this individual. He was not born to live socially. Alone, in a condemned wood, the branch of a tree reaches out to him. So that he can hang himself . . . .

And since he appealed to the witness of those who were there, we must complete the degradation of Judas for the benefit of our brother Frenchmen, rob him of something more, better than an epaulette or a chevron, of the truth which seems to have escaped him.[8]

The culmination of all this denial and anti-humanism, this rejection of anything which generalizes laws, morals, or principles impartially, is nihilism. The attitudes which have been found associated with anti-Semitism are, as the name implies, essentially negative—hostile, resentful, and restrictive. Anti-Semitism is not arrived at by nice balancings of pros and cons. It comes from within, from a rush of the blood. It is the most extreme form of aggressive self-expression. The anti-Semite needs a clear-cut dichotomy between absolute power and absolute submission. Since he feels himself surrounded by evil powers plotting his destruction, only the thought of their destruction can help him.*

---

* Sometimes the destruction is quite vicarious and borders on fetishism, such as the desecration of Jewish cemeteries.

Modern anti-Semitism may have begun as a conservative religious and social force, opposing the liberal challenge to older values. It has throughout remained anti-liberal, but has also, in its later stages, been affected by the assault Liberalism had made on conservative and religious values. This is why it is correct to say that latter-day anti-Semitism rejected all the values of Western civilization. It could find satisfaction in neither of its main streams. It is the full flowering of what Albert Camus has called *la terreur irrationelle,* of which sadism is an essential ingredient. Modern Fascist anti-Semitism is related to this double negation, not to the earlier and milder varieties, although this historic legacy of Jew-hatred provided it with indispensable foundations.

REFERENCES

1 A. Hitler, *Mein Kampf* (trans. J. Murphy, London, 1939), p. 273.
2 *Ibid.,* p. 460.
3 M. Schön, *Die Geschichte der Berliner Bewegung* (Leipzig, 1889), p. 60.
4 Massing, *Rehearsal for Destruction,* p. 34.
5 H. Arendt, *The Origins of Totalitarianism* (2nd ed., New York, 1958), p. 107.
6 P. de Lagarde, *Schriften für das deutsche Volk* (Munich, 1934), Vol. II, p. 239.
7 H. Schmitz, "Aus Pater Abels Erinnerungen an die christlich-soziale Frühzeit," *Volkswohl,* Vol. XIV, No. 12 (Vienna, 1923), pp. 342–3.
8 Barrès, *Scènes et Doctrines,* Vol. I, pp. 142–4.

8

The Cult of Grass Roots

Another important factor in political anti-Semitism, which may be deduced from the fear of liberal values and of the complexities of modern, competitive life, is nostalgic primitivism, noble savagery—a rejection of the elaborate, sophisticated, intellectual, and legalistic urban concepts which we associate with nineteenth-century civilization. The leaders of that civilization were not democrats. They believed in an aristocracy of the intellect, alone among all the classes of society capable of judging rationally and disinterestedly the interests of all. They feared rule by the masses, whom they regarded as ignorant and unenlightened. We have only to read Liberal Victorian intellectuals like J. S. Mill, Matthew Arnold, and Bagehot on this point. They were devoted to an economic system, allowing great differences of wealth, which they considered as part of a *natura semper sibi consona*.*

Yet a great many ordinary people, in Central and Eastern Europe more than in Britain and the West, were unimpressed. The system brought them no benefits, but increased their insecurity. Government by the clever, they remained convinced, led them nowhere. But they had been stirred, as the slogans of 1789 and 1848 percolated to them, into a realization that they too ought to be heard, and they were attracted more easily by the illiberal democracy of Rousseau's simple, unspoilt man. The people, the *Volk*, the *narod*, meant those untouched by the modern Babylons in which Jewish stockbrokers, Jewish editors, Jewish lawyers, and Jewish deputies had usurped power; and in this democracy of the lowest common denominator and the most mediocre achievements the mass appeal of radical, racial anti-Semitism found an echo. As in much grass-roots propaganda

* A flawlessly consistent natural order.

63

the radicalism is restricted to words. Essentially the approach was conservative, a revolt against the innovations of nineteenth-century confidence and optimism. Its appeal was small town and agrarian; its admiration for the ethos of Cold Comfort Farm is expressed by Schönerer:

> The land of the Boers is in God's wide world the last refuge to which the humble poetry of peasant life had withdrawn itself, that poetry of the manly warrior who, without prospect of honours or decoration, cold-bloodedly goes to his death for family, home, his holding and freedom. In this happy state of contented proprietors gold and diamonds are to be found too. And, as the clean flame attracts the fluttering pests of the night, so the glitter of gold called out the scum of the earth, and particularly the revoltingly greedy speculations of the English stock-holder.[1]

Twenty years earlier a peasant paper in Lower Austria had written:

> The peasant movement is nothing else than a war of the rural population of primitive peoples, against the free spoilers of the world in the cities, who will be victorious over the townees as surely as the robust Germans overcame the refined, softened Romans, and the peoples of the steppes the civilised but degenerate nations.
>
> It is a struggle for existence, a struggle by Nature against the enemies of the rights of nature who must at all times be defeated, and that is something our men of book-learning, our German Jew-scribes and insulters of peasants and burghers, do not know.[2]

Indeed the Jew's enmity toward agriculture is one of his worst vices. For Lagarde coexistence between Jews and Germans was undesirable:

> The more so as Jews have, as a matter of principle, an aversion from those occupations which seem to me to be important above all others, agriculture and stockbreeding.[3]

For Otto Glagau, his contemporary, the matter was simpler still: "all Jews and persons of Jewish descent are born opponents of agriculture."[4]

From the 1890's onward, this rural romanticism was accompanied by "back to nature" movements and the deliberate revival of pagan customs (midsummer and Yuletide festivals). In the twentieth century the Youth Movement, in all its manifold variety, expressed this urge to resist and escape from urban civilization. It had in it elements of both the anarchist left and the authoritarian right, with its mixture of vegetarian pacifism and blood-and-soil mystique, elements which rejoined in that ill-explored no-man's-land where extremes meet, subsisting in an earnest Lawrentian puritanical promiscuity. Julius Langbehn, perhaps the earliest prophet of this trend, hoped that

> in the end it may happen that the farmer will kill the professor; that what is innate in the nature of the German will predominate over what is artificial and conquer it.[5]

Yet another curious aspect of this noble savagery was a distaste for applying the discoveries of science to everyday life. Inoculation, vaccination, and (later) blood transfusion were objected to for reasons which may be guessed.* Even today we can note a connection between extreme right-wing politics and the opposition to adding fluorides to drinking water.†

Plain superstition also played its part, as it has done in more modern anti-Semitism; it is, after all, quite consistent with the belief in Jewish-Masonic plots, in secret symbols, in cabalistic numbers, and in the Protocols of the Elders of Zion. L. B. Hellenbach, an early anti-Semite pioneer, was also the author of numerological and spiritual works,[6] and Josel Gersdorff, a Protestant hymn writer, describes in detail the supernatural means by which Jews destroy those who have stumbled on to their secrets:

---

* The German journal *Versöhnung* ("Reconciliation") considered that compulsory inoculation, in force since 1874, "derived from an un-German way of thought." (*MVA*, May 13, 1896, pp. 193–4). Anti-Semitic leaders as diverse as Nietzsche's brother-in-law, Bernhard Förster, and the Viennese editor Ernst Vergani were vigorous opponents of inoculation and supporters of homoeopathy (W. Buch, *50 Jahre antisemitische Bewegung*, p. 60; G. Kolmer, *Parlament und Verfassung in Österreich*, Vol. V, p. 318).

† Cf. the campaign against fluorides in the British anti-Semitic publication *Gothic Ripples* ("We do not care how many Jews you poison with your fluorides . . ."), Nov. 5, 1955, Dec. 22, 1955. For an analogous situation in the United States, see *The Economist*, Dec. 22, 1955, pp. 1177–8. According to the Australian *The New Times* the tentacles of the Jewish world conspiracy include the Bank of England, the Salk vaccine, and artificial manure (*Nation*, Sydney, Nov. 26, 1959).

After the name of the victim has been called out three times, but so softly that only a most sensitive ear can be aware of it, a list of his actual or alleged sins is rehearsed, after which the verdict is, "You *must* die . . . ."

Then it goes, "I curse you! Be cu-u-ursed!—oh, horror—you shall die of blood-poisoning. I poison you with blood taken from cats and dogs; I poison you with spilt blood, with blood taken from human hearts. I poison you with spilt innocent blood from human hearts!—in twice twenty-four hours you will be dead!"[7]

J. C. F. Zöllner, a professor of physics at Leipzig and the only professor to sign the anti-Semitic petition of 1880,[8] also dabbled in spiritualism, and he conducted experiments with the fraudulent American medium, Henry Slade.[9] And Lanz von Liebenfels, the Austrian racialist, kept the true date of his birth secret in order to balk unauthorized persons who might try to cast his horoscope.[10]

French anti-Semites showed similar preoccupations. The Chevalier de Gougenot des Mousseaux, whose *Le Juif, le Judaïsme et la Judaïsation des Peuples Chrétiens* of 1869 was one of the earliest French right-wing anti-Semitic tracts, wrote voluminously on magic, demons, and spirits.[11] Drumont was reputed to consult palmists and always to carry a mandrake root on his person, and two members of the staff of *La Libre Parole* founded and edited *L'Écho du Merveilleux,* a journal devoted entirely to sorcery.[12] Charles Maurras, on his own confession, was persuaded by a female astrologer in June 1940, that he ought to collaborate with the Nazis.[13] The Third Reich is the only European or Western state in modern times whose leaders have openly resorted to horoscopes.

The uneducated were joined in their beliefs by their fellow citizens in the universities. Obsessed by the primacy of the blood, they were anxious to reject as foreign importations all values inconsistent with it. The Rights of Man were French, Christianity was Jewish (or "Etrusco-Syrian"), and sophistication was Mediterranean. Any community with loyalties beyond the boundaries of the chosen group was suspect—not only Jews, but Freemasons, Catholics,* or whoever came to hand. Particularly

* The counteraccusations of the nationalists of different countries are worth examining. Thus Germans are anti-Catholic and denounce human equality as a French idea; the French are anti-Protestant and denounce "Kantism" as German; the Klu Klux Klan is anti-Negro, anti-Semitic, and anti-Catholic.

strong was the anti-Mediterranean propaganda, since the Mediterranean, generally regarded as the cradle of European civilization, was the most dangerous source of rival values. Hence (in
part) the rejection of Roman law, Wagner's diatribes against
Italian music,[14] the elevation of Arminius to a national hero,*
and the warnings which the *alumni* of Berlin University imbibed
from the lips of Treitschke about the facts of life south of the
Alps: it is "quite in accordance with Nature that the Northern
temper should be deeper and fuller" and "the sensuality of the
Southern races go hand in hand with their idleness."[15] Hence,
too the exaltation of instinct over reason, of the moral over the
intellectual, of the physical over the cerebral,† which was the
meeting point for all classes.

This was the form which the emotion of nationalism had
taken by the end of our period. In so far as anti-Semitism
underwent changes in the fifty odd years we have studied, they
parallel exactly those we observe in nationalism. To the
Romantic English liberal of the nineteenth century, from Byron
to Trevelyan, no idea appeared more noble than that of national
renaissance—the surge of an ancient people against dynastic
despots, prescriptive magnates, and obscurantist clerics. As long
as the system of Metternich endured the confusion of two
principles could persist; a common enemy disguised the diversity
of aims.

Once in power, nationalism ceased to be liberal. Within a
generation it succeeded in drawing to itself the traditional
conservative classes, who were ready to forgive the dispossessions
their fathers had suffered and to appreciate, in the clearer light of
the middle distance, how partial this dispossession had been. Few
Liberals had the prescience to write, as Acton did, in 1862:

> Nationality is founded on the perpetual supremacy of the
> collective will, of which the unity of the nation is the necessary
> condition, to which every other influence must defer, and against
> which no other obligation enjoys authority, and all resistance is
> tyrannical. The nation is here an ideal unit founded on the race, in

* The battle of the Teutoburg Forest came to be bracketed with festivals
celebrating the victory of Sedan.
† This is illustrated by the part played by gymnastic clubs, from Jahn to
Henlein, in nationalist ideology.

defiance of the modifying action of external causes, of tradition, and of existing rights. It overrules the rights and wishes of the inhabitants, absorbing their divergent interests in a fictitious unity; sacrifices their several inclinations and duties to the higher claim of nationality, and crushes all natural rights and all established liberties for the purpose of vindicating itself. Whenever a single definite object is made the supreme end of the State, be it the advantage of a class, the safety and power of the country, the greatest happiness of the greater number, or the support of any speculative idea, the State becomes for the time inevitably absolute . . . . The co-existence of several nations in the same State is a test, as well as the best security of its freedom. It is also one of the chief instruments of civilisation; and as such it is in the natural and providential order, and indicates a state of greater advancement than the national unity which is the ideal of modern liberalization.[16]

Perhaps it is no accident that Acton was a Catholic as well as a liberal; we have the evidence of G. M. Trevelyan how such views could astonish an impressionable young liberal even of a later date.[17]

How important, in its practical effect, was the change from pre-liberal, backwardlooking to post-liberal mass-based anti-Semitism? The audience's vague and irrational image of the Jew as the enemy probably did not change much when the orators stopped talking about "Christ-slayers" and began talking about the laws of blood. The difference lay in the effect achieved. It enabled anti-Semitism to be more elemental and uncompromising. Its logical conclusion was to substitute the gas chamber for the pogrom. (But it must be remembered that the gas chamber was an invention of the leaders, not spontaneously demanded by the masses, even though they may have acquiesced in the accomplished fact.)

If anti-Semitism in German Central Europe is especially virulent and especially worthy of attention, this is because here nationalism was defensive as much as aggressive and optimistic, as was the outlook of important groups and classes within that area. The role of Jews in the life of those countries was not the decisive factor in formulating the dissatisfactions expressed in anti-Semitism; it did help to determine, however, the particular form which that expression took.

The Germans had suffered the effects of late national unification which even then was incomplete—over twelve million Germans in Europe lived outside the empire's bounds—and which, within the national state, left discontented Polish, Danish, and Alsatian minorities. They were faced with the ever-present threat of encirclement in the form of a Franco-Russian alliance and with the image they had formed of themselves as Europe's outer rampart against Asia. In Austria, the position of the German was even more insecure, for although they were politically and culturally the dominant nationality, they amounted to only one-third of the population of the western half of the empire. They could remind themselves daily of Metternich's saying that Asia begins on the *Landstrasse* (then an eastern suburb of Vienna).

The more strongly nationalist emotion gripped people's thought, the less it had to do with the concrete problem of relations between Gentiles and Jews. Both nationalities were considered entirely as entities, rarely as individuals. This increased as assimilation proceeded from 1870 and the individual Jew became less and less recognizable. Cases of violence against Jews such as pogroms and riots were rare in both Germany and German-Austria. Between 1867 and 1914 there were twelve ritual murder trials in the two empires, eleven of which collapsed although the trials were by jury.* More and more, anti-Semitism was directed against "mythical" rather than "real" Jews, even against abstractions, such as "das Judentum." How little connection this had with individual, live Jews is shown by Dr. Reichmann who points out that even after 1933, when most legal and moral restraints on mob violence had been removed in Germany, instances of popular anti-Jewish outbursts were rare.[18]

But whatever changes of emphasis or intensity there may have been in the propaganda of anti-Semitism, what is most striking is the continuity in the main assumptions of anti-Semitic thought and the main motives for anti-Semitic action since 1870. Hardly one of the qualities we can discover in the age of the

---

* The exception was the famous Polna case in 1899, in which the accused, Leopold Hilsner, after two trials, was found guilty of murder but not ritual murder. The case aroused considerable public attention, including an appeal for revision by Thomas Masaryk. Hilsner was pardoned by the Emperor Charles I in 1917.

psychologically gifted demagogues of our day will be found lacking in the simpler tub-thumpers of the 1880's.

REFERENCES

1 *UDW*, April 1, 1902.
2 *Mittelstrasse*, Aug. 1, 1881.
3 P. de Lagarde, "Über die gegenwärtigen Aufgaben der deutschen Politik" (1853), *Schriften für das deutsche Volk*, Vol. I, p. 41.
4 O. Glagau, *Deutsches Handwerk und historisches Bürgertum* (Osnabruck, 1879), p. 44.
5 A. J. Langbehn, *Rembrandt als Erzieher* (38th ed., Leipzig, 1891), p. 235.
6 *Die Magie der Zahlen* (1882), numerological; *Die Logik der Tatsachen* (1884) and *Die neuesten Kundgebungen einer intelligiblen Welt* (1881), spiritualist.
7 J. Gersdorff, *Das internationale Judentum und die schwarze Magie* (Usingen, 1899), p. 14.
8 J. C. F. Zöllner, *Beiträge zur deutschen Judenfrage, mit akademischen Arabesken* (Leipzig, 1894), p. xxii.
9 J. C. F. Zöllner, *Naturwissenschaft und christliche Offenbarung. Populäre Beiträge zur Theorie und Geschichte der vierten Dimension* (Leipzig, 1881), *passim*.
10 W. Daim, *Der Mann, der Hitler die Ideen gab* (Munich, 1958), p. 43.
11 For example, his *La Magie au XIX siècle, ses agents, ses verités, ses mensonges; Les Médiateurs et les Moyens de la Magie, les hallucinations et les savants, le fantôme humain et le principe vital; Les hauts phénomènes de la Magie; Moeurs et pratiques des démons ou esprits visiteurs.*
12 Byrnes, *Anti-Semitism in Modern France*, pp. 144–5.
13 Arendt, *Origins of Totalitarianism*, p. 110.
14 R. Wagner, *Beethoven* (1870), *passim*.
15 H. von Treitschke, *Politics* (trans. Dugdale and de Bille, London, 1916), Vol. I, 209–10. See also *ibid.*, Vol. I, pp. 206, 231.
16 Lord Acton, *Essay on Nationality* (1862); *Essays on Freedom and Power* (London, 1956), pp. 153–60.
17 G. M. Trevelyan, *An Autobiography and other Essays* (London, 1949), p. 131.
18 E. Reichmann, *Hostages of Civilisation* (London, 1950), p. 234; H. H. Rothfels, *Die deutsche Opposition gegen Hitler* (paperback, Frankfort, 1958), p. 36.

GERMANY 1867–1900

9

The Conservative Intellectuals

On July 13, 1878, Bismarck signed the Treaty of Berlin. He thus made the German Empire one of the guarantors of religious equality in Rumania, Serbia, and Montenegro,[1] largely—as it happened—at the instigation of the Jewish bankers in his entourage.[2]

It was in the same year that the first attempt was made in Germany to organize a political party on a basis of opposition to precisely those legal provisions of religious equality which had now been statutory for nine years. Up to the midseventies this opposition had been largely restricted to romantic conservatives who were Prussian particularists, or federalist Greater Germans, or both. At any rate they were totally out of sympathy with the plutocratic, centralized Bismarckian Reich. In three of their representatives—Frantz, Meyer, and Lagarde—we can follow the evolution of their ideas.

Konstantin Frantz was born in 1817, the youngest of eight children, near Halberstadt in the heart of Germany. His father was a Lutheran pastor, his mother came from a Huguenot family.[3] He studied at the universities of Halle and Berlin, coming at first under the influence of Hegel, which at that time dominated German learning, but very soon rejecting it when he found that it failed to satisfy his religious needs. Although he often hankered after an academic career, he never accepted a university appointment. He was for a time employed by the Prussian Foreign Service and traveled widely, but in his later years he lived independently. He died in 1891.

Frantz was initially an admirer of Bismarck, and he broke with him only when Bismarck decided on a solution of the German problem which excluded Austria. Gradually the idea of the nation-state grew increasingly repugnant to him; the most considerable of his later writings deal with his proposals for a European federation (under the Habsburgs) to counter-balance the growing power of Russia and the United States.[4]

Of all the critics of Bismarck and the German Empire he was the most thoroughgoing. There was not a single item, political, social, or economic, which did not excite his distaste. Nor was he primarily an anti-Semitic writer. In many of his writings he does not mention the Jews; of the two essays which are directed specifically at Bismarck and the National Liberal régime, only one is anti-Semitic, though it is his most sustained attack on the Jews.

Frantz had already occupied himself with the Jewish question in a short pamphlet published at the beginning of his career, at a time when the stirrings of constitutionalism in Prussia attracted many contributions to the subject.* He is, in this pamphlet, concerned with the moral basis of political life: the only surety for this is faith, and therefore a completely moral communal life presupposes the acknowledgement of a common religion.[5] Since the authority of modern states rests on the acknowledgment of Christ, Jews must be excluded from citizenship, barred from public offices, and restricted to closed communities where they can maintain their own religion.[6]

There is nothing new or original here, either as a theory of the state or as an argument against emancipation. Where, then, does its significance lie? In the first place there is no trace of racialism. In the second, the pious, old-fashioned Jew is at any rate tolerated—the enemy, by implication, is the secularized Jew, the chief apostle of radical politics. In the third place, Frantz rejects nationality as the basis of the state. It is this contention that inspired his onslaught on the Bismarckian revolution.

His major works on this are *Die Religion des National-liberalismus* (1872) and *Der Nationalliberalismus und die Judenherr-schaft* (1874); in them he sees the principles of National Liberalism as simply the child of the secularizing tendencies since the Renaissance,[7] and Bismarck and his henchmen as the old Ghibellines writ large.[8] Their law forbidding priests to use the pulpit for propaganda hostile to the state ignores the prior claim

---

* Including a pamphlet by Marx in 1843 and a debate in the Prussian United Diet of 1847.

of religion on the conscience.[9] Against them is Christianity, essentially universal and opposed to the spirit of national egoism. The new empire cannot have the moral basis of the old Holy Roman Empire, for its prestige rests on the incorporation not of justice but of military power.[10] It was founded by the Prussian Army and the *Zollverein,* and there is not so much as a mention of religion in the Imperial Constitution.[11]

The natural consequence of governing according to National Liberal principles is Jewish domination.[12] Jews benefit from the new commercial code: "It is for this mobile element that we have shaken the solid foundations."[13] Jews benefit from parliament-arism: "Nothing suits the Jewish point of view better than . . . the so-called constitutional state."[14] Jews benefit from the *Kulturkampf,* which helps to separate the state from Christian-ity,[15] and from the atheism of the Social Democrats:

> Jewry may well smile at the fact that it was once more two of its men who first initiated the German *Michel* into Socialism. It draws an even greater advantage from being able to use Socialism itself as a battering ram against Christianity . . . . Is not the budget of Jewry one hundred times as great as that of the Church, since Rothschild alone must possess more than all the German priests together?[16]

In succumbing to Jewish financiers, Germany is repeating the mistakes France made under the July Monarchy and the Second Empire:

> The building of the tower of Babel, which was then attempted on the banks of the Seine, is now being undertaken along the Spree.[17]

The state has been leased out to the financial oligarchs:

> In the end it will not even be able to mint coins, but will have to leave this, too, to the bankers, and in future Bleichröder or Rothschild will appear on our currency . . . . Indeed it might be best if this were already so, for then everyone would know who governs in present-day society.[18]

"Social monarchy," Frantz concludes, has more to offer Germany than "constitutional monarchy";[19] only a return to Christianity can save Germany from National Liberalism and Jewish domination.[20] Toward the end of his life he grew increasingly skeptical of any constitutional or spiritual cure for the Jewish plague.

> The steadily growing Jewish domination will gradually lead to such an intolerable situation that we shall, in the end, see an outbreak of popular fury . . . . Neither the police nor even the army would offer the Jews any protection against such a great popular movement,[21]

he wrote in 1883.

This outburst apart, Frantz was something of a dreamer. He was essentially backward-looking, unwilling, perhaps unable, to come to terms with industrial civilization. In this respect he was in a different category from those conservative monarchists associated with the State Socialist movement. They, too, were bitterly hostile to the capitalist constitutionalism of the Bismarckian Reich, but they were more open-minded toward modern processes. They hoped to produce a synthesis of industrialism and the traditions of the Prussian state, and they played some part in leading Bismarck away from Liberalism, and toward protection and welfare laws in the late 1870's.

Not all of them were anti-Semites. Even Adolf Wagner, the editor of the *Staatssozialist* and close collaborator of Stöcker,* was opposed to giving the Conservative party an anti-Semitic program. Since it was impossible to expel Jews from Germany, and pointless to exclude them from particular professions, anti-Semitism was mere slogan-mongering:

> Of course it is less trouble to say, "It's his fault, throw him out, then everything will get better."[22]

The most extreme anti-Bismarckian, anti-Semitic State Socialist was Rudolf Meyer, who was never formally a member of the *Kathedersozialist* group. Born in 1839, he was a scholar of considerable attainments who, notwithstanding his sentimental notions of the powers of monarchy to relieve the sufferings of the poor, genuinely exerted himself on their behalf. He published a detailed, well-informed, and sympathetic account of the labor movement in various European countries and United States. It was a pioneer work on the subject.[23]

He was a fierce and embittered man; he was, as we have seen,

* See Chapter 10.

prominent in the *Antikanzlerliga,* and he thundered against Bismarck in the *Berliner Revue,* which he edited, and other journals. In 1875 he challenged the Liberal leader Ludwig Bamberger to a duel. His *magnum opus,* denouncing the whole *Gründer* period, which he published in 1877, caused him to leave the country and he spent the rest of his life first in London, then in Canada as a farmer, and then in Vienna, where he died in 1899.

He grew disillusioned with the Conservatives when they appeared to do nothing for the working classes and complained that "so-called Conservatives had played an unhandsome game" with him.[24] In the 1890's he frequently contributed articles on agriculture to *Neue Zeit,* the Marxist weekly, a connection which he probably owed to his meetings with exiled Socialist leaders in London.* Mehring, Engels, and Bebel all thought highly of his book against the *Gründer.*[25]

In the 1870's he still pinned his faith to the Conservatives and the monarchy;† he strove to awaken the ruling class from a sterile regret of a bygone, patriarchial order of society,[26] so that they could take up their new mission of rescuing the poor. In France, where the third estate had emancipated itself, the possessing classes had lost all; in Prussia, where the monarchy had emancipated them, the aristocracy was still powerful.[27] So far, the growing misery among the workers was being exploited only by the Social Democrats who would sweep away both aristocracy and bourgeoisie.[28] The new social order must be Christian; the Catholics were beginning to appreciate this, but the Protestants showed little sign of doing so.[29]

From this general reminder to the Conservatives and the Emperor, Meyer moved into the full-scale attack against the Bismarck system in *Politische Gründer und die Korruption in Deutschland,* published in 1877. It is a thorough and scathing exposition of the speculations, bubbles, and frauds which

---

* In London he amused himself by going to Marx's house straight after visiting Cardinal Manning (Engels' letter to Bebel, Dec. 22, 1882. Engels, *Briefe an Bebel,* p. 72).

† Exactly how conservative Meyer was is difficult to determine; Vogelsang was not impressed. "In reality," he wrote, "conservatism is identical with the historical continuity of ideas, of which no trace is to be found with either Dr. Rodbertus or Dr. Wagner" (*Vaterland,* April 2, 1883).

constituted the economic history of Germany during the preceding decade; of the administration of the French indemnity and the *Welfenfonds*;* of the unwholesome influence exercised by the two giant banking houses, Bleichröder and the *Disconto-Gesellschaft* of Hansemann; and of the gradual filling of parliament and even the cabinet with the placemen of the financial powers:†

> The government is not only quite undisturbed about the formation of two mighty financial powers in the state, but favours their transactions, although the dishonesty of these was already partly known at the time. It loses one efficient servant after another, who leaves its service to enter the more lucrative service of the bankers; it knows that one parliamentarian after another, even diplomats, entrusted with the most important and secret affairs of state . . . fall into the dependence of banking houses and tolerates this; it not only recognizes financial agents as politicians but listens principally to their advice, although it is plain that this must be distorted by business interest. The ministers themselves mix with these blood-stained *Gründer* in the most intimate way.[30]

Meyer concludes that the responsibility for Germany's misfortunes is entirely Bismarck's, since he has concentrated all power in his hands and given the *Gründer* free rein.

> As long as Prince Bismarck remains its most powerful idol, the German nation will be sacrificed for the sake of the *Reich,* the *Reich* for the sake of the Chancellor, and the Chancellor—is owned by the Jews and the *Gründer.* For our political course, therefore, only one way remains open: elimination of the present system and its carrier.[31]

Frantz and Meyer represented the relatively moderate and intellectually honest opposition to Liberalism of the 1870's. They pointed out—generally in a sober and reasonable way—the objections to the Liberal society which had been introduced in

---

* This was the confiscated exchequer of the Kings of Hanover which Bismarck used as a chest for distributing political largesse.
† The replacement of von der Heydt as Finance Minister by Camphausen in 1869, after Heydt had opposed the *Disconto-Gesellschaft*'s plan to issue shares for 100 million Thaler, and the growing influence of Johannes Miquel, also of *Disconto*, in the National Liberal Party are good examples.

1867 and whose values had before then been winning increasing support. They were not haunted, as their successors were, with the paranoiac's hallucination of the Jewish demon lurking behind every misfortune, every evil, and every unbalance in economic and cultural life. They did not deny to Jews the title of human beings. The essential weaknesses of their argument from the anti-Semitic point of view were that it was too much bound up with admiration for outworn political forms, too much hedged with humane qualifications, so that it would, in another generation, lose its appeal.

If Meyer differed from Frantz in accepting the industrial revolution, Lagarde differed from him in accepting nationalism, and with these beginnings of nationalist anti-Semitism we see the beginnings, however tentative, of the abandonment of civilized values.

Paul Bötticher, who later adopted his great-aunt's name, de Lagarde, lived from 1827 to 1891. His father, like most of his ancestors, was a Lutheran minister and he himself was also destined for the Church. But he preferred the study of philology, became a leading scholar of Semitic and Near Eastern languages, and a prolific author of learned works. His quarrelsome temperament kept him from a university post until 1869, when he was appointed to a chair at Göttingen. His writings on religion, the state, and the Jews were neither systematic nor consistent; the most important of them were collected under the title of *Deutsche Schriften* and published in 1886, and since then have been reprinted innumerable times.[32]

He hated Catholicism because it was foreign to the German spirit, and left the Protestant Church as a young man because he felt that it had become spiritually dead. Thereafter he placed his faith in a new Germanic deism. He was a conservative who celebrated the revolutions of 1848 by sporting the black-and-white cockade of the Prussian Right, but who remained on persistently bad terms with all right-wing parties. He rejected all idea of human equality,[33] he despised legislatures based on universal suffrage because they atomized the nation,[34] and he was a nationalist for whom the social whole and the linguistic community were more important than the state. Like Frantz, he initially supported Bismarck, whose anti-Liberalism he admired, and turned against him only in 1871 out of horror at the nature of the German Empire. Like Frantz, he condemned the *Kulturkampf;* here was sectarian Protestantism at its worst, dividing the nation.[35]

In public, as in private life, he never tired of uncovering a new conspiracy. All of this led logically to anti-Semitism. He declaimed it passionately, but could never make up his mind between segregation and assimilation as answers to the Jewish question. In condemning the economic and political role of the Jews in Liberal society his language was completely conventional:

> For the sewer of the speculations and influence of the stock exchanges the world has to thank the Jews.[36]
> To let the Jews into the Prussia of today, the Prussia of Altenstein and Falk,* is to turn Prussia into Palestine.[37]

Like Socialism and Catholicism, Liberalism was an international conspiracy, not red or black, but grey. The Grey International "is, like all its sisters, without a fatherland, and therefore of the greatest danger to every nation."[38]

This denunciation of internationalism is a valuable clue to Lagarde's attitude to the Jews. He did not merely oppose them on religious grounds, as Frantz had done, or on economic, as Meyer had done. He was not a racialist as Marr and Dühring were; for him the dividing line between Germans and Jews was cultural, not biologically predetermined.

> The Jews are a nation, not a religious community—at least they are the latter only because they are the former.[39]

Lagarde's dream for the salvation of the German nation was a Central Europe under German hegemony, based on the dissolution of the Habsburg Empire, the colonization of the East, and the forcible transfer of the indigenous Slavs and Jews.[40] ("All remaining non-German tribes of the Danubian Empire, very much including the Magyars, are merely a burden for Europe. The faster they go under, the better it will be for us and them.") This pan-Germanism, which was relatively unpopular at the time that Lagarde was most active, was naturally in opposition to

---

* Altenstein, a follower of Hegel, was Prussian Minister of Education in the 1820's and 1830's; Falk was the minister responsible for the *Kulturkampf* legislation.

the Bismarckian state, which had failed to unite Germans geographically and atomized them politically and socially. Like all Conservatives, Lagarde exaggerated the Jacobin characteristics of the constitution of 1871; nevertheless the distinction between the folk community and the constitutional state is clear enough.

But expansion abroad is useless if the Jews, as a culturally separate group are allowed to survive among the Germans: "It is impossible to tolerate a nation within a nation."[41]

> The Jews will become Germans only when they continually hear from us that they have not yet achieved this, and that, as Jews, they are for us a repulsive burden, useless for history.[42]
>
> We are anti-Semites because the Jewish community living among us betrays, in the nineteenth century and in Germany, views, customs and ways of speech which go back to the period of the separation of the peoples after the Flood, and because they do so, appear as extraordinary amongst us as flint axes and arrow heads. We are anti-Semites, not enemies of the Jews, because in the midst of a Christian world Jews are Asiatic pagans.[43]

If the Jews have survived as a group, this is a sign of German weakness:

> . . . this circumstance proves that life in Germany is not yet sufficiently energetic and serious . . . . Every objectionable Jew is a grave reproach to the genuineness of our Germandom . . . . However, the nation cannot live energetically and seriously, if the governments do not remove from its neck the burden of well-meaning but simple-minded liberalism which they press upon it.[44]

That the Jews are as much a menace to Germany's world mission as they are to national unity is evident:

> The Jews . . . know that every German is an enemy, not of the individual Jew, but of Israel as Israel. The stronger German being becomes, the more entirely Israel is finished. That is why Israel tries to hinder a Central European federation.[45]

Lagarde was both a romantic conservative and an ultra-modern Imperialist. He believed both in aristocracy and pluralism, and in integral tribalism. Unlike those who regarded the Jewish question as merely religious or economic or constitutional, he believed that there had to be a final solution. But because he was not a racialist, he favored—except for an occasional indulgence in genocidal fantasies—assimilation. (See p. 62.)

The Jews as Jews are a grave misfortune to every European people. It follows for Germany that the Jews must either emigrate from Germany, or become Germans within it.[46]

REFERENCES

1 Articles V, XVII, XXXV, XLIV.
2 See N. M. Gelber, "The Intervention of German Jews at the Berlin Congress, 1878," *Leo Baeck Year Book VI* (London, 1960), pp. 221–48.
3 E. Stamm, *Konstantin Frantz' Schriften und Leben* (Heidelberg, 1907), pp. 1–2.
4 *Der Föderalismus al das leitende Prinzip für die soziale, staatliche und internationale Organisation* (Mainz, 1879); *Die Weltpolitik, mit besonderer Bezugnahme auf Deutschland* (Chemnitz, 1882–3); *Deutschland und der Föderalismus* (posth.).
5 K. Frantz, *Ahasverus, oder die Judenfrage* (Berlin, 1844), p. 18.
6 *Ibid.*, pp. 20, 35.
7 Frantz, *Die Religion des Nationalliberalismus*, p. 79.
8 *Ibid.*, p. 82.
9 *Ibid.*, p. 93.
10 *Ibid.*, p. 196.
11 *Ibid.*, pp. 2, 9–10.
12 Frantz, *Der Nationalliberalismus und die Judenherrschaft*, p. 8.
13 *Ibid.*, p. 35.
14 *Ibid.*, p. 21.
15 *Ibid.*, p. 22–3.
16 Frantz, *Der Untergang der alten Parteien*, pp. 57–8.
17 Frantz, *Die Religion des Nationalliberalismus*, p. 253.
18 Frantz, *Der Untergang der alten Parteien*, p. 105.
19 *Ibid.*, p. 94.
20 Frantz, *Der Nationalliberalismus und die Judenherrschaft*, p. 65.
21 Frantz, *Die Weltpolitik, Vol. III*, p. 115.
22 *NDAZ*, April 9, 1895, p.m. See also S. R. Tirrell, *German Agrarian Politics after Bismarck's Fall* (New York, 1951), p. 149.
23 R. Meyer, *Der Emanzipationskampf des vierten Standes* (Berlin, 1874–5).
24 R. Meyer, *Heimstätten- und andere Wirtschaftsgesetze* (Berlin, 1883), p. 560.
25 Engels to Bebel, Nov. 24, 1879. F. Engels, *Briefe an Bebel* (E. Berlin, 1958), p. 48; Engels to Kautsky, Nov. 27, 1891. K. Kautsky, *Aus der Frühzeit des Marxismus* (Prague, 1935), p. 303.
26 R. Meyer, *Was heisst konservativ sein? Reform oder Restauration?* (Berlin, 1873), pp. 18–19.
27 *Ibid.*, p. 14.
28 *Ibid.*, pp. 10, 13.

29 *Ibid.*, p. 17.
30 R. Meyer, *Politische Gründer und die Korruption in Deutschland* (Leipzig, 1877), pp. 110–11.
31 *Ibid.*, p. 204.
32 F. Stern, *The Politics of Cultural Despair. A Study in the Rise of the Germanic Ideology* (Berkeley–Los Angeles, 1961), pp. 19, 83.
33 A. de Lagarde, *Paul de Lagarde, Erinnerungen aus seinem Leben* (Göttingen, 1894), p. 38.
34 P. de Lagarde, "Über die gegenwärtige Lage des deutschen Reichs" (1875), *Schriften*, Vol. I, pp. 137–41.
35 Lagarde, "Zum letzten Male Albert Ritschl" (1890?), *Mitteilungen*, Vol. IV, p. 406.
36 Lagarde, "Juden und Indogermanen" (1887), *Mitteilungen*, Vol. II, p. 343.
37 Lagarde, "Programm für die konservative Partei Preussens" (1884), *Schriften*, Vol. I, p. 424.
38 Lagarde, "Die graue Internationale" (1881), *Schriften*, Vol. I, p. 358.
39 Lagarde, "Uber die gegenwärtigen Aufgaben der deutschen Politik" (1853), *Schriften*, Vol. I, p. 41.
40 *Ibid.*, pp. 129–31.
41 *Ibid.*, p. 41.
42 Lgarde, "Juden und Indogermanen," *Mitteilungen*, Vol. II, p. 331.
43 *Ibid.*, p. 330.
44 Lagarde, "Die graue Internationale," *Schriften*, Vol. I, p. 370.
45 Lagarde, "Juden und Indogermanen," *Mitteilungen*, Vol. II, p. 350.
46 Lagarde, "Programm für die konservative Partei Preussens," *Schriften*, Vol. I, p. 422.

10

Stöcker and the Berlin Movement

Frantz and Meyer reached only a small audience, and Lagarde's influence became dominant only after his death. If anti-Semitism, therefore, were to become an important factor in politics, if the campaign to revoke emancipation were to result in legislation, an appeal would have to be made to the broader public. Once the impact of the 1873 crash had registered, anti-Semitism appeared more frequently in press articles, and periodicals devoted entirely to "anti-corruption" propaganda were founded. In 1875 the organs of extreme Prussian conservatism and of the Centre Party each carried a series of anti-Semitic articles. In the *Kreuzzeitung** the agrarian publicist, F. F. Perrot, wrote on "The Era of Bismarck, Delbrück and Camphausen" and a great many people who had never heard of worthy conservative academics could read:

> Bank, share and stock exchange privileges are, as things stand, Jews' privileges. They are therefore protected and pushed with all their might by the Jewish press, by Jewish scholars and Jewish deputies.[1]

So successful were these five articles that they were reprinted separately. In the Catholic campaign against the absolute Liberal majorities in the Reichstag and the Prussian Diet, *Germania,* wielded the anti-Semitic weapons, but with the end of the *Kulturkampf* and the decline of parliamentary

---

* This paper, later edited by Freiherr von Hammerstein, was founded in 1848 and represented the extreme right of Prussian conservatism. This faction was sometimes referred to as the *Kreuzzeitungspartei.*

Liberalism* official Catholic anti-Semitism became a rarity. Joachim Gehlsen, a colleague of Meyer's in the *Antikanzlerliga* and already the editor of other anti-Semitic journals, founded, in 1874, the *Deutsche Eisenbahnzeitung* (later renamed *Die Reichsglocke)*, so called because railway finance had produced some of the most blatant scandals.

The most important in its immediate impact on public opinion was the series of articles contributed from December 1874 to December 1875 by Otto Glagau to the *Gartenlaube,* a lower middle-brow magazine circulating among the Pooters and Podsnaps of Berlin,† precisely those sections of the population who were now suffering under the Liberalism to which they had hitherto given a somewhat emotional and unreflective support.

Glagau was a first-class journalist, with a fluent and witty style, who, his opponents alleged, has lost all his money in speculations during the *Gründerzeit.* The articles were an immediate and immense success and were reprinted, with augmentations, in two volumes.[2] He made and defended statements such as that 90% of all *Gründer* and stock exchange speculators were Jews[3] and relentlessly fed the despondency and pessimism of his readers:

> How much has the German people lost in fame and reputation; how quickly has the glory, so recently won, paled and waned! How great are its losses in honesty and morality, in virtue and religion, in industry and thrift, in propriety and manners! The most serious and unnatural crimes are the order of the day, murder and robbery, burglary and theft make town and country unsafe, fraud and embezzlement spread like the plague, suicide has assumed epidemic proportions. Beggars and vagabonds roam about in droves, the prisons and penitentiaries are full, the number of civil and criminal trials, of bankruptcies, seizures and enforced sales is legion.[4]

There are even echoes of Marx in his Jeremiads to the despairing *Mittelstand*:

* In the Reichstag elections of 1874 the national Liberals won 155 seats out of 397 and the Progressives 50. They lost this majority in 1877. In Prussia they held a majority from 1873 to 1879. For a further discussion of Catholic anti-Semitism, see Chapter 29.
† Its circulation in 1875 was 382,000, quite exceptionally large for those times (H. Zang, *Die Gartenlaube als politisches Organ,*1935, p. 14).

The abolition of guild privileges has torn every bond between master, mate and apprentice, and ruined the artisan class which once formed the core of the bourgeoisie.*

Like Frantz and Lagarde he also blamed the *Kulturkampf* on the Jews.[5]

Into this political and moral disorientation, born of economic distress, stepped Adolf Stöcker. Stöcker's father was a blacksmith who had become a soldier and, after thirty-seven years' service in the ranks, a prison warder. He himself had been enabled, through the sacrifices of his parents, to study theology and become a pastor of the Lutheran Church. He spent a number of years as tutor to a noble German family in Courland; and during the Franco-Prussian war he was an army chaplain. Thanks to his exceptional patriotic fervor he was recalled to Berlin when the war was over and attached to the cathedral there with the post of court preacher.

This position at the capital, and the favor he appeared to be enjoying from the very highest circles, encouraged him to take up the political work for which he had always had a taste. He was appalled by the extent to which German society had become secularized and by the indifference, not to say hostility, to the traditional values of the Prussian state which he saw in Berlin.† His ideal in politics was monarchic and aristocratic. He wanted a Christian state which not only taught the virtues of obedience but inspired its rulers to take the weaker and poorer classes under their wing.

The two great enemies of all he stood for were the Progressive and Social Democratic parties, which between them commanded the political loyalties of almost the whole of Berlin. In particular he felt the call to save the capital from atheist Marxism, not only because it was a subversive force, but because

---

* *Op. cit.*, Vol. II, p. xxxii. Cf the *Communist Manifesto*: "The bourgeoisie has . . .destroyed all feudal, patriarchal, idyllic relationships. It has ruthlessly torn asunder the motley feudal ties that bound men to their 'natural superiors' . . . . It has drowned pious zeal, chivalrous enthusiasm and humdrum sentimentalism . . . . It has degraded personal dignity to the level of exchange value."

† In 1875, only 27.3% of marriages between Protestants in Berlin were solemnized and 65% of Protestant births baptized: five years later the figures had risen to 41.5% and 74.8% respectively (*Zeitschrift des Königlich Preussischen Statistischen Bureaus*, Vol. XXI, pp. 352–4).

he saw very clearly that under universal suffrage the only hope for the Conservatives was to go into the streets and enlist the mass support of the workers, fellow sufferers and natural allies in the struggle against Liberalism.

So it was that early in January, 1878 posters appeared on the hoardings of North Berlin, inviting the public to a meeting for the purpose of founding a Christian Social Workers' Party. Stöcker was not the first Protestant conservative to agitate for social reform. Adolf Wagner's *Verein für Sozialpolitik* had been founded in 1872, and other literature had begun to appear on the subject.[6] But Stöcker was the first to take the social gospel to the masses. Alas, the meeting was a pitiful fiasco. The Social Democrats turned up in force and took over. After a long and violent harangue by Johann Most* a resolution was passed by acclamation, condemning the Church for having done so little, in 1900 years, to end poverty and misery and expressing confidence in the Social Democratic Party as the only workers' party.

Later meetings suffered a similar fate. To Stöcker's arguments, borrowed from Adolf Wagner, that Socialism was not the equivalent of materialism and republicanism there was no response. The workers were suspicious of priests; they feared and distrusted the whole enterprise as an attempt to neutralize them politically. The Social Democrats had taught them that their salvation lay in their own hands and that none but they themselves could help them; and this they believed.

The first test for the strength of Stöcker's appeal came with the general election in the autumn of 1878. The Christian Social Party contested three of the capital's six seats and fought on an independent program which demanded professional corporations and compulsory arbitration, old age and invalid pensions, factory legislation, restoration of the usury laws, progressive taxation, and taxation of stock exchange dealings and luxuries. It appealed to the clergy to participate "lovingly and actively" in the people's struggle for betterment, and to the possessing classes for

* Most was the leader of the Berlin Social Democrats. He was a man of extremely violent temperament, an anarchist rather than a Marxist, and was excluded from the party in 1880 for advocating terrorism. He had sought asylum in England in 1878, but was expelled in 1882 after having publicly welcomed the assassination of Tsar Alexander II.

willingness to meet half-way the justified demands of the have-nots.[7]

They were shatteringly defeated. The Progressives won 86,411 votes and five seats, the Social Democrats 56,146 votes and the sixth seat. The Conservatives had 12,196 votes, the Christian Socials 1422. The results of this election were decisive for the future of the party; but so were its circumstances.

· Normally the Reichstag elected in 1877 would not have been dissolved until 1880. Although the Liberal parties had lost their absolute majority they were still strong enough to bargain with Bismarck on the composition of his ministry and the formulation of policy. They had served Bismarck's purpose well enough during the crucial years of unification, but he now resented their increasing opposition to such issues as tariffs, the army vote, and freedom of the press.

Then, in the summer of 1878, two attempts were made, within three months of each other, on the life of the emperor. These two attempted assassinations made a considerable emotional impact on the nation. Bismarck had, after the first attempt, presented a bill to the Reichstag to outlaw the Social Democrats, whose agitation and revolutionary teachings were blamed for the outrage, but the bill was rejected. The second attempt, which unlike the first, severely injured the aged emperor, gave Bismarck the chance he wanted. Determined to impale the National Liberals, he dissolved the Reichtag, on the sole issue of the "defense of the realm" against Red terror. The anti-Socialist bill was resubmitted to the new Reichstag receiving the numb assent of those National Liberals who were elected by their promise to support it. It remained in force for twelve years.

This general election and its outcome represented a permanent change in the balance of power in German politics. It was a blow from which the National Liberal Party never recovered. Political exigencies henceforth exerted a continuous pressure on it to put patriotism before Liberalism, and the economic crisis provided a powerful incentive to compromise with the principles of free trade. Thus the Christian Social Workers' Party, formed with the intention of tapping mass support for the Right, appeared at a most auspicious moment on the political scene.

If it was to play the part it had set itself, however, it would have to revise its tactics and the nature of its appeal. It obviously had little future with the workers. It had not prevented the Social Democratic vote from doubling in eighteen months;* the retaliatory move launched by Johann Most, a campaign to urge workers to leave the Church, though not a conspicuous success from the Socialist point of view, was ominous enough for Stöcker.

There were, however, others beside the workers who had reason to complain of Liberalism or to feel discontented in some other ways—traders, artisans, shopkeepers, officials—classes which, though capable of spasmodic radicalism, were basically loyal to Church and State. Moreover, unlike the workers, who knew that the answer lay in the dialectic, they were susceptible to anti-Semitism. And when Stöcker's meetings began to fill with them instead of the workers, he made his partly an overtly anti-Semitic one. So, on September 19, 1879, "filled with Christian charity,"[8] he devoted a speech to this subject for the first time, entitling it, "Our Demands on Modern Judaism."

It contained nothing that others had not said before. It was couched in ironical and half-conciliatory tones. His three demands were "a little more modesty, a little more tolerance, a little more equality."[9] But having thus made anti-Semitism part of his platform, even though he might have intended it to take only a subordinate part, he could never again renounce it, for in the 1880's it became a highly competitive business.

It is arguable that Stöcker's party was bound, sooner or later, to embrace anti-Semitism. Stöcker himself, it is clear, did not originally have this intention. The Jewish question had indeed been canvassed once or twice during the election campaign on the initiative of the rank and file,[10] but Stöcker committed himself on it only in the last paragraph of his election manifesto.

> We respect the Jews as fellow citizens and honour Judaism as the lower step of divine revelation. But we firmly believe that no Jew can be leader of Christian workers in either a religious or an economic capacity. The Christian Social Party inscribes Christianity on its banner.[11]

By 1879, however, Stöcker had nothing to lose by embracing anti-Semitism. The workers had turned a deaf ear and the Liberal

---

* In 1877 it received 27,889 votes, and in 1878 it received 56,147 votes.

press and politicians of Berlin, both comprising numerous influential Jews, had been hostile from the start. They resented not only his clericalism and his conservatism, but also his social program which threatened their moneybags. Indeed, his defenders have argued that the continuous barrage of criticism, some of it less than just, to which he was subjected from the *"Judenpresse,"* was the starting point of his anti-Semitic campaign.

If the Liberals and Socialists now had added incentive to attack and despise him, the Conservatives had reason to revise their attitude. Originally most of them had been lukewarm, even severely critical, toward his venture. They disliked his "democratic" methods of agitation and feared the attacks he was making on the privileges of the rich, and when the Social Democrats discovered and gleefully published the fact that Hödel, one of the would-be regicides, had for a time actually been a member of the Christian Social Party, voices were not lacking which advocated extending the terms of the anti-Socialist bill to the Court Preacher's party.

In general, however, the turn of the tide for the Conservatives in 1878 and Bismarck's change of front put the Christian Social Party in a different light. It appeared as a potential ally in the assault on the hitherto impregnable Progressive citadel of Berlin, all the more so since Stöcker was no longer the only politician hawking anti-Semitism as a panacea round the beer halls of Berlin.

The most important of his prospective rivals, or allies, were Bernhard Förster, Max Liebermann von Sonnenberg, and Ernst Henrici. Förster was a brother-in-law of Nietzsche and a schoolmaster who had already gained a certain amount of notoriety by being involved, with a colleague, Dr. Jungfer, in a disturbance on a tramcar in which a Jewish businessman was beaten up.[12] Sonnenberg was a minor aristocrat and ex-officer whose own financial embarrassments—he had frequent difficulties in honoring his checks[13]—no doubt helped him toward the contempt in which he held attempts at mere economic reform. He saw Germany's salvation in nothing less than the

material and moral rebirth of German *Volkstum,* intensification of German being, stimulation of the practical application of the Christian Doctrine.[14]

Förster and Sonnenberg formed the *Deutscher Volksverein* in March 1881, and attracted 6000 people to its first meeting.[15] It was, if anything, to the right of Stöcker. For Sonnenberg, parliament was "the source of all evil;"[16] the party's program demanded the restoration of guilds for both artisans and industrial workers.[17]

Henrici, like Förster, was a schoolmaster.* He was the first politician to popularize the purely racial propaganda of Marr and the *Antisemiten-Liga*. He was only twenty-seven years old when his first meetings, toward the end of 1880, created a tremendous sensation by their completely uncompromising and unscrupulous arguments. He described himself, and the *Soziale Reichspartei* which he founded in 1881, as *"freisinnig-antisemitisch."*† Stöcker had based himself on religion and loyalism; Henrici appealed to the radical and nationalist traditions of Berlin. He argued that Berlin had no sympathy with clerics and Junkers and that there was no need to give up what had been won since 1867 in liberal institutions in order to stop the Jews from taking excessive advantage of them.

His program demanded a prohibition of Jewish immigration, the exclusion of Jews from all public office, and the resumption of a special census for Jews. In the economic sphere it went further than Stöcker's in demanding a ten-hour day and the abolition of direct taxes for lower income groups.[18] But what was really significant about it was the insistence that the core of the Jewish question was racial. "If it is a question of racial characteristics, then both body and spirit must be kept in mind."[19] Stöcker's solution, the conversion of Jews to Christianity, was as impracticable as it was undesirable: "The religion of the Jews is a racial religion."[20] A visit, with speeches, by Henrici to the Pomeranian town of Neustettin resulted in anti-Jewish

---

* Förster, Jungfer, and Henrici were all dismissed from their teaching posts by the Berlin City Council.

† There is no exact equivalent for "freisinnig" in English. It is sometimes rendered as liberal, a word which in this context is obviously misleading. it really implies a mixtue of social radicalism and anti-clericalism, with the emphasis on a rationalist intellectual attitude. The German left-wing liberals called themselves "freisinnig" from 1884 to 1910; one of the principal Swiss parties of today is called "Freisinnige Partei" in German and "Parti Radical" in French.

riots and the burning of the synagogue—events altogether rare in Imperial Germany.

Förster, Sonnenberg, and Henrici were jointly the organizers of the Anti-Semitic Petition, the inspiration for which had come to Förster during the Bayreuth Festival of 1880. Its purpose was to gain signatures for what were by now the standard anti-Semitic demands—the suspension of immigration, the exclusion of Jews from public positions, and the restoration of a special census. The Delphic reply which the Prussian Minister of the Interior gave to a Progressive deputy when asked about the government's attitude to the petition then circulating, and which did not contain the official rebuke the interpellation had intended to provoke,[21] encouraged rather than deterred the organizers. In April 1882, they presented the petition to Bismarck; it had been signed by 225,000 persons, the bulk of them from northern and eastern Prussia. Bavaria contributed 9000 names, and Württemberg and Baden between them contributed 7000.[22]

These various trends of Berlin anti-Semitism found a cover organization in the *Berliner Bewegung,* a half-political, half-missionary body, comprising Christian Socials, Conservative State Socialists, and generally reformist and anti-Semitic tendencies. Its fate depended to a considerable degree on the favor it could find in Bismarck's eyes.

Any coolness Stöcker encountered from the Emperor or the Chancellor was due to his rabble-rousing tactics. Stöcker was not content with attacking yellow journalism in the radical Berlin press or the Jewish leaders of the Social Democratic Party, he also averted the hungry eyes of his listeners to the wealth of bankers like Bleichröder. The Jewish *haute bourgeoisie,* as Bismarck knew very well, were pillars of established society; anti-Semitism directed against them could hardy help to serve the cause Stöcker claimed to have at heart. His antipathies were restricted to the Jews prominent in the left-wing politics of Berlin.

Much ink has been expended on the question of Bismarck's relationship with anti-Semitism. It is certain that he no longer held, in the 1880's, the views he expressed in his *Landtag* speech of

---

* The bulk of the immigrants came from Austria and Russia, and Bismarck was certainly not willing to antagonise either power by discriminating against its citizens for so small a price.

1847, when he opposed emancipation. His later remarks about Jews being a valuable "mousseux" and about "bringing the Gentile stallion together with the Jewish mare"[23] probably represent his sincere opinion. One of the writers who reproach his failure to condemn anti-Semitism quotes him as saying that "in their polemics against me the Jews have never been as mean as my Christian opponents."[24] The banker Bleichröder was one of his few intimate friends, and both his doctor (Cohen) and his lawyer (Philip) at Friedrichsruh were Jews.[25] It was his association with Jewish bankers and businessmen that had so incensed the early anti-Semites; when, in the 1890's, a later generation joined in the general adulation of the ex-chancellor, the pioneers were deeply grieved.

> At that time [wrote Gehlsen in 1894] the opposition of many circles to Bismarck as well as to the Jews was identical; today, however, a section of the German anti-Semites seek support in some imaginary anti-Semitism on the part of the ex-Chancellor.[26]

Another claimed that only since the retirement of "this bosom-friend of Bleichröder" had anti-Semitism truly flourished.[27]

The truth is that Bismarck had a sense of proportion, and by no stretch of the imagination could the Jewish question be called the most serious issue of the day. In the political context of 1880 and 1881, however, Bismarck saw that some advantage could be reaped from a tactical alliance with anti-Semitism. He was occupied with following up his anti-Socialist legislation with measures of social security designed to take the wind out of the Socialist sails; and for this his most reliable allies were the Conservatives and the Centre who had only so recently combined their anti-Semitism with a hatred of the Chancellor. Above all he was continuing to pursue his aim of weakening and isolating both wings of the Liberal Party. The Berlin Movement, and its political agency, the Conservative Central Committee, qualified for support on both counts. Privately[28] he expressed the hope that Stöcker would win and he seems to have tolerated the violently anti-Semitic articles which his press secretary, Moritz Busch, was writing in the *Grenzbote*[29] at that time. He bestowed no public blessing on Stöcker, but there was no anathema either, and it was widely believed that money from the

Welfenfonds was finding its way into the coffers of the C.C.C.

For the 1881 elections the Conservative Central Committee adopted four well-known anti-Semites among its six candidates. They were Adolf Wagner, the *Kathedersozialist*, Liebermann von Sonnenberg, Joseph Cremer, a Catholic and reputed to have been the author of the *Germania* articles, and lastly Stöcker himself who stood against Rudolf Virchow, a pathologist, one of the most eminent German men of science and a leader of the Progressive Party. "Herr Professor Virchow," Stöcker informed the electors,

> has defended Jewry and signed an appeal in favour of Jewish usurers [i.e., the Declaration of the Notables]; he has always attacked and despised Christianity. A Progressive manifesto has called him a representative of *Kultur* and the candidate of the educated world. I desire no *Kultur* without Germandom and Christianity; that is why I am fighting against Jewish predominance.[30]

Sonnenberg, more flamboyantly, stood as "the candidate of German Christian faith, the supporter of Prince Bismarck's social reforms" against "the rich *Gründer* and Manchester man, the Jew Ludwig Löwe."[31]

The election did not bring the Berlin Movement the success it had hoped for. The Progressives won all six seats in the capital, but the C.C.C. had succeeed in beating the Social Democrats, disabled by the discriminatory laws, into third place.* Stöcker himself was elected on the Conservative ticket at Siegen in Westphalia, a constituency which, with one break, he continued to represent until 1908. Since 1879 he had also sat in the Prussian Diet for the neighboring constituency of Minden. His election, in that loyalist, pietistic part of the country, was a victory "not for the social agitator, but for the Churchman."[32]

For all the disappointment that the elections brought to the Christian Social Party, its achievement represented a considerable improvement on any previous performance by the Conservatives in Berlin. Stöcker had succeeded in leading into the conservative camp those disgruntled members of the *Mittelstand,* the "small men" whose fathers had manned the barricades in 1848 and who, since the crash of 1873, had really been politically homeless. He

---

* The Progressives received 89,000 votes, the C.C.C. 46,000, and the Social Democrats 30,000.

had also secured considerable support from civil servants and professional men, now that anti-Semitism had apparently become "house-trained."* The word "Workers" had been removed from the party's name at the beginning of 1881.[33]

These classes, once disillusioned with Liberalism, remained permanently estranged from it; they were thus a prize Stöcker and his successors would continue to enjoy. On the other hand, they also represented the limits of the possibilities of his success. Except in 1887, when the circumstances of the *Kartell* election favored the Right, the Conservative anti-Semitic bloc never really improved on its 1881 figures; it never during the whole of its existence succeeded in capturing a Reichstag seat in Berlin.†

For Bismarck, the outcome of the election had been most satisfactory. The National Liberals, weakened by the defection of those, who, like Lasker and Bamberger, objected to the increasingly servile attitude of the party, had sunk in seven years from first place to fifth. The social legislation he had planned, praised by the emperor as according with the "moral bases of Christianity," went through the Reichstag without any difficulty, sped on its way by a fulsome, if perhaps superfluous, commendation by Stöcker.

Stöcker, in fact, did not cut a very important figure in parliament. Bismarck lost interest in him now that the man had shown his limitations as well as his usefulness and Stöcker sought his company more and more among the backwoodsmen of the *Kreuzzeitungspartei*. He suffered, too, from being out-flanked by the more radical anti-Semites. His beliefs and his social position made it impossible for him to emulate them. For the Marxist virtue is a matter of class, for the racialist a matter of blood; but for the Lutheran pastor it can only be a question of faith and grace. "The Christian spirit," he said, "penetrates the barriers of

* Treitschke's articles had been published in 1879 to 1880. See Chapter 27.
† The strength of Christian-Social support among the lower middle class of Berlin is shown by the 1883 elections to the City Council, the electorate being divided into three classes.

	Progressive Votes	*Anti-Semitic Votes*	*Social Democrat Votes*
Class I	1,871	434	
Class II	6,989	2,288	
Class III	32,101	25,074	8,000

race, and when the Israelites are baptized they become our brothers."[34] Nor would he tolerate attacks on the Old Testament for it "is as sacred to us as the New, and whoever attacks the latter, breaks with positive Christianity," though this did not prevent him from quoting the Prophets to show how unsatisfactory the children of Israel were in the eyes of God.[35]

He saw the Jewish question as neither merely racial nor merely religious, it was *"sozial-ethisch:"*[36]

> I see in unrestrained capitalism the evil of our epoch and am naturally also an opponent of modern Judaism on account of my socio-political views. But it would never have occurred to me to take up my stand against purely economic errors, if this frivolous chase against all Christian elements in our life were not connected with them.[37]

In one matter, however, he was cool and realistic. He resisted any attempts to cut the knot of the problem by demanding a revocation of emancipation.

> Emancipation is a fact, not only amongst us, but amongst all civilised nations. That we have to reckon with.[38]

And in this he was a realistic politician.

Contemporaries agree that Stöcker's personality and fervor —he was hailed as the "second Luther"—had a remarkable effect on his audiences. Indeed they must have had, for this alone can account for his success. His arguments, read in cold blood, seem tortuous and tentative, their presentation prolix and unctuous. The Liberal logic-choppers seized on the constant contradictions in his utterances, so as to defeat anti-Semitism with reason. That this is the weakest of arms against it was a lesson not then learnt.

Unlike Förster and Sonnenberg, whose *Volksverein* avoided the rowdyism of Henrici and who succeeded in making their peace with the C.C.C., Henrici remained high and dry. In 1881 he stood independently in Berlin and polled 843 votes. Though his whole political career was a mere flash in the pan, he was symptomatic of a permanent and increasingly important direction in the German anti-Semitic movement. He and Stöcker represented its two wings: the "democratic" and the "conservative," and all the parties and organizations which sprang up at or after this time can be fitted into one or the other of these categories.

REFERENCES

1 F. F. Perrot, *Die Ära Bismarck-Delbrück-Camphausen* (Berlin, 1876), p. 17.
2 Vol. I: *Der Boïrsen- und Gründungsschwindel in Berlin* (Leipzig, 1876); Vol. II, *Der Börsen- und Gründungsschwindel in Deutschland* (Leipzig, 1877).
3 *op. cit.*, Vol. I, p. xxiv.
4 *Ibid.*, Vol. II, pp. xvii–xviii.
5 O. Glagau, *Des Reiches Not und der neue Kulturkampf* (Osnabrück, 1879), p. 265.
6 For example, Pastor R. Todt's *Der radikale deutsche Sozialismus und die christliche Gesellschaft* (1877).
7 Stöcker, *Christlich-Sozial*, pp. 21–2.
8 *Ihid.*, p. 359.
9 *Ibid.*, p. 362–7.
10 K. Wawrzinek, "Die Entstehung der deutschen Antisemitenparteien," *Historische Studien 168* (Berlin, 1927), p. 22.
11 *"An die Wähler Berlins,"* Stöcker, *op. cit.*, p. 127.
12 C. Fischer, *Antisemiten und Gymnasiallehrer. Ein Protest* (Berlin, 1881), p. 3.
13 H. von Gerlach, *Von Rechts nach Links* (Zürich, 1937), p. 111.
14 Wawrzinek, *op. cit.*, p. 40.
15 Liebermann von Sonnenberg, *Beiträge*, p. 73.
16 Wawrzinek, *op. cit.*, p. 41.
17 Liebermann von Sonnenberg, *op. cit.*, p. 81.
18 Wawrzinek, *op. cit.*, pp. 38–9.
19 E. Henrici, *Was ist der Kern der Judenfrage?* (Berlin, 1881), p. 5.
20 *Ibid.*, p. 4.
21 *StPrA*, 2. Sess., XIV. Leg, Per. (1880–1881), *Anlagen* Vol. I, pp. 735–6.
22 Wawrzinek, *op. cit.*, p. 38.
23 J. H. M. Busch, *Tagebuchblätter* (2nd ed., Leipzig, 1902), Vol. II, p. 33.
24 Popper-Lynkeus (i.e., J. Popper), *Fürst Bismarck und der Antisemitismus* (Vienna, 1886), p. 24.
25 E. Eyck, *Bismarck, Leben und Werk* (Zürich, 1941–44), Vol. III, p. 361.
26 J. Gehlsen, *Aus dem Reiche Bismarcks* (Berlin, 1894), p. 57.
27 Anon., *Die Antisemiten und Bismarck. Dazu etwas über alten und neuen Kurs, Bedientenhaftigkeit u.s.w.* (Leipzig, 1892), pp. 6, 35.
28 In a letter to his son Wilhelm, reproving him for speaking publicly in favor of Stöcker during the campaign. Massing, *Rehearsal for Destruction*, p. 224.
29 The articles were published anonymously and also appeared in book form. In later editions the authorship was acknowledged. Busch's numerous other writings include translations of Mark Twain.
30 *"An die Wähler des zweiten Berliner Wahlkreises,"* Stöcker, *op. cit.*, p. 345.
31 J. Jacobs, *The Jewish Question, 1875–84. A bibliographical Handlist* (London, 1885), p. 7.
32 W. Frank, *Der Hofprediger Adolf Stöcker*, p. 72.

33 *Ibid.*, p. 71.
34 Speech on Jan. 3, 1881. Wawrzinek, *op. cit.*, p. 37.
35 Speech on Jan. 5, 1880. Stöcker,*op. cit.*, pp. 383–4.
36 Speeches on Jan. 3, May 27, 1881. *Ibid.*, p. 405.
37 Speech on Sept. 26, 1879. *Ibid.*, p. 377.
38 speech on May 27, 1881. *Ibid.*, p. 411.

11

National and International
Organization

For most of the 1880's political anti-Semitism was in the doldrums, and the promises held out by the debut of the 1881 election remained unfulfilled. Attempts to spread the movement beyond Berlin were equally unsuccessful. Alexander Pinkert's *Deutsche Reformpartei* in Saxony (1881) took up feelers with Stöcker and the Conservatives and helped a Right-wing coalition to gain control of the Dresden city council, defeating the only Jew on it, but it soon became a mere adjunct of Social Conservatism and there was no trace of it in 1885.

At first sight it would have seemed that Saxony was in any case unreceptive ground for such agitation. Its Jewish population in 1880 was 8755 or ¼% of the total.[1] It was, however, one of the most highly industrialized parts of Germany with a numerous and economically insecure *Mittelstand;* there was considerable response to the idea of reform on mildly State Socialist lines and in the 1890's anti-Semitism made appreciable headway here. But at this stage its appeal was not yet strong enough to succeed where the Jew was not a readily visible villain.

Pinkert's other activities included the "First International Anti-Jewish Congress" which he organized at Dresden in 1882, with delegates from several parts of Germany, Austria, and Hungary. It met under the shadow of the ritual murder trials of Tísza-Eszlár in Hungary and the platform was decorated with a portrait of Esther Solymossi, the victim of the alleged murder, which Ivan Simonyí, one of the Hungarian participants, had brought with him. A standing committee was elected with a certain Schmeitzner, chairman of the Chemnitz Reform Association as "plenipotentiary"; he converted the organization into an

98

Alliance Antijuive Universelle (an allusion to the *Alliance Israëlite Universelle,* founded in Paris in 1860).

A second congress in Chemnitz the next year attracted delegates from Austria, Hungary, Russia, Rumania, Serbia, and France.[2] When the fundamental racialists tried to force the acceptance of Dühring's book as the basis of the whole anti-Semitic movement, the meeting split, and the moderate, Christian elements were excluded from subsequent congresses.* Like all attempts at anti-Semitic unity it and the Kassel congress of 1886 merely demonstrated the incompatibility of the two wings of the movement.

Of greater importance was the loose confederation of *Reformvereine* which sprang up in the 1880's on the basis of Pinkert's at Dresden. By 1885 there were 52 of these, by 1890 there were 136,[3] representing every possible shade of anti-Semitism. The extreme view, associated with Dühring, predominated in Westphalia, where Dr. König was a leading figure. In Hesse, one of the poorest parts of Germany, economic grievances were stressed and the Kassel association founded a paper called the *Reichsgeldmonopol* because it regarded an imperial monopoly of the right of issue as the essential basis of economic reform. A good indication of the Reform Movement's social composition is given by the Chemnitz association which constituted itself simply by changing its name from "Association for the Defense of Artisans' and Traders' Interests."[4] The most important branch, however, from the point of view of the movement's history, was that at Leipzig, with a membership of 1500, under the chairmanship of Theodor Fritsch, for it provided the continuity between the first and second waves of anti-Semitism. Meanwhile the wranglings between the various factions continued, based as much on temperamental as ideological incompatibilities. One by one, the leaders became too discouraged to carry on. Henrici retired after only two years and his organization was taken over by the Dühringites. He went to America and returned with a wife who was reputed to be "of mixed blood."[5] Förster left for Paraguay, where he attempted to form a *judenreine* colony, but Thor on the pampas proved too much for him and he committed suicide in 1889.[6] In 1885

* See illustration 1.

Sonnenberg's *Deutsche Volkszeitung* ceased publication. Other parties were founded only to collapse again.

It would be wrong to suppose that the disunity among the organizers was alone responsible for these failures. This was a symptom rather than a cause, for when conditions are favorable neither the incoherence of the program nor the criminal records of the leaders★ are an obstacle to widespread public confidence. The excitement of the late 1870's was over now, the political confusion of those years had given way to a new party alignment which was providing stable government, Bismarck's social legislation had taken the edge off discontent, and the country had recovered from the worst of the slump. Fritsch was hardly exaggerating when he wrote that by 1885 the anti-Semitic movements had "by all appearances come to a complete standstill, indeed an undeniable retreat."[7]

The germ of revival was in the *Reformverein* of Leipzig. Fritsch had from the start rejected Pinkert's moderate approach and had no sympathy with Bismarck's policy of social reform without anti-Semitism. He was an unqualified fanatic who subordinated every issue to the supreme necessity of Germanic racial purity.

Taking it upon himself to revive anti-Semitism from the total decline with which it was threatened, he bought out Schmeitzner's publishing house and from it edited the *Antisemitische Correspondenz.* He was also instrumental in popularizing Lagarde's *Deutsche Schriften.*[8] Warned, perhaps, by the failure of previous attempts at party organization, he regarded himself purely as a propagandist. In his view:

> Anti-Semitism is a matter of *Weltanschauung* which can be accepted by anyone, no matter what party he belongs to . . . .

★ As a general point about extremist parties this hardly needs elaborating. As far as German anti-Semitism is concerned, see the careers of Ahlwardt and Schack. Hellmut von Gerlach, the Junker who died as a pacifist exile in Switzerland and knew many of the anti-Semitic leaders of this period at first hand, has left the following verdict on them: "Among the anti-Semitic leaders I got to know only a few really decent people, and those whose character was spotless were so ignorant and uneducated that I was appalled when I had the opportunity of observing them at close range. They were demagogues one and all, some against their better judgment, others for lack of judgment" (Gerlach, *Von Rechts nach Links,* p. 114).

Our aim is to permeate all parties with the anti-Semitic idea. . . .
As soon as we present ourselves as a party we shall naturally
have not only the Jews, but all other political parties against us.[9]

His journal, intended to be a forum ("Sprechsaal") for all shades
of anti-Semitic opinion,[10] in fact—and this was inevitable—soon
edged out the conservative side.

The first success of anti-Semitism had been to a large extent
engineered from above. It took its form because the Conservatives had decided to seek as allies the discontented among the
lower middle classes. The second was organized from below, and
in terms of noise, votes, and deputies it was much the more
formidable. It distinguished itself from the Conservatives who,
while no doubt predominantly sharing anti-Semitic sentiments
and making use of them from time to time, did not look upon
them as the core of their political principles.

The *Deutsche Antisemitische Vereinigung,* which was the fruit of
Fritsch's contacts with fellow spirits in western Germany, might
have gone the way of all its predecessors had it not succeeded in
recruiting an enthusiastic young man from Hesse, whose
irruption into political life, in a blaze of abuse and demagogy,
was to effect a complete transformation of the anti-Semites'
political prospects. This man was Otto Böckel.

REFERENCES

1 Krose, *Konfessionsstatistik Deutschlands,* p. 78.
2 *Schmeitzners Internationale Monatsschrift,* Vol. II, No. 5 (1883), pp. 255, 262.
3 *Deutsche Reform,* July 30, 1885, quoted by M. Broszat, *Die anti-semitische
   Bewegung im wilhelminischen Deutschland* (unpublished dissertation, Cologne,
   1953), p. 67; T. Fritsch, "Vom parteipolitischen Antisemitismus" in *Neue
   Wege,* p. 283.
4 Wawrzinek, *Die Entstehung,* p. 56.
5 Massing, *Rehearsal for Destruction,* p. 114.
6 *Deutsche Antisemitenchronik,* p. 23.
7 *Antisemitische Correspondenz* No. 1 (October, 1882).
8 A. de Lagarde, *Paul de Lagarde,* p. 106.
9 Fritsch, *Neue Wege,* pp. 280–1.
10 The paper was headed, "Anti-Semitic Correspondence and Forum for
   internal matters. Distributed only to reliable party comrades."

12

Böckel and Ahlwardt

Böckel was a librarian at the University of Marburg in Upper Hesse. His chief hobby was the collection of folk songs and folk tales, and for this purpose he traveled much round the countryside, thus gaining the intimate acquaintance with the peasants' condition of life which proved so valuable in his campaign.* Hesse† was one of the poorest and most backward regions of Germany, which had derived few advantages from annexation by Prussia to compensate for the higher taxation and conscription. It had also a comparatively large Jewish population which was occupied mainly in moneylending, land and corn brokerage, and general trade, and seems to have been on the same cultural level as its Gentile neighbors.‡

Böckel's attention to the Jewish question had first been drawn, he claimed, by a trial resulting from the murder of a

* The fruits of some of his researches claimed him when he had become famous. In 1889, having since married, he was sued by his former housekeeper for the maintenance of her illegitimate children (*Antisemitenchronik*, p. 19).

† The principalities annexed by Prussia became the province of Hesse-Nassau; the Grand Duchy of Hesse-Darmstadt remained independent. Anti-Semitism was confined to the northern part of the region covered by these two states.

‡ The percentage of self-employed among gainfully occupied adults may be taken as a rough indication of the economic and social backwardness of a region or of a Jewish community within that region. In the Grand Duchy of Hesse, 66.0% of Jews were classified as self-employed in the occupational census of 1895, compared with an average of 57.6% for the whole of Germany [Ruppin, "Die sozialen Verhältnisse der Juden in Preussen und Deutschland," *Jahrbuch für nationalökonomie und Statisktik*, Series III, Vol. XXIII/6 (1902), p. 869; Ruppin, "Die berufliche Gliederung der Juden in Hesse," *ZDSJ* Vol. IV/4 (1908), p. 50]. Hesse was also one of the few regions of Germany with a large Jewish rural population. As late as 1910 45% of Jews in the Grand Duchy lived in rural areas, compared with 31% in Bavaria, 28% in Baden, and 12% in Prussia. (J. Kreppel, *Juden und Judentum von Heute*, p. 341.)

Jewish moneylender, at which unsavory details about the methods of Jewish usurers had come to light.[1] He was a contributor to the *Antisemitische Correspondenz* under the pseudonym of "Dr. Capistrano"* and in 1886 participated in the founding of a Hessian anti-Semitic party which remained affiliated to Fritsch's parent organization. In 1887 he contested the constituency of Marburg on a radical social program which in some respects was indistinguishable from that of the Social Democrats. He thundered against Junkers and the Church. He declared himself to be *"politisch freiheitlich"*[2] (i.e., "liberal"), came out against religious education, for complete freedom of speech, and the extension of universal suffrage to provincial elections. He favored an income tax to strengthen the legislature against the executive,[3] he opposed government monopolies for the same reason and he voted against the brandy tax on the same side as the "Jew parties."[4] He was the only anti-Semitic deputy in 1899 to vote for a reduction in the standing army.

If he railed against the Conservative anti-Semites, he was in turn attacked—not only by Stöcker but also by Fritsch[5]—for his political similarity with the parties of the Left. The argument that there was essential common ground between agitators of all colors had been traditional with Conservative and Liberal opponents of anti-Semitism and, with the sudden resurgence of anti-Semitic social agitation, it too was soon to be revived. A well-to-do Hessian Jew wrote:

> Everywhere this anti-Semitic fury signifies nothing more and nothing less than the beginnings of the social revolution. Let it be clearly understood by all who support anti-Semitism openly or secretly, or who merely tolerate it; it is not a question of the Jews at all, it is a question of subverting the entire order of life, society and the state! Let no-one believe that one can throw the Jews as meat to the revolutionary beast and thus meanwhile salve oneself.[6]

Böckel might begin by merely whipping up the peasants by exploiting their financial dependence on the Jews:[7] but sooner or later he would have to write in his *Reichsherold,* much to the joy of the Social Democrats,

* Capistrano was a fifteenth-century Franciscan, a preacher of crusades against both the Crescent and the Star of David.

The money-greedy capitalist, never mind whether Jew or non-Jew, is the destroying angel of our people, whose opportunity to work he takes from them. The hoarding of great wealth must lead to impoverishment and stagnation.[8]

Böckel's novel and original campaign, and still more his victory in what had for long been considered a safe Conservative seat, awakened all the dormant anti-Semitism in other parts of Germany. The Dresden Reform Party was revived and Sonnenberg, ever seeking fresh windmills to tilt against, contested another Hessian constituency, but could not dislodge its Conservative incumbent.

One effect of this new lease of life for both wings of the party was to revive acutely the question of their mutual relationship. It came at a particularly awkward time for the Conservatives, for 1887 to 1890 was the period of Bismarck's *Kartell,* a coalition of the two Conservative parties and the National Liberals. In fact, however, the radicals showed little disposition to compromise. They forced Paul Förster (the brother of Bernhard) to persevere in his candidature, sponsored by the *Kreuzzeitung,* in a by-election in Berlin against the official *Kartell* candidate.*

Another, and final, attempt to form a united national anti-Semitic party failed at Bochum in 1889. From it emerged the *Antisemitische Deutschsoziale Partei,* led by the Förster-Fritsch-Sonnenberg wing, which gained the blessing of the *Kreuzzeitung* as an ally in fulfilling the Imperial Message of 1881 and in fighting the *Kartell;* and Böckel's followers, who at Erfurt constituted themselves as the *Antisemitische Volkspartei.* Their program is typical of the "national Socialist" appeal which drew on both chauvinism and economic discontent, a synthesis which has become a more important factor in twentieth-century policy.† But in so far as they drew on genuinely popular, as opposed to paternalistic forces, they had correspondingly greater hopes of expansion. It is significant that Walter Frank, the Nazi historian and biographer of Stöcker, regards Böckel's anti-Semitism as the politically more realistic and preferable.[9]

As the 1890 election approached, an agreement between the

---

* In the even Förster polled more votes than the *Kartell.* The seat was won by Liebknecht for the Social Democrats.

† See Appendix II; see illustration 1.

1. Poster for the German Anti-Semitic Conference of 1889. Speakers included Georg von Schönerer and Hungarian and French delegates. (*Österreichisches Verwaltungsarchiv*, Vienna).

Conservatives and the *Deutschsoziale,* though desirable from the point of view of both, was impossible because the *Kartell* was still in force; but since the happy hunting ground for anti-Semitism was Hesse, the various anti-Semitic parties decided at the last moment not to cut each other's throats and to divide the spoils in the likeliest constituencies. Böckel had even threatened to oppose Stöcker. Hesse yielded five seats and sizable minorities were achieved in other constituencies, mainly Hessian or West-phalian.* This was better than the anti-Semites had done in any previous election, but could only be described as disappointing in relation to the effort they had expended on an energetic and, at times, eccentric campaign.†

At a by-election in 1892 the anti-Semites in the Reichstag were joined by a new recruit, who in vehemence, radicalism, and hysterical mendacity could be described only as a second Böckel. He was Hermann Ahlwardt. Ahlwardt[10] was born into a family of poor circumstances in Pomerania. He entered the teaching profession and finally became *Rektor* of a primary school in Berlin. His serious financial difficulties involved him first in more and more complicated dealings with moneylenders and finally led him, in 1889, to embezzle funds collected for the children's Christmas party at his school. For this he was dismissed,‡ and it was then that his anti-Semitic career began.¶ His first opus, *Der Verzweiflungs- kampf der arischen Völker mit dem Judentum* ("The struggle of despair between the Aryan peoples and Judaism"), was in the apocalyptic, cataclysmic school of Marr and gave a hair-raising account of the sinister omnipotence of Jews in every conceivable walk of life. Nearly one hundred pages consist of a minute account of his dealings with Jewish usurers,[11]"a weird example of self-humiliation combined with persecution mania."[12]

He followed this with *Der Eid eines Juden* ("The oath of a

---

* In addition Stöcker, as the sole representative of the Christian Social Party, continued to sit on the Conservative benches.

† Böckel, for instance, informed the burghers of Giessen that the Rothschilds had bought up the world's oil (*Deutsche Antisemitenchronik,* p. 35).

‡ His former profession entitled him to be called "Rektor a.d." (i.e. Rektor ausser Dienst—"Headmaster [retd.]"). his admirers transformed this into "Rektor aller Deutschen."

¶ In a letter of January 25, 1885 to *Oberinspektor* Crohn, explaining his financial difficulties, he had specifically stated that the majority of the usurers he had dealt with were Christian (*MVA,* April 13, 1893, p. 192).

Jew"), which purported to be an account of Bleichröder's corrupt dealings with the police in an alimony case. Ahlwardt was prosecuted and, unable to produce the slightest evidence for his charges, sentenced to four months' imprisonment. Hardly out of prison, he committed his most audacious coup yet: a leaflet entitled *Judenflinten* ("Jew-rifles"), which claimed that arms supplied to the German forces by the Jewish manufacturer Loewe (a brother of the former Progressive deputy) were—in accordance with a Franco-Jewish plot to paralyze Germany military—defective. The whole story was again proved to be pure fantasy and he was sentenced to a further five months' imprisonment. But he had by this time become a member of the Reichstag and parliamentary immunity saved him from serving the second sentence.

He had been sent to parliament by the peasants of Arnswalde-Friedeberg, a district in Brandenburg near the Oder, and virgin territory to anti-Semitic evangelism. He had neither funds nor organization. But he went from farmstead to farmstead, telling the peasants and the laborers that their misery was due to the Jews and the Junkers; and indeed they were the double victims of the new industrialism and the old agrarianism.

It would be a mistake to evaluate the election of men like Ahlwardt in terms of modern parliamentary politics. Its assumptions had not penetrated to areas like Arnswalde, one of those regions (Hesse was another) where a normally passive and apathetic conservatism is periodically interrupted by brief outbreaks of violent rebellion.* Campaigns like those of Ahlwardt or Böckel are more in the nature of a *jacquerie*, reminiscent of those bloody and hopeless peasant risings which punctuate the history of medieval and Reformation Germany.†

* In 1848, for instance, Hesse was one of the regions with the most severe anti-Semitic disturbances, but in the elections to the Frankfort Parliament moderates were, with one exception, successful [V. Valentin, *Geschichte der deutschen Revolution von 1848–49* (Berlin, 1930–1), Vol. I, pp. 355, 362; Vol. II, pp. 5–6.
† There is an echo of the Anabaptists in the leaflet, circulating in Baden in 1847 and 1848, which demanded:
    1. The nobility must be annihilated.
    2. The Jews must be expelled from Germany.
    3. All Kings, Dukes, and Princes must disappear and Germany become a free republic like America.

Ahlwardt had more in common with the great social highway-men of Europe folk memory—Robin Hood, Schinderhannes, and Giuliano. Their credentials and motives were not too closely examined. Their enemies were those of the peasants—the city in general, the law, and money in particular. Occasionally, according to the variations of time and place, the enemy was associated with the Jews.

Intimidated by the Junkers whom they hated, yet on whom they depended, the peasants were in no position to analyze the true sources of their miseries or to discriminate between those who seemed to be saying in public what they had only dared to murmur in private. The Progressives' pious hot air was as much over their heads as the Marxists' complicated explanations of why they were poor and bound to get poorer. They admired courage more than wisdom; that the wealthy and powerful should use the courts to silence a critic was further proof of his virtues.

There was at this time no organization through which the peasants could protect their interests or press their claims, and no mechanism for co-operative marketing, for absorbing small savings, advancing mortgages, or insurance cover at moderate rates. In the absence of any constructive lead, they naturally persisted in modes of political expression which were essentially prenineteenth century. It should not be forgotten that even the Mother of Parliaments could nurture a Horatio Bottomley. Ahlwardt received twice as many votes as his Conservative opponent but not an absolute majority. A second ballot was therefore necessary, in which the defeated candidate threw his support into Ahlwardt's scales.* Although the *Kreuzzeitung* later said of Ahlwardt that no Conservative could vote for him,[13] his own opponent had declared, "I prefer ten Ahlwardts to one Progressive."[14] The traditional anti-Junker agitators among the poorer peasants of this region were the Progressives;[15]

---

4. All civil servants must be murdered."
(Valentin, *op. cit.*, Vol. I, pp. 344–5.)

* The voting was as follows:	1st ballot	2nd ballot
Ahlwardt	6,901	11,206
Progressive	2,917	3,306
Conservative	2,815	
Social Democrat	942	

and presumably rural demagogy backed by a powerful urban radical movement was considered more dangerous than the free-lancing subversion of an Ahlwardt who, equally abusive of the national Left, would one day have to decide whom he hated more. Ahlwardt's success proved that the election of Böckel had been no isolated phenomenon. The Böckel formula had been used again, and again found successful—in an area where there were few Jews. But as a parliamentarian Ahlwardt was a failure. His calumnies knew no measure, his denunciations no bounds. Böckel was an intelligent man who knew when to roar and when to smile. Moreover, he did practical work for his peasants and by organizing co-operatives undoubtedly helped to save them from the evil consequences of their fecklessness.[16] (His *judenrein* cattle markets were less successful.)[17] Ahlwardt had only one accomplishment, the ability to rant. He was from the start regarded as a liability and an embarrassment to his party colleagues, and they cut him in Parliament. After a period in the United States and a number of unsuccessful business ventures he launched, in 1907, the *Freideutscher Bund* whose goal was "the augmentation of the sum of general happiness." Membership was open "without distinction of sex, denomination, or party allegiance." Its activities were directed against Jesuits and Freemasons.[18] In 1909 he was sentenced for blackmail and he died in 1914 from injuries sustained in a traffic accident.

Even Böckel's triumph did not last all that long. Although worshiped for a decade or more by his constituents as the "peasant king of Hesse" and the "peasants' liberator," he was defeated in 1903 by Hellmut von Gerlach of the National Social Union, a Protestant State Socialist organization which had split away from Stöcker and abjured anti-Semitism, and in which Friedrich Naumann and Max Weber were active. He withdrew, an impoverished recluse, to a hamlet in Brandenburg, an object of curiosity and pity to the villagers. He dragged out a penurious existence until 1923, and his death passed unnoticed.[19]

But before these whimpering ends came the "bangs" of 1893, the year of the anti-Semites' biggest success.

REFERENCES

1 Böckel, *Die Juden—Könige unserer Zeit*, p. 7.
2 Wawrzinek, *Die Entstehung*, p. 67.
3 *Ibid.*, p. 67.
4 *StBr*, April 13, 1887, 7. leg., I. Sess., 41. Sitz., p. 913;*Ibid.*, 46. Sitz., pp. 1113–15.
5 Wawrzinek, *op. cit.*, p. 67.
6 J. Rülf, *Entstehung und Bedeutung des Anti-Semitismus in Hessen* (Mainz, 1890), pp. 20–1.
7 He quoted, *inter alia*, from Bismarck's famous Landtag speech of 1847. *Op. cit.*, p. 4.
8 *Vorwärts*, May 13, 1894.
9 Frank, *Hofprediger Adolf Stöcker*, pp. 236–40.
10 For details of Ahlwardt's life, see Massing, *Rehearsal for Destruction*, pp. 92–6, 113–4; W. Buch (i.e., W. Buchow), *50 Jahre antisemitische Bewegung. Beiträge zur ihrer Geschichte* (Munich, 1937), pp. 14–17, 23.
11 H. Ahlwardt, *Der Verzweiflungskampg der arischen Völker mit dem Judentum* (Berlin, 1890), pp. 66–164.
12 Massing, *op. cit.*, p. 92.
13 "Für den kann ein konservativer Mann nicht stimmen," May 30, 1893 (p.m.).
14 *Deutsche Antisemitenchronik*, p. 122.
15 F. Paeske, *Die Reichstagswahl in Friedeberg-Arnswalde* (Reetz, 1892), *passim*.
16 P. Scheidemann, "Wandlungen des Antisemitismus," *Neue Zeit*, Vol. XXIV, Pt. 2 (1906), p. 635.
17 Gerlach, *Von Rechts nach Links*, pp. 170–1.
18 L. Curtius, *Der politische Antisemitismus von 1907 bis 1911* (Munich, 1911), pp. 58–9.
19 Massing, *op. cit.*, pp. 239–40; Buch, *op. cit.*, pp. 22–3.

13

The Changing Role of the
Conservative Party

Twice German anti-Semitism had visions of glory, from 1880 to
1881 and in 1893. In each instance external circumstances had
favored them. In 1880 there were economic distress and
Bismarck's breach with the Liberal parties, and in 1893 the
Conservatives had a quarrel with Caprivi. The second time,
indeed, it looked as though a permanent community of interest
between Conservatism and anti-Semitism had been established;
what prevented this from coming to fruition was the change
which overcame the political position of the Conservative Party
between 1892 and 1896. Sections of it had not been too happy
about their part in the Bismarckian system of the 1880's. The
Kreuzzeitung group, with which Stöcker was associated, could
reconcile itself neither to the parliamentary regime nor to the
Kartell, the alliance with the National Liberals who until so
recently had been the party of Jewish finance. Stöcker fell more
and more from grace, first because his silencing was part of the
price the National Liberals exacted for entering the coalition,
partly because he was involved in the intrigues with Field
Marshal von Waldersee and the later Emperor William II.[1]
When in 1888 both William I and his son Frederick III, Emperor
for only ninety-nine days and the hope of the Liberals,* died and
William II ascended the throne, the Conservatives' prospect of
persuading the apparently favorable new monarch to their plan
of an absolute, "social" monarchy seemed to be bright. But apart
from dismissing Bismarck he did little to please them, for

* He is credited with the statement that "anti-Semitism is the disgrace of the
century."

III

Stöcker, forced at last to choose between the pulpit and the hustings, went too, and so did von Waldersee. William dreamt of being the benevolent and well-loved emperor of all the Germans and appointed the conciliatory Caprivi as chancellor.

The course of Caprivi's chancellorship soon determined the Conservatives to stop at nothing to secure his dismissal. They had four main grievances against him: a law granting greater self-government to municipal authorities in Eastern Prussia, a series of low-tariff treaties with foreign countries, the apparent indifference with which he accepted the defeat of a bill to reintroduce denominational schools in Prussia, and his friendliness to the Polish minority. Over the School Bill he was forced to resign the premiership of Prussia; but his biggest crime was the tariff revisions—passed with Social Democrat votes—and the Conservatives were appalled by the extent to which "Jewish" influence had revived within two years of Bismarck's retirement.

Their only immediate hope, now that William appeared to have turned his back on the idea of an Imperial *coup d'état,* lay in the 1893 elections, and it was to prepare for these that they summoned a public conference, the first since the party's foundation, for December, 1892. It met in the Tivoli Hall in Berlin, under the shadow of Ahlwardt's election, faced with the problem of drawing up a program which could command mass support. It was thus that Stöcker seemed, after fourteen years, to be on the brink of capturing the Conservative Party for his ideals. Fourteen years earlier he had prophesied:

> Under the prevailing universal suffrage [it cannot] be doubted that the Conservative Party will gain its strength only in the social question.[2]

Now paragraph one of the Tivoli Program contained the statement:

> We combat the widely obtruding and decomposing Jewish influence on our popular life.
> We demand a Christian authority for the Christian people and Christian teachers for Christian pupils.[3]

A motion condemning the "manifold excesses of anti-Semitism" secured only seven votes. A much-applauded speech of the haberdasher Ulrich, of the Dresden *Deutsch-sozialer Verein,* who complained that the cause which had won the people's greatest enthusiasm should be denounced as demagogy.[4] The economic section of the program contained the familiar Christian-Social and Reformist claims, but they were claims which had never before appeared in a Conservative program. In becoming the first major party to go on record as being anti-Semitic, the Conservatives took a significant but not a decisive step. They had long been regarded as *de facto* anti-Semitic; as early as 1883 one of their members had claimed:

> We have taken on ourselves the entire odium of the anti-Semitic movement in order to revitalize the Christian conscience of the people and lay the ethical foundation for the solution of the social question.[5]

The *Preussische Jahrbücher* correctly observed:

> Basically the Conservatives have always been anti-Semitic . . . . By becoming anti-Semitic, the Conservative Party has turned into . . . nothing new in its content, but it has become demagogic . . . . The enormous significance of the transformation of the Conservative Party is to be found in this, and in this alone: that anti-Semitism is, and must by nature always be, demagogic.[6]

In one sense the Conservative conversion to anti-Semitism came ten years too late, for it was not in itself an answer to the most promising campaign issue of 1893—the fall in corn prices caused by Caprivi's tariff policy. This demanded a somewhat sterner reaction than emanated from the Tivoli Conference. Two months later a body constituted itself which was to exert a powerful influence on the politics of the next two decades. It was the *Bund der Landwirte* (Agarian League) which, part political party, part pressure group, proved an invaluable ally to both Conservative and anti-Semitic candidates. Its field of action did not completely coincide with that of the Conservatives, though the two overlapped. The Conservatives represented not merely the Junkers of eastern Prussia, but especially the most backward section of that class, the so-called *Krautjunker*, or "cabbage-Junkers," who had failed, in the main, to keep pace with the political and economic changes of the past thirty years. Hence it was easy for them to sympathize with the sufferings of distant factory workers; they could as cheerfully approve Stöcker's social reform as Tory squires could vote for Shaftesbury's

---

Factory Acts. They disliked the rich in the new towns; they had no reason for hating the poor.

They felt, too, that their future could be better secured by a Stöckerian social policy than by too close an association with Agrarianism. This was a miscalculation. The days when the proletariat could be wooed by "social monarchism" were long past; meanwhile the Conservatives were missing the opportunity of an alliance with those landowners who had made their peace with the empire and with industrialism.

With stability depending more and more on extra-parliamentary forces, on the Prussian structure adapted to imperial needs, a sound agriculture answered long-term political ends as well as short-term class interests. Such an accession of strength to the Right could be obtained only through the Agrarian League. By camouflaging the divergence of interest between the magnates of the Northeast and the peasant proprietors of the South and West with a rallying cry against free trade and the corn jobbers,* it secured a response from the most varied recruits and helped to extend the influence of Prussian Conservatism where this had hitherto been weakest.

The election of 1893, then, was fought in very different circumstances from that of 1890. With the *Kartell* in ruins and an enemy of the Right as chancellor, there was sufficient sympathy between Conservatives and anti-Semites, even if there was no official co-operation, to make the result a joint Conservative–anti-Semitic victory. Anti-Semitic candidates won 263,000 votes (2.9% of the total) and sixteen seats—eight in Hesse, six in Saxony, and two in Prussia east of the Elbe (both won by Ahlwardt). A seventeenth was added at a by-election in 1895; this was Waldeck, a small principality bordering on Hesse-Nassau. And though Böckel and Ahlwardt exploited hatred of the Junkers, the Conservatives guessed, or hoped, that they

---

* The structure of agriculture was radically different east and west of the Elbe. The percentage of the total area taken up by holdings of various sizes is shown in the following table:

	West of Elbe	East of Elbe
Up to 50 acres	62%	31 %
50 to 250 acres	30	28.5
Over 250 acres	8	40.5

(H. Heaton, *Economic History of Europe*, New York, 1936, p. 460.)

would be able to use the sentiments unleashed against the Progressives and the Social Democrats. Allegedly there had even been abortive negotiations between Ahlwardt's staff and Hammerstein and Mannteuffel, the leaders of the extreme Conservatives, regarding a limited electoral truce.[7]

In fact, since the Tivoli Conference, the general political views of a considerable number of Conservatives were quite indistinguishable from those of Right-wing anti-Semites. Fritsch calculated that, considering the number of Conservative candidates known to be anti-Semitic, the total number of anti-Semitic votes must be estimated nearer 400,000.[8] He names seven victorious candidates, five in Prussia east of the Elbe and two in Saxony, who associated themselves with the Conservatives only after the election. Two more, one in Pomerania and the other in Saxony, are named by other authorities, as well as several unsuccessful candidates.[9] *The Times,* commenting on the "growing popularity of the anti-Semitic cry," wrote that in the Prussian rural districts such seats as the Conservatives had gained or retained were mostly to be credited to the widespread contacts and agitation of the anti-Semitic or Agrarian machines, lubricated with Conservative money. Elsewhere, anti-Semitism had succeeded largely in displacing Conservatism.

> It is a not unsatisfactory nemesis that many of their successes appear likely to be gained at the expense of the Conservatives who have dry-nursed them to their undoing.[10]

In fact, of their eleven gains, eight were from the Conservatives, from which the *Kreuzzeitung* drew the conclusion:

> There is no denying that anti-Semitism's mighty powers of recruitment leads many back into the loyal camp who would otherwise have had to be considered irremediably lost to Liberalism or Social Democracy.[11]

Perhaps the most notable feature of the election was the success of the anti-Semites in Saxony. It was especially ironical that at the very moment when Stöcker's views seem to have conquered in the Conservative Party, the radical anti-Semites should here gain almost exclusively at the expense of the Right. In Saxony, where the number of Jews was negligible, an anti-Semitic vote was mainly a protest by the *Mittelstand* against the ineffectiveness of the traditional bourgeois parties. It was particularly from the two Liberal parties that the anti-Semites had gained their votes, as comparison with the 1890 figures shows:

	Conservatives (both wings)	National Liberals	Progres- sives	Anti- Semites	Social Democrats
1890	160,407	112,514	52,776	4,708	241,187
1893	135,709	35,741	30,439	116,013	273,000

Even more relevant to the future policy of the Conservatives than the success of anti-Semitism were the spectacular advances made by the Social Democrats. In 1878, the year of the Anti-Socialist Act, they had polled 437,000 votes; and in 1890, the year in which it lapsed, their strength was 1,427,000. In 1903 they polled three million votes; and in 1912 four and a quarter, more than one-third of the total.

The first effect of the 1893 elections, when one German in four voted for the party of subversion and atheism, was to disillusion the Kaiser. His honeymoon with the lower orders was over, and he returned to his first love, the staple weapons of the German ruler, blood and iron. Caprivi had shown himself to be increasingly ineffective and his Army Bills had been passed after the election only with the help of Polish votes.* He was dismissed in 1894 and Hohenlohe was appointed in his place.

The implacable mood of the workers—who were now out to revenge themselves for the indignities to which their movement had been subjected for twelve years—the dismissal of Caprivi, and the sudden rise to influence of the Agrarian League all changed the face of German politics and the role of the Conservative Party in it. Real power was moving more and more into the hands of the hard-faced and hard-headed business-men who directed the policy of nationalism and chauvinism during the two decades before the outbreak of the war. The success of such a policy—colonial expansion, naval supremacy, suppression of Polish separatism, a "place in the sun," national

---

* The Polish Party, varying in strength between fifteen and twenty members, would normally have opposed any measures designed to strengthen the executive, but, impressed with Caprivi's moderate policy towards them, wanted to keep him in power.

unity in face of the Social Democrat menace—depended on a coalition of all the "state-conserving" forces, from the National Liberals to the extreme Right, and a neutralization of the Reichstag. The "national" coalition included the two Conservative parties, the anti-Semites, the Agrarians, and that unique organization, small in numbers but great in influence, the *Alldeutscher Verband*.* This inclusion in a broad Right meant in turn a rapid weakening of "democratic" anti-Semitism.

German government was now impossible without the Conservatives. The growth of Socialist strength—81 seats in 1903, 110 in 1912—and the unreliability, from the "national" point of view, of the Centre made Conservatism the sheet anchor of every administration from Hohenlohe through Bülow to Bethmann-Hollweg.

> It would be impossible to govern Germany [wrote one Conservative commentator] were it not for the uneven demarcation of constituencies and the graded Prussian franchise.[12]

The true source of power of Imperial administrations was in fact the Prussian Diet with its automatic Conservative predominance, not the Reichstag, which might, and sometimes did, have majorities "hostile to the Reich."

This "national" coalition was ready to use anti-Semitism as a platform device; it objected, however, to its social reform program. The Conservatives, who in 1892 had hoped to ride to victory on a program of "social Conservatism" found, by the middle of the 1890's, that such ideas were unwelcome to the "industrial Junkers" and the manufacturing magnates who were now the dominant political force. Hohenlohe, seventy-five years old when appointed and no more familiar with the ins and outs of Berlin politics than his predecessor, was never more than a figurehead. The period of his chancellorship was often referred to as the "Stumm era" after Baron Stumm-Halberg, a Saar steel magnate and personal friend of the Emperor, who was famous for his uncompromising opposition to political democracy and the workers' right to unionize.

Stumm, symbolizing the new materialism, had no fiercer opponents than the Protestant social reformers, such as Adolf

---

* Its exact relationship with anti-Semitism is discussed in Chapter 25.

Wagner and Stöcker's newspaper, *Das Volk,* which was often quite vehemently radical. Moreover, the rural labor question was troubling the Conservatives as much as the urban. From 1893 onward some of the younger Christian-Social intellectuals, such as Max Weber, began taking up the cause of agricultural workers,[13] which was naturally offensive to the Junkers.

Under such circumstances, Stöcker, who had seemed to carry all before him at the Tivoli Conference, had to be sacrificed. The Conservatives' task was made much easier by the Hammerstein scandals and the "pyre letter" which, in 1894 and 1895, sadly tarnished the prestige of the extreme Right. Hammerstein's administration of the *Kreuzzeitung* had been accompanied by embezzlements and forgeries amounting to 600,000 marks, a matter which, when it could be hushed up no longer, naturally damaged Stöcker, his intimate associate. But the cup was filled by the Socialist daily which chose this moment to publish a letter he had written to Hammerstein in 1888, advising him, in terms more worthy of Don Basilio than the second Luther, how to cast his editorials with the aim of estranging the new Emperor from Bismarck:

> If the Kaiser realises that we want to sow discord between him and Bismarck, he will be antagonised . . . . If we feed his discontent in matters where he is instinctively on our side, we shall basically strengthen him without causing personal irritation.[14]

Like many of the elect, he could be no less cunning than the serpent, leaving others to be as harmless as doves. In 1896 he was ordered by the Conservative Pay to sever all relations with *Das Volk* if he wished to remain in the party. This he could not do, and preferred a breach with his former patrons. Both the pro- and anti-Stöcker factions agreed that the cause of the rupture was the labor question.[15]

Nor did the other anti-Semitic parties, despite their undoubted electoral success, show more staying power. There was a rapid turnover of deputies, most of whom were men of inferior caliber, and the various organizations failed, as they had done hitherto, to unify themselves in one movement.

Thus within three or four years of seeming within grasp of victory, anti-Semitism was once more tamed and forced into a role of subordinate usefulness. After 1900 the parties specifically devoted to anti-Semitism declined in importance, while the number of parties and movements which adopted anti-Semitism as part of their general outlook increased. Their fortunes are examined in Chapter 21.

REFERENCES

1 Prince O. von Bismarck, *Gedanken und Erinnerungen* (Stuttgart, 1921), Vol. III, p. 48.
2 Frank, *Hofprediger Adolf Stöcker*, p. 70.
3 Salomon, *Die deutschen Parteiprogramme*, Vol. II, pp. 71–2.
4 *Deutsche Antisemitenchronik*, p. 122.
5 Speech by von Rauchhaupt, Feb. 22, 1883, *AZJ*, Sept. 25, 1883.
6 *PJ*, Jan. 28, 1893, Vol. LXXXI, pp. 385–7.
7 *Vossische Zeitung*, June 12, 1893.
8 T. Fritsch, *Antisemiten-Katechismus* (25th ed., Leipzig, 1893), pp. 346–7.
9 *KZ*, May 16, 1893, p.m.; Anon., *Herr Liebermann von Sonnenberg als Parteiführer und Gesinnungsgenosse. Von einigen Deutschsozialen* (Leipzig, 1893), p. 108.
10 *The Times*, June 18, 1893.
11 *MVA*, Jan. 15, 1894, p. 23.
12 G. von Below in Sarason D. (ed.), *Das Jahr 1913. Ein Gesamtbild der Kulturentwicklung* (Leipzig, 1913), p. 5. He amplifies this point in his *Das parlamentarische Wahlrecht in Deutschland* (Berlin, 1909), pp. 82, 128.
13 K. Buchheim, *Geschichte der christlichen Parteien in Deutschland* (Munich, 1953), pp. 285–6.
14 *Vorwärts*, Nov. 3, 1895
15 See L. Kynades, *Herkules am Scheidewege, oder Stöcker und die konservative Fraktion* (Leipzig, 1896), favorable to Stöcker; Col. von Krause, *Zum Austritt Stöckers aus der konservativen Partei* (Berlin, 1896), unfavorable.

AUSTRIA 1867–1900

14

The Failure of Liberalism

Superficially, the history of anti-Semitic movements in Austria would seem to follow much the same pattern as in Germany— the first foundations in the 1870's, a period of uncertainty in the 1880's, and political triumph in the 1890's, followed by a general acceptance in respectable circles and a decline in vitality. There were, however, important differences, in particular in the roles played by nationalism and the Church.

The German Empire was the product of national unification and an intoxicating military victory. True, much of the coarseness and arrogance of German nationalism was due to a feeling of insecurity and a lack of self-confidence. Nevertheless, nationalism was, for better or worse, a unifying force. In Austria it was disruptive. The Dual Monarchy was born of defeat. For the Germans within it, it meant final separation from the main body of their co-nationals; for the other nationalities, a chance to salve as much as possible in a jungle war of all against all.

Such unifying factors as there were, were surpra-national and historical. They were the dynasty, the Army, the bureaucracy, and the Church. The cisleithan half of the Empire was over-whelmingly Catholic,[1] one of Bismarck's reasons for excluding it from the new Germany. Where the Catholic Church is in a minority, it is inclined to favor constitutionalism; committed to opposing discrimination, it must do so on grounds of principle if it is not to be discredited. But in a country where it has almost no rivals, and where its chief enemy is not heresy but secularism, it will incline to the support of absolute authority.

A third difference from Germany lay in the number and situation of the Jews. In Germany, although scattered territori-ally, they formed a fairly homogeneous society. Although only a small minority was wealthy, there was not the overwhelming contrast in status and culture with a multitude of paupers. In Galicia, where Jews numbered 11% of the population, they had hardly emerged from the ghetto and occupied an economic position which, in keeping with the conditions of those regions, was medieval. They fared better only than their co-religionists in Russia.

It was the perpetual triangular struggle among the Church, constitutionalism, and nationalism and the close link between Liberalism and German-Austrians that determined the role of the Jews in Austrian politics. The tussle between centralism and federalism was really one for supremacy in the state between the executive and the nobility and goes back to the era of Joseph II. The enlightened despotism of Joseph and his chief minister, Kaunitz, in many ways foreshadowed the policies of the Liberals. It was typical of the European enlightenment in being anti-clerical and anti-ultramontane, without, however, being specifically anti-religious. By substituting the bureaucracy for the aristocracy as the instrument of government and standardizing the language of administration, Joseph inevitably favored the German element in his dominions. He granted limited toleration to Protestants and Jews, partly out of genuine humanitarianism, but partly because discrimination was stupid and inefficient.*

His modernization of government naturally antagonized the Church and the magnates who saw their strength in the historic institutions of the realm. The experience of those years explains why the German Liberals always looked back to "Josephinism" as the golden age; why the other nationalities saw their hope in federalism and conservatism; and last why Austrian Liberalism, which, as the creed of the civil service, was never really "anti-authority," was only skin-deep.

To this must be added the experience of 1848. The Liberals of Austria, like those of the rest of the German Confederation, were in revolt against the system of Metternich. They were nationalist and, with few exceptions, had no sympathy with the aspirations of the other Austrian nationalities.[2] They paid dearly for their

---

* The *Toleranzpatent* opened with the words: "Convinced on the one hand of the perniciousness of all religious intolerance, and on the other hand of the great advantage of a true Christian tolerance to religion and the state . . ."

blindness, and the specter of Jellačić haunted them to the end of their days.

The Jews, in so far as they were politically articulate, sided with the Liberals, and in Vienna they were prominent in the Liberal cause. This inevitably meant that there was an anti-Semitic note in some of the counterrevolutionary propaganda, aimed especially at the Jewish *café literati* who were producing the multitude of journals, gazettes, and broadsheets then flourishing.

Die Geissel, which printed frequent anti-Semitic anecdotes, ridiculed constitution making in an article in mock Yiddish on "Die grausse Konstitution, so hot gmocht fer Oestraich der David Abraham Levysohn."[3] *Schild und Schwert* complained that:

> By constantly making concessions . . . to the Jews we reinforce the party of subversion, which is proved by the fact that all Jews who, since the March days have been very skilful at exploiting the general confusion in hunting for positions, have become arrogant deputies, impudent hate-mongers and agitators.[4]

Outright opposition to emancipation, or freedom of the press, was rare,[5] but even the *Wiener Kirchenzeitung,* which at that time was one of the more moderate publications, found fault with

> those Israelites who owe their significance in modern society solely to the combination of Jewish disbelief with poisonous hatred against Christian doctrine and Catholic practice.[6]

Throughout the 1860's and 1860's the Catholic and Conservative forces reinforced the battle they were waging against Liberal demands with touches of anti-Semitism. Not all prelates were like the Bishop of Przemyśl, who, in 1860, threatened excommunication to any Christian girl who went into Jewish employment;[7] on the other hand the Liberals sometimes practiced "tolerance" in a way calculated to offend Catholic sensibilities. On September 23, 1863, the day of the Jewish New Year, Parliament adjourned in deference to its two Jewish members, but had earlier in the year decided to hold a sitting on the Feast of Corpus Christi.[8]

The constitutional struggles, the repudiation of the Concordat, and the Old Catholic split after the Doctrine of Infallibility had been proclaimed, all touched Catholics to the quick.

Never again shall we entrust the protection of our liberties [wrote Fr. J. Greuter, the leader of the Tyrolean Conservatives, after the Imperial prorogation of 1865] to a Parliament sitting under the guns of the *Judenpresse* which so many fear more than the loss of their manly honour or their convictions.[9]

and *Vaterland*, the official Conservative organ wrote:

It is they, too, who, as in the days of the Roman Emperors, set going all campaigns against the Church, against the clergy and against the religious order, and incite the deluded masses to acts of violence. It is they who, in our tines also, do battle on the side of the enemies of the Catholics and similar sects and urge them on to an open breach, not out of sympathy, but as battering rams for their own purposes.

Always and everywhere they are on the side of political and ecclesiastical revolution and defend its causes, so as to be able to exploit it for their own ends and the extension of their power . . .

The weapons which Jewry uses to reach its sole object, domination of the Christian world, are its money, its commerce, and its newspapers. With its money and its commerce, Jewry has in its power almost all princes, all governments and all peoples. All laws which stand as obstacles in the way of its speculative and usurious tendencies had to be repealed in the interests of the Jews; all barriers which protected Christianity torn down; the craft guilds dissolved, freedom of enterprise introduced, the partition of landed estates legally permitted; the usury laws declared null and void. More and more the Christian social order is being dissolved by Jewry. Workers and craftsmen are wandering into the factories, landed property into the hands, houses into the possession, and the wealth of peoples into the pockets of the Jews. Through the electoral laws they dominate elections, politics and the Reichsrat, consequently legislation and the ministry; a few more years of such "progress" and Vienna will be called New Jerusalem and old Austria—Palestine.[10]

Austrian Catholicism was fortunate in securing as an advocate Karl Freiherr von Vogelsang, one of the leading conservative social and political theorists of the day. He was born in 1818 into a Protestant family from Mecklenburg—an almost exact contemporary of Konstantin Frantz with whom, indeed, he had much in common. His experiences in the 1848 revolution made a deep impression on him:

Whoever would be genuinely conservative, not out of consideration for his money-bags but from reasons of conscience, will find it his constant duty to let his personality be determined by conservative principles and gladly to submit himself to all consequences. Therefore, in order not to belong even with the tips of my fingers to revolution and the spirit of negation, I renounced all error and disbelief, and was received into the bosom of the Holy Catholic Church in the year 1850 at Innsbruck.[11]

Like other Romantic converts to Catholicism—such as Adam Müller and Friedrich von Schlegel—he was drawn to Vienna and lived there, with intervals, from 1859 until his death in 1890.

Writing in Austria, where Liberalism had always been weaker and the Church correspondingly stronger than in Germany, and in the only Catholic temporal power of any consequence to survive the holocaust of the 1860's, he had naturally much more hope of successfully influencing practical politics than his German contemporaries. The political climate in which he wrote is shown by the trial of a priest in 1896 who, charged with defamation of the Jews in his sermons, successfully pleaded:

I know that in almost all European countries the Jews are at present emancipated . . . and that formally this emancipation is legally established. It is granted to them in accordance with the constitution, and the Jews insist on it, like Shylock on his bond. But Christian society has not yet ratified this total equalisation of Jews with Christians, and will not, as long as a spark of Christian belief and national self-consciousness glows within it.[12]

In 1875 he was appointed editor of *Vaterland,* a paper which had been founded in 1869 with the slogan, "May our struggle be against the spirit of 1789!"[13] He had no sooner taken up his appointment than he was immersed in political controversy. His first attack on the Auersperg administration[14] was quickly followed by one aimed specifically at Dr. Julius Glaser, a baptized Jew who was Minister of Justice.[15] But his chief interest was always in social and economic problems and these he discussed at length in the *Österreichische Monatsschrift für Gesellschaftswissenschaft und Sozialreform* which he founded and edited.

Vogelsang's ideal was the restoration of the Christian economic order. He was anti-Semitic only incidentally, inspired in this respect by the *Germania* articles of 1875, and only in so far as the Jews represented the advance guard of capitalist ideology and practice. As a Catholic he completely rejected racial anti-Semitism, nor did he attack the Hebrew religion as such. Like many others, he distinguished between the "Jewish" (i.e., wicked, Talmudic) and "Israelite" (i.e., traditional, Old Testament) religions, regarding the two as being in a sense contradictory.[16] He wanted Jews to abjure Talmudic teachings and return to the religion of their fathers. He abominated above all the *Reformjude* who "infects all nations among whom he settles with his godlessness and greed."[17]

He does not delude himself that Jews have a monopoly of immorality:

> If by some miracle all our 1,400,000 Jews were to be taken from us, it would help us very little, for we ourselves have been infected with the Jewish spirit.[18]

The reason for this is that people have turned from God. Liberalism—atheism—nihilism: these are the fruits of religious indifference. Only in a Christian society are the people safe from the domination of the Jews:

> A people which keeps this Christian ethos in its political and social institutions is safeguarded against Jewish domination, as it is now showing itself in so many European states. The truly Christian people will be able to receive and absorb the Jew without becoming judaised; but one which has fallen away from Christianity in faith, law and morals must crawl, with no hope of rescue, through the Caudine yoke of serfdom, and will be robbed, dominated and made into a pariah by the Jews."[19]

His scheme for reform, is, in fact, as complete a return as possible to the principles of medieval society. Machine production cannot be abolished, but the old relationship between work and property should be restored by producers' associations and cooperatives, by compulsory guilds with apprentice training, and by opening trades only to those who have certificates of skill.[20] Protective tariffs for producers would replace the laws of those who were dazzled by "the *fata morgana* of a world market."[21] His sympathy for the poor, and the industrial proletariat in particular, was genuine. It was a courageous step for a Catholic-conservative newspaper openly to support the great weavers' strike in Brno in 1875,[22] even if the decision was made easier by most of the employers' being Jewish. He did not hesitate to point out that the anarchist outrages of the 1880's had their roots more in misery than in wickedness.[23] "Appoint proper factory inspectors," his friend and fellow convert Emil Bülow, S.J., wrote to him, "and hang a few dozen Jews instead of the Anarchists—then Anarchism will soon stop."[24] Within the reformed society, Jews would have their place, just as they did in the Middle Ages.[25] But it is essential that emancipation should he rescinded; to grant the Jews equality is to submit to domination by them.[26] Without these political and economic reforms the Jews will continue "to exterminate the artisan,"[27] the people will continue to be led to ruin by "the temptations of an incredibly insolent *Judenpresse,* mocking all order, human and divine," the progenitor of nihilism.[28] "That is Catholic anti-Semitism, the only moral, the Christian and therefore the only efficacious one."[29] The trumpets of *Vaterland* alone would not have sufficed to destroy Austrian Liberalism. As in Germany, it was weakened by its own failures. It was because constitutionalism, administrative centralism, religious tolerance, and private enterprise appealed insufficiently to the peoples of the empire, because Liberalism appeared to provide inadequate answers to both the empire's economic needs and the clash of nationalities, that it failed as a political force. And because the Jews had staked more on its success than any other group in the monarchy, they felt its failure most keenly.

On the one hand the lack of scruples connected with the *Gründer* boom, the failures even more spectacular than the successes, and the crash of 1873 discredited it, and even within the "Left" there was dissatisfaction with the *"Veriwaltungsrats-partei"*[30]—the company directors' party.* Both the democrats and the young guard of German Nationalists tried to introduce a more popular element.[31]

On the other hand the German Nationalists were undermining the other foundation of Liberalism. Although primarily

* Of the 167 members taking part in the Reichsrat's deliberations—most of the Right were boycotting it—46 held 125 directorships (H. Hartmeyer, *Die führenden Abgeordneten des Liberalismus in Österreich, 1861–1879* [unpublished dissertation, Vienna, 1949], p. 110.

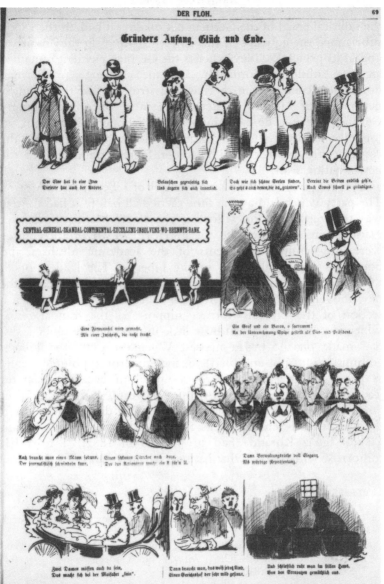

2. "The *Gründer*'s Progress. Anti-Semitic cartoon from the Viennese satirical paper *Der Floh*, 14 April 1872, shortly after the opening of the new Stock Exchange building.

the political creed of the German nationality, it had, in the 1860's proclaimed the equality of the different nations in the empire as one of its principles. Nevertheless the German element remained *de facto* politically dominant, and the challenge to German dominance contained in the national struggles led the younger generation of Liberals to demand a more uncompromisingly German policy. The extremists under Schönerer soon split off together, but the "Left" continued to be weakened by the constant struggle between the older Liberal tradition and the newer nationalism.

By 1914, practically nothing was left of Liberalism in Austria. The party which had at one time carried all before it had to give way to three new political forces. They were Marxist Socialism, Nationalism, and Catholic social reform. Two of these three were anti-Semitic, opponents of the academic idealism and bourgeois cosmopolitanism of the Liberals. The leaders of all three had begun their political careers as Liberals. As each of the new movements branched off from Liberalism it took with it a section of the Liberals' former support; as the franchise was widened it became evident how little impression the Liberal idea had made on the broad masses. When, in 1878, the Liberal administration split and, in 1879, the emperor appointed Taaffe as prime minister, the failure of liberalism became apparent. Taaffe remained in power for fourteen years, at the head of an "iron ring" of Conservatives and Slavs, and during that period the various anti-Semitic parties fulfilled what the veteran Jewish Liberal Ignaz Kuranda had prophesied in 1882: "I fear that tomorrow will destroy what has been created today."[32]

REFERENCES

1 Ninety-one per cent of the population were Roman Catholic or Greek Uniate in 1900.
2 For a detailed discussion, see R. J. Rath, "The Viennese Liberals of 1848 and the Nationality Problem," *JCEA*, Vol. XV, No. 3 (1955).
3 *Die Geissel*, Sept. 21, 1849.
4 *Schild und Schwert*, Sept. 10, 1848.
5 P. Klein, *Der Antisemitismus in der Wiener Presse von 1848 bis 1873* (unpublished dissertation, Vienna, 1938), pp. 21–23; also Fuchs, *Die Juden in der Karikatur*, pp. 120, 125, 228–31.
6 *Wiener Kirchenzeitung*, April 29, 1848.
7 G. Franz, *Liberalismus. Die deutschfreiheitliche Bewegung in der Habsburger*

Monarchie (Munich, 1955), p. 477.

8 *Wiener Kirchenzeitung,* Jan. 18, 1873.

9 Letter to Count Thun, Nov. 9, 1865; Molisch, *Briefe zur deutschen Politik,* p. 29.

10 *Vaterland,* Dec. 20, 1871. The accusation that the Jews were behind the Old Catholic schism was repeated on April 6, 1873.

11 Allmayer-Beck, *Vogelsang,* p. 25.

12 J. Deckert, *"Der wahre Israelit" vor den Wiener Geschworenen* (Vienna, 1896), p. 95.

13 Allmayer-Beck, *op. cit.,* p. 44.

14 *Das Ministerium Lasser, genannt Auersperg* (1875), first published anonymously. It was seized by the censorship in Prague.

15 *Ein offenes Wort an Herrn Justizminister Glaser* (Amberg, 1877).

16 M. Saner, *Freiherr Karl von Vogelsangs Gesellschafts- und Wirtschaftslehre* (Fribourg, 1939), p. 143.

17 *Vaterland,* April 8, 1888.

18 *Ibid.,* Oct. 10, 1875.

19 Klopp, *Die sozialen Lehren,* p. 187.

20 *Ibid.,* pp. 438–41.

21 *Ibid.,* p. 433.

22 *Vaterland,* July 2, 13, 17, 20, 25, 1875.

23 *Ibid.,* Aug. 12, 1886.

24 Klopp, *Leben und Wirken,* p. 277.

25 Klopp, *Die sozialen Lehren,* p. 193.

26 *Ibid.,* p. 189.

27 *Ibid.,* p. 436.

28 *Ibid.,* p. 36.

29 *Ibid.,* p. 194.

30 G. Kolmer, *Parlament und Verfassung in Österreich* (Vienna, 1902–14), Vol. II, p. 302.

31 P. Molisch, "Die Stellung Wiens in der deutschösterreichischen Politik von 1848–1918," *Jahrbuch des Vereins für die Geschichte der Stadt Wien,* Vol. III (Vienna, 1942), p. 187.

32 O. Karbach, "The Founder of Modern Political Anti-Semitism," *Jewish Social Studies,* Vol. VIII, No. 1 (1945), p. 19.

15

The Nationality Question

The Jews of East-Central Europe traditionally identified themselves with the "historic" nations, and *a fortiori* with the Germans. Hence, in the Habsburg Empire, they identified with German Liberalism. Not only were the Liberals the party of religious toleration and equality before the law, but the other cisleithan nationalities opposed their centralizing (i.e., Germanizing) policy—so that a victory for Slav federalism would endanger Jewish civil rights.

The legal question of their language and nationality also helped to determine the Jews' political attitudes. At the time of the Compromise the Jews in the western crownlands tended to speak German, and those in the Carpathian crownlands Yiddish (a debased form of German).[1] Article XIX of the Austrian Fundamental Laws defined, but did not specify, nationalities and the same was true of Hungary;[2] later judgments of the *Reichsgericht,* going right down to 1911, consistently denied the claims of Jews to legal nationality status, and of Yiddish to language status.[3]

One of the major grievances against Jews throughout East-Central Europe was that they were carriers of rival cultures; expediency, therefore, as well as the increasing anti-Semitism of German Nationalists, caused Jews gradually to assimilate themselves with the nationality of their immediate environment. But their occupational structure, their generally higher standards of literacy, and their need for political security made it easier to associate with the dominant, "historic" nationalities (Poles, Magyars, Russians) than with the submerged, peasant, "non-historic" nationalities (Czechs, Slovaks, Ukrainians, Lithuanians, for example). In Galicia and Hungary, therefore, they rid themselves of the stigma of being Germans, though this did not help them much with the races whom the Poles and Magyars were in turn oppressing.

The swing of the Jews to Polish nationality is illustrated by the census returns. In 1880, 5.4% of the Galician population declared themselves as German, in 1910 it was 1.1% (The percentage of Jews in Galicia remained fairly constant at 11% that of German-speaking Gentiles at 0.5%.

In Hungary forcible Magyarization would in any case have been difficult to resist. The 1848 revolution had begun with a number of pogroms, notably in Bratislava, as part of the nationalist enthusiasm. At Győr the students narrowly averted a pogrom;[4] and, despite the opposition of Kossuth, the Jewish members of the National Guard had to be suspended in both Bratislava and Budapest.[5] A dispatch to Vienna reported that

> here it is not merely the Palestinian or Jewish nationality of the Jews which is feared; here one trembles rather at their German nationality . . . . The Hungarian Jew is part and parcel of the German element. In his German sentiment and manners of thought and action, with his political and social upbringing, with his religious and literary progressiveness, he is rooted in Germanism.[6]

The situation was similar in Prague and Poznania, though here too, anti-Semitism was deprecated by the revolutionary leadership,[7] and it is an oversimplification to suggest, as some German historians do, that anti-Semitism in 1848 was a specifically Slav phenomenon.[8]

In 1880, 59.1% of the Jews of Budapest adhered to the Magyar nationality and 35.4% to the German; by 1905 the figures were 90.3% and 8.2%.[9] Similarly in Galicia Germanization soon ceased. Of the four Polish Jews elected to the Reichsrat in 1873, three joined the Liberals and one the Polish *Klub*. After the death of Nathan von Kallir in 1886 they were all either in the Polish *Klub* or, in the case of a handful of Jewish Nationalists, remained independent.[10] Jewish support was vital to the Poles, since they held the balance between Poles and Ruthenians, but Jews in the Polish *Klub,* like the Jews in the Hungarian Independence Party, were tolerated only on the understanding that they did not further sectarian interests. The struggle was more bitter in the Czech provinces, where the majority of the

Jews continued to consider themselves German until the outbreak of the First World War.* In Prague and several other cities the German minority would have disintegrated but for Jewish support. One writer records that in the *Altstädter Gymnasium* of Prague which he attended (after 1918) there were only two non-Jews in his class.[11] We have seen the reasons for this stubborn anti-Czech attitude among Jews. It in turn, lay at the root of much Czech anti-Semitism. Rieger, the venerable leader of the Old Czech Party, mocked the excessive Germanophilia of many Jews by asking, "Are perhaps only those to be regarded as Germans whose ancestors' cradles stood on the Jordan?"[12] And in 1899, in a debate on anti-Jewish riots in Moravia, Czech deputies complained that

> the worst opponents of the Czech people in political matters have been Jewish fellow-citizens, who have consistently maintained Germandom.[13] and that

> in the linguistically mixed areas they are at the head of the oppressors of our Czech minorities.[14]

On the other hand, Czechization was fostered by the *Národní Jednota česko-židovská*. As early as 1883, two Czech Jewish candidates narrowly defeated two German Jews in the Jewish quarter of Prague in an election for the Bohemian Diet.[15] One Jew, Alois Zucker, sat as an Old Czech in the Reichsrat and a small number of Jews were even connected with the Slovak nationalist movement from its very beginning.[16] In Galicia organized anti-Semitism flared up in the 1880's, stimulated by the wave of pogroms which marked the accession of Alexander III in Russia (directly, by way of example, indirectly by the influx of refugees they caused). In Hungary organized anti-Semitism was founded in 1875 by Victor von Istoczy. With Géza von Önody and Ivan Simonyí he represented the movement at Pinkert's International Anti-Semitic Conference in 1862. The ritual murder trial of Tísza-Eszlár in the same year, which was followed by pogroms, marked the emotional climax of the movement. Politically it declined after having succeeded, in

* In 1900 the proportion of German-speaking Jews was as follows: Bohemia, 44.6%, Moravia, 77.4%, and Silesia, 80.7% (Rauchberg, *Der nationale Besitzstand*, Vol. I, pp. 389–91).

1884, in electing twenty-one members of the Hungarian parliament and capturing the Bratislava town council.

Political anti-Semitism had little chance of success in Hungary for a number of reasons. Because the Hungarian aristocracy and gentry were fairly evenly divided between Catholics and Calvinists there was a well-established freedom from religious prejudice. Moreover, the Jewish bourgeoisie was considered useful in performing economic functions which the nobility disdained. There was therefore co-operation rather than rivalry, and the Jews owed their emancipation and relatively secure position to the protection of the ruling classes. If the virtual monopoly of some branches of commerce that Jews enjoyed caused the hostility of the poorer classes, they were generally too well under control to be able to express this. The anti-Semitic Christian Social movement which Count Zichy unfolded in the 1890's made little headway. Characteristically, Zichy supported the Slovaks' resistance to the Liberal policy of Magyarization.

In Galicia, the first stirrings came from the Ruthenian side.[17] In the main, however, it was a Polish phenomenon, religious, national, and economic in origin; and it was generally aimed as much against Ruthenians as against Jews. "Agricultural associations" were formed to preserve land in Polish ownership, and in 1883 the Catholic Congress in Cracow proclaimed a fight against Orthodoxy and Judaism.[18] The main vehicles of anti-Semitism were the National Democratic Party (which, unlike other bourgeois nationalist parties in the Habsburg Empire, was, under the inspiration of Roman Dmowski, pro-clerical)[19] and Father Stojalowski's Christian People's Party. Stojalowski was one of the pioneers of the Polish peasant movement in the 1870's but achieved no success until the 1890's. His agitation against the magnates and their Jewish bailiffs aroused the displeasure of both the civil and ecclesiastical authorities and he had finally to organize his campaign from Hungary. He himself was elected at a by-election in 1898 after a campaign of great violence accompanied by over thirty pogroms.[20]

In general we may draw the following conclusions about anti-Semitism in its connections with the nationalities problem:

1. It was stronger in ethnically homogeneous than in "mixed" regions, where the need for allies counterbalanced the

sharper tempers and greater mutual suspicions. 2. It was stronger among "unhistorical" nations than among "historical" ones, the exception being the German Austrians who had more to lose and were less secure than the other "master races" of the Empire. 3. Where it flourished among historical nations it was at the same time a social revolt aimed at the Jews as the allies of the native ruling class.

Anti-Semitism in the eastern regions of the Habsburg Empire most thickly populated by the Jews was spasmodic and incoherent, and it did not play an important part in either Poland or Hungary until after 1918—at any rate in comparison with the proportions it was assuming during our period in the German provinces and particularly in Vienna.

REFERENCES

1 A. Ficker, "Die Volksstämme der österreichisch-ungarischen Monarchie," *Mitteilungen aus dem Gebiete der Statistik*, Jahrgang XV, Heft 4 (Vienna, 1869), pp. 688, 723.
2 Hugelmann, *op. cit.*, p. 91; C. A. Macartney, *Hungary and her Successors, 1919–1937* (Oxford, 1937), pp. 79, 203.
3 Hugelmann, *op. cit.*, pp. 232, 723; M. Rosenfeld, *Die polnische Judenfrage. Problem und Lösung* (Vienna, 1918), pp. 136–7, 145; R. A. Kann, *The Multi-National Empire* (New York, 1950), Vol. , p. 359.
4 R. J. Rath, *The Viennese Revolution of 1848* (Austin, Texas, 1957), p. 103.
5 S. W. Baron, "The Impact of the Revolution of 1848 on Jewish Emancipation," *Jewish Social Studies*, Vol. IX, No. 3 (1949), pp. 226–7.
6 *Der Wanderer*, Nov. 20, 1849; quoted by Klein, *Antisemitismus in der Wiener Presse*, p. 31.
7 L. B. Namier, *1848: The Revolution of the Intellectuals* (Oxford, 1958), pp. 58–9.
8 For example, G. Rhode, *Geschichte der Stadt Posen* (Neuendettelsau, 1953), pp. 116, 120–21; M. Hartmann, *Revolutionäre Erinnerungen* (ed. H. H. Houben) (Leipzig, 1919), pp. 25–8.
9 *Statistisches Jahrbuch der Haupt- und Residenzstadt Budapest*, Vol. V, p. 23.
10 S. R. Landau, *Der Polenklub und seine Hausjuden* (Vienna, 1907), pp. 37–9; F. Freund, *Das österreichische Abgeordnetenhaus* (Vienna, 1907, 1911).
11 F. Weltsch, "The Rise and Fall of the German-Jewish Symbiosis," *Leo Baeck Year Book I* (London, 1959), p. 258.
12 Speech in Reichsrat, Feb. 16, 1882. *StPA*, IX. Sess., 195, Sitz., p. 6573.
13 Speech in Reichsrat by Začek, Nov. 8, 1899, *StPA*, XVI. Sess., 9. Sitz., p. 533.
14 Speech in Reichsrat by Adamek, Nov. 8, 1899, *StPA*, *loc. cit.*

15 *Prager Tagblatt*, July 1, 1883. But by 1901, at the height of the linguistic furore, these, too, had become dispensable; one was dropped before the election, the other between the first and the second ballot. *Ibid.*, Oct. 16, 1901; *ÖW*, Oct. 4, 1901.
16 J. Lettrich, *A History of Modern Slovakia* (Lond, 1958), p. 174.
17 J. S. Bloch, *Erinnerungen aus meinem Leben* (Vienna, 1922), p. 289.
18 Dubnow, *Neueste Geschichte*, Vol. III, pp. 79–80.
19 W. Feldman, *Geschichte der politischen Ideen in Polen seit dessen Teilungen* (Munich, 1917), pp. 348, 351–2; *Cambridge History of Poland*, Vol. II, p. 456.
20 P. Brock, "The Early Years of the Polish Peasant Party, 1895–1907," *JCEA*, Col. XIV, No. 3 (1954), p. 222.

16
Economic Anti-Semitism

Of all the aspects of the post-1867 order, it was economic liberalism that placed the heaviest immediate burden on the population; it was with this that Jews were most prominently associated, exposing themselves if not to hatred, then to ridicule and contempt. This often came from non-Conservative sources, especially the humorous press, which was in general Liberal and devoted most of its space to lampooning priests and the efforts of Czechs and Hungarians to cope with the German language. But the opening of the stock exchange was an opportunty too good to miss, and the Jewish *Gründer parvenu* supplied regular material.* *Der Floh* ran a feature "Aus dem Tagebuche der Madame Eleonore de Veitelbaum, née de Pinkeles," *Figaro* on "Der Bankier Moriz Feigelstock beim Morgenkaffee."

But there was a serious side to this. While the average rate of interest during the years of the *Gründer* period ranged from 12 to 22% (the *Wiener Bankverein* paid 80% in 1872,[1]) one artisan business after another was seized for default† and mortgage commitments forced tens of thousands of peasant holdings on to the auction market.‡ The crash of 1873 seemed, in the popular mind, to prove the Jews' wickedness; and that the House of Rothschild, which had kept its hands clean during the speculations, emerged unscathed from the chaos proved the Jews' cunning.¶

---

* See illustration 2.

† The number was 35,000 in Vienna alone in the thirty years which followed the abolition of guild privileges in 1859 (F. Funder, *Aufbruch zur christlichen Sozialreform*, Vienna, 1953, p. 37).

‡ There were 74,725 between 1870 and 1810 (*Ibid.*, p. 36).

¶ The oldest established houses fared best. Of the six pre-1868 foundations in Vienna none suffered harm. Of the seventy later ones, 62 crashed (Eder, *Liberalismus*, p. 221).

It was some time, however, before an anti-Semitic movement emerged in response to these events. Conservative and clerical anti-Semitism suffered under the general atmosphere of tolerance and religious indifference which the Liberal era had spread. Religious prejudices were tainted with the brush of Habsburg absolutism. Only in the 1880's were the fulminations from above fused with the rumblings from below into a combined assault on political Liberalism.

This was voiced, louder and more effectively than Catholic deputies or editors could do, by the Viennese artisans. Anti-Semitism had for long gone together with a defense of their rights. In 1848 the shoemakers' guild had complained that emancipation* would increase their already great poverty.[2] *Die Geissel* asked:

> If it has been possible for the Jews in a condition of dependence and oppression to raise themselves almost to becoming the money-lords to the whole world, what will happen when the last barriers are down which still impede their unshakeable spirit of speculation?[3]

Now, in 1880, on November 11, a meeting was called in Vienna (attended by, among others, Lueger and Grübl, a later Liberal mayor) [4] with the slogan, "Craftsmen against the pedlars' trade!" One of the orators, the clockmaker Joseph Buschenhagen (later a follower of Schönerer), exclaimed:

> Who are the pedlars? They are mainly Polish, Hungarian and fugitive Russian Jews. They damage the artisan and none of them has learned a trade.[5]

It was resolved to set up a permanent "Society for the Protection of Artisans" *(Gesellschaft zum Schutz des Handwerks)*.[6]

From 1881 onward, other artisans' conventions were held, demanding the restoration of compulsory guilds. Of these organizations the most important was the *Österreichischer Reformverein* founded in 1882, which later absorbed the Society for the Protection of Artisans.[7] A speech by Schönerer at the initial meeting was followed by one from Robert Pattai, a lawyer, who

---

* There was a similar petition from the artisans of Leipzig against emancipation and the "subversion of egalitarianism" (Valentin, *Geschichte der deutschen Revolution*, Vol. II, p. 102).

had been elected vice-president and a year later became president. The connection between the purpose of the meeting and the Jewish question was for him self-evident:

The ubiquitous and dumb-founding rise to prosperity of the Jews in these days [he explained] seem to me to be but an illustration of the theories of the Manchester school, to which I am most strongly opposed . . . . It is a fact that the unconditional sovereignty of the . . . Manchester theory is in every respect linked with surprising growth in the Jews' prosperity, just as we find them represented above all in those walks of life whose purpose is not so much actual production but solely the transformation of existing property relations. If we now see that today the Jews have, under the rule of their theories, risen to almost a hegemony in the economic sphere, then from this loftier point of view the Jewish question appears as but a symptom of the general economic disease . . . .

Should it not be possible to cut the root of the Jewish question through these necessary reforms, then the discriminatory laws, . . . demanded from so many sides, will become necessary.[8]

The *Reformverein* was for many years the main anti-Semitic organization of Vienna and the battleground for the various trends of anti-Semitism that were emerging. It did much of the preliminary work in providing the later parties with their lower middle-class clientèle. Kronawetter's Democrats, who had hitherto based their following on precisely these classes, tried to condemn the anti-Semitic element in the economic agitation,[9] but they were fighting a losing battle. Within four months the *Reformverein* had 1000 members,[10] and after the meetings during the Northern Railway controversy in 1883 and 1884, which developed into pitched battles between the Democrats and the anti-Semites, their fate was sealed.

REFERENCES

1 Charmatz, *Österreichs innere Geschichte*, Vol. II, p. 11.
2 Tietze, *Die Juden Wiens*, p. 197.
3 *Die Geissel*, March 6, 1849.
4 *DVB*, Dec. 13, 1908.
5 E. Pichl, *Georg Schönerer und die Entwicklung des Alldeutschtums in der Ostmark* (Oldenburg, 1938), Vol. II, p. 25.
6 K. Skalnik, *Dr Karl Lueger, der Mann zwischen den Zeiten* (Vienna–Munich, 1954), p. 41.

7 *Ibid.*, p. 42.
8 *ÖV*, Feb. 19, 1882.
9 *DZ*, April 13, 1882.
10 Pichl, *op. cit.*, Vol. II, p. 26.

17

Schönerer and the Liberal Split

The settlement of 1867 inevitably produced a conflict between loyalty to "the German national idea' and "the German-Austrian idea of state, constitution, and freedom."[1] Yet paradoxically, because the Germans in Austria and the creators of the new state were the same body of people, the history of their political organization, "the Left," is one of the continuous conflict between Liberalism and Nationalism. Because their enemies, clericalism and Habsburg absolutism, were the same, for reasons which, as we have seen, date back to Joseph II, the two irreconcilables worked together in the *Verfassungspartei*. Their inclination to split was rivaled only by their desire to coalesce again, and in 1910 they were, as they had been in 1867, once more one party—though the father is unlikely to have known his own child.

The constitution which this party was pledged to defend was, for all its libertarian elements, weighted to favor the Germans. Ernst von Plener, the scion of a famous Liberal family, admits this in his memoirs:

> The representation by interests (i.e., curias) in the February constitution was no doubt open to many objections, but its fundamental political idea was, to be honest, the attempt to secure the historic and political position of the German nation, which, as is well known, does not constitute the majority of the population of Austria, but which, through historic labor, education, prosperity and the burden of taxation towered above all others. For that reason it was foolish on the part of radical and German Nationalist tendencies constantly to carp at these electoral provisions and, conversely, equally wise for those genuinely concerned with the leading position of Germandom in the state, to maintain the electoral system as far as possible.[2]

Yet it was precisely against the comfortably ensconced Liberal oligarchy that the radicals and nationalists were campaigning. In the 1873 Reichsrat, the first to be directly elected, they formed themselves into a *Fortschristtsklub* of fifty-seven members, but in all essentials co-operated with the majority of the Left in providing the majority for the Auersperg administration.* After the Liberals lost power, however, the conflict between the two wings grew stronger. At the 1879 conference of the party in Lower Austria, Schönerer unsuccessfully demanded that the party commit itself to autonomy for Dalmatia, Galicia, and Bukovina, to placing the newly acquired territory of Bosnia and Hercegovina under the regency of an archduke and to introducing universal suffrage.[3]

The next year Friedjung, whose first book,[4] strongly critical of the Hungarians, caused his dismissal from his post at the *Handelsakademie,* again tried, equally unsuccessfully, to steer the party on to a more pronouncedly nationalist course.[5] The old guard of the Liberal leadership was unsympathetic, partly because such notions were too closely connected with popular agitation and democracy, partly because the Liberal Party at that time still contained non-Germans.†

The pacemaker for both nationalism and anti-Semitism within the Left was Georg Ritter von Schönerer. He was born in 1842, the son of the most notable of Austria's early railway engineers who had been ennobled for his services. The father retired to his estate at Rosenau in Lower Austria, near the Bohemian frontier, which young Schönerer took over after his father's death. In 1873 he was elected to the Reischsrat for his home constituency (Waidhofen-Zwettl) in the fourth *curia* (i.e., rural communes). In parliament he joined the *Fortschrittsklub,* but left it after three years, considering its attitude too tame on both national and economic questions.

It was economic questions that mainly claimed his attention at this time. He was an "improving landlord" who took a beneficial

* The main unit of Austrian party organization was the *Klub* or parliamentary group. A national party might subdivide into a number of *Klubs.* On the other hand, several parties or independent members might coalesce into one *Klub.*
† The Liberal deputy Skene declared in 1879 that he was proud to have been elected by both Czechs and Germans (*NFP*, October 7, 1879. See also, Plener, *op. cit.*, Vol. II, pp. 9, 218).

interest in the welfare of his neighboring peasants. It was his expert knowledge and personal popularity that insured his election and re-election as a local man, at any rate during the earlier part of his career. Even his anti-Semitism—at this stage a subordinate element in his political thought—was economic rather than racial. He deplored the effect of "Jewish" capitalism on peasants and artisans; he deplored the "Jewish" press and the "Jewish" Liberal Party for the support which they gave to these undesirable developments. His first anti-Semitic remarks in the Reichsrat were made in a speech on March 7, 1878, when he attacked the government for adopting a tone "such as might otherwise be more usual in non-Christian coffee-house establishments"[6] He followed this three weeks later by claiming to be "undisconcerted by the paid, selfish, and repulsive yapping of the greater part of the Viennese Jewish and government press."[7]

His 1879 election address gives a clearer insight into his developing political philosophy. In it he demanded:

1. universal and direct suffrage;
2. the substitution of the present *Ausgleich* with Hungary by a purely dynastic union;
3. economic and political union with Germany;
4. the maintenance of secular education;
5. the nationalization of the railways.

> Above all, the interests of landed property and of productive hands are in future to be resolutely promoted, and opposed to the hitherto privileged interests of mobile capital and the hitherto Semitic dominance of money and words.[8]

Although Schönerer was still nominally a Liberal—he had been nominated by the Liberal *Landes-Wahlcomité*[9]—he did not join any of the Liberal *Klubs* in the new *Reichsrat*. Together with a fellow-spirit, Fürnkranz, elected for the neighboring constituency of Krems, he formed a two-man party.

The new element which appeared in his manifesto was the desire to stress the Germanity of the German-Austrians and their dislike of any further commitments with non-Germans to the south or east. Already in 1878 he had caused an uproar in the Reichsrat by exclaiming, "If only we already belonged to the German Empire!"[10] The full formulation of his pan-German

came in 1882 with the publication of the Linz Programme,[11] the
main points of which were:

1. Those parts of the Austro-Hungarian Monarchy which
had belonged to the German Confederation to form an independent unit; all connections with Hungary except the dynastic to be
severed; autonomy for Galicia; annexation of Bosnia and Dalmatia
by Hungary.
2. To preserve the German character of the territories which
formerly belonged to the Confederation, German is to be the
only official language in them.
3. The constitution is to be safeguarded; universal suffrage
introduced; "interested" persons, e.g. priests, civil servants or
directors of companies with state contracts, to be excluded from
Parliament.
4. Maintenance of civil rights and press freedom, but
"effective action against the moral rottenness of the press," if
necessary by nationalizing press advertising; defense of lay
education.
5. Settlement of the Hungarian debt.
6. To make the state "independent of money powers,"
introduction of a progressive income tax, unearned income tax
and luxury tax.
7. Customs union with Germany; compulsory artisans' and
workers' unions.
8. Nationalization of railways and insurance; insurance for
old age and injury.
9. Support for home industries and "honest labour;"
compulsory training certificates for artisans; prohibition of
house-to-house peddling; factory legislation; "quick and cheap
justice," with regulation of lawyers' fees.
10. Maintenance of "sturdy peasantry;" low-interest agricultural credit; homestead law.
11. Special treaty to strengthen the alliance with Germany.

This mixture of nationalism with semi-socialism is a familiar
feature of racial anti-Semitism, though here the anti-Semitism is
still to come. Politically the document is markedly liberal, indeed
much more radically so than the official Liberal policy. In its
economic proposals, however, we have a well-developed statement of the antithesis between "honest" and "harmful" capital
and a denunciation of the professions notably associated with
Jews.

The Linz Programme was so called because it was to have been given to the world at a meeting in Linz, but this was banned by the *Statthalter*. It was the logical outcome of the nationalist struggle within the Liberal Party and had many points of similarity with the program of the *"Jungdeutschen"* adopted in Graz in 1871.[12] Its immediate inspiration came from the failure of the nationalist faction to carry the 1879 and 1880 party conferences. Schönerer and Friedjung thereupon joined forces and formed a *Deutscher Klub* out of which grew the *Verein der Deutschen Volkspartei.** Friedjung himself had already published his own *Programmentwurf für die Deutsche Volkspartei* in 1879, many parts of which were incorporated in the Linz Programme.[13] The combination of constitutional and social reform in the group's aims was adumbrated in 1881 in Schönerer's manifesto for the *Verein*:

> We want to give lively expression to the feeling of solidarity of the German nation in Austria, not only in contending with Slavdom, but also in a struggle against the exploitation of the noblest forces of the people to the advantage of a few . . .[14]

It seems doubtful whether Hitler in his enthusiastic approval of Schönerer[15] knew that his chief collaborators in compiling the Linz Programme were Heinrich Friedjung and Victor Adler, both Jews. A half-Jew, Dr. Serafin Bondi, a friend of Schönerer from university days,[16] was also on the committee of fifteen which did the preliminary work.[17] It may be asked how Jews could become the collaborators of a known anti-Semite. Both were no doubt incautious and soon realized whom they were dealing with. But we have to understand that neither Friedjung nor Adler was conscious of being primarily a Jew (Adler was baptized); they were Germans, and as Liberals were indifferent to religion. Moreover, Schönerer's occasional anti-Semitic utterances assume a bigger importance if his career is viewed in retrospect. In the context of 1880 they were no more than regrettable.

Very soon, however, anti-Semitism became a major plank in his platform. On July 2, 1882, at the first meeting of the *Deutschnationaler Verein*, which was founded to succeed the

* These were both extraparliamentary organizations and should not be confused with later political parties of the same name.

Volkspartei, now banned by the government, a motion to exclude Jews was passed.[18] Pernerstorfer, Adler's friend, was chairman at the meeting, and he accepted the motion in the hope, as he afterwards claimed, of later influencing the *Verein* in another direction.[19] By April, 1883 his relations with Schönerer had reached the breaking point on a number of issues and he resigned the chairmanship with the complaint that

> the form of anti-Semitism which seems today to be, or at least to be becoming, party dogma, is in my view quite unacceptable.[20]

In 1885 the twelfth, and most famous point was added to the Linz Programme:

> The removal of Jewish influence from all sections of public life is indispensable for carrying out the reforms aimed at.[21]

In his economic reforms, too, Schönerer had been adopting a more anti-Semitic note. He had been one of the speakers at the foundation meeting of the *Reformverein* and was chairman of a meeting on April 1, 1882 which was dissolved by the authorities after anti-Semitic speeches.[22] His big chance came, however, with the Northern Railway controversy. The Northern Railway, connecting Vienna with the industries of Northern Bohemia and the first to be built in Austria, had been financed by Salomon Rothschild. He had been granted a fifty years' concession by Imperial patent in 1836, and in 1884 the government was proposing to renew the privilege. To Schönerer this was a clear case of Jewish influence putting private profit before the public good.

The controversy dragged on for over a year. In April, 1884 it opened with a public meeting in the Town Hall of Vienna, addressed by both Schönerer and Lueger,[23] in favor of nationalization. The next month, when the Reichsrat began the first of its debates on the future of the railway, Schönerer presented a petition with 33,896 signatures demanding nationalization:[24]

> It would be a good action of parliament and the government [he said] if it paid attention for once to the voice of the people instead of the voices of Rothschild and partners.[25]

A year later, when neither the Reichsrat nor he had yet exhausted the subject, he claimed:

Things have come to such a pass that the population would not be at all astonished if it were to hear that at the end of the debate and on the acceptance of this Bill the cry had gone out unanimously from here: "Long live our allies, the corruptible and Judaised Viennese press! Long live the Northern Railway Jews and their comrades![26]

His irretrievable adoption of anti-Semitism had two effects. First it secured him an increased electoral following, especially after the extension of the franchise to the "five-florin men."* In 1885 he and two followers were elected. By-elections brought the number up to six by 1887. All had been candidates in the third or fourth *curiae*. The second effect was a considerable diminution in the quality of his movement's leadership. Disgusted by his intolerance and fanaticism, which extended to personal, not only doctrinal matters, those who had hopefully gathered round him in 1882, in an attempt to revivify Liberalism, left him one after the other. Adler founded the Austrian Social Democratic Party in 1889 and he was joined later by Pernerstorfer. Pattai found a more congenial haven among the Christian Socials and through them eventually became vice-president of the Chamber of Deputies. Friedjung remained faithful to his idiosyncratic brand of Liberalism.

Schönerer never commanded a mass movement and never achieved large-scale electoral success. At the height of his popularity, in 1885, his paper, the *Unverfälscht Deutsche Worte*, had a circulation of under 1700, and membership of the *Deutschnationaler Verein*, at the time of its dissolution in 1889, was about 1200.[27] This did not disturb him unduly; he was concerned more with the spreading of an idea than leading a party, and it was partly through his influence that nationalism and anti-Semitism made considerable strides forward among the Liberals in the 1880's.

During Taaffe's long administration, the bitter bread of opposition, with which the party had become unfamiliar, caused them to hunger for more palatable policies than the Liberalism

---

* The electorate for the Reichsrat was divided into four *curiae*: the landed proprietors elected 85 members, the chambers of commerce 21 members, the urban communes 118 members, and the rural communes 129. In 1882 the minimum annual taxation for the franchise was reduced from ten to five florins.

with which, it appeared, Austria was sated. Taaffe's "iron ring" policy* was especially conciliatory to the non-German nationalities. The Polish and Czech landed nobility who controlled about a hundred seats in the chamber were the mainstay of his majority. Thus by proposing political and social reforms, the German Nationalists hoped to enlist the support of the economically weak against the privileged classes whose policy was in the main federalist and anti-nationalist.

The 1885 elections brought the nationalist wing within the Left further reinforcements. Unable to get the *Vereinigte Linke* as a whole to accept an uncompromisingly German policy, it decided to set itself up as a separate party and formed the *Deutscher Klub,* fifty members strong. The moderate element, numbering eighty-one, constituted the *Deutsch-Österreichischer Klub.* The Jewish question played no part in this split, but it inevitably came to the surface when the tension within the *Deutscher Klub* increased.

The trouble first arose over the question of the party press. In 1886 the *Klub* made the *Deutsche Zeitung,* with Friedjung as editor, its organ. From the start there were voices against appointing a Jew as chief spokesman,[28] but as late as January 31, 1887, only a fortnight before it split, the *Klub* reaffirmed its confidence in its editor by thirty-four votes to seven.[29]

The storm finally blew on an anti-Semitic motion by Schönerer which he moved in Parliament on February 12, 1887. Eighteen of the *Klub* voted for it, and twenty-three voted against. The real question at issue was the *Klub's* relationship with the Schönerer faction. The battle was fought out at a number of *Klub* meetings. Otto Steinwender, a schoolmaster from traditionally anti-clerical Carinthia, leading the extreme wing, proposed that, notwithstanding the *Klub's* opposition to Schönerer, it was

a logical conclusion of our national and economic convictions to take arms against the harmful influence of Judaism where it does exist.

Pernerstorfer, in reply, wanted the *Klub* "to reject anti-Semitism

---

* The expression was intended to convey an inexorable encirclement of the German minority by the other nationalities.

as a party principle." Eventually the *Klub* agreed on a compromise whereby it declared itself as resolutely opposed to corruption as to "wild class and racial hatred," and rejected any community with "bodies which elevated this hatred into a political principle."[30]

However, the compromise did not work, and seventeen radicals left the *Klub* on February 14 and 15. They complained that the Left was too much concerned with regaining office and not enough with the long-term defense of Germandom. On the Jewish question it demanded that

> everyone should be permitted to proceed with complete freedom, following only his own conscience and his conception of duty by the German people . . . [31]

In May the rebels formed themselves into a new *Klub,* sixteen strong, named the *Deutschnationale Vereinigung,* out of which developed the later German National Party. On the Jewish question it laid down:

> Neither anti-Semitism nor resistance to it will be adopted as parts of the programme; the matter is left to the individual conscience of members.[32]

This ambiguity had its obvious advantages. It enabled the party's speakers to blow hot or cold according to the audience and even, under certain circumstances, to angle for Jewish votes. But it was also sheer necessity, for the new *Klub* was not united on the anti-Semitic issue. Its core consisted of those who had voted for the Schönerer motion in February, but two deputies —Pernerstorfer and another—who had voted against joined too, and four of the motion's supporters declined. In fact, there was a general feeling that the Jewish question was, in Steinwender's words, "by no means the most urgent."[33]

The new *Klub,* like the old, found co-operation with Schönerer impossible. Explaining why they were unable to support his bill for the restriction of Jewish immigration, they wrote:

> Above all [we] cannot accept the sentence, "Whereas it is in our view only a question of a short while before the Jews already in the country are subjected to special legislation . . ."[34]

But in the long run the 1887 debate decisively altered the whole course of Liberal politics.[35] Even if less than one-fifth of the Left deputies put themselves in a position of declared extremism, the whole party was forced to become more openly national and "soft" on anti-Semitism. Above all there was the reappraisal, which had begun with the Friedjung episode, of the role of the Jews as a constituent part of the German nationality. The rump of the *Deutscher Klub* reamalgamated with the majority of the Liberals into a *Vereinigte Deutsche Linke* of 110 members—the first time that the entire Left acknowledged itself as being German. In 1885 the Liberal program specifically

condemn[ed] . . . most decisively all loathsome agitations against individual classes of civil society, but especially the anti-Semitic movement, unworthy of a civilised country.[36]

In 1891 it was silent on this point.*

The failure of the Liberals' economic appeal also meant that they had to base themselves more on the lower middle classes. An analysis of the constituencies of those who voted on the 1867 Schönerer motion is revealing. The forty-one votes of the *Deutscher Klub* were distributed as follows:

	For	Against
Sudeten lands	7	17
Vienna region	3	3
Alpine provinces	8	4

The new *Deutschnationale Vereinigung* consisted of nine Alpine deputies, three from the Vienna region, and four from the Sudeten lands. This might seem surprising, considering how much more evident the "Slav menace" must have been in Bohemia and Moravia, and how few Jews there were west of Vienna. The explanation, however, lies elsewhere. The ground was never really receptive for Liberalism in the Alpine provinces.

* This appears to have been a last-minute decision. A printer's proof of the manifesto in the Plener papers *(ÖSA,* fol. 34) reads: "Let us leave aside all schisms, let us conduct the elections with noble means, let us abjure the tactics of personal accusations and of hatred against particular Classes and denominations . . . ." The published version omitted "and denominations' ("und Confessionen").

The "Liberal" voters were mainly traders, notaries, and horse doctors in towns of which even the biggest were provincial and the majority little more than glorified villages. They were concerned to counterbalance their predominantly agrarian surroundings and were jealous of the priest's influence. If they were state employees their loyalty was to a "Josephinian" bureaucratic machinery. They had no time for the enlightened and cosmopolitan ideals of Liberalism and no interest in a free economy. The Sudeten lands were different. They were industrialized, with a prosperous (partly Jewish) capitalist class and an old cultural and intellectual tradition. They could afford to combine quite vehement national feeling with a self-confident and even complacent largeness of ideas. After the mid-nineties, Liberalism had disappeared as a force from the Alpine provinces.[37] In Bohemia, and still more Moravia, it hung on until 1914, even if sadly diluted by a need to take account of the downward extension of the franchise and an increasing tendency to compromise on anti-Semitism.

The changing attitude toward Jews inside German National ranks is best illustrated by events in the *Deutscher Schulverein*. Throughout the 1860's and 1870's, when there was consistent anti-Jewish sniping from the Right, the Left regarded the Jews as its allies on national as well as constitutional issues. Old Plener might snort that the Young German movement in Vienna was run by Max Menger, *"ein schlesischer, wasserpolackischer Jude,"*[38] but more typical was the view, for instance, that German-Jewish schools in Galicia should receive official support against the pro-Polish authorities.[39] Jewish Liberal politicians often made a parade of their German loyalty—Friedjung was by no means isolated examples[40]— and strongly national views among Gentiles could, as we have seen, be quite consistent with pro-Jewish feelings. Joseph Kopp who became, with Menger, the leader of the *Deutscher Verein* in Vienna in 1870, represented Rabbi Bloch in the famous Bloch-Rohling trial.

The *Deutscher Verein* was largely instrumental in 1880 in the foundation of the *Deutscher Schulverein,* whose purpose was to give support to German schools in areas threatened with de-Germanization. Two questions were soon raised.

1. Should the association support Jewish denominational

schools when these preserved the teaching of German in threatened areas?

2. Should Jews be admitted as members at all?

Jews had been prominently associated with it from the start; in 1882 the committee of twenty-four included Adler and Bondi.[41] Eight Jewish schools were subsidized in 1861, twelve in 1886, and five in 1886. About 9% of the *Verein*'s expenditure went on these schools in the first seven years.[42]

An offensive against Jewish participation was started in 1885 by Schönerer, who was piqued at not being re-elected to the executive committee. Anti-Semitic motions by the Vienna and Graz university branches were overwhelmingly rejected by the annual conference[43] and the offending groups were expelled. Schönerer resigned the next year from *"diesen verjudeten Verein"*[44] and formed his own anti-Semitic *Schulverein für Deutsche,* but it was a failure and the authorities dissolved it in 1889. However, the *Schulverein,* like the Liberal Party, had to move with the times. The 1896 conference rejected by 674 votes to 305 a motion to exclude Jews,[45] but the 1899 conference allowed branches to fix their own rules of membership and more than one branch to exist in one place.[46]

Some respite was given to the Left in these fierce debates in 1888, when the German Nationalists were relieved of the liabilities of Schönerer's leadership under characteristic circumstances. On March 8 he and some companions invaded the editorial offices of the *Neues Wiener Tagblatt* whose early evening edition had published a premature announcement of the death of the Emperor William I. Incensed that the "insolent Jewish press" should not scruple to play fast and loose with the truth even in such sacred matters as the life and death of a Hohenzollern emperor, they laid about the staff with sticks—an exploit for which he was sentenced to four months in prison and the loss of political rights for five years. His patent of nobility was also cancelled. The *Deutschnationaler Verein* was dissolved the next year.

Schönerer's eclipse brought about a temporary relaxation in the controversy on nationalism within the parliamentary Left. In the 1891 elections only two of his followers and twenty-one of Steinwender's group (now called *Deutsche Nationalpartei)* were elected. The United German Left maintained its precarious unity with 109 deputies. But his eclipse also left the leadership of the anti-Semites more open than it had been for some time and gave to Schönerer's rival, Karl Lueger, the opportunity he had been waiting for.

REFERENCES

1 *NFP*, May 13, 1873. Quoted by P. Molisch, *Geschichte der deutschnationalen Bewegung in Österreich, von ihren Anfängen bis zum Verfall der Monarchie* (Jena, 1926), p. 86.
2 E. Baron von Plener, *Erinnerungen* (Stuttgart–Leipzig, 1911–21), Vol. III, pp. 90–1.
3 *DZ*, Oct. 5, 1879.
4 *Der Ausgleich mit Ungarn* (1877). See E. Zailer, *Heinrich Friedjung. Unter besonderer Berücksichtigung, seiner politischen Entwicklung* (unpublished dissertation, Vienna, 1949), p. 30.
5 *Der VI. deutschösterreichische Parteitag. Abgehalten zu Wien am 14, November 1880* (Vienna, 1880), p. 5.
6 Speech on March 7, 1878. *StPA*, VIII. Sess., 352, Sitz., p. 11453.
7 Pichl, *Schönerer*, Vol. I, p. 61.
8 "Mein Programm," *NP, ÖVA*, Box 35, fol. 1.
9 "An die Herrn Wähler der niederösterreichischen Landgemeinden," *NP, ÖVA*, Box 31.
10 Speech on Dec. 18, 1878. *StPA*, VIII. Sess., 409. Sitz., p. 13112.
11 Pichl, *op. cit.*, Vol. I, pp. 113–22.
12 Julius Sylvester in *Österreichische Volkzeitung*, Dec. 25, 1913.
13 For an exact comparison of the two texts, see Zailer, *op. cit.*, p. 52.
14 "Deutsche Stammesgenossen!" *NP, ÖVA*, Box 35, fol. 1.
15 Hitler, *Mein Kampf*, pp. 93–5.
16 Pichl, *op. cit.*, Vol. I, p. 107.
17 *DZ*, Jan. 13, 1901.
18 Pichl, *op. cit.*, Vol. II, pp. 73–4.
19 *DW*, April 16, 1883.
20 Letter to Kautschitsch, the deputy chairman, April 6, 1883; *DW*, June 16, 1883. See also *ibid.*, July 1, July 16, Aug. 1, 1883 for the general controversy.
21 Pichl, *op. cit.*, Vol. I, pp. 122, 175.
22 *Ibid.*, Vol. II, p. 28.
23 Skalnik, *Lueger*, p. 43.
24 Pichl, *op. cit.*, Vol. I, p. 251.
25 Speech on May 2, 1884, *StPA*, IX Sess., 364. Sitz., p. 12636.
26 Speech on March 27, 1885, *StPA*, IX Sess., 429. Sitz., p. 14983.
27 Pichl, *op. cit.*, Vol. II, pp. 59–67, 109.
28 H. Friedjung, *Ein Stück Zeitungsgeschichte* (Vienna, 1887), pp. 6, 7, 9.
29 *Ibid.*, p. 12.
30 *DZ*, Feb. 11, 1887; *Deutsche Volkszeitung*, Feb. 25, 1887.

31 *DZ*, Feb. 16, 1887.
32 *DZ*, May 24, 1887.
33 *DZ*, Dec. 5, 1885.
34 Letter of May 26, 1887, from Steinwender and five others, *NP*, *ÖVA*, Box 35, fol. 2.
35 For further details of the debate, see P. G. J. Pulzer, "The Austrian Liberals and the Jewish Question, 1867–1914," *JCEA*, Vol. XXIII, No. 2 (1963), pp. 135–6.
36 *Rechenschaftsbericht der Vereinigten Linken des Abgeordnetenhauses, 1885* (Vienna, 1885), p. 25.
37 Kolmer, *Parlament und Verfassung*, Vol. VI, p. 175.
38 Letter to Ernst Plener, April 11, 1872; Molisch, *Briefe zur deutschen Politik*, p. 80.
39 *DZ*, Nov. 3, 1872.
40 For example, the speech by Rudolf Auspitz in 1880, *Der VII. deutsch-mährische Parteitag in Brünn, abgehalten am 19, September, 1880* (Brno, n.d.), pp. 42–5.
41 *MDS*, June, 1882, p. 9.
42 This constituted 8830 florins out of a total expenditure of 1M. florins. *MDS*, Oct., 1882.
43 *MDS*, April, 1886, p. 2.
44 *UDW*, April 16, 1886.
45 F. G. Schultheiss, *Deutschnationales Vereinswesen. Der Kampf um das Deutschtum*, Heft 2 (Munich, 1897), p. 70.
46 A. Ritter von Wotawa, *Der deutsche Schulverein, 1880–1905. Eine Gedenk-schrift* (Vienna, 1905), p. 26.

18

Lueger and the Catholic Revival

Nationalist anti-Semitism was only one symptom of the reaction to the failure of Liberalism; another equally portentous, was provided by its oldest opponent, Catholicism. The two had, as we have seen, been embattled since the end of the eighteenth century. But Josephinian ideas had left their mark even on unenlightened Habsburg despots, so that during the nineteenth century there were two parties in Austrian Catholicism. One consisted of the majority of the hierarchy, who, pursuing a conciliatory and opportunist policy, were prepared to regard themselves as partners in state authority; the other was an "opposition" who condemned the hierarchy for rendering too much unto Caesar and wished the Church to pursue a more independent and aggressive policy. They accused the hierarchy of being apathetic and impregnated with "Josephinism," and indeed two prelates, the Archbishop of Salzburg and the Abbot of Melk, actually sat with the Liberal peers in the *Herrenhaus*.[1]

It was this opposition, which welcomed the 1848 revolution,* stressed the social mission of the Church, and stringently opposed any concessions on educational or other matters, that brought anti-Semitism into Catholic political propaganda. The movement was derived from the Catholic Romantic movement which, like Romanticism in general, was a reaction against the Enlightenment. Its local father was the Redemptorist saint and apostle Clemens Maria Hofbauer (1751–1821) whose pupils—or rather pupils' pupils—provided the popular basis for the "Catholic Renewal" movement in 1848. It included men like Veith,

---

* cf. *Wiener Kirchenzeitung*, Nov. 14, 1848: "Will the Church . . . intended by its nature and purpose to be free, now lose the shameful fetters under whose pressure it has groaned since the days of Joseph II?"

Gruscha, and Brunner,[2] a circle which contained a surprisingly large number of Protestant and Jewish converts.[3] It was from this circle that the bulk of Catholic journals and periodicals emanated (*Wiener Kirchenzeitung, Österreichischer Volksfreund, Kapistran, Gegenwart*), mostly edited, published, or directed by the tireless Albert Wiesinger and Sebastian Brunner,[4] whom Kuranda accused in 1860 of having chosen agitation against the Jews as his literary specialty.[5]

More dubious assistance came to the Catholic anti-Semitic cause from Canon August Rohling, whose *Der Talmudjude* of 1871 made him a center of controversy for some fifteen years. The book was a rehash of Eisenmenger's *Entdecktes Judentum* of 1708, and sought to prove the depravity of the Jews by means of extracts from the Talmud. He scored an initial success with it; the *Bonifatius-Verein* of Westphalia distributed 30,000 copies of it gratis, and he was appointed to the Chair of Semitic Language at Prague thanks to the efforts of an influential well-wisher. His work was well received by the Catholic press of Austria;[7] and it had sufficient standing as a work of scholarship to secure the acquittal, in 1882, of Franz Holubek, a *Reformverein* orator, who, accused of utterances likely to bring the Jewish faith into disrepute, based his defense on Rohling.

His exposure soon followed, however. He was accused by Joseph Bloch, a Viennese rabbi newly arrived from Galicia, of ignorance and incompetence, and was challenged to undertake an unseen Hebrew translation in open court.[8] Eminent theologians like Professors Delitzsch of Leipzig, Nöldeke of Strasbourg, and Wünsche of Dresden testified against Rohling. He was finally forced to withdraw his plaint against Bloch in 1885,* a blow from which he never recovered. His *Der Zukunftsstaat* of 1898 was placed on the Index and he died in 1931 a forgotten man. He was altogether too disreputable to provide academic respectability for the anti-Semitic campaign. His equally vehement anti-Protestantism disqualified his work from use in Germany, and he was disowned by part of the Catholic press.[9] However, no fewer than three translations of *Der Talmudjude*

* In the trial Rohling was represented by Pattai, and Bloch by the Liberal deputy Kopp. Lueger had offered his services to Bloch, who was warned by Fischhof not to trust him (Bloch, *op. cit.*, p. 88).

were published in France at the time of the Dreyfus Case[10] and the work also circulated in Russia.[11] He added no new ammunition to the "Talmudic" argument against the Jews; he may, however, have done something to revive its popularity. But in an age in which religion mattered less than it had mattered in Europe for 1500 years and which was more inclined to listen to economic or nationalist arguments, this can never have been more than a secondary influence.

It was particularly to its attention to the social question that the Catholic minority faction owed its growing support, although reformist zeal was not necessarily their primary motive. A memorandum to the hierarchy argued:

> In the first place the social question is the question of the possibility of, and the means towards, the living re-Christianisation of society; only in the second place is it for us a question of the viable reform of existing economic and social conditions. In the second place for this reason: because such reforms are not possible without liberating the peoples from spiritual and moral anarchy.[12]

Nevertheless, reform remained the trump card of that group of which Vogelsang had become the political philosopher and Karl Lueger the party leader.

Lueger was Schönerer's junior by two years. He was born in Vienna, lived there all his life, and died there. On his father's side he was descended from peasants in Lower Austria. His father, being the second son, became a soldier during the Napoleonic wars, and after his retirement an attendant at the Polytechnic. His mother was the daughter of a carpenter. After her husband's death she opened, with her daughters, a tobacco kiosk.[13] In Lueger's quarterings we may read the composition of his future political following.

He had hardly graduated and qualified as a lawyer when he immersed himself in public affairs. The rough-and-tumble of Vienna suburban politics appealed to him and remained his love for all his life. Although he became a member of the Reichsrat and Deputy *Landmarschall* of Lower Austria, his heart remained in Viennese politics and his following, throughout his career, came from the "little man" of the growing and teeming suburbs of the capital.

The dominant political philosophy of Vienna was Liberalism. Clericalism and Conservatism counted for next to nothing (in 1868 the Council had petitioned unanimously for the abrogation of the Concordat), and such differences of opinion as existed were fought out within the Liberal ranks. The Liberals of the Town Hall and the political clubs were the most loosely-knit of parties—an association of like-minded individuals rather than a specific organization. The political leadership was provided by the *haute bourgeoisie* of the city, who were educated and cultured men, broadminded, citizens of the world, but out of touch with the great social and economic transformation Vienna was then undergoing, ignorant of, rather than selfishly opposed to, the more democratic yearnings of the masses. Nor was corruption on a modest scale lacking in their somewhat easy-going administration of the capital's services and finances.

But even the radicalism which was then fermenting in the industrial districts grew out of a desire to go beyond rather than react against, the principles of 1867. It formed a ginger-group, not an opposition. It was in such political circles that Lueger found himself in the third district, and it was to represent their interests that he was elected to the city council in 1875 in the second *curia*.* In the council chamber he adopted a critical attitude to the majority and joined with an idealistic but erratic Jewish lawyer, Julius Mandl, in asking awkward questions about laxity and corruption.† The two grandiloquently formed the *Fortschritts- und Wirtschaftspartei*. Its political effectiveness was restricted to the third district, based on the *Eintracht* club, but it had a mouthpiece in Mandl's *Fortschritt,* one of the capital's less distinguished journals. He was re-elected in 1878, this time for the third *curia,* and joined with a number of other radical-minded councilors in a group named the United Left, but their essentially negative attitude and the death, in 1881, of their leader, the Democrat Schrank, robbed the faction of

* The municipal electors of Vienna were divided into three *curiae*, according to the amount they paid in taxes and rates.
† Among the scandals unearthed were: that the sand delivered for building the Ringstrasse was not of the quality paid for; that the snow-clearers' wage list at the Central Cemetery was identical with the list of those to be buried; and that the wardens of two orphanages had their footwear repaired at the public expense.

any cohesion and by 1882 it was dissolved.

Lueger had placed high hopes on the ability of the United Left to transform the city government. He appreciated that its failure would for the time being leave him little scope within the confines of municipal politics and he therefore sought wider fields of action. We have already seen him at artisans' conventions* and at the Northern Railway meetings. The next year, 1885, he decided to enter Parliament. He was elected for the fifth district and in the Reichsrat associated himself with the band of Democrats led by Ferdinand Kronawetter. The Democrats, sitting on the extreme Left, considered themselves advanced Liberals, but their interest in social reform and hostility to nationalism made them more benevolent toward Taaffe. Thus it was not too difficult for Lueger to take up contact with anti-Semites and Catholic reformers.

It is next to impossible to trace accurately Lueger's development toward the acceptance of either anti-Semitism or religious belief. There is virtually no evidence in favor of supposing either conversion to have been sincere, and there is a good deal of evidence against. According to Kronawetter, he remarked at this time, when reproached with going over to the anti-Semites, "Well, we shall see which movement will become the stronger, the Democratic or the anti-Semitic. One will have to accommodate oneself accordingly."[14]

In May 1887 he was one of nineteen deputies who voted in favor of Schönerer's bill to restrict the immigration of Russian and Rumanian Jews,[15] an action which caused Kronawetter to break with him.[16] He also took part in the cortège of sympathy which paraded past Schönerer's house the day on which he began his imprisonment, and he had signed two motions which Schönerer was planning to put to the Reichsrat, one to deplore the premature announcement of William I's death in the "*Judenpresse*," and the other to limit the right of Jews to change their names.[17]

Of more immediate importance was the fact that he was being drawn into the meetings of the Catholic reform movement.

* In 1881 he proposed that the city council officially welcome the artisans' congress [H. Miko, *Die Vereinigung der Konservativen in der Christlichsozialen Partei* (unpublished dissertation, Vienna, 1949), p. 18].

Vogelsang's ideas were speedily gaining popular support in the 1880's, not only because of the undoubted need to counter the neglect which social problems were suffering, but also because of the contact which Vogelsang was able to establish with widely divergent political forces. First, inspired by the example of such figures as the Comte de Mun and the Marquis de la Tour du Pin in France, a few Conservative noblemen, notably Prince Alois Liechtenstein, were interesting themselves in the idea of reform. Second, a number of clergymen, including Franz Schindler, A. M. Weiss, and Adam Latschka, were attaching themselves to the same ideas. Third, Vogelsang was in touch almost from the beginning with the artisans' reform movement in which the clerical wing was led by Holubek and Schneider.[18] In Parliament, Liechtenstein was instrumental in the revision of artisan legislation and securing the five-florin franchise. The relationships among these various men, all of them aiming at some sort of reform, was largely personal and informal. Thus Lueger was introduced to Vogelsang by his friend, and later second-in-command, Albert Gessmann, then an employee at the University Library, who in turn had been introduced by Schneider.[19]

Lueger began taking Christian-Social ideas seriously after the foundation, in 1887, of the *Christlich-sozialer Verein* by two priests, Adam Latschka and Ludwig Psenner, the editor of the anti-Semitic *Österreichischer Volksfreund*. In general, the younger clergy predominated in this circle, including, for instance, Fr. Rudolf Eichhorn, who had published a pamphlet on the working conditions of the tramway employees.[20] The Society of Jesus was also strongly represented and there were two future cardinals among the young reformers.[21] In September 1887 he was persuaded to attend a meeting of the union; and what happened there is related by Psenner and recorded by Klopp in his biography of Vogelsang:*

> At this meeting the first speaker was the Hungarian anti-Semitic leader Dr. Komlossy, who was received with an ovation lasting several minutes, and, constantly interrupted by cries of assent, made a strongly anti-Semitic speech . . . . Lueger, as the second speaker, was meanwhile sitting near the chairman,

* See Appendix II.

Psenner, and asked him anxiously what he should speak on so as not to fall foul of Komlossy. Psenner's advice was that he could become the hero of the evening only if he outdid Komlossy in his anti-Semitism. Lueger appreciated this at once and, amid storms of applause, made a speech which, as Psenner said, set the seal on his transformation from a Democrat into an anti-Semite.[22]

If Lueger was converted to anything that night, it was not the truth or validity of anti-Semitism but its usefulness as a political weapon.

Lueger's connection with the Christian-Social Union and Volegsang grew closer after this. They met informally for the first time at the beginning of 1888 in Princess Metternich's villa.[23] His speech at the Catholic demonstration the next month in celebration of Leo XIII's fifty years of priesthood—a purely religious, not reforming or anti-Semitic occasion—so impressed Vogelsang that he afterward exclaimed, "Now we have our leader! Lueger must be our leader!"[24] He became a regular visitor to the study group which, beginning in 1889, met weekly at the *Goldene Ente* inn under the presidency of Schindler and became known as the *Entenabende*.[25]

The 1880s marked the turning point for the Catholic reform movement. and it brilliantly seized the opportunity which was to lead it to success not only against Liberalism but also against a "crypto-Josephinian" hierarchy. It did this by taking up feelers with the anti-Semitic and anti-Liberal movement generally—the artisans, the Nationalists, and even Schönerer's party. Its instrument was the temporary alliance which these disparate groups formed under the name *Vereinigte Christen* (United Christians).

REFERENCES

1 Franz, *Liberalismus*, pp. 413–4.
2 R. Till, *Die Anfänge der christlichen Volksbewegung in Österreich*, Jahrbuch der Leo-Gesellschaft, 1937 (Vienna, 1937), pp. 57–8, 65.
3 R. Till, *Hofbauer und sein Kreis* (Vienna, 1951), p. 107.
4 Klein, *Antisemitismus in der Wiener Presse*, pp. 49–50, 72.
5 Franz, *op. cit.*, pp. 422, 513.
6 Bloch, *Erinnerungen*, p. 22.
7 For example, *Vaterland*, Jan. 1, 1872; *Tribüne*, Dec. 11–13, 1882.
8 In articles in the *Wiener Allgemeine Zeitung*, Dec. 22, 1882, Jan. 10, 1883.
9 For example, *Kölner Volkszeitung*, Feb. 10, 1897.
10 Byrnes, *Anti-Semitism in Modern France*, pp. 91–2.

11 Dubnow, *Neueste Geschichte*, Vol. III, p. 69.
12 Funder, *Aufbruch zur christlichen Sozialreform* (Vienna, 1951), pp. 11–12.
13 Skalnik, *Lueger*, p. 17; H. Schnee, *Bürgermeister Karl Lueger* (Paderborn, 1936), pp. 7–9.
14 *NFP*, March 11, 1910.
15 Pichl, *Schönerer*, Vol. I, pp. 351–3. The measure was based on the Chinese Exclusion Bill passed by the United State Congress in 1882.
16 Skalnik, *op. cit.*, p. 57.
17 Pichl, *op. cit.*, Vol. I, p. 355.
18 Vogelsang's correspondence with Schneider dates from 1882. Klopp, *Leben und Wirken*, p. 292.
19 *Ibid.*, p. 293.
20 *Die weissen Sklaven der Wiener Tramwaygesellschaft* (Vienna, 1885).
21 A. M. Knoll and J. Triebl, "Österreichs Katholisch-soziale Literatur zur Zeit des *Rerum Novarum*," *Volkswohl* (Vienna), Vol. XXII, Nos. 7 and 8 (1931), pp. 268–72, 286–93.
22 Klopp, *op. cit.*, p. 306.
23 Skalnik, *op. cit.*, pp. 63–4.
24 *Ibid.*, p. 65.
25 F. M. Schindler, "Neun Jahre Entenabende," *Volkswohl*, Vol. XIV, Nos. 3 (1923).

19

The "United Christians"

The 1880's were the melting pot of Austrian political parties. In the various radical and reformist circles, dissatisfaction with disintegrating Liberalism and the "masterly inactivity" of Count Taaffe found expression in movements and organizations which seemed doomed to ineffectiveness if only by their very multiplicity. Schönerer, Adler, Pernerstorfer, Mandl, Lueger, Kronawetter, Schneider, and Pattai—Jews and anti-Semites, clericals and pan-Germans, ex-Liberals and future Socialists rubbed shoulders, jockeyed for positions, and prayed for ideas.

The chief organization for canalizing these sentiments, the *Reformverein,* was a microcosm of the quarrels and patched-up alliances of the movement. The first struggle was between the Pattai-Schönerer wing, Nationalist in inspiration, and Vogelsang's friend, Schneider, who led the Catholic wing. The Catholics were profoundly disturbed by the pan-Germanism and irredentism of some of the extreme Nationalists:

> Let me tell you honestly and without reservation [Schneider wrote to Schönerer] that I am an Austrian in body and soul and could never, never reconcile myself to being subject to a Prussian government. I would sooner go to America.[1]

But the Nationalists also had reason to be dissatisfied, particularly when the *Reformverein* opposed a customs union with Germany which would obviously have been damaging to the less efficient small producers in Austria. Schönerer finally walked out with his closest followers, "since the *Reformverein* does not primarily pursue anti-Semitism, but has as its aim the support of the Taaffe régime."[2] The next year, 1885, Schneider narrowly defeated Pattai for the presidency.

In addition the Democrats must be considered. They had,

during the 1870's, been the spokesmen of the small man's discontent with Liberal big business, and had in their ranks worthy veterans of 1848, such as Steudel. But their reluctance to embrace anti-Semitism, particularly during the battles of 1884 and 1885 to divest the Rothschilds of their railway concessions, led to large-scale desertions by both leaders and rank and file. Many later luminaries of the Christian-Social Party entered public life as Democrats, including Lueger's lieutenant, Albert Gessmann.[3] Indeed, according to Kronawetter, the Democrats' leader,[4] Lueger was largely responsible for drafting their 1884 program with its specific endorsement for "the principle of the equality of all denominations.[5]

The chief organs at the disposal of the anti-Liberals were two weeklies. The *Österreichischer Volksfreund,* revived in 1881 after its demise in 1877, became, in 1882, the *Organ der Österreichischen Reformpartei* and in 1884 was bought by Ludwig Psenner, a Christian-Social priest. It was partly financed by the Countess of Chambord (the Archduchess Maria Theresa),[6] who had also been an intimate of the Franch banker, Étienne Bontoux. (His unsuccessful and fraudulent *Union Générale* had been an attempt to break the Jewish–Protestant monopoly of French banking.) It claimed among its readers seven members of the imperial family, three generals, seven bishops, and 101 clergymen, as well as hundreds of professional and businessmen.[7]

The *Österreichische Wählerzeitung* was close to the Democrats. Its occasional anti-Semitism was rather subdued. The two co-operated, involuntarily to some extent, in the campaign to unseat Liberal representatives in parliament and the city council. In the annual elections to the city council, the *Volksfreund* made and unmade reputations. Opposition to Liberal "corruption" was the primary criterion. Occasionally it refused to endorse Democrats who were not also anti-Semites;[8] at other times it was more latitudinarian.[9] Lueger, at this time still associated with Julius Mandl, was consistently given support,[10] even by the Conservative *Vaterland,*[11] although a minority of Nationalists objected to this.[12] However, during the period of Schönerer's imprisonment, even his supporters were prepared

to vote together with Clericals as the occasion demands, for instance when it is a question of defeating the Jew-Liberals.[13]

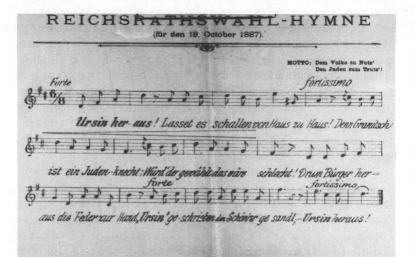

3. Anti-Semitic Election Song, in favor of the pan-German Josef Ursin. His Liberal opponent is described as "a slave of the Jews". (*Österreichisches Verwaltungsarchiv*, Vienna).

There was an element of the unreal and even ridiculous in these carefully edited messages of advice from party headquarters. The real electoral decisions were generally made by small caucuses meeting over a beer table, actuated as much by personal as party considerations, and executed by a fairly unsophisticated electorate.

The formal appearance of the "United Christians"[14] dates from two by-elections at St. Pölten in 1887, one to the Reichsrat and the other to the provincial Diet of Lower Austria. There were three candidates in the first ballot, the Conservative and the Schönerian Josef Ursin being presented as "both men of honest labor and differing in only *one* point of their program;"[15] in the second ballot the Conservatives withdrew in favor of Ursin and the verdict on his success was, "The United Christians have been victorious over the united pseudo-Liberals "[16]

The grand alliance had been forming for some time. In 1884 the Nationalists had suggested that Psenner should be approached to help in the distribution of their literature through the *Volksfreund*,[17] and to Vogelsang the need to make common cause between Schönerer and the Conservatives against the Liberals in Northern Bohemia justified "the use of Beelzebub to drive out the Devil."[18]

As a party label, "United Christians" was useful. At the time of the St. Pölten by-elections Lueger had proposed that Democrats, anti-Semites, and Conservatives should, since their economic programs were almost identical, unite themselves into an anti-Liberal league;[19] but "anti-Liberal" could be interpreted as meaning opposition to constitutional liberties. "Christian" was acceptable to Nationalists and even in Vienna, where "clericalism" was still in bad odor; even the heterodox Schönerer approved

> the title . . . for the electoral coalition of all anti-Semitic and also those Conservative elements who fight against Jewish-Liberal candidates . . . Shortly after Ursin's election [reported Pattai] Herr von Schönerer told me expressly, "We do not like the name anti-Liberal league, because it is open to misinterpretation, but United Christians is all right," and asked me to inform Dr. Lueger of this, which I did.[20]

Vogelsang wryly remarked, "Nowadays we have to start rejoicing once people call themselves Christians."[21]

In 1889 the first official program of the United Christians was published. It demanded (apart from the usual claims on behalf of artisans and peasants) a restriction on Jewish immigration; the exclusion of Jews from the civil service, the judiciary, the army, the law, medicine, pawnbroking, retail trade, and the teaching of Gentile pupils; a customs union with Germany; and denominational schools.[22] The last two points no doubt represented an attempt to reconcile the two wings of the movement. By 1890 the Democrats had been virtually eliminated as a force and remained a small rump, led by Kronawetter, drawn increasingly to reliance on Jewish Liberal voters. The Reformers had also purged themselves of their remaining Jews. Mandl was expelled from the *Eintracht* club in 1889, after some token resistance from Lueger,[23] and forced to seek refuge with the Liberals. Heinrich Friedjung confessed to Rabbi Bloch that he had broken with all Nationalists, not only Schönerer, who had "become a laughing stock," but also Steinwender who was "coquetting with anti-Semitism."[24] Sigmund Mayer, who was Liberal agent in the second district (the Jewish quarter of Vienna), kept separate registers of Jewish and Gentile voters, and noticed that each year fewer Gentiles voted Liberal.[25]

It was not only the undoubted economic distress and their skillful propaganda that helped the United Christians to success; they were also aided by the 1882 electoral reform enfranchising the five-florin men—precisely the class most likely to support them. The electorate was thereby increased from 15,385 to 45,695 voters.[26] An illuminating analysis of the occupations of the new voters in one district is given in the *Gemeindezeitung*:[27]

7591	artisans
2833	clerks in private employment
588	municipal officials
472	teachers
455	municipal porters
221	servants
152	roast-chestnut men
61	hawkers
35	itinerant knife grinders
43	clerks of works
13	journeymen
9	interior decorators
4	bootblacks
3	Sedan chair carriers
1	maker of wicker chairs
1	dog trimmer

Even more helpful to the United Christians was the extension of the city's boundaries in 1891, increasing the number of voters to 78,387. In the seedy suburbs which formed the nine newly incorporated "districts," 77% of the electorate belonged to the third *curia*, compared with 62% in the area of the old city;[28] only 5.2% of them were Jews, compared with 12% in the old city[29]—an important difference if we remember that a Jewish vote was almost automatically a Liberal vote. As in Berlin, the anti-Semites' main strength lay in the third *curia*, that of the Liberals among the well-to-do. In the first elections to the enlarged city council the anti-Semites polled almost as many votes as the Liberals;* only the graded franchise gave the Liberals a two-to-one majority in seats.

Under Lueger's leadership the anti-Semites had united themselves in the *Bürgerklub,* and after the 1891 Reichsrat elections Lueger also became the leader of the "Free Union for Economic Reform on a Christian Basis," a grouping of the anti-Semitic parliamentarians who now numbered eighteen. The great prize, the object to which all his political wanderings were to lead, was in sight.

REFERENCES

1 Letter of April 4, 1882, *NP ÖVA,* Box 37.
2 *UDW,* March 15, 1884.
3 R. Kuppe, *Karl Lueger und seine Zeit* (Vienna, 1923), p. 90.
4 *NFP,* March 11, 1910.
5 *Österreichische Wählerzeitung,* Dec. 14, 1884.
6 Bloch, *Erinnerungen,* p. 22.
7 *ÖV,* Jan. 15, 1882.
8 *ÖV,* March 15, May 17, 1885.
9 *ÖV,* April 29, 1884; March 7, March 28, April 4, April 11, 1886.
10 *ÖV,* March 9, March 23, 1884; March 7, March 28, April 4, April 11, 1886; March 20, 1887.
11 *Vaterland,* March 20, 1884.
12 *UDW,* April 1, 1884; April 16, 1886.
13 *UDW,* April 1, June 1, Oct. 16, Nov. 1, 1888.
14 Mgr. Josef Scheicher is credited with the actual invention of the name. N. Miko, *Die Vereinigung der Konservativen in der Christlich sozialen Partei* (unpublished dissertation, Vienna, 1949), p. 20.
15 *Vaterland,* Oct. 13, 1887.
16 *Ibid.,* Nov. 25, 1887.
17 Nov. 29, 1884, *NP ÖVA,* Box 40. This letter was written less than eight months after Schonerer had left the *Reformverein* in the highest dudgeon.
18 Letter to Becredi, Dec. 17, 1887. Molisch, *Briefe zur deutschen Politik,* p. 296.
19 G. Schmitz, *Die Entwicklungsgeschichte der christlichen Volksbewegung in Österreich, 1875–1891* (unpublished dissertation, Vienna, 1938), p. 196.
20 Letter to Vergani (probably March, 1889), *NP ÖVA,* Box 18, fol. 2.
21 Klopp, *op. cit.,* p. 307.
22 *DVB,* February 20, 1889.
23 Kuppe, *op. cit.,* pp. 191–2.
24 *ÖW,* March 20, 1891.
25 S. Mayer, *Ein Jüdischer Kaufmann, 1831 bis 1911. Lebenserinnerungen* (2nd ed., Berlin–Vienna, 1926), pp. 374–6, 392.
26 Kuppe, *op. cit.,* p. 139.

* Liberals received 29,005; and Anti-Semites received 27,858.

27 Skalnik, *Lueger*, p. 44.
28 *Vaterland*, March 4, 1891.
29 *Statistisches Jahrbuch der Stadt Wien* (Vienna, 1892), pp. 36–7.

20

The Battle for Vienna

When that the poor have cried, Caesar hath wept:
Ambition should be made of sterner stuff.

To Lueger, as to many others, this contradiction did not apply. In a country without ministerial responsibility the mayoralty of Vienna was the most important elective office, and he had early fixed his eyes on it. Already in 1882, at the age of thirty-seven, in the days of the United Left, he had been a candidate for the vice-mayoralty; now, in 1891, he was the determined leader of an active opposition in the council chamber.

He conducted his campaign with vigor and skill; eschewing the orotund periods and classical allusions of the Liberal orators, he employed a deliberately popular mode of speech, with slang expressions, grammatical solecisms, and a strong Viennese accent. None could feel the popular pulse more sensitively, none tell his audiences with more unerring accuracy what they wanted to hear. He promised better conditions for civic employees, he promised to free the city's services from the stranglehold of "Jewish" private interests and middlemen. Civic pride was not a rare virtue in Vienna, and much had been done for the capital under the Liberals. Under Dr. Kajetan Felder the old fortifications had been demolished and the Ringstrasse laid down in their place; the first aqueduct, supplying the city's pumps and taps with the delicious water of the Alpine springs, was laid down: but it was not enough. Between 1870 and 1890 the population of the municipal area had tripled, transport facilities had failed to keep pace with the expansion and over one-third of the population lived in dwellings of two rooms or less,[1] so that Vienna had one of the highest tuberculosis rates in Europe.

Lueger was secure as leader of all anti-Semites and anti-Liberals in Vienna. A bandwagon was being built, and as its roadworthiness and the direction of its journey became evident, people were jumping on to it. Nothing succeeds like success, and electoral success is what the United Christians were beginning to achieve. It was useless for Steinwender to complain that, for all the party's soundness on economic questions, Lueger's personality as well as the clericalism now bedding itself down among the United Christians makes it impossible for us to come to an agreement with them,"[2] and it was useless for Schönerer's esquire Türk to mock that Lueger could not sleep without the black and yellow flag over his bed.[3] Schönerer's political impotence, his sullenness and petulance, caused desertion after desertion. Pattai left him in 1888; by 1890 Ernst Vergani, valuable as the owner of the *Deutsches Volksblatt*, whose circulation reached 50,000 in the mid-nineties,[4] was to all intents and purposes in the wake of Lueger.

Furthermore, he enjoyed the growing support of many sections of the clergy. True, the majority of the nobility and the hierarchy disapproved of him, but Prince Alois Liechtenstein had, in 1891, abandoned his safe seat in Styria to do battle for Lueger in Vienna, and the Jesuit preacher, Fr. Abel, entertained his audiences with ditties of his own composition:

> Die Presse führt das Publikum
> Gemütlich an der Nas' herum,
> Die Loge führt hinwiderum
> Die Presse und das Publikum.
> Und Presse, Loge, Publikum
> Wird rumgeführt vom Judentum.*

The decisive year for Lueger's career was 1895. In March and April municipal elections were due. Lueger already dominated the third *curia;* the first was, in general, beyond his reach. The battleground was the second, which was to be re-elected in its entirety. It was the *curia* of teachers, civil servants, and the more modest professional men. It prided itself on the name *"Intelligenz-Kurie."* On April 1 it swung against the Liberals and unseated them from power, leaving the city council without a working majority.

* The press gently leads the public by the nose, and the Lodge in its turn leads the press and the public. And press, public and Lodge are led around by the Jews" (Kuppe, *op. cit.*, p. 244).

On May 14 the newly elected council met to choose a deputy mayor; and at the fourth ballot Lueger achieved an absolute majority. Thereupon the Liberal mayor resigned and the deputy mayor automatically succeeded him. The Liberals' plan was to give the inexperienced Lueger and his heterogeneous party enough rope to hang themselves.

But Lueger's enemies were more numerous than merely his electoral rivals and the press. He had also, like the radical anti-Semites of Germany, to face the hostility of established authority such as the Emperor, the hierarchy, and the aristocracy. After the fall of Taaffe in 1893, the Conservatives and Liberals, both disturbed by lower middle-class radicalism in their ranks, had combined to form the Windischgrätz-Plener coalition. The mere possibility that Lueger might become mayor of the Imperial capital was the occasion of a major political crisis which lasted for over a year, for no election to that office was valid without Imperial confirmation:

> The government alone will occupy itself with the question whether it considers it to be in keeping with the interests and reputation of the Empire that Vienna should be the only great city in the world whose administrator is an anti-Semitic agitator[5]

the *Neue Freie Presse* hinted. The incidents in the street on May 29, when the crowd pursued and insulted well-known Liberal councilors, gave an added argument to those who felt that the exercise of the Imperial prerogative was the only solution.

The Cabinet did indeed occupy itself with the question. The coalition was committed to the assuagement of national and social passions; therefore

> Wurmbrand and I were opposed to confirmation [the Liberal leader records in his Memoirs] because this would be regarded as condoning his [Lueger's] demagogic agitation; a government which had made opposition to radical opinion as part of its programme could not possibly allow the spokesman of a movement bordering on the revolutionary to assume, with the Emperor's approval, the administration of the Imperial capital.[6]

Already when the city boundaries had been enlarged in 1891 it had been hinted that the filling of so important a dignity should not be left to the arbitrament of popular passions. How much better were these things ordered in France, where the prefect of the Seine department was a government appointee.

Lueger had, however, by his actions forestalled the debates of others. Declaring that the party deadlock made administration impossible, he declined his election, leaving the government no option but to dissolve the council. New elections were ordered for September and their circumstances could not have been more favorable to the anti-Semites. The maneuvers of the Liberals had been as unsuccessful as they had been discreditable. It was a challenge to the voters which could not go unanswered that it had been so much as proposed to bar the elect of the people (or of those of them who paid five florins in taxes) from office. With slogans against the capitalists, the press, the governent and the Jews, the campaign ran its course. The Liberals lost twenty-eight seats, including their ten remaining seats in the third *curia:*

> Vienna has delivered itself to the mortal enemies of its freedom, its intelligence, its progress . . . with an overwhelming majority the third curia has gone over to the Viennese Boulanger[7]

lamented the Liberal press. The Liberals received 22,868 Viennese votes; the anti-Semites received 43,776. In the council chamber, Lueger had a two-to-one majority (ninety-two to forty-six). The elections had solved none of the government's or the bishops' difficulties.

Not that the bishops were pro-Jewish—but they looked with growing distaste on the excesses and dangerous radicalism of the Viennese agitators. Above all anti-Semitism was tarred with the brush of Schönerer and pan-Germanism; it was a title Schönerer had first claimed for himself. An example of the Church's difficulties was the case of Fr. Josef Deckert, an occasional speaker at Schindler's *Entenabende,* whose scurrilous anti-Semitic sermons and pamphlets landed him several times in conflict with the courts. Plener records that on one of these occasions

> the Emperor, who for all his ecclesiastical inclinations, strongly condemned excesses on the part of individual clergymen, himself proposed that should Deckert not be convicted, the government was to request the Archbishop to relieve him of his appointment, which would enormously strengthen episcopal authority against disobedient clergymen.[8]

Plener himself, significantly enough, was skeptical of the value or any prosecution "since anti-Semitism was very widespread not only in the jury-box but among the younger members of the judiciary."[9]

The whole Lueger crisis illustrated the split in the Austrian Church, between the energetic and popular Christian-Social movement and a Conservative hierarchy which, as a pillar of the state, felt more drawn to the equally state-conserving Liberal bureaucracy and a "Josephinian" compromise than to the rumbustious and often ill-disciplined movement of the streets. They were inclined to view Lueger through the spectacles of the police presidency who reported that

> the Christian-Socials have, from easily recognisable motives, appeared at their public meetings as ostentatious patriots and stressed, in the most varied contexts, their unconditional loyalty and attachment to the most noble dynasty.
>
> None the less, part of their programme, as well as the nature of their agitation must, out of considerations of state, arouse the gravest misgivings; for the Christian-Social party also appeals, as does the Social Democratic party, to the coarse instincts of the lower orders and collaborates in a dangerous manner in the stirring-up and incitation of the people.[10]

It was in a sense a class struggle within the Church, with much of the lower clergy, often poorly paid and always hard worked, in arms against ecclesiastical princes whom they considered indifferent to their sufferings as well as those of the secular poor.

It was these considerations that caused the cabinet to act. Plener notes that

> a not uninteresting episode was our attempt to enlighten the Roman Curia about the Christian-Social movement and to make representations against any support of the anti-Semites.[11]

Madejski, the Minister of Education, and Windischgrätz drew up a memorandum on the subversive and insubordinate activities of the party and transmitted them to Rome through diplomatic channels. At the same time, in February 1894, the Archbishop of Prague, Cardinal Schönborn, a brother of the Minister of Justice, arrived in Rome to present a memorandum from the hierarchy.

Rome, however, was by no means displeased with the

Christian-Social movement. The *Osservatore* occasionally criticized its excesses,[12] but in the main appreciated that, thanks to its connection with the lower clergy, it was doing valuable work in re-evangelizing the masses. Neither Leo XIII nor his Secretary of State, Rampolla, the driving force behind *Rerum Novarum,* had much time for the Austrian bishops, whom they regarded as spineless and conservative. Their contact with the ecclesiastical "opposition" in Vienna was the Nuncio, the indiscreet Agliardi, whose interventions in Hungarian politics finally caused his recall to Rome, where, however, a Red Hat awaited him. Already in 1892 the Pope had sent a blessing to the *Katholikentag* in Linz, which in fact turned into an anti-episcopal demonstration and from which the Bishop of Linz had disassociated himself. In 1894 the first number of the *Reichspost,* the new Christian-Social daily, which the same bishop had banned from seminaries, carried a Papal blessing. Rampolla took an almost proprietary interest in the party. "*Vedete, abbiamo trionfato!*" he is said to have exclaimed on receiving news of the Viennese municipal elections.

The hierarchy, indeed, was so slow to appreciate how it could turn the anti-Semitic movement to its own advantage that it had prepared a pastoral letter in condemnation of it. It was held back only so as not to prejudice the Schönborn negotiations.

Meanwhile, the Christian-Socials, kept fully posted by their friend Agliardi, drew up a statement of aims for the benefit of the Vatican. It was the work of Prelate Franz Schindler, who had inherited the intellectual leadership of the movement from Vogelsang,[13] and received general, if qualified approval from Rampolla.[14] It was therefore not surprising that the Schönborn mission returned to Vienna empty-handed. Indeed the reply to their request, received in July, ordered them not to publish the intended pastoral letter and to assist the Christian-Social Party even if it extended its agitation into Conservative territory.[15]

By February 1895, Church and government were equally disturbed by the spread of Stojalowski's party in Galicia and the growth of the anti-Semitic Catholic People's Party under Count Zichy in Hungary.* Another mission from the hierarchy therefore arrived in Rome that month, again led by Schönborn and consisting also of the Bishops of Brno and Székesféhervar.

* See p. 135.

The bishops received a somewhat dusty welcome and were left in no doubt that they were regarded as merely emissaries of the government. But their complaint was attended to, and the Christian-Social organization was called upon to reply to the bishops' accusations.

The main charges were political subversion, ecclesiastical insubordination, economic radicalism, and general addiction to excesses, such as anti-Semitism.[16] Once more it fell to Schindler to draft a reply. Expressions injurious to the Christian spirit might have been used in the heat of the battle, but the Christian-Social idea, he insisted, owed its origins to eminent Catholics like Vogelsang and Liechtenstein, and its principles were based on *Rerum Novarum*. Nobody attacked the Christian-Socials more strongly than the Social Democrats for defending the legitimate order and intending to create peace between the proletariat and the entrepreneurs. On anti-Semitism, felt to be one of the most damaging counts in the accusation, he made it clear that

> we do not countenance a certain radical anti-Semitism which is directed against the Jewish race as such and which our party, in accordance with its programme, has nothing to do with.[17]

The reply was completed within seven days of Schönborn's being received in audience. Schindler himself went to Rome. He, too, was received by the Pope and departed with a message for Lueger. The Holy Father sympathized with Christian-Social aims and sent Lueger his blessing.[18] In adopting this attitude, the Holy See merely confirmed the estimate which the majority of the Viennese clergy had already made of Lueger (and of which the hierarchy complained so bitterly). At the celebrations of his fiftieth birthday in October 1894, he was presented with an address from five hundred priests in the capital.[19]

Thus his battle with the Church was on the point of being won when he entered on the crucial round of his battle with the state. The September elections had forced the government to make a definite decision: to confirm or not to confirm. On October 28 the council met to elect a mayor; ninety-three votes were cast for Lueger, and forty-four ballots were blank. The thing had happened: the stock market reported the worst fall since May 1873. Merchants at the international corn exchange were insulted by the public who had been whipped up against "foreign capitalists," and the market finally moved to Budapest. Wealthy Jews, trembling for their safety and their property, threatened to do the same. Only an assurance from the Emperor that he would protect all his subjects indiscriminately prevented them from taking flight.[20] The Hungarian Prime Minister, the Protestant Baron Bánffy, incensed at Lueger's tirades against the"*Judäomagyaren,*" pointed out that negotiations for the renewal of the *Ausgleich* were due to begin shortly.[21]

There had also been a change of government. The coalition had fallen under the impact of the Celje school controversy, which was a question of whether the high school of that German enclave in the Slav-speaking part of Styria should provide classes in Slovene as well as German. The new prime minister was Count Badeni, a former governor of Galicia. He was hated by the Christian-Socials as a member of the pro-government Polish nobility, and because he had built up good relations with the Jews in a province which Fr. Deckert had described, with sacerdotal delicacy, as *vagina judaeorum*.

Badeni prevailed on the Emperor not to confirm Lueger in his mayoral office. The further re-election of the city council which this necessitated merely increased the anti-Semitic majority by a further four seats. Only in the inner, bourgeois districts, and in the upper *curiae* did the Liberals retain a narrow lead. Elsewhere, in the newly incorporated suburbs, the anti-Semites' majorities were overwhelming.

The mayoral crisis was solved in the only way possible. Lueger, after an audience with the Emperor, agreed to step down. A puppet named Josef Strobach assumed the chief magistracy. A year later Strobach quietly retired and on April 8, 1897 Lueger was elected mayor for the fourth time. On April 16, to nobody's surprise, the Imperial confirmation was announced. For between the spring of 1896 and the spring of 1897 important constitutional changes had taken place which made Lueger's position appear in a very different light.

The need to extend the franchise somehow, and to make at any rate limited concessions to the call for universal suffrage, was becoming increasingly evident, and with the formation of the Social Democratic Party in 1889 pressure was becoming persistently stronger. In 1896 Badeni presented to the Reichsrat a

4. The "millions" behind Lueger and the "millions" behind Richter. *Kikeriki*, 28 April 1895.

5. Jewish voters being unloaded outside a Liberal committee room. The entrance is marked "Kosher". *Kikeriki*, 28 April 1895.

proposal to add a fifth *curia* to the already existing four, comprising seventy-two seats, to be elected by universal manhood suffrage. At the general election in March 1897, three-and-a-half million newly enfranchised Austrians voted for the first time. The Social Democrats, though denouncing Badeni's reforms as inadequate, entered the electoral battle with the aim of making an impressive show of strength in the fifth *curia* and of demonstrating how shaky was Lueger's claim of popular support. They overestimated their strength. Of the fourteen seats which they won, none came from Lower Austria; Lueger, King of Vienna, was crowned once again by the masses. Nevertheless, the voting figures showed how artificial had been the fight the previous year. In Vienna the Christian-Socials had 117,000 votes, the Social Democrats 88,000, the Liberals 6000, and the Pan-Germans 2500. The Liberal candidates were nominal only. The party had been concerned with saving what it could in the privileged *curiae;* in the general *curia* it had abandoned the fight to the Social Democrats. In the whole province the Christian Social Party received 245,000 votes, and the Social Democrats received 123,000.

> It would be a mistake [the anti-Semitic commentator Julius Patzelt rightly observed] to regard the 250,000 votes which the anti-Semitic candidates have received in Lower Austria as being necessarily anti-Semitic. The party formed a crystallising point which attracted all anti-revolutionary elements. It proved itself to be fitted, and strong enough, to draw to itself all the elements of law and order in the common fight against Social Democracy.[22]

The apparent alliance between the party of property and the party of revolution was hailed by the anti-Semites as proof of Jewish duplicity:

> The Liberals and the party of the *Sozialpolitiker**—a creation of Jewish democracy in the Inner City—had not only failed to take up the fight against Social Democracy, but in the majority of districts worked for the Social Democratic candidates. It was demonstrated quite clearly that the bourgeois, so-called Liberal progressive, parties were dominated entirely by Jewish influence.

* This was a left-wing Liberal ginger-group which had its origin in the *Gesellschaft der Fabier*, and was led by the ex-Democrat Kronawetter and Julius Ofner, a later Jewish deputy.

PARTY REPRESENTATION IN VIENNA CITY COUNCIL, 1896

Curia	1894		April 1895		September 1895		March 1896	
	Anti-Semites	Liberals, etc.	Semites	Anti-Liberals	Semites	Anti-Liberals	Semites	Anti-Liberals
Seats								
1st	6	40	6	40	14	32	18	28
2nd	15	29	24	22	32	14	32	14
3rd	35	11	36	10	46	....	46	....
Votes								
1st			....	....	1,420	2,679	1,677	2,753
2nd			8,864	9,433	11,079	9,088	11,796	9,332
3rd			....	....	31,277	11,101	33,556	9,074
TOTAL					43,776	22,868	47,029	21,159

The leading Jewish-Liberal paper of Vienna, the *Neue Freie Presse* took up its position before the elections in an article which had proclaimed that Liberals and Social Democrats "had a common interest and a common battle-cry: against reaction and for the free school." The paper looked forward "full of pleasure" to the expected successes of the Social Democrats . . . . So the *Neue Freie Presse* has admitted that Jewish Liberalism begot Social Democracy and hoped that Social Democracy would arise to avenge Liberalism.[23]

In Austria, as in Germany, anti-Semitism had, despite its stormy past, become "state-conserving." Lueger the firebrand had had within twenty-four months turned into Lueger the dam against Red Revolution. Never had poacher become gamekeeper so quickly and so successfully.

By the turn of the century the build-up of specifically anti-Semitic parties was complete. Thereafter parties played an increasingly smaller and social or semi-political organizations a larger part in political anti-Semitism. Above all, the spread of pan-Germanism makes it difficult to study the two empires separately after that date.

REFERENCES

1 W. A. Jenks, *Vienna and the Young Hitler* (New York, 1960), p. 37.
2 Letter to Dobernig, March 23, 1890; Molisch, *Briefe zur deutschen Politik*, p. 304.
3 Letter to Kaiser (?), October, 1890, *NP ÖVA*, Box 40. Black and yellow were the Austrian Imperial colors.
4 Jenks, *op. cit.*, p. 127.
5 *NFP*, May 30, 1895.
6 Plener, *Erinnerungen*, Vol. III, p. 257.
7 *NFP*, Sept. 18, 1895.
8 Plener, *op. cit.*, Vol. III, p. 259.
9 *Ibid.*, Vol. III, p. 172.
10 Quoted by Miko, *Die Vereinigung der Konservativen*, p. 208.
11 Plener, *op. cit.*, Vol. III, p. 219.
12 *Ibid.*, Vol. III, p. 220.
13 F. Funder, *Vom Gestern ins Heute* (Vienna, 1952), p. 131.
14 Funder, *Aufbruch*, p. 105.
15 Funder, *Vom Gestern*, pp. 143–4.
16 *Ibid.*, p. 145.
17 *Ibid.*, pp. 145–6.
18 *Ibid.*, p. 147.
19 Pichl, *Schönerer*, Vol. IV, p. 33.

20 A. J. May, *The Hapsburg Monarchy, 1867–1914* (Cambridge, Mass., 1951), p. 310.

21 Compare Lueger's speeches on June 21, 1891, and July 2, 1895, and Schlesinger's reference to the Hungarian government as a "Judaeo-Magyar mob of sewage navvies." Kolmer, *Parlament und Verfassung*, Vol. VI, p. 108.

22 J. Patzelt, *Österreichisches Jahrbuch*, Vol. I (Vienna, 1897), p. 24.

23 *Ibid.*, p. 21.

GERMANY AND AUSTRIA
1900–1914

THE DECLINE of the overtly anti-Semitic organizations after 1900 is deceptive. In Germany the various parties quarreled and vegetated; at the same time anti-Semitism was more openly accepted than before by several other parties, an increasing number of political and economic interest groups, and many nonpolitical bodies, such as students' corps or athletic or mountaineering clubs. The spillover of anti-Semitism into semi- or nonpolitical groups was equally characteristic of Austria. The Austrian anti-Semitic parties, far from declining, became, after the introduction of universal suffrage, some of the major constituents of the Reichsrat. But the net effect of this on public opinion was not much different from that in Germany: a decline in sectarian fanaticism and in the vehemence of anti-Semitic propaganda, combined with the widespread acceptance of mild, almost incidental, anti-Semitic opinions.

21

German Parties After 1900

The sixteen deputies elected in 1893 represented every shade of anti-Semitic opinion, from Böckel on the extreme Left, to Sonnenberg on the far Right, with Oswald Zimmermann's *Deutsche Reformpartei* somewhere in the middle. However, they succeeded in 1894 in forming themselves—Böckel and Ahlwardt apart—into a single party.[1] In the 1898 elections they secured twelve seats and about the same number of votes as in 1893 (284,000); a thirteenth seat was added at a by-election.

Unity within the new *Deutschsoziale Reformpartei* was more apparent than real. The big stumbling-block was relationship with the Agrarian League. It was only to be expected from its social composition and the interests it represented that the League should lean to anti-Semitism. The program of its predecessor, the *Vereinigung der Steuer-und Wirtschaftsreformer,* had been drawn up in 1876 by the anti-Semitic Niendorf,[2] and Perrot (of the *Kreuzzeitung* articles) was one of its prominent advisers.[3] The League's original manifesto had been silent on the Jewish question, but at its first general assembly in 1894 membership was restricted to Christians,[4] and its statement of *Zweck und Ziele* proclaimed:

> It aims at the presentation and development of our present political order on a Christian monarchic foundation, and places its principles on the basis of just and thorough consideration for the interests of the whole of creative labour. . . . For this reason also it is an opponent of Jewry, which has become altogether too mighty in our country and has acquired a decisive say in the press, in trade and on the exchanges.[5]

According to the League's handbook for the 1898 elections, the candidates of the DSRP would always receive the endorsement of the Agrarians,[6] Conservative candidates "almost always,"[7] but those of the *Reichspartei* (in which industrialists like Kardorff were prominent) would need a thorough clearance.[8]

An ultra-Conservative anti-Semite like Sonnenberg who dreamt of a grand right-wing coalition consisting of his own group, the Christian-Socials, the Conservatives, and the Agrarians, could only welcome the word of Freiherr von Wangenheim at the League's opening congress:

> Just imagine what an enormous accession of strength the parties of order would receive if we were to attract the whole of the apathetic mass which has hitherto stayed away from elections, if we come to the elections with forces as never before.[9]

The radical anti-Semites, however, dissented. Böckel denounced Sonnenberg's followers as "an appendage of the Conservative party"[10] and the annual conference of his party unanimously rejected co-operation with the League in 1895.[11] The *Deutsche Volkswacht,* the Hessian anti-Semitic paper, warned:

> Peasants, take care! The Agrarian League is making ready to catch peasants.[12]

Four weeks later it referred to the Agrarians as a "League of Windbags."

It was, in fact, resentment at Agrarian tutelage that split the party again in 1900 when Sonnenberg, defeated for the presidency, reformed the *Deutschsoziale Partei.* To the complaint of the DSRP *Staatsbürgerzeitung* that

> the masses were put off by the Junker-like character of the Agrarian League's leadership,

the Conservatives retorted:

> Messrs. Bindewald and Bruhn are worthily joining the ranks of those of their party friends who have already done estimable preliminary work for the Social Democrats.[13]

Böckel also had in 1900 reorganized his following in the *Deutsche Volksbund* which was constituted strictly on the leadership principle. He, Förster and a third man named Hans von Mosch were the grand masters who, together with seven masters and thirteen aldermen (appointed by the grand masters), formed the Council of Twenty-three. The council, in turn, appointed elders and agitators who were called "knights"; well-wishers who wanted to remain anonymous were made "friends."[14] The mere multiplication of parties did not strengthen the movement.

> The anti-Semitic deputies [Böckel told the *Volksbund* in 1901] are divided not into two but into four parties. None would wish the other a crumb. It is really enough to discourage anybody. Every single one wants to be a ruler without subjects. . . . Many of these deputies are not serious deputies at all.[15]

The original membership of the *Volksbund* was 5000 but by 1906 it had dwindled to 2000.[16] Förster succeeded in combining his tenure of office with membership of the DSRP until 1907, when all *Volksbund* members were expelled.[17]

On military issues the division among anti-Semites was equally deep. For the Right, military and naval expansion were great and noble objects, but according to the Hessian *Deutsche Volkswacht:*

> The peasants have no enthusiasm whatever for world-power policies and a naval power of the first rank.[18]

Yet, these differences notwithstanding, the anti-Semites had, by 1903, simply melted into Bülow's majority and were, whether they liked it or not, increasingly dependent on quasi-political bodies like the Agrarian League, the German National Employees' Union,* and the *Mittelstandsvereinigung.* Indeed, after 1903 deciding who was and who was not an anti-Semitic deputy was an academic point. For instance, two seats won by the Agrarian League in 1907 were won by the same candidates in 1912 as Conservatives.[19] In 1903 eleven proclaimed anti-Semites were elected, and another three at subsequent by-elections. The three German-Social and two Christian-Social deputies joined with the Agrarians and the representatives of the Bavarian Peasant Party into a *Wirtschaftliche Vereinigung* whose statutes did not mention anti-Semitism and in which the specifically anti-Semitic deputies were outnumbered by those with predominantly economic interests.[20] The *Wirtschaftliche Vereinigung* was also joined by deputies of the *Mittelstandsvereinigung,* founded in

* See pp. 214–16.

1904, which was not specifically anti-Semitic, though its first chairman was Theodor Fritsch.[21]

The radicals of the DSRP and *Volksbund* remained aloof from any combination though after 1907 the DSRP affiliated to the *Reichspartei* in Parliament. It secured six seats in 1907 and three in 1912. The *Wirtschaftliche Vereinigung* secured nineteen and ten respectively.

Geographically the success of anti-Semitism was limited. Its strongholds were Hesse and Saxony-Thuringia. It also gained scattered victories in Northwestern Germany and east of the Elbe. South of the Main it had next to no footing. Only a minority of successful anti-Semitic candidates had ever to contend with Conservative or even National Liberal opposition, though there was occasional throat cutting among rival anti-Semitic parties. In the twenty-four constituencies of the Hesse-Waldeck region there was, in 1907, only one Conservative candidate, although the Conservatives had held five seats in 1887 and three in 1890. The extent to which anti-Semitic candidates had to fight other right-wing* candidates from 1903 to 1912 is analyzed in the following table:

TABLE 6. SUCCESSFUL ANTI-SEMITIC CANDIDATES

	Total	Conserva-tive	Opposition National Liberal	from Other anti-Semitic	None
1903–1907†	14	5	7	3	3
1907	25	2	11	3	11
1912	13	1	7	1	5

Equally instructive are the number of constituencies in the chief areas of anti-Semitism such as Hesse-Waldeck (twenty-four seats) and Saxony-Thuringia (thirty-five seats) in which only one right-wing party put up a candidate.

Gentlemen's agreements among the Right are almost universal in Saxony and Thuringia since this, one of the most

---

* National Liberals, *Reichspartei*, Conservatives and all anti-Semites.
† Including by-elections.

heavily industrialized regions of Germany, was a stronghold of the Social Democrats. In fact the number of anti-Semitic successes denotes not the waxing or waning of the popularity of anti-Semitism but simply the wider swing of opinion between Left and Right.

TABLE 7. JOINT RIGHT–WING CANDIDATURES

(a) Saxony and Thuringia

	Conservative- Anti-Semite	Conservative- Anti-Semite National Liberal-
1903	3	25
1907	1	20
1912	2	19

(b) Hesse and Waldeck

	Conservative Anti-Semite	National Liberal- Conservative- Anti-Semite
1903	4	4
1907	5	8
1912	11	6

TABLE 8. ANTI–SEMITES AND SOCIAL DEMOCRATS ELECTED IN SAXONY AND THURINGIA

	Anti-Semites	Social Democrats
1898	3	16
1903	1	29
1907	6	8
1912	1	27

The apparent upsurge of anti-Semitic strength in 1907 is nothing more than the product of Bülow's *Block* policy. The overriding importance of the struggle against the Social Democrats led to more than one curious result. For instance, at

Frankfort-on-Main, in the second ballot in 1903, the anti-Semites voted for the Progressive, a Jew named Bruck, against the Social Democrat.[22]

The growing tacit acceptance of mild anti-Semitism by the Liberal parties is the best indication of the declining virulence of anti-Semitism in national politics. Tables 7 and 8 show how the growth of Social Democracy and the unreliability of the Centre on patriotic issues were forcing the other parties more closely together. Ever since Lasker and Bamberger had left the National Liberal Party in 1880, its attitude had been ambiguous. On the one hand its delegate conference in 1894 denounced anti-Semitism,[23] and Rudolf Gneist, a *Kathedersozialist* and one of the founders of the *Verein zur Abwehr des Antisemitismus,* was a National Liberal deputy. Bassermann and Stresemann, the party's leaders in the 1900's, both had Jewish wives. On the other hand, as early as 1881 one National Liberal candidate was accused of having made use of anti-Semitic election literature.[24] Professor Hasse, the first president of the Pan-German League, wrote in 1906:

> The decisive factor in the field of humanity and for the political demands of the future lies in the fact that the races, as they exist today, desire to become homogeneous and permanent, and that they therefore wish to expel foreign elements not yet assimilated . . . . In these fundamental considerations lies the essence of nationalism and the justifiable aspect of anti-Semitism.[25]

In 1893, faced with the danger of opposition from an anti-Semitic candidate in his constituency, he had promised to vote for the prohibition of Jewish immigration, the expulsion of non-naturalized Jews and the prohibition of ritual slaughtering.[26] Hasse was a parliamentary affiliate, though not an official candidate, of the National Liberal Party, but a great many other National Liberal deputies were members of the Pan-German League, the Evangelical League, *Burschenschaften,* and other organizations which coquetted with anti-Semitism.

Even the Progressives, whose program specifically condemned anti-Semitism, found themselves in this position. During the *Block* elections of 1907, when Bülow, in defense of his navy bills, formed a united front from the Progressives to the extreme

Right, against the Centre and the Social Democrats, they supported four anti-Semitic candidates in the second ballots, three of them successfully.[27]

The Liberals had not been converted to racial hatred. It was merely that anti-Semitism, now regarded as obviously endemic, had ceased to be a vital issue. In so far as it had political importance it was, as the passage from Hasse shows, an integral (and subordinate) part of nationalism and pan-Germanism.* The emotions and ambitions which had been canalized into anti-Semitism during the 1880's and 1890s now found more promising outlets.

A more serious blow to organized anti-Semitism was that many of the most idealistic social reformers foreswore it altogether. One of the most prominent of Stöcker's younger followers was the Protestant pastor Friedrich Naumann. Under the spell of Stöcker he had been one of the founders of the anti-Semitic *Verein deutscher Studenten*† but by the mid-1890's he had become disillusioned with the Christian-Socials' attachment to conservatism and agrarianism. In 1896 he led his group out of Stöcker's party and formed the National Social Union. In 1903 he told the *Verein deutscher Studenten:*

> I have not kept my anti-Semitic views, and consciously not kept them, because a great people must be capable of assimilating elements of foreign nations, be they Jews or Poles, and to incorporate them into its history, instead of adopting a closed-shop point of view towards such elements.[28]

In the era of *Weltpolitik* there were so many external enemies, so many issues and crises outside Germany's borders to absorb the full attention of the xenophobe, that the Jews were sometimes quite forgotten. Africa, China, the South Seas, dreadnoughts and the Kiel Canal, then Dual Entente, the Triple Entente, pan-Slavism, the railway to Baghdad, South American markets, Middle Eastern markets—how much more exciting, how much more rewarding than Jew-baiting. In 1906 Bebel could write of anti-Semitism:

> It is a consoling thought that it has no prospect of ever

* See Chapter 24.
† See p. 109, and p. 248.

exercising a decisive influence on political and social life in Germany.*

It was, at the time, a reasonable assumption to make. But the symptoms were deceptive: anti-Semitism was not moribund, merely dormant. Its sudden and violent resurgence after 1918 shows the apparent enfeeblement of anti-Semitism in the immediately preceding period in its proper perspective.

Meanwhile, as the generation of original anti-Semitic leaders disappeared from the scene, no successors emerged. Böckel and Ahlwardt retired after electoral defeat, gradually to sink into the *Lumpenproletariat;* Schack was sent to prison for sexual offenses and Hirschel for embezzlement. Stöcker died in 1909, Zimmermarm in 1910, and Sonnenberg in 1911. Of the new champions for the old cause the most pathetic was Count Pückler, a deranged landowner who rode into Berlin with a guard of mounted yokels, threatening violence to any Jew who might show his face. For a brief period he was all the rage, for many Berliners willingly paid twenty pfennigs to witness this *outré* entertainment.

Those propagandists who had all along opposed making racialism a party matter, such as Class and Fritsch, agreed that the personalities of most anti-Semitic politicians were a major reason for the popular failure of their doctrine.[29] In 1914 one of the remaining anti-Semitic deputies, Ferdinand Werner, succeeded in uniting most of his colleagues into a *Deutschvölkische Partei.* Fritsch himself devoted his energies to nonpartisan burrowings. In 1904 he founded the *"Hammer* communities," discussion and propaganda groups based on his journal, *Hammer-Blätter.* By the outbreak of the war there were nineteen of these, grouped in the *Reichshammerbund.*[30]

---

* Bebel, *Sozialdemokratie und Antisemitismus*, p. 38. Already in 1901, writing to Victor Adler, he had declared, "Bei uns hat er nicht nur den Höhepunkt überschritten, er ist fertig." July 8, 1901 (F. Adler, *Viktor Adler, Briefwechsel mit August Bebel und Karl Kautsky*, Vienna, 1954, p. 359).

REFERENCES

1 Anon., *Antisemiten im Reichstag* (Berlin, 1903), pp. 5–6.
2 Author of *Die Sittenlehre des Talmud*.
3 J. Croner, *Die Geschichte der agrarischen Bewegung in Deutschland* (Berlin, 1909), pp. 30–1, 174.
4 *Ibid.*, p. 42.
5 *Kleines Wahl-ABC des Bundes der Landwirte* (Berlin, 1898), p. 33.
6 *Ibid.*, p. 7.
7 *Ibid.*, p. 8.
8 *Ibid.*, p. 8.
9 O. von Kiesenwetter, *25 Jahre wirtschaftspolitischen Kampfes* (Berlin, 1918), p. 24.
10 Scheidemann, *Wandlungen des Antisemitismus*, p. 635.
11 *Antisemiten im Reichstag*, p. 19.
12 *Deutsche Volkswacht*, Nov. 29, 1899, quoted in *op. cit.*, p. 20.
13 *Ibid.*, pp. 20–1.
14 *Der politische Antisemitismus von 1903–1907. Herausgegeben vom Verein zur Abwehr des Antisemitismus, Berlin* (Berlin, 1907), pp. 30–1.
15 *Antisemiten im Reichstag*, p. 9.
16 *Der politische Antisemitismus*, p. 38.
17 L. Curtius, *Der politische Antisemitismus*, pp. 44–5.
18 Scheidemann, *op. cit.*, p. 635.
19 Electoral data in this chapter taken from J. Kürschner, *Der neue Reichstag* (Berlin–Leipzig, 1903, 1907, 1912).
20 Specht and Schwabe, *Die Reichstagswahlen*, pp. 434–6.
21 C. Bürger, *Die politische Mittelstandbewegung in Deutschland* (Gross-Lichterfelde, 1912), p. 16.
22 R. Michels, "Psicologia e statistica delle elezioni generali politiche in Germania," *Riforma Sociale*, Vol. X, No. 13 (Turin, 1903), p. 28.
23 *MVA*, Oct. 6, 1894, p. 317.
24 *AZJ*, Nov. 29, 1881.
25 A. Geiser (ed.), *Deutsches Reich und Volk. Ein nationales Handbuch* (Munich, 1906), p. 8.
26 *Herr Liebermann von Sonnenberg als Parteiführer*, p. 106; *MVA*, July 2, 1893, p. 266.
27 G. D. Crothers, *The German Elections of 1907* (New York, 1941), p. 174.
28 T. Heuss, *Friedrich Naumann. Der Mann, das Werk, die Zeit* (2nd ed., Stuttgart, 1949), p. 312.
29 Fritsch, *Neue Wege*, p. 287; D. Frymann (i.e. H. Class), *Wenn ich der Kaiser wär* (5th ed., Berlin, 1914), p. 214.
30 R. H. Phelps, "'Before Hitler came': Thule Society and Germanen-Orden", *Journal of Modern History*, Vol. XXXV, No. 3 (1963), pp. 248–9.

22

Austrian Parties After 1900

By 1897, with the capture of Vienna, anti-Semitism had won its major battle and seemed safely entrenched as a permanent force in the country. It ceased to be a major issue and lost some of its magic as a catchword. With the exception of the Social Democrats, no party could afford to adopt an overtly friendly attitude to the Jews and even the Social Democrats tended to avoid one. Indeed, the increasingly large Jewish element in the Socialist movement made some form of anti-Semitism more necessary than ever to the bourgeois parties. Of most interest during the last seventeen years of peace was the relationship between the various anti-Semitic groups.

Victory in Vienna necessarily meant the break-up of the "United Christian" alliance. The 1897 Reichsrat elections had shown that the Christian-Social movement had grown beyond Vienna. By means of Peasant Unions it was succeeding in organizing the peasants, especially in Lower Austria and the Tyrol, into becoming its second pillar of electoral support.* With its slogans against the corn brokers and the land jobbers it convinced them, as it had convinced the artisans a decade earlier, that it was the Jews who were at the back of the system that was ruining them, and that if the Jews were removed their problems would be solved.

---

* The Peasant Unions, like the Austrian trade unions, were organized from above as a means of political recruitment, not from below as spontaneous economic combinations. In Lower Austria the clergy were prominent in organizing the Peasant Union, notably Mgr. Scheicher and Fr. Döller. In the Tyrol, where the Conservatives were stronger, the clergy were forbidden to associate themselves with it until 1909 (Miko, *Die Vereinigung der Konservativen*, p. 52). When the Lower Austrian *Bauernbund* was reconstituted in its present form, thirteen of the eighteen officers and committee members were also holders of political office (Kraus, *Niederösterreichischer Bauernbund*, pp. 189–90).

Secure in command of his impregnable majority, Lueger could now turn against the Nationalists in his own ranks and convert his party into a purely Christian-Social one. Estimates of the number of anti-Semitic Nationalists elected in 1895 vary from twenty-seven to thirty-two;[1] in 1896 there were twenty-eight. Schönerer had ordered his followers to boycott Lueger's movement, but a group of dissident pan-Germans, round Karl Wolf, had decided to support him, as did the majority of Steinwender's *Volkspartei*. A split came in 1896 over the candidature for second deputy mayor. The pan-Germans wanted their man Pacher, but Lueger would accept only Neumayer, the chairman of the Viennese *Volkspartei*.[2] Eleven of the Nationalist councilors resigned from the *Bürgerklub*[3] and formed themselves into a *Deutschnationale Vereinigung,* the remaining seventeen deciding that it would be political suicide to defy Lueger.[4] Of these twenty-eight councilors, sixteen had been elected in the crucial second *curia*. It is obvious that without Nationalist support Lueger could never have risen to his eminence. The hopes of the *Vereinigung* to constitute a third force in the city council, supporting Lueger on economic questions, but opposing him on the clerical issue, were short-lived. Lueger "reorganized" the franchise for the various *curiae* beyond all recognition. Ministers of religion were promoted *en bloc* to the second *curia,* the *Vereinigung's* main source of strength, and by 1900 it had no councilors left.[5] Indeed, incredible as it may sound, the pan-Germans were driven in 1900, by their hatred of Lueger, into a number of alliances with Liberals—all of them unsuccessful—in opposition to the official anti-Semitic list of Christian-Socials and pro-Lueger Nationalists.[6] By 1900 the Christian-Socials had a virtual monopoly of seats, 131 out of 154. Indeed, the only districts that regularly returned Liberal candidates were the first, second, and ninth, which between them contained over half the city's Jews.

A similar development, with similar tactics, can be seen in the simultaneous struggle for the control of the diet of Lower Austria. This province, with a population of 3½ million, at that time included Vienna. Its diet was elected by four *curiae;* the landed proprietors (twelve seats), the chambers of commerce (four seats), the urban communes (thirty, later thirty-five, seats), and the rural communes (twenty, later twenty-one, seats).

Before 1890 the Liberals enjoyed an overwhelming majority, the only opposition coming from the followers of Schönerer. Attempts to form a Schönerer-Lueger alliance for the 1890 election foundered;[7] the Liberal majority was reduced, but the anti-Semites were split into six groups. In 1896, the year of the tidal wave, the United Christians were triumphant. An *Antisemitisches Zentralwahlkommittee,* of which Lueger was chairman, and Richter of the *Volkspartei* vice-chairman,[8] drew up a list of candidates for the two lower *curiae.* The majority of their candidates had a clear run against their Liberal opponents; the remainder had no difficulty in overcoming scattered adherents of Schönerer and Wolf.[9] Altogether twenty-seven Liberals and fifty-one anti-Liberals were elected, but only thirty-three of the fifty-one joined Lueger's *Antisemitische Vereinigung,* the Nationalists mainly staying aloof[10] and thus depriving him of an absolute majority.

In the countryside the Christian-Socials were still relatively weak. After 1896 they therefore concentrated on gaining a secure hold on the peasantry, and succeeded in doing so through the *Landesverband der Landwirte* (later known as the *Bauernbund).* This originally nonpartisan body declared its formal support for the Christian-Social Party in 1901,[11] and in 1902 the party fought nine of the twenty-one rural seats with candidates who were also *Landesverband* functionaries.[12]

The 1902 elections were largely a civil war within the anti-Semitic ranks. The Lueger machine did its work, and the Nationalists, whether pan-German or of the *Volkspartei,* were steam-rollered out of the diet. The Christian-Socials made a clean sweep of Vienna and the rural seats. The Liberals by this time relied for their representation almost entirely on the upper *curiae*: the members elected by a relatively wide suffrage were overwhelmingly anti-Semitic and in the main Christian-Social. And with the elimination of the Liberals the Nationalists became the chief guardians of the anti-clerical heritage, which was more tenacious in the provincial towns than in Vienna.

Lueger was by now well established in the favor of the Imperial Party. There had always been a wing of the Conservative Party which looked with favor, even if not wholehearted support, on the more aggressively Catholic and socially conscious forces round Vogelsang and Liechtenstein, led by anti-Semitic

Conservatives like Ebenhoch of Upper Austria and Dipauli of the Tyrol.[13] They formed the *Katholische Volkspartei* in 1895 out of protest against Badeni's refusal to recommend Lueger's confirmation, but disagreed with the Christian-Social Party's opposition to Badeni's language ordinances. In 1901 they reunited with the Conservatives.

The relationship between the Conservatives and the Christian-Socials was radically altered by the introduction of universal suffrage in 1907. The Christian-Socials rose from twenty-three to sixty-seven seats, but even more important was the Social Democrats' leap from ten to eighty-seven. Ebenhoch had already declared before the election that he would lead his own Conservative followers into one *Klub* with Lueger, and the remaining Conservatives were left with no choice, so that with a strength of ninety-six the Christian-Socials became the largest *Klub* in the first democratically elected Reichsrat. This unification had already been foreshadowed by an electoral truce between the two parties, which operated everywhere except in the rural seats of the Tyrol and there the Conservatives were uniformly beaten.[14] In 1911, Gustav Piffl, one of the bright, young Christian-Social priests of the 1880's became Archbishop of Vienna; in 1912 *Vaterland* was amalgamated with the *Reichspost*. The Christian-Social Party was what it had been tending to become for many years—the Conservative Party of Austria.

Few parties have been so unequivocally the work of one man. Lueger was the most skilled politician, and certainly one of the most popular men, in the late Empire. His imposing presence (he was universally known as *"der schöne Karl")*, his command of the vernacular, his sense of occasion, and his solid achievements made him beloved in Vienna. If he had one sincere emotion it was love for his native city. He bought out the British-owned utility companies and replaced their antiquated services with a municipal gasworks and an electrified tramway system. He expanded the water supply, built hospitals, schools and a publicly owned abattoir, and founded an employment exchange and savings bank—all in a spirit of municipal Socialism that would have warmed the hearts of the Webbs. (On the other hand we can only be grateful that his project for building an Acropolis on the crest of the Vienna Woods was never carried out).

TABLE 9. PARTY STRENGTHS IN LOWER AUSTRIAN DIET, 1890–1902

Curia	1890			1896		1902			
	Liberals	Christian Social	German Nationalists	Liberals	Anti-Semites	Liberals	Christian Social	German Nationalists	Social Democrats
1st	15	…	…	12	4	13	3	…	…
2nd	4	…	…	4	…	4	…	…	…
3rd	18	9	3	10	24	2	25	7	1
4th	4	16	…	…	21	…	21	…	…
Others	1	2	…	1	2	1	2	…	…
Total	42	27	3	27	51	20	51	7	1

He knew that in Vienna anti-Semitism drew its strength from neither racial nor religious springs, but from economic springs. "The fears or hatred of pious souls virtually vanished beside the significance of the indignation at empty pockets."[15] Anti-Semitism was "co-terminous with the struggle against that capitalism which overruns, oppresses and entwines itself with everything."[16] In any case, what he said in public and thought in private were different matters. "I dislike the Hungarian Jews even more than I do the Hungarians," he told one of the leaders of Viennese Jewry,[17] "but I am no enemy of our Viennese Jews; they are not so bad and we cannot do without them. My Viennese always want to have a good rest, the Jews are the only ones who always want to be active."

How deep his anti-Semitism went is shown by his most famous utterance, "I decide who is a Jew"—"*wer ein Jud ist, das bestimme ich*"—which he made in reply to criticisms of the frequent hospitality he accepted at Jewish tables.* It is a summary of his whole character, cynical and opportunist in public, genial and informal in private. In his thirty-five years of public life he had sat on both sides of every fence. He began as a Liberal and reached his highest office as an anti-Liberal; he founded a two-man party with a Jew and a one-man party based on anti-Semitism. As late as 1888, Fr. Abel informs us, "he would hear nothing of Church or religion"[18] and there is no evidence that he experienced a conversion later. Nevertheless, his portrait adorned the Pope's desk for many years.

Neither Lueger nor his party, nor the Conservatives, nor the Church could afford to regard anti-Semitism as more than a means to an end. Racial anti-Semitism was out of the question, and would have been even without Theodor Kohn as Prince-Archbishop of Olomouc. Julius Porzer, who was partly Jewish, became deputy mayor in 1904—something that had never happened in the thirty-four years of Liberal rule; one of the movement's leading lawyers was Max Anton Löw, the grandson of a Bratislava rabbi.

Lueger kept his hold on the population to the end. At every

---

* He is also said to have said to Kielmansegg, *Statthalter* of Lower Austria in the 1890's, that his anti-Semitism only went as far as the Fichtegasse, the editorial offices of the *Neue Freie Presse* (Molisch, *Die Stellung Wiens*, p. 196.

popular consultation, from 1895 to his death in 1910, under whatever system of voting, his party came first. The bulk of his support came from the middle and lower middle classes, but there is no doubt that many working men, especially those in municipal employment, voted for him too. "He was the first bourgeois politician," wrote Friedrich Austerlitz, the editor of the Socialist daily, "who recognized the importance of the masses in politics."[19] How much his party relied on his personality is shown by the 1911 general election, when it lost 35,000 votes in Vienna and held only four of the city's thirty-three seats.

Lueger's anti-Semitism has been the subject of much debate and his most recent biographers have been at pains to minimize it:

> After Auschwitz and Maydanek one may speak of this subject . . . only with seriousness. Dr. Karl Lueger can maintain himself before the verdict of history. In 1880, 1890, 1900, life ran inside such a well-defined order, that one could afford, among other political escapades, to play with anti-Semitism, without at the same time breaking the principles of civilised humanity and falling into a daemonic abyss.[20]

In the 1930's the historian Oskar Karbach asked Emmerich Czermak, then chairman of the Christian-Social Party, how it had defined the term "Jew" in its early history. "He answered, after some hesitation that it never occupied itself with the problem — an answer which, though probably untrue, is none the less significant."[21]

On the other hand, he was quite willing to be feted as a member of the anti-Semitic international. He professed to be a great admirer of Drumont,[22] and Léon Daudet, in his goodwill message on Lueger's sixtieth birthday, wrote: *"Je me contente donc de crier, "A bas les Juifs!"*"[23]* Above all, unknown to him, his audience included from time to time a frustrated young architect from Upper Austria who, rootless and embittered, was tramping the streets of Vienna and spending his idle afternoons in the gallery of the Reichsrat. Hitler's own statement that he knew nothing of anti-Semitism at home[24] and learnt its significance only from Lueger[25] must be treated with the same reserve as most autobiographical assertions in *Mein Kampf*. His friend Kubizek claims that "Hitler already came to Vienna a determined

* "I will merely cry, 'Down with the Jews!'"

anti-Semite" and that once, passing a synagogue, he had remarked, "Linz is no place for that."[26]* There is no doubt that what Hitler did learn from Lueger was what Lueger learnt from Komlossy—the political effectiveness of anti-Semitism.

The completeness of Lueger's success within the limited field he had set himself should not blind us to the steps anti-Semitism was making on the bourgeois Left.

On the extreme Left there was still, or perhaps one should say, again, Schönerer. Having been expelled from his original stalking-ground in Lower Austria by the Christian-Socials, he established his forces, on his return to political life, in the Sudeten lands—North Bohemia and Austrian Silesia—in those proud, centuries-old bastions of Germandom on the Slav frontier, Eger, Reichenberg, Leitmeritz, and Troppau.

Where Lueger had the pliable, moody, opportunistic, genially unprincipled outlook of the Viennese, Schönerer was unbending in all his hates, and he had many. His anti-Semitism he derived from Dühring, mainly through his university contacts. When, in the 1880's, the Jewish question was splitting the *Deutsche Klub* he was racked by no doubts:

> In contrast with the gentlemen of the German and German-Austrian *Klubs,* we . . . make no secret of regarding anti-Semitism not as a regrettable symptom or disgrace, but as the main prop of national thought, the chief means of promoting a disposition genuinely based on the people, and thus the greatest achievement of the century.[27]

* As Franz Jetzinger has shown in his scholarly critique (*Hitler's Jugend. Phantasien, Lügen und die Wahrheit,* Vienna, 1956), Kubizek's account is at least as unreliable as Hitler's own. However, Kubizek's assertion that Hitler's father's circle of friends and some masters at his school were "openly anti-Semitic and pan-German" is inherently plausible and Jetzinger's claim that no schoolmaster would ever make an anti-Semitic remark in class under the Habsburgs (*op. cit.,* pp. 119, 243) is a wild idealization of that age. Nevertheless, the eulogy heaped on Hitler's history master, Poetsch, in both *Mein Kampf* and other Nazi writings (e.g. G. A. von Metnitz, *Die deutsche Nationalbewegung,* p. 115) seems misplaced. Although undoubtedly pan-German (he served as a German Nationalist town councilor for many years) he was in no way proud of numbering Hitler among his ex-pupils. He passed his complimentary copies of *Mein Kampf* to a local monastery library and, alone among Hitler's surviving teachers and classmates, declined to send his signed photograph to Hitler when asked to do so in July, 1936 (Jetzinger, *op. cit.,* pp. 107–8).

Such creeds, together with his fawning on Prussia, remained the property of an esoteric sect. When, in 1902, he ended a speech in the Reichsrat with the call *"Hoch und Heil den Hohenzollern!"*[28] general disgust was evoked.

Typical of his failure to judge public feelings was his *Los-von-Rom* movement. The language of his original manifesto,* with its unqualified denunciations and its vision of enemies all around was characteristic of his party's response to any question. The campaign cannot be considered a success; the open support it received from German organizations, such as the *Gustav Adolf-Verein,*† was only a liability. Schönerer himself and his son went over to Protestantism in April, 1900 after the first 10,000 converts had preceded them (over half of them in Bohemia);[29] in ten years the number of converts reached 85,000.[30]

The majority of Austrians were not attracted by the slogan, *"Ein Gott, ein Kaiser, ein Volk";* they were not disposed to dismantle the Habsburg Empire, however discontented they might be within it, or subscribe to his speech in 1901 when he said that the dissolution of a state might bring the redemption of a people.[31] In contrast with the Liberals, whose *raison d'être* was the defense of the constitution, with the Conservatives who preached federalism, and with the Church which could not accept racialism, he had to make his anti-Semitism so extreme that to accept both it and the existing structure of the multinational state was impossible. The Habsburgs, shrewder than they are sometimes given credit for, appreciated this, and for a long time held themselves aloof from, and even hostile to, all forms of anti-Semitism.

Schönerer's own attitude to religion was obscure. At the same time that he embraced Lutheranism he installed an interdenominational chapel at Rosenau; but he also declared—and this was probably nearest the truth—that he "was and remained a pagan."[32] This mixture of Protestantism and Teuton paganism was evident in the many quasi-political organizations with which he was associated, such as gymnastic clubs, cycling clubs, the Union of German Women, the *Burschenschaften,* and the *Bund der*

* See Appendix IV.
† See pp. 226–7.

Germanen. A glance at the names of some of the branches of the *Bund*[33] illustrates this hodge-podge:

Odin, Ulrich von Hutten, Ekkehard, Martin Luther, Kornblume, Eiche, Blücher, Wartburg, Kriemhilde.

He tried to introduce a new calendar dating from the battle of Noreia (118 B.C.) when the Cimbri defeated the Roman legions under Parpirius Carbo—the first entry of the Germans on the stage of history—and organized a festival in the Wachau to inaugurate the year 2001 n.N. He tried to revive the old Germanic names of the months; Midsummer and Yuletide festivals were held, as well as celebrations to commemorate the battles of Sedan and the Teutoburg Forest.

All this went some way toward compensating him for the lack of direct political success. He came to regard representative institutions with disdain; his eyes were fixed on the distant horizons of blood and race, not on the parish pump. For the spreading of the faith it was much more useful to have "front organizations," infiltrate the major parties, form "direct action" bodies like the *Volksräte* and, by means of a constant barrage of slogans and programs for joint platforms, force all other German parties to be perpetually looking over their left shoulders. Had Schönerer been a rational politician, he could have become a major popular leader and been to the Germans of Bohemia what Lueger was in Vienna. Especially after 1897, under the shadow of the Badeni language ordinances, a surge of Nationalist extremism went through all classes of the population and the German parties in the Reichsrat obstructed all business. He might well have secured a mass following among Sudeten workers who were anti-capitalist, anti-clerical, and anti-Czech. But the pan-German movement had apparently become too involved in the defense of *Mittelstand* interests to be able to take advantage of this opportunity,[34] and emotionally Schönerer was closer to the beer-swilling adolescents of the university clubs than to dour and hardened railwaymen or coal miners.

He did taste political victory once, in 1901, when twenty-one of his followers were elected to the Reichsrat. But the *Alldeutsche Vereinigung* which they formed soon broke up; the latent hostility between Schönerer and Wolf, coupled this time with revelations about Wolf's more than disreputable private life, erupted within twelve months and at the end of the parliamentary period twelve of its members had rallied to Wolf's German-Radical group.[35]

If Schönerer and his dwindling band appeared pathetic and ludicrous, the feelings which they tried to spread, or exploit, were gaining ground. By 1897, all other German parties, including the Christian-Socials, were forced to acknowledge "national" aims and to disassociate themselves from Jews.

The *Deutsche Volkspartei* of Steinwender came into being in 1895 and 1896, under the impulse of the Celje school controversy, and gained forty-two seats in 1897. It co-operated with Lueger in Lower Austria, as we have seen. West of Vienna it quickly replaced what remained of Liberalism as the chief opposition to the Conservatives, and in Bohemia it made some headway too. Although its manifesto was substantially the same as the Linz Programme it was less vehemently anti-Semitic than the pan-Germans', demanding only "liberation from . . . the predominant Jewish influence."[36] It was not specifically anti-Church[37] and later favored the partition of Bohemia,[38] a proposal which was *anathema* to Schönerer who saw Bohemia as indivisible and German.

Its collapse in Vienna and to the West restricted Liberalism to the Sudeten lands, and there the *Fortschrittspartei* constituted what was in effect a more moderate *Volkspartei*. Its *Klub* in the newly elected parliament excluded Jews and was reluctant to have anything to do with the remaining Viennese representatives.[39] The four German Jewish deputies and those of the second *curia* (what remained of specifically capitalist representation) formed a *Klub* of their own. In 1901 the *Fortschrittspartei* reunited and once more accepted Jews in its ranks. There was some trouble about this, but no actual resignations.[40]

After 1901 the intensification of the linguistic struggle and the success which the "anti-national" parties (Christian-Socials and Social Democrats) were having among the economically depressed led to the formation of two more *völkisch* parties. In 1903 the *Deutsche Arbeiterpartei* was formed to wean the workers from international Jewish Marxism, and in 1905 the *Deutsche Agrarpartei* to loosen the hold of the Church on the peasants.

Their programs, though mainly pan-German in inspiration, contradicted each other on a number of points, in particular on suffrage reforms; [41] both were more successful in the Sudeten lands than elsewhere. The *Arbeiterpartei* is of historical interest. In its ideology it owed something to Dühring[42]— probably the only political party ever to do so—but its class separatism made it unwelcome to Schönerer.[43] Its Nationalism was directed mainly against Czech competition in the labor market, its anti-Semitism against "the dishonesty of Social Democracy, led by Jews and related to mobile big business."[44] It became, in May, 1918, the *Deutsche Nationalsozialistische Arbeiterpartei;* after the collapse of the empire the Czechoslovak and Austrian successor parties became the nuclei of Nazi organization in those states, in close liaison with the German party.[45]

Thus, not counting the Liberals, there were five Nationalist parties when the 1907 elections were approaching. All calculations were, however, nullified by the government's decision—in a last attempt to make the parliamentary system, riven by intractable Nationalist passions, work—to "shoot Niagara" and give the vote to every male Austrian over twenty-four. The election brought sweeping changes: it showed that strident Nationalism had been typical only of the classes and parties entrenched in the second and third *curiae,* where commercial and professional competition was fiercest. Reduced for the first time to a parliamentary representation more proportionate to their real strength, the *Fortschrittspartei, Volkspartei,* and Young Czechs seemed less mighty than the debates of the previous decades had suggested.*

Anti-Semitism, however, in so far as it was an electoral force outside Vienna, suffered no setback. Of the 233 seats allotted to the German regions, 131 fell to anti-Semitic parties. With Schönerer gone, the Liberals reduced to a shadow and Lueger leading the anti-Semites to Church, there seemed little left to divide the remaining German parties. United by a desire to defend the German language and by varying degrees of anti-Semitism and anti-clericalism, they formed themselves, in 1910, into a tactical alliance, the *Deutscher Nationalverband,* without giving up their individual identities.

This meant that the position of the Liberal Jewish deputies once more needed settling. Already in 1907 there had been talk

---

* The Liberals sank from 41 to 15, the *Volkspartei* Nationalists from 51 to 29, the Young Czechs from 53 to 18 seats.

of uniting all "national" parties into one organization. Wolf's German-Radicals and the Agrarians immediately objected to the inclusion of any Jewish or Viennese deputies.* After some embarrassing negotiations[46] the Viennese deputies concluded that:

> In the formation of the *Verband* the demands of Liberalism will not have the effective representation . . . which from our point of view would be an indispensable condition of united action.[47]

and lost interest; Redlich and Licht, however, had no difficulty in staying in the party.

When the whole affair was over Gustav Gross, the leader of the Liberals, complained disingenuously of the difficulties caused by the "ill-fated Jewish question" ("der unglückselige Judenpunkt")[48] but the issue had in fact become confused with the generally bad relations between the Viennese and Sudeten Liberals. The Viennese Liberal electorate was not entirely Jewish, but undoubtedly its most influential section was. The *Österreichisch-Israelitische Union,* founded in 1886 because the Liberals could no longer be relied upon to fight anti-Semitism,[49] endorsed and sometimes even selected candidates on behalf of Jewish voters. These were not necessarily Jewish or even Liberal. Kronawetter was supported, as was Masaryk. In the general election of 1897 in Vienna it supported Liberals and *Sozialpolitiker* for the privileged *curia* and the Social Democrats for the universal *curia.*[50] But it did mean that the *Union* was the biggest power in Viennese Liberalism. Moreover, Ofner and Hock were well to the Left of the *Fortschrittspartei,* a matter on which Redlich's views were much more sound.†

With the virtual eclipse of pan-Germanism, the moderate Nationalists wanted to include the Christian-Socials in the alliance of German anti-Socialist parties and to exclude those sections of the Liberal party suspected of being "crypto-Social

---

* Those concerned were Josef Redlich and Stefan Licht, both baptized Jews who sat for Moravian constituencies, and three Viennese, Paul von Hock, the son of a convert, Kamill Kuranda, son of Ignaz, and Julius Ofner, both Jews. Ofner was not an official Liberal candidate.

† "I must say that I am moving away ever more from '*Judenliberalismus*' à la Hock[8] and the Social Democrats," he recorded in his diary in January 1908 (*Tagebücher,* ed. Fellner, Graz, 1953, Vol. I, p. xvii).

Democrat,"[51] or which were too fearful of agrarian predominance in such an alliance.[52] It was therefore obvious that neither
the Viennese Liberals nor the Christian-Socials would agree to
serve in a coalition with each other. In Moravia things lay
differently. The Liberal tradition was stronger here, and racial
feeling less intense, than elsewhere. This had made possible the
German–Czech compromise of 1904. Before that Jews literally
held the balance for control of the diet in six or seven marginal
constituencies,[53] and even afterwards could make the decision
between one party and another in a number of German seats.*
Jewish manufacturers were still a force in the Progressive Party.
In 1902 the *Bund der Deutschen in Nordmaähren* postponed for five
years the ticklish question of whether to be *judenrein;* ten years
later the German-Radical *Deutsches Nordmährerblatt* could still
write:

> When Jewish influence helps to keep a village, a town or a
> chamber of commerce German, it would be more than folly to
> combat such "influence" . . . it is, moreover, in any case a matter
> for rejoicing for the German public to see any instance in
> Moravia where, through the joint work of all parties, a bulwark
> is held.[54]

In the diet the only Jewish member, Fischel, sat in the same *Klub*
with German-Radicals.

The 1911 elections raised the same issues and evoked the same
responses. Although anti-clericalism had figured largely in the
"national" parties' campaign, they decided that in the second
ballots it was the duty of the German "bourgeois" parties to
come to each others' aid. This plan was sabotaged by the
Viennese Liberals. The *Neue Freie Presse* called on its readers, as it
had done in 1907, to vote, where necessary, for the Social
Democrats on the grounds that "one can vote for one's
opponents but . . . not for one's enemies."[55]

This time eight Liberals were elected in Vienna. The question
of asking Hock, Kuranda, and Ofner to join the *Nationalverband*
did not arise;[56] two others were considered too Left-wing by the
Radicals and Agrarians; and the remaining three, who could not

---

* In three of them, Jewish voters exceeded 25% of the total (*MIU*, Dec. 1905,
pp. 4–5.

Mittheilungen

der

Oesterreichisch-Israelitischen Union.

Herausgegeben von dem Vorstande dieses Vereines.

Das monatlich einmal erscheinende Vereinsblatt erhalten die Vereins-Mitglieder unentgeltlich.

Zuschriften und Tausch-Exemplare erbittet man unter der Adresse:

Wien, I., Schottenring 23.

Vereinskanzlei: I., Schottenring Nr. 23.

| Nr. 94. | März | IX. Jargang 1897. |

WIEN, 16. März 1897.

Euer Wolgeboren!

Der Verein „Oesterr.-Israel. Union" hat für die **Samstag, den 20. März d. J.** stattfindenden **Reichsrathswahlen** für den **I. Bezirk** die Herren:

Dr. Ferdinand Kronawetter, Magistrats-Rath und Landtags-Abgeordneter, VIII. Lerchenfelderstrasse 122,

Constantin Noske, General-Secretär u. Landtags-Abgeordneter, I. Bäckerstrasse 22,

Dr. Julius Ofner, Hof- und Gerichts-Advokat und Landtags-Abgeordneter, I. Wollzeile 12,

Carl Wrabetz, Gemeinderath, I. Tuchlauben 18

und für den IX. Bezirk:

Herrn **Dr. Eugen v. Philippovich,** k. k. Univ. Professor und Landtags-Abgeordneter, XIX. Colloredogasse 8

nominirt und bitten wir Sie diesen Candidaten ausnamslos Ihre Stimme zu geben, da eine Stimmenzersplitterung leicht den Sieg der Reactionären herbeiführen könnte.

Wie Euer Hochwolgeboren aus dem umstehenden Referate des Herrn Landesschulrathes Dr. Gustav Kohn ersehen, sind unsere Bemühungen, zwischen den beiden fortschrittlichen Parteien der inneren Stadt eine Einigung anlässlich der bevorstehenden Reichsrathswahlen zu erzielen, leider erfolglos geblieben.

6. Electoral recommendation to Jewish voters in Vienna, from the *Österreichisch-Israelitische Union.* (*Österreichische Nationalbibliothek, Vienna*)

be accused of progressive views on anything, were admitted.* Licht and Redlich remained members.

By 1911 the Austrian political spectrum, which had been shifting since the 1880's, was once more set and the distribution of "Reds" in industrial Vienna, "Blacks" among the Viennese middle classes and Alpine peasants, and "Nationals" among the provincial middle class persisted into the 1930's and still applies, with qualifications, to the present day. Of the German parties in 1911, the Christian-Socials got 37%, the Social Democrats 32%, and the *Nationalverband* 31% of the vote—in other words, over two-thirds of the German electorate, whether or not out of anti-Semitic motives, cast its vote for anti-Semitism.

It would be wrong to suggest that anti-Semitism in Austria was a monopoly of the Germans. We have already mentioned Stojalowski and the periodic outbreaks of Czech anti-Semitism. Dr. Baxa, a Czech Radical deputy and, after 1918, mayor of Prague, had been a private prosecutor in the Hilsner ritual murder trial, and during the Dreyfus Affair Masaryk had to complain that almost all Czech papers, including *Narodni Listy,* were anti-Dreyfus.[57] Among the nonhistoric nations, anti-Semitism was principally a protest against Jewish association with the economic and political oppressors. As Dr. Stefánek, a prominent Slovak leader, put it:

> How does the village Jew live and what is his social situation? He is the merchant and the innkeeper of the village. He constitutes a distinct community with his co-religionists, a community tied up by religion, but even more by common economic interest. The Jew lives quite apart from the people. Only on the economic terrain does he have intercourse with them, and he has not the slightest sympathy with their religious or social endeavours. . . . The more the schools progressed in the field of Magyarisation, the more aggressive and active the Jew became in party politics, and the deeper the antagonism became between him and the people surrounding him. Today they are considered the exponents of the Magyars, an auxiliary troop of the sheriffs, of the village officials and the gendarmerie, and they are feared everywhere.[58]

---

* Two of these were artisans and therefore really unrepresentative of Viennese Liberalism (Molisch, *Die Stellung Wiens,* p. 191).

Similarly Ruthene anti-Semitism was, in Hungary, basically anti-Magyar[59] and in Galicia anti-Polish. One Ruthene politician listed the following enemies of the Ruthene peasant in influencing his vote: the district captain, the district prefect, the mayor, the landlord, the tax inspector, and "the cunning Jew."[60]

Nevertheless, it was among German Austrians that the creed became not merely a party principle but a common link that was widely taken for granted. In becoming part of a general political attitude it had sacrificed most of its dynamic; from being stigmatized as a form of social and political subversion it was becoming almost *de rigueur* in polite circles.

The various schools of anti-Semitism often differed from each other profoundly. Once traditional Liberalism and Conservatism had been overthrown, the working alliance of the United Christians was bound to break up, for the various factions were now fighting each other for the same middle-class clientèle. In so far as it is possible to generalize, Catholic anti-Semitism appealed more to the commercial *Mittelstand,* while Nationalist anti-Semitism appealed to the professional *Mittelstand.* Catholic anti-Semitism was the more tradition-bound of the two. It flourished more easily among groups with the largest tradition of anti-Jewish feeling and it was in a strong position when it came to enrolling the peasants. In Vienna itself it was able to base itself on a tradition of Catholic popular preaching—demagogic, anti-intellectual[61] and anti-Semitic—which goes back at least two centuries to Abraham a Santa Clara.[62]

The professional classes were more conscious of Slav as well as Jewish competition, and they were attracted by the intellectual superstructure and the anti-clericalism that Nationalism had inherited from the Liberals. The anti-clerical issue became increasingly important in the last decade of the Empire, especially on the academic plane. Lueger had thrown out a challenge at the *Katholikentag* of 1907 when he spoke of the remaining task, "the conquest of the universities,"[63] at a time when there was heavy pressure for the establishment of a Catholic university at Salzburg to counteract the prevailing anti-clericalism of Austrian academic life. A grave blow was struck at academic freedom by the dismissal of Professor Wahrmund in 1909 from his chair of Moral Theology at Innsbruck because of a pamphlet in which he had expressed his "doubts."

But when all is said and done, whenever there was a critical challenge from an outside foe, the anti-Semites closed their ranks, whether against the Slav majority or the Social Democrat workers; anti-Semitism was part and parcel of the wider *malaise* of insecurity, insufficiency, and resentment of uncontrollable superior forces.

REFERENCES

1 Pichl gives the number at 32: *Schönerer*, Vol. IV, p. 52; Molisch as 30: P. Molisch, *Geschichte der deutschnationalen Bewegung*, p. 183; Badeni in a confidential report to the Emperor as 27: Miko, *Die Vereinigung Konservativen*, p. 211.
2 *DZ*, Jan. 24, 1897.
3 *ODR*, Oct. 20, 1896.
4 *DVB*, Oct. 26, 1896.
5 O. Pohl, "Die Wiener Gemeinderatswahlen," *Neue Zeit*, Vol. XVIII, Pt. 2 (1900), p. 335.
6 *Wiener Zeitung*, May 26, 1900; *UDW*, April 16, 1900.
7 Manuscript minutes of the meeting, *NP, ÖVA*, Box 32, fol. 1.
8 *DVB*, July 24, 1896.
9 *DVB*, Oct. 22, Oct. 26, 1896; *ODR*, Oct. 21, Nov. 1, 1896; *UDW*, Oct. 16, 1896.
10 Pichl,*op. cit.*, Vol. IV, pp. 82–3.
11 T. Kraus, *Die Entstehung des niederösterreichischen Bauernbundes* (unpublished dissertation, Vienna, 1950), p. 162.
12 *Ibid.*, p. 169.
13 Compare an article by Dipauli welcoming the Christian-Social Party (*Reichspost*, Jan. 13, 1894) and a speech strongly favorable to anti-Semitism on Dec. 10, 1895, *StPA*, XI. Sess., 439. Sitz., pp. 21969–70; and Ebenhoch's obituary on Vogelsang in the *Linzer Volksblatt* (quoted in Klopp, *Leben und Wirken*, p. 371).
14 Miko, *op. cit.*, p. 71.
15 R. Charmatz, *Deutsch-österreichische Politik. Studien über den Liberalismus* (Leipzig, 1907), p. 93.
16 Schnee, *Bürgermeister Karl Lueger*, p. 20.
17 S. Mayer, *Die Wiener Juden* (Vienna, 1917), p. 345.
18 H. Schmitz, *Aus Pater Abels Erinnerungen*, p. 345.
19 F. Austerlitz, "Die Wahlen in Wien," *Neue Zeit*, Vol. XXIX, Pt. 1 (1911), p. 510.
20 Skalnik, *Lueger*, p. 82.
21 Karbach, *The Founder of Modern Political Anti-Semitism*, p. 25.
22 F. Bournand (i.e. J. de Ligneau), *Les Juifs et nos Contemporains. L'Antisémitisme et la Question Juive* (Paris, 1898), p. 265.
23 *DVB*, Oct. 23, 1904.
24 Hitler, *Mein Kampf*, p. 55.

25 Ibid., pp. 95, 113–4.
26 A. Kubizek, Adolf Hitler—Mein Jugendfreund (Graz, 1953), p. 113.
27 Speech on April 18, 1887, StPA, X. Sess., 136. Sitz., p. 4963.
28 Speech on March 18, 1902, StPA, XVII. Sess., 112. Sitz., p. 10546.
29 Pichl, op. cit., Vol. VI, p. 388.
30 Karbach, op. cit., p. 21.
31 Molisch, op. cit., p. 210.
32 Pichl, op. cit., Vol. VI, p. 389.
33 Ibid., Vol VI, pp. 550, 551, 568, 587, 603.
34 See Whiteside, Austrian National Socialism, pp. 61–6, 81–2.
35 Pichl, op. cit., Vol. V, pp. 82, 87–8, 95.
36 Programm der deutschen Volkspartei, I, 4.
37 Ibid., II, 2–3.
38 Molisch, op. cit., p. 178.
39 Kolmer, Parlament und Verfassung, Vol. VI, p. 217.
40 Kolmer's statement (ibid., Vol. VIII, p. 295) is incorrect.
41 Molisch, op. cit., p. 213.
42 Whiteside, op. cit., pp. 102–3.
43 Pichl, op. cit., Vol. VI, p. 288.
44 Iglau Programme of 1913. Whiteside, op. cit., p. 100.
45 A. Ciller, Deutscher Sozialismus in den Sudetenländern und der Ostmark (Hamburg, 1939), pp. 142–3.
46 See Pulzer, "The Viennese Liberals and the Jewish Question,", p. 139.
47 Letter to Funke, chairman of Fortschrittspartei, NFP, June 6, 1907.
48 Speech in Iglau, June 9, 1907, Tagesbote (Brno), June 10, 1907.
49 MIU, April, 1910, pp. 12, 17.
50 Mayer, Ein jüdischer Kaufmann, pp. 410–12, 448–9; ÖW, March 19, 1897; MIU, Feb. 1903, p. 2; ibid., March, 1897, pp. 1–2, 5.
51 Reichspost, May 30, 1907.
52 Österreichischer Volkswirt, Vol. III, No. 38 (1907), p. 756.
53 Mayer, Die Wiener Juden, p. 473.
54 Deutsches Nordmährerblatt, Sept., 1912.
55 NFP, May 19, 1907, June 16, 1911.
56 Pulzer, op. cit., pp. 141–2.
57 MVA, Nov. 11, 1899, p. 353.
58 O. Jászi, The Dissolution of the Habsburg Monarchy (Chicago, 1929), p. 175. See also R. W. Seton-Watson, A History of the Czechs and Slovaks (London, 1943), p. 322.
59 Jászi, op. cit., p. 235; Z. A. B. Zeman, The Break-up of the Habsburg Monarchy (Oxford, 1961), p. 7.
60 J. Romanczúk, Die Ruthenen und ihre Gegner in Galizien (Vienna, 1902), p. 13.
61 For Christian-Social anti-intellectualism, see Kolmer, op. cit., Vol, V, pp. 318ff., Vol. VII, pp. 32, 250, 256.
62 For Abraham a Santa Clara's anti-Semitism, see R. A. Kann, A Study in Austrian Intellectual History. From late Baroque to Romanticism (London, 1960), pp. 57, 76–9, 104.
63 Skalnik, op. cit., p. 143.

23

The Para-Political Organizations

The decline in the virulence of organized party anti-Semitism was matched by its increasing pervasion of social life, semi-political bodies, and ideological and economic pressure groups. The German Agrarian League which, by virtue of its participation in elections is best considered as a political party, has already been discussed. Other good examples are the National Union of Commercial Employees, the anti-feminist movement, and gymnastic clubs. Pan-Germanism is reserved for a separate section.

Of the various quasi-political bodies from which anti-Semitism derived strength after 1900, one of the most interesting was the *Deutschnationaler Handlungsgehilfenverband* (DHV). It represented a class which at the same time that it was growing numerically, was economically and socially hard-pressed.

The *Verband* was not anti-Semitic or reactionary by accident or implication only. Its name revealed its purpose, for the word "national" in German political parlance meant not "nation-wide" but patriotic and exclusive of nonnationals.* It was founded in 1893 in Hamburg to create a "fighting organisation of commercial employees against Social Democracy"[1] and "a defence against the dangers of proletarisation."[2] German commerce, it claimed, consisted of "two nationalities, Germans and Jews" and "hostility to Jews contributed materially to the expansion of our union."[3]

The importance of racial purity was made clear in the constitution:

* Similarly any organization advertising itself as "Christian" could be counted on as having at least an anti-Semitic tinge. When the Secretary of the American Y.M.C.A. visited Hungary in the 1930's, he was welcomed by Admiral Horthy who expressed delight at meeting the head of "such an important anti-Semitic organization."

Since the union aims at raising the status of commercial employees on national lines, Jews or persons whose character is not blameless cannot acquire membership of any kind.[4]

and this importance was emphasized still further by the amendments to the constitution in 1909. The relevant paragraphs are 7 and 57.

7. Jews and those belonging to nations and races in conscious antithesis to Germandom cannot acquire membership of any kind.

57. Section 2. A majority of three-quarters of those present is necessary for any resolution which contains an amendment of the constitution or purposes the dissolution of the union, with the exception of §§ 7 and 57 which require, in addition, the unanimous approval of the executive committee and management committee for their amendment.[5]

The reason for these stringent regulations was, according to Zimmermann, the

unpleasant Jewish qualities, namely lack of courage, greed for profits, sultry sensuality, lack of honesty and cleanliness . . . . The German concepts of fidelity and faith [are] essentially different from Jewish concepts of commercial honesty.[6]

Zimmermann and his fellow-*Reformpartei* deputy Giese were prominent at the foundation of the union, and its connection with the anti-Semitic parties remained close. At the 1897 congress, addressed by Sonnenberg and Hasse,[7] the chairman of the Pan-German League, it resolved:

Commercial employees should furthermore feel themselves obliged to give their votes, at elections to legislative bodies, only to those nationally-minded men, without distinction of party, who are prepared to support the justified demands of commercial employees.[8]

In 1903 it gave the money for another DSRP candidature, that of Raab, and also provided support for Hasse.[9] Its secretary. Schack, was elected in a by-election in 1905 on behalf of the German-Social Party and held his seat until 1910, when he was imprisoned for sexual offenses against young girls.

The union was, indeed, an ever-present help to the anti-Semitic parties in their endemic financial difficulties, and the

Deutsches Blatt, the organ of the united *Deutschsoziale Reformpartei* during the 1890's, was printed and entirely financed by the publishers of *Handelswacht,* the union journal.[10] Sonnenberg's plans for including the union in his projected coalition of "state-conserving" forces was one of the constant causes of quarrels in the anti-Semitic ranks. One of the rival leaders states that all Sonnenberg could think of after the party's setback in 1898 was to ask Schack how much more help the union could be to the party.[11]

Although the union's interventions on behalf of its members for better wages and conditions were sometimes an embarrassment to employers who had hitherto rejoiced at the quiescence of white-collar workers, it represented in the long run a reinforcement of the Right and a strengthening of the defense against proletarian Social Democracy. The union deliberately and successfully appealed to the bourgeois class-consciousness of commercial employees. By 1913 its membership was 148,079, compared with 12,380 for the Social Democrats' clerks' union (over half of whom were women).[12] The editor of the union's journal, Alfred Roth, contested the 1912 elections, sponsored jointly by the German-Social Party and the Agrarian League.

A cardinal point in the union's program was opposition to female emancipation, in particular to vocational education for women. The inundation of male professions by women was deleterious to *"deutsche Art und deutsches Wesen,"*[13] and Schack maintained that "for women to earn their livelihood in men's professions is never a *Kulturfortschritt.*"[14] Here the Union was merely following in the footsteps of the *Sozialer Arbeiterverein,* a trade union formed by Stöcker's followers in the 1870's. It, too, in strong contrast with the Social Democrats, opposed equal rights for women.[15]

There was indeed a strong link between anti-Semitism and anti-feminism; most anti-Semites were anti-feminists and most anti-feminists were, if not actively anti-Semitic, at least strongly Nationalist at a time when this was coming to mean almost the same thing. According to Dühring,

> this deformed, ephemeral phase of thought may be put down in
> the main to the discredit of Hebrew women.[16]

and his pupil Schönerer was equally adamant that women were destined for *Kinder, Kirche und Küche:*

> The really bourgeois women, the women of the *Mittelstand,* but also those of the thinking working man, decline to have anything to do with the question of female suffrage, since they have, after all, retained the greater part of their feminity. In general, it is unoccupied women who devote themselves to the idiocy of female suffrage *(Frauenstimmrechtstrottelei),* women who have failed in their calling as women or who have no wish to answer it—and Jewesses. They naturally get the support of all the old women of the male sex and of all "feminists," that is, those men who are no men.[17]

Indeed, all the standard Right-wing objections to modern feminism were summarized by Oswald Spengler when he contrasted the *Urweib* (for example, the peasant woman) with the *Ibsen-weib:* one produces children, the other spiritual conflicts.[18]

Pastor Josef Werner's *Christlich-nationale Gruppe zur Bekämpfung der modernene Frauenemanziparion* rested "on the basis of German-national sentiment and Christian *Weltanschauung.*"[19] It yielded in importance to the *Deutsche Bund zur Bekämpfung der Frauenemanzipation,* founded in 1912:

> That it rests on a national and patriotic basis may be deduced from its purpose and aims, from the dangers which called it into existence.[20]

Ludwig Langemann, its chairman and editor of its journal, wrote:

> The modern feminist movement is, like Social Democracy, an international, foreign body in our national life.[21]
> Both movements are, considering the great participation of the Jewish element, international in origin and fight, with equal fanaticism, against all fundamentals of the people's life.[22]

The identification of the feminist movement with Jewesses was no doubt inspired by the fact that most of the leading female advocates (outside the Social Democrat Party at least) were Jewish—Anita Auersperg, Lydia Heymann, and Regina Deutsch.

Before 1918, openly anti-Semitic references in the *Monatsblatt* were rare,[23] though the *Bund* claimed the sympathy and support of numerous anti-Semitic newspapers, including, of course, the

Deutsche Handelswacht.[24] After the German defeat, however, it became suddenly and violently anti-Semitic,[25] and Langemann produced anti-Semitic and anti-Catholic pamphlets.[26] With the introduction of female suffrage under the Weimar constitution, the *Bund* admitted that its cause was lost, and it reconstituted itself as *Deutscher Bund für Volksgesundung*.

One consequence of the more purely ideological and less partisan nature of anti-Semitism was that organizations covering both Austria and Germany became increasingly important. The DVH attempted to extend its membership to Austria. In 1903 the *Gau Ostmark*, with its own *Gauleiter*, was constituted in Vienna; by 1913 its membership was 9065.[27]

Two bodies which had always ignored the frontiers of 1867 and 1871 were the *Deutsch-österreichischer Alpenverein* of 1874 and the *Deutsche Turnerschaft* of 1861;[28] both were typical in that the impetus toward extreme nationalism and anti-Semitism came from the Austrian branches. Anti-Semitism had an easier passage among the gymnasts than among the mountaineers. The gymnasts, after all, could trace their movement to the ardent nationalism of "Father" Jahn; the *Turnerschaft* was a consciously patriotic body in a way that the *Alpenverein* was not. The Austrian branches of the *Turnerschaft* were grouped in *Kreis* 15. In 1887 the eight branches in Lower Austria (including that of Vienna University) went *judenrein*, with the result that they were expelled from *Kreis* 15 and formed an independent *Deutscher Turnerbund*.[29] In 1901, however, *Kreis* 15 itself disaffiliated all Jewish branches as well as individual Jewish members of other branches; these (fifty branches with about 7000 members) were then recognised by the parent *Turnerschaft* as *Kreis* 15b.[30] Three years later *Kreis* 15, with 525 branches and over 50,000 members,[31] seceded altogether and formed a *Turnkreis Deutsch-österreich*.[32] Goetz, the chairman of the *Turnerschaft*, deploring the reasons for the secession, declared:

> The *Deutsche Turnerschaft* rests on a national, not a political or partisan basis . . . . Any political partisanship must be kept strictly away from gymnastic clubs as such; the formation of clear-cut political attitudes is the duty and concern of the individual gymnast.[33]

In the *Alpenverein* the anti-Semitic victory was delayed until after 1918, but the pattern was similar. In 1921 the Austrian section voted by a majority of two-to-one in favor of an *Arierparagraph*, whereupon the Jewish members formed their own section, *Donauland*. By 1924 there was a sufficient majority in the whole of the *Alpenverein* to secure the disaffiliation of the Jewish section.[34]

Another organization in which Austrian radicalism made rapid headway was the *Wandervogel* youth organization founded in 1901. By 1913 the Austrian section had succeeded in excluding "Slavs, Jews, and Latins,"[35] at a time when the racialist wing in Germany was still fighting an uphill battle. The struggle within these nation-wide bodies was reflected in local clubs and societies which made it a point of pride to be *judenrein*. The smaller the likelihood of Jewish members, the greater the ease with which this was done. The Tyrolean Cycling Union reconstituted itself in 1900 on a "German-Aryan" basis;[36] the danger of inundation from Jewish cycling enthusiasts in the Tyrol cannot have been pressing.

REFERENCES

1 W. Schack, *Wie und was wir geworden sind. Schriften des deutschnationalen Handlungsgehilfenverbandes, Band 16* (Hamburg, 1903), p. 22.
2 H. Irwahn, *Bilder aus der Urgeschichte des DHV* (Hamburg, 1920), p. 5.
3 Schack, *op. cit.*, p. 38.
4 *Der deutschnationale Handlungsgehilfenverband. Mitteilungen des Verbandes zur Abwehr des Antisemitismus* (Berlin, 1911), p. 27.
5 *Ibid.*, p. 31.
6 *Jahrbuch für deutschnationale Handlungsgehilfen, 1908*, quoted in *op. cit.*, p. 31.
7 *Verhandlungsschrift über den 3. deutschen Handlungsgehilfentag am 11. April in Leipzig. Schriften des deutschnationalen Handlungsgehilfenverbandes, Band 2* (Hamburg, 1902), pp. 7–10.
8 *Ibid.*, p. 9.
9 *Der deutschnationale Handlungsgehilfenverband*, p. 28.
10 W. Giese, *Die Herren Raab und von Liebermann in der deutschsozialen Reformpartei* (Berlin, 1900), p. 108.
11 *Ibid.*
12 H. Schuon, *Der deutschnationale Handlungsgehilfenverband. Sein Werdegang und seine Arbeit* (Jena, 1914), pp. 236–8.
13 *Ibid.*, p. 78.
14 Anon. (i.e. W. Schack), *Die Frauenarbeit im Handelsgewerbe. Schriften des deutschnationalen Handlungsgehilfenverbandes, Band 21* (Hamburg, 1904), p. 8.
15 Schön, *Geschichte der Berliner Bewegung*, pp. 118–9.
16 Döll, *Dühringwahrheiten*, p. 145.

17 *Alldeutsches Tagblatt*, Jan. 15, 1907.
18 Quoted in E. J. Jung, *Die Herrschaft der Minderwertigen, Ihr Zerfall und ihre Ablösung durch ein neues Reich* (2nd ed., Berlin, 1930), p. 201.
19 J. Werner, *Die Gefährdung des deutschen Hauses und der christlichen Familie. Flugschrift der christlichnationalen Gruppe gegen die moderne Frauenemanziption*, No. 1. Only one issue appeared.
20 *Monatsblatt gegen die Frauenemanzipation*, May, 1913, p. 37.
21 L. Langemann, *Auf falschem Wege. Beiträge zur Kritik der radikalen Frauenbewegung* (Berlin, 1913), p. 13.
22 *Ibid.*, p. 25.
23 *Monatsblatt*, May, 1913, p. 39; December, 1913, p. 107.
24 *Berliner Neueste Nachrichten, Leipziger Neueste Nachrichten, Reichsbote, Hammer, Staatsbürger-Zeitung. Monatsblatt*, Oct. 1913, pp. 83–4.
25 *Ibid.*, Jan. 1919, pp. 2–3.
26 L. Langemann, *Deutschlands Erniedrigung und das Zentrum* (Göttingen, 1918); *Der deutsche Zusammenbruch und das Judentum* (Göttingen, 1919).
27 H. Schuon, *op. cit.*, pp. 222–4.
28 Geiser, *Deutsches Reich und Volk*, p. 176.
29 *ATB*, Vol. XVII, No. 12 (1904), p. 439.
30 *Ibid.*, pp. 434–5.
31 *ATZ*, Oct. 15, 1904, p. 312.
32 *ATB*, Vol. XVI, No. 9 (1903), p. 266.
33 *ATZ*, Nov. 1, 1904, p. 335.
34 *MIU*, Vol. XXXI, No. 7, April 9, 1921; *Mitteilungen des deutschen und österreichischen Alpenvereins* (Munich), Vol. XLVIII, July, 1922, p. 58, Vol. XLVII, Aug. 1921, p. 70; Vol. LI, Jan. 1925, p. 20.
35 W. Z. Laqueur, *Young Germany. A History of the German Youth Movement* (London, 1962), p. 76.
36 Pichl, *Schönerer*, Vol. VI, p. 560.

24

Pan-Germanism

The interrelationship between German and German-Austrian anti-Semitism shows the extent to which Nationalism had, by the beginning of the twentieth century, become the main driving force behind anti-Semitism. This German Nationalism took various forms according to the intellectual preferences of the devotees and the different political exigencies of the Hohenzollern and Habsburg Empires. It ranged from the *Weltpolitik* of the Pan-German League, through the relatively sophisticated theorizing of the "political anthropologists," to small bands of fanatical racialists. Often, as in the journals of the student corps, the various strands were inextricably mixed. Yet, as far as the anti-Semitic content of these various pan-German schools was concerned, there was little that was unfamiliar. The justifications, the rationalizations, and the "superstructure" were different from those of the 1870's and 1880's, but the values of *Judenliberalismus* which were attacked were the same, and the traditional *Mittelstand* was evoked as the backbone of the nation just as Glagau had done thirty years earlier.

The assumption that any German Nationalist should, as a matter of course, be anti-Semitic—in however mild a form—nevertheless represented a change from earlier attitudes. In 1848 it was, in the main, the anti-Nationalist Right which was anti-Semitic, and as late as the early 1880's quite vehemently Nationalist Liberals in Germany or Austria were outspoken opponents of anti-Semitism. The Nationalist line at this stage was that Jews should cut their ties with Judaism and become assimilated. *"Sie sollen Deutsche werden!"*[1] Treitschke had demanded, echoing Paul de Lagarde's words, *"Um Gottes Willen, ganz herein mit ihnen oder ganz heraus."*[2]★ "Friendship," according to Lagarde, "is possible with individual Jews, but only on one condition, that he ceases to be a Jew. Jewishness as such must disappear."[3]

The most important and the most influential of the various bodies which existed to propagandize German Nationalist ambitions was the *Alldeutscher Verband.* In its ambivalence toward the Jewish Question and its latent, implicit anti-Semitism it was equally typical of much of middle-class opinion. It was founded in 1893; its predecessor, the *Allgemeiner Deutscher Verband,* derived its immediate impetus from the treaty which Caprivi signed with Britain in 1891, exchanging Zanzibar for Heligoland.† The purpose of the League was to draw attention to Germany's need to expand overseas and pursue active colonial, military, and naval policies.

The League's power and backstair influence in Germany before and during the First World War have been often and inconclusively discussed; a final verdict is impossible precisely because a pressure group does not document its intrigues. Some indications of its aims we may, however, derive from the speech made by Heinrich Class, its second chairman, on taking over his post in 1908; they were "to form a national political officer corps, at whose head is to stand a general staff consisting of the Leadership *(Hauptleitung)* and executive committee *(Geschäftsführender Ausschuss).*' [4]

The semi-authoritarian constitution lent much support to this analysis. The presidents of the local and regional groups *(Ortsgruppen* and *Gauverbände),* together with co-opted members, formed the general praesidium *(Gesamtvorstand),* which elected the Leadership, consisting of up to six members, and the executive committee of thirty whose purpose was to help the Leadership.[5] In fact, Class's long tenure of office made him the virtual dictator of the League. In contrast with Hasse's equivocal attitude‡ Class was a strong anti-Semite. Hasse had been opposed to the exclusion of Jews, on the grounds that if they subscribed to

---

★ "For God's sake, let them come right in, or stay right out."
† The Pan-German League, the Agrarian League and the Commerical Employees' Union were all founded in the same year, at the height of the Right-wing reaction to Caprivi.
‡ See p. 192.

nationalist policies they should be welcomed. Qualifying its admiration for Schönerer, the League's journal had at that time pointed out:

> It is clear that neither in Germany nor in Austria can the League's program be represented by a political party, because a political party must adopt a number of policy aims on which the League, for very good reasons, refuses to commit itself, e.g. the Jewish Question, the Break-with-Rome movement, and others.[6]

While the Berlin branch was from the outset anti-Semitic,[7] extreme racialists were initially dissatisfied with the League's record.[8] From about 1907 onward, the *Alldeutsche Blätter* became markedly more anti-Semitic. Jewish association with any of the League's *bêtes noires* is more and more frequently discussed— Left-wing literati and journalists,[9] Social Democracy,[10] Slavism in the Habsburg Empire,[11] and even opposition to the Flemish cause in Belgium.[12]

However, it was under Class's presidency that the League became an instrument for extreme militarist and authoritarian agitation and pursued the policy outlined by Class in his pseudonymous book *Wenn ich der Kaiser wär ("If I were Emperor")*, published in 1912.

A war would, in his view, increase the chances of a military dictatorship[13] and assure the overthrow of the universal suffrage which he detested. "Self-assertion is the first duty of the state."[14] During the First World War the League was prominent in the agitation to dismiss Chancellor Bethmann-Hollweg, and Class was involved in Ludendorff's plot for a military *coup d'état*.[15]

Of the Jews he wrote:

> A recovery of the health of our popular life, in all its fields, cultural, moral and economic, and a maintenance of this regained health, are possible only if Jewish influence is either excluded completely or driven back to an extent that makes it safe and tolerable.[16]

Class confessed himself to be equally indebted to Lagarde, Gobineau, and Houston Stewart Chamberlain.[17] He was a friend of Böckel, and several anti-Semitic deputies were members of the League. So were Chamberlain and Schemann, the translator and popularizer of Gobineau, and Lagarde's widow.[18]

It was in its distinguished membership, which included politicians, highly placed officials, and university lecturers that the strength and influence of the League lay—hence also the difficulty of assessing the exact extent of its impact on affairs. Between 1894 and 1914 a total number of sixty Reichstag deputies belonged to it, fifteen anti-Semites, nine Conservatives, eight from the *Reichspartei,* and twenty-eight National Liberals.[19] The Centre, Social Democrats, and Progressives were unrepresented. The leaders of the National Liberal Party, Bassermann and Stresemann, belonged to the League; Conservative members included Count Kardorff,[20] founder and chairman of the German Industrialists' Federation. In general, however, there were few representatives of big business and heavy industry; in the individual membership the professions predominated.*

In 1905, 101 organizations had corporate membership, and through individual members the League had contacts with the *Flottenverein* (Navy League), *Wehrverein* (Army League), *Kolonialgesellschaft,* the Reich Association against Social Democracy, and the *Deutsche Arbeiterpartei* of Bohemia.[21] At the 1912 annual conference representatives from Nationalist student societies attended.[22] Speakers from Schönerer's pan-German movement regularly appeared, but the League did not agree with its irredentist program, appreciating, as Bismarck had done, that this would diminish rather than increase German influence in Southeast Europe.

During the first twenty years of its existence, the Pan-German League, like the German Right in general, was more interested in Imperialism than anti-Semitism. Some sections of it were actually opposed to it, others accepted it, without a great deal of noise, as an integral part of their political outlook. Neither side was prepared to insist on rigidity in a matter which was no longer a major issue of politics or conscience. But under the determined leadership of the extreme Class and the impact of defeat and revolution in 1918, the anti-Semitism inherent in all German Conservatism showed itself fully in the League.

If the Pan-German League was the largest organization of its kind, it was also the most moderate. At the other extreme, hardly concerned, it seems, with immediate political success and

* See p. 275.

dominated by the millenarian purity of its racial doctrine, was the *Deutschbund*. It was founded in 1894 by Friedrich Lange, editor of the *Deutsche Zeitung*. Its membership, recruited from readers of the newspaper, reached 800 by 1905.[23] (Heinrich Class was a founding member.)

Lange's anti-Semitism was uncompromising. According to the statutes:

> The Jew cannot belong to the *Deutschbund,* nor become eligible by baptism, because his circumcision harbours his nature. Rather, whoever belongs to the *Deutschbund* testifies to his enthusiasm by all legally permissible vigilance against Jews.[24]

Other nations, with well-defined areas of settlement and specific gifts to bestow on mankind, it is possible for Germans to respect.

> But the nation of the Jews is excluded from our respect, because it does not wish to live in any other way than in dispersal among other nations and the exploitation of their creative forces. We do not tolerate Jewish blood in our *Bund;* rather is it one of our duties by pure Germandom to beat off the deleterious influence of Judaism on us and our people. The long history of an unavailing struggle by German and other nations has, however, taught us that Judaism has entwined itself too strongly and too closely for us to separate ourselves from it by sound and fury. Therefore the command of wisdom against cunning is to wage a defensive battle with calm collectedness, quietly but thoroughly; for only then—if it is the will of providence—will the day dawn in the far distant future on which our people will once more be free from degeneration by Jewish blood and Jewish money.[25]

Lange was, however, prepared to acknowledge that however indispensable anti-Semitism might be "it can be only *one* element, and by *no means the most important,* of a much wider and higher-reaching *Weltanschauung* and policy."[26]

Like so many other Nationalist bodies, the *Bund* "unconditionally recognises, not only in practice, but formally, the authority of its leading men."[27] Membership was by secret election, with a three-month probation period, confirmed by a hand-clasp "to symbolize an oath of faith and enthusiasm."[28] The lodge-like structure and the mystery-mongering of the *Deutschbund* and Böckel's *Volksbund* gave them a strange similarity to the Freemasons, whom they affected so greatly to fear and to despise. But the closest approximation to a racialist freemasonry, and the most important of its kind, was the *Germanen- und Wälsungsorden* (the Order of Teutons and Volsungs), founded in 1912. Its activities were closely co-ordinated with Fritsch's *Hammerbund*, and office-holding in the two organizations tended to overlap. The Order's journal *Runen* was decorated with the swastika,[29]

Similar organizations, springing up almost every year, need be no more than mentioned. The *Urda-Bund* of Munich aimed to base racial consciousness on the study of the Eddas.[30] There was the *Germanischer Volksbund* of 1897, which later amalgamated with Böckel's *Volksbund*[31] and in turn became the *Kulturbund für Politik*. It was led by Gustav Simons, a retired artillery captain and veteran of Henrici's *Sozialer Reichsverein*,[32] who had developed a new type of wholemeal loaf, hailed by Lanz von Liebenfels as "bread fit for heroes."[33] Then there was the *Deutschvölkische Vereinigung* of Stuttgart (1902) which aimed at "pure Germandom in manners and morals, in faith, art and law, in letters and language. . . . Awakening of the sentiment of interdependence and community (*Zusammengehörigkeit und Gemeinbürgschaft*) of all Germans."

> For the fulfilment of these tasks the combating and removal of every foreign influence, especially the Jewish and Roman, is indispensable in all areas of public life.[34]

Jewish and Roman: it follows that the Catholic Church had to be disinterred as the traditional enemy of the German nation. This revived *Kulturkampf* was due partly to the Church's identification with an intensified Polish national movement, partly to the role of the Centre in exposing the colonial scandals, and as the Social Democrats' allies in the 1907 elections. The main motive, however, was the allegedly anti-German and pro-Slav policy of the Church and dynasty in the Habsburg Empire. Anti-Catholicism thus became a necessary ingredient of pan-Germanism; and, as was usual in joint Austrian-German enterprises, the main impulse to radicalism came from Austria.

The oldest of the militantly anti-Catholic organizations, the *Gustav Adolf-Verein*, founded in 1844, was not originally pan-German in outlook. It proclaimed its field of activity to be "the diaspora of evangelical Christians who find themselves in a minority among those of other beliefs, in particular Roman Catholics,"[35] though Protestant enclaves in eastern and southern

Europe, the main beneficiaries, tended to be predominantly German and the emotional links with German Protestants were obviously closer. However, even in the Habsburg Empire, Czech as well as German Protestants were given subsidies until well toward the end of the century.[36]

A more specifically nationalist organization was the *Evangelischer Bund*; within it individual members like Professor Witte and Pastor Bräunlich (secretary after 1904) initiated a campaign to come to the aid of German-speaking Protestants and to associate the *Bund* with the *Los-von-Rom* movement and thus with Schönerer.[37] A special *Ausschuss zur Förderung der evan- gelischen Kirche in Österreich* was created.[38] Faced with this pressure from an organization with which its links were in any case close,[39] the *Gustav Adolf-Verein* also became more specifically pan-German. In 1899 it voted a grant of 6100 marks for the Austrian *Los-von-Rom* movement "since in the great conflict of nationalities the Roman Church has placed itself on the side of Slavdom."[40]

Lay organizations in Germany for the support of Austrian pan-Germanism, like the *Verein der Deutschvölkischen in Bayern*, were little more than branches of the Schönerer movement and resembled it in their open anti-Semitism as well as their anti-Romanism. The opening meeting of the *Verein der Deutschvölkischen* was addressed by Karl Wolf[41] and other Austrian anti-Semitic deputies were speakers at meetings and contributors to publications of pan-German bodies in Germany.[42]

An important link between these bodies with their varying degrees of explicit anti-Semitism was the publishing house of Lehmann in Munich, who were publishers to the Pan-German League, the *Evangelischer Bund*, and the *Verein der Deutschvölkischen* as well as for individual anti-Semitic and nationalist works.

Except in the most extreme of these organizations, explicit anti-Semitism was not a part of the program, though it is obvious that the ethnocentrism, the attacks on internationalism, and on human equality or universal morality were inconsistent with a tolerant attitude toward Jews. A significant indication of how inadequate anti-Semitism had by this time become as an independent motive force is the extent to which openly anti-Semitic parties had to base their appeal more and more on general nationalism. The DSRP at its 1899 congress declared its devotion to *"Alldeutschland von der Königsau bis zur Adria;"*[43] after 1901

227

Professor Ruhland, the pan-German ideologue, became political adviser to the Agrarian League.[44] On the international and colonial issues which increasingly dominated German politics after 1900, anti-Semites generally took an extremely chauvinistic line.[45] Often anti-Semitism was simply presented as the logical concomitant of patriotism:

> The rejection of all Jewish influence presents itself as the complement of the conscious cultivation of German national ways.[46]

It thus suggested a mere continuation of the work of unification.

In this respect the space devoted to the several enemies of German national interests in typically nationalist journals is significant. The *Akademische Turnzeitung* carried, between 1904 and 1906, twelve anti-Polish, one anti-Czech, and one anti-Magyar articles, as well as four objective articles on Zionism; Volume XXIV of *Burschen Heraus!* [1911-12] two anti-Czech, two anti-Polish, one anti-British, one anti-French, and one anti-Italian. Neither contained any anti-Semitic material; yet they were organs of bodies which refused to admit Jews. *Burschenschaftliche Blätter* between 1910 and 1912 contained one anti-Semitic article[47] as against two anti-Czech and four directed against internationalism and Marxist Socialism. Hugo Böttger, its editor, was elected National Liberal deputy in 1912.

REFERENCES

1 *Preussiche Jahrbücher*, Vol. XLIV (1879), p. 573.
2 Lagarde, "Über die gegenwärtigen Aufgaben der deutschen Politik," *Schriften*, Vol. I, p. 42.
3 Lagarde, "Juden und Indogermanen." *Mitteilungen*, Vol. II, p. 346.
4 H. Class, *Wider den Strom. Vom Wachsen und Werden der nationalen Opposition im alten Reich* (Leipzig, 1932), p. 131.
5 A. Kruck, *Geschichte des Alldeutschen Verbandes, 1890–1939* (Wiesbaden, 1954), pp. 13–4.
6 *ADB*, Sept. 7, 1901, p. 411.
7 M. S. Wertheimer, *The Pan-German League, 1890–1914* (New York, 1924), p. 39.
8 *MVA*, July 30, 1898, p. 245.
9 *ADB*, May 25, 1907; Dec. 7, 1918, pp. 392–3.
10 *ADB*, July 1, 1911, p. 219.
11 *ADB*, Nov. 2, 1907, p. 376; March 30, 1912, p. 109; Nov. 2, 1912, pp. 389–91.

12 *ADB*, May 25, 1912, p. 182.
13 Frymann, *Wenn ich der Kaiser wär*, p. 65.
14 *Ibid.*, pp. 40, 55.
15 Kruck, *op. cit.*, pp. 102–4.
16 Frymann, *op. cit.*, p. 74.
17 Class, *Wider den Strom*, p. 87.
18 Kruck, *op. cit.*, pp. 19, 130–1; O. Bonhard, *Geschichte des Alldeutschen Verbandes* (Leipzig–Berlin, 1920), p. 46.
19 Wertheimer, *op. cit.*, pp. 134–5.
20 Kruck, *op. cit.*, p. 19.
21 *Ibid.*
22 Wertheimer, *op. cit.*, p. 62.
23 Broszat, *Die antisemitische Bewegung*, p. 145.
24 Schultheiss, *Deutschnationales Vereinswesen*, p. 72.
25 F. Lange, *Reines Deutschtum* (5th ed., Berlin, 1904), p. 353.
26 *Ibid.*, p. 109.
27 *Ibid.*, p. 352.
28 Schultheiss, *op. cit.*, pp. 72–3.
29 Phelps, "Before Hitler Came," *Journal of Modern History*, Vol. XXXV, No. 3, pp. 248–50.
30 Buch, *50 Jahre antisemitische Bewegung*, p. 27.
31 Geiser, *Deutsches Reich und Volk*, p. 181.
32 Buch, *op. cit.*, pp. 24, 27.
33 Daim, *Der Mann, der Hitler die Ideen gab*, p. 121.
34 *PAR*, Vol. II, No. 9 (1903), p. 759.
35 H. F. von Criegern, *Geschichte des Gustav Adolf-Vereins* (Hamburg, 1903), p. 209.
36 Schultheiss, *op. cit.*, p. 12.
37 P. Bräunlich, *Was die Los-von-Rom-Bewegung in Böhmen erlitt und erkämpfte, Berichte über den Fortgang der Los-von-Rom-Bewegung, 2. Reihe, Heft 8* (Munich, 1906), pp. 30–1.
38 *Ibid.*, p. 34.
39 Criegern, *op. cit.*, p. 147.
40 *Ibid.*, p. 156.
41 *Odin. Ein Kampfblatt für die alldeutsche Bewegung* (Munich), Nov. 4, 1899.
42 Türk and Hofmann von Wellenhof wrote pamphlets for the Pan-German League's series, *Der Kampf um das Deutschtum* and Türk for Böckel's *Deutsche Volksbibliothek*. He also paid frequent oratorical visits to Germany. Broszat, *op. cit.*, p. 122.
43 *Ibid.*, p. 127.
44 *Ibid.*, p. 108.
45 *Ibid.*, pp. 127–30.
46 Schultheiss, *op. cit.*, p. 6.
47 *Burschenschaftliche Blätter*, Oct. 15, 1911.

25

New Ideologies for Old Causes

Most of the pan-German propagandists took the truth of racial theories for granted. Others were more concerned with substantiating them. Gobineau's neglected work was reissued, and a German version appeared in 1898. The translator, Ludwig Schemann, who had come under the spell of Lagarde while a librarian at Göttingen University,[1] had four years earlier founded a *Gobineau-Vereinigung*. Houston Stewart Chamberlain's *Die Grundlagen des 20. Jahrhunderts* was published in 1899. A more immediately influential school of thought was that of the "political anthropologists" whose main organ, from 1902 onward, was the *Politisch-Anthropologische Revue,* edited by Woltmann and Buhmann. This journal, besides publishing a great deal of new and even pioneering sociological and penological material, was also devoted to questions of racial vitality and degeneration, and to proving the virtues of racial purity and Germanic superiority. It was not explicitly anti-Semitic, but its other assumptions were, in the climate of opinion of the time, easily open to anti-Semitic interpretations.

The *Revue's* arguments were elaborated in Woltmann's major work, *Politische Anthropologie*. The premise is that human races and human society must be discussed in the light of Darwinism. Unlike fully blown racial anti-Semites he does not deny the Jews' right to respect and human consideration; with complete consistency he is pro-Zionist. But "the Jewish question is an anthropological question" and there must be no intermarriage with Jews whose race "is in a state of physical decline.'[2] Faced with the problem of Jewish intellectual prowess, and the contributions made by non-Germans in art and thought, his answer is simple. Intellectually gifted Jews must have Amorite blood;[3] the giants of the Renaissance and of the Enlightenment

—Leonardo da Vinci, Galileo, Canova, Voltaire—are of Lombard or Frankish descent.[4] Napoleon was of Vandal origin.[5] The civilizations of the Middle East and Southern Europe

> are entirely the work of Nordic tribes. Indians, Persians, Greeks, Romans were originally the genuine sons of the fair, light race.[6]
>
> The whole of European civilisation, even in the Slav and Latin countries, [is] an achievement of the Germanic race. Franks, Normans and Burgundians in France, Visigoths in Spain, Ostrogoths, Lombards and Bajuvari in Italy, planted the anthropological seeds of the mediaeval and modern culture of these states. The Papacy, the Renaissance, the French Revolution and Napoleon's world domination were great deeds of the Germanic spirit.[7]

More important, however, are the implications of these doctrines for internal political and social policy. Here it is best to consider Woltmann together with his contemporary, Otto Ammon, and other pan-Germans already mentioned. In doing so, we shall find, in the main, new arguments for familiar policies—opposition to the Liberal tenets of internationalism, human equality, or even the rights and duties derived from citizenship; in their place, the claims of national and social differentiation, political authority, and racial consciousness.

Lange categorically states that "Nationality is not the same as *Volkstum*"[8] and the basis of all pan-German movements was that Germans who were citizens of other states had a prior loyalty to their people. Within Germany, too, equality was denied. Since "the development of social and political forms is a biological process,"[9] society needs a differentiation in the conditions of development "not only according to vocation and ability, but according to sex, race and class."[10] Ammon, the more extreme of the two, even opposed a policy of generous university scholarships, on the grounds that this would merely serve to import the proletarian mentality into the ruling class.[11]

Increasingly the argument of race was invoked to defend a class. Gobineau had already shown how to do this, but for him it was aristocracy and Aryanism which went together. The popular appeal of such an argument was clearly limited and the new racialists harnessed Aryanism to the defense of the third estate, the *Mittelstand*. Woltmann complained that because of backward conditions in the countryside, all elements capable of culture are driven to emigrate into the cities or abroad. The emigrants are in the first place Germanic elements. They are replaced by more easily satisfied Slav workers, a fifth estate, on whom the German language is imposed by an ill-advised policy and who are thus captured for a spurious Germandom.[12]

Economic aid was therefore necessary to peasants "especially in those regions . . . where the purely Germanic race has been preserved."[13] Ludwig Kuhlenbeck, Professor of Law at Kiel, told the Pan-German League that the *Mittelstand* was

> the veritable reservoir of racial worth, from which the great men of the nation, . . . who form the true embodiment of the collective power of the race, have emerged almost without exception.[14]

Like Woltmann, he deplored the fact that industrialization led to the migration of dolichocephalic types to the towns, and to "the freedom of movement accorded to workers which one-sidedly benefits capitalist-industrialist interests and imposes on us predominantly Slav, brachycephalic elements."[15] Lange similarly sees in peasants and artisans "the most deeply-rooted genuine representatives of our nationhood."[16] Paul Förster, launching his appeal in 1904 for a *"völkisch* general staff" saw as its ideal "a nation consisting, as it were, entirely of *Mittelstand";*[17] and both Class and Fritsch speak in very similar terms.[18]

It follows that democracy, and *a fortiori* Social Democracy, infected not only with egalitarianism but also with *morbus internationalitatis,*[19] were unacceptable:

> For us Germans, wedged between hostile nations, universal suffrage becomes, through Social Democracy, a great national peril.[20]

The answer is Social Aristocracy:

> For a German Social Aristocracy there is only one commanding principle, and this is, *"Deutschland, Deutschland, über Alles!"*[21]

Lange's anti-Socialism led him to found the *Reichwahlverband* out of which grew, in 1904, the *Reichsverband zur Bekämpfung der Sozialdemokratie,*[22] and the anti-Semitic deputy Ferdinand Werner was instrumental in 1908 in founding the *Deutscher*

Jugendbund, the purpose of which was also to combat Social Democracy.[23]

Sometimes the Christian religion, not merely Catholicism, was castigated for the same sins as Socialism:

> In the eyes of Christianity there is no *Volk,* caste or national character, only humanity. . . . These forces must, under all circumstances, be preserved not only against Social Democracy but against its Christian allies.[24]
>
> Is war evil? . . . In the light of this question we have clear proof that the Christian commandment contradicts the natural sentiment of our people.[25]

Even more influential, because it secured a mass readership, and in a very different vein, was Langbehn's work. While the pan-Germans, the Imperialists, and the political anthropologists based their aggressiveness on self-confidence and muscle flexing, Langbehn's was rooted in despair. He was a Conservative; but far from wishing to take on the world, he wanted Germany to turn back on herself. Like almost all romantic Conservatives he thought in terms of the folk, not the state. Even to call him conservative is in one sense misleading. Although his political influence was profound and lasting, he was not himself interested in politics, and certainly very ignorant of it. The most one can say is that he hoped to achieve nonpolitical ends by political means.

August Julius Langbehn was born in 1851 in Schleswig-Holstein, where his father was a schoolmaster. On his mother's side of the family there was a history of mental disturbance, and his mother was confined to an asylum for some time.[26] He began studying chemistry but he was drawn to the history of art and archaeology. He was moody, impulsive, and egocentric; he quarreled with, and insulted, most of his friends and well-wishers. His relationships with Lagarde and Nietzsche were as unsatisfactory as those with the less eminent. In 1890 he published anonymously, and at the uneconomic price of two marks, his prophetic tract, *Rembrandt als Erzieher.* None of his later publications, which included essays and some highly erotic poems had the same impact. He entered the Catholic Church in 1900, having already left the Lutheran Church in the 1880's. He died in 1907 of cancer of the stomach.

Rembrandt als Erzieher was an instantaneous and lasting success. By 1945, over 150,000 copies had been sold.[27] Langbehn said what had been said before, but said it with a new ferocity; he was listened to, as Lagarde or Nietzsche had not been, because the *malaise* of which he was an example, the doubts and apprehensions about German culture and German society, were now widespread. He was a herald in Germany of that international intellectual revolution which took place in the last decade of the nineteenth century, the revolt against positivism.[28] The re-evaluations on which that generation embarked took many forms, but they all had in common the re-instatement of unreason, if not as a guide to be followed, at least as a phenomenon to be sympathetically studied.

Langbehn despised the "false objectivity" of the natural sciences, the musty academicism of German education, the materialism and corruption of the big cities, and the formal egalitarianism of the law which ignored all other human relationships.

> The final end of false science is to establish facts, the final end of true science is to deliver value judgments. . . . The activity of most modern scholars is of the first kind. . . . Their "objectivity" which treats all matters as equally valid is as untruthful as that modern "humanitarianism" which treats all men as equal.[29]
>
> The professor is the German national disease. Today's education of German youth is a kind of massacre of the innocents . . . . Nowadays you can see German children carrying whole libraries under their arms on their way to school.[30]
>
> The teacher ought to be an artist and is a manufacturer.[31]
>
> The crude cult of money is a North American, and at the same time Jewish, trait, which dominates Berlin more and more. . . . Spiritually and politically the provinces should be mobilised and ordered to march against the capital.[32]
>
> Equality is death, hierarchy is life.[33]

These evils of modernity could be abolished by a revival of art, instinct, and innocence. The great antinomy to the narrow specialization of the schools and universities, to the vulgar monumentality of official art, and to the meticulous naturalism of the younger generation was Rembrandt. His art was anti-classical, filled with mystery and religious feeling, spontaneous, unconventional, faithful to the contradictions of human experience. He was "the most German of German artists"; his "influence . . . on the art of the German people is unthinkable without its simultaneous influence on the moral and intellectual life of the whole nation."[34]

Rembrandt as a German? Yes, because he belonged to that tribe in which the Germanic virtues of simple faith and artistic vitality were best represented and preserved, the *Niederdeutsche* of the Northwest, tall, blond, strong, and blue eyed, of whom Langbehn, too, was one. It was there that the true, lasting basis of political and cultural regeneration, *Volkstum,* was still to be found; it was there that the class which was its most reliable repository, the peasantry, had survived. With *Volkstum,* the original, unsophisticated culture of a people, we are back at that favorite myth of the romanic anti-Liberal—noble savagery. "Whoever wants to raise German art, will first have to raise German *Volkstum* . . . the new German art will have to base itself on the peasantry, the best and simplest expression of the *Volkstum.*"[35]

This notion of the simple, static *Volk* was not merely the antithesis of modern politics, which Langbehn neither understood nor sympathized with, but of all politics. In the society that the primitivists envisage there will be no conflict, because there will be no desire for change. It follows that Langbehn's politics for the unsophisticated are authoritarian and hierarchic. Germany's savior will be an unspecified *Führer,* a "Caesaristic-artistic . . . individual," the "secret Emperor [36] who recurs in so much Germanic mythology. The people he will lead will be dominated by "a social aristocracy based on historical and traditional relations and hence at one with the healthy elements of the lower classes."* Thus all the evil effects of the French Revolution would be finally counteracted.

Anti-Semitism was an inescapable corollary of this social and political philosophy; what is interesting is that it took him some time to discover this. Initially he has little to say on the subject, and he was indeed full of praise for the pious, orthodox Jews whom Rembrandt had known and painted so well.[37] But

---

* *Rembrandt,* p. 158. This will have the further merit of being the only lasting and effective antidote to Social Democracy. "The corporative principle which is now gradually returning to favour in Germany . . . is *the* aristocratic principle. . . . All Germany is replete with latent social aristocracy."

Langbehn could have no sympathy for the secular *Reformjude,* any more than he had for the liberal Protestant or the modernist Catholic. Moreover, the Jew in Wilhelmine society was not only a symbol of all the forces and attitudes which Langbehn detested; he had helped to make things so. Very quickly an ever more strident, almost racialist anti-Semitism was introduced as the book went through its various printings. The thirty-seventh edition of 1891 contained two whole new anti-Semitic chapters:

> The modern, plebeian Jews are a poison for us and will have to be treated as such. . . . They are democratically inclined, they have an affinity with the mob; everywhere they sympathise with decay.[38]

The "'Secret Emperor' will have to intervene actively in . . . the Jewish Question; he will have to point his sceptre and separate the sheep from the goats."[39] The forty-ninth edition was more vitriolic still.[40] By 1892 he was listing his enemies as "Jews and idiots, Jews and scoundrels, Jews and whores, Jews and professors, Jews and Berliners."[41] He had, by then, passed into the final, bacteriological phase of all anti-Semitism: "For us, the Jews are only a passing pest and a cholera."[42]

It was to youth that Langbehn made his greatest appeal. Much of what he attacked was undoubtedly worth attacking, such as the bookishness of German education, the ugliness of her industrial towns, the disaffection of the working class, the aimlessness of her policies, and the impotence of the party leaders. In this he was in the tradition of Lagarde. Indeed, the first, anonymous edition of his book was widely attributed to Lagarde. But his style was more lyrical, his scholarship was lighter. No single writer had a greater influence on that most extraordinary of neo-Romantic outbursts, the German Youth Movement, in which the schoolboys and students of the most urbanized nation on the European continent sought to rediscover a rural, small-town past.

What connection is there between the cultural primitivism, the withdrawal, and the deliberate innocence of Langbehn, and the brassiness of the *Weltpolitik* ideologues? No doubt it was an exaggeration for one contemporary to see the anti-Semitic gains in the 1893 elections as the translation of the Rembrandt book "into the will of the people, expressed in parliamentary language."[43] But it must be remembered that the Agrarian League, the pan-Germans, and the Commercial Employees' Union were as keen as Langbehn on *Volkstum* and racial purity in their "internal imperialism," and as opposed as he was to parliamentary politics, high finance, and intellectualism. And in his exaltation of all things German (on his own, highly imaginary, terms) he very much fitted the mood of the Imperialists. He corresponded with Fritsch,[44] was praised by Lange,[45] and declared that "*Rembrandt als Erzieher* is a pan-German book."[46] Expansion, and the gospel of world mission, would strengthen the ties of the folk community. As an addition to anti-Semitic literature, Langbehn's book was of secondary importance. Its real significance lay in its suggestion that anti-Semitism was consistent with, and logically derived from, the intolerant causes that were winning public enthusiasm.

The most interesting development in anti-Semitic thought after the turn of the century was a shift to the South in its center of gravity. Before 1900 the only major contribution from South of the Main had been Vogelsang's, and he was North German in origin. Both anti-modernist conservatism and imperialist chauvinism fitted fairly comfortably into the structure of the Second Empire. The Germany of Bismarck and William II had enough of the features of a conventional nation-state to satisfy anyone reared in the traditions of Prussian statehood. To be sure, pan-Germanism and *völkisch* ideas had their followers all over Germany; but extreme racialism, in its full-blooded chiliastic decadence, had a more congenial home in Bavaria and Austria, where the political pointlessness of Wittelsbach and Habsburg rule pervaded the intellectual atmosphere. For the seminal ideas of the post-war period we must therefore look to Vienna and Munich.*

This is true, for instance, in the elaboration of "Aryan" symbolism. The swastika was revived by the poet Alfred Schuler in Munich in the 1890's, and Lanz von Liebenfels hoisted a swastika flag over his Austrian castle, Burg Werfenstein, in 1907.[47] In Schuler's poem, *Epilogus Jahwe-Moloch,* the swastika makes its first appearance as the instrument of genocide.[48] Guido von List, Liebenfels' Viennese contemporary, discovered secret

---

* See p. 330.

race messages in the ancient Germanic runes and the *Kabalah* (wrongly thought to be Jewish).[49] The wildest fantasies of all, about the origins of the world and the human race, and the role of women and monkeys in degenerating it, appeared in Liebenfels' journal *Ostara*. This, "in an age which carefully cultivates all that is female and of inferior race and ruthlessly exterminates blond, heroic mankind," devoted itself to "actually applying the discoveries of racial science in order to combat socialist and feminist subversion."[50] His solution of the Jewish question was of the simplest: "We would never dream of preaching pogroms, because they will come without encouragement."[51] The racial struggle must be carried on "as far as the castration-knife."[52]★

The coteries and societies over which these men presided were deeply immersed in spiritualism, astrology, and many other kinds of occultism; Dühring or Chamberlain were, by contrast, almost exemplars of Victorian positivism.

REFERENCES

1 L. Schemann, *Paul de Lagarde, Ein Lebens- und Erinnerungsbild* (Leipzig, 1919), pp. 369–85.
2 L. Woltmann, *Politische Anthropologie* (Eisenach–Leipzig, 1903), p. 309.
3 *Ibid.*, pp. 288–9.
4 *Ibid.*, p. 255.
5 *Ibid.*, p. 294.
6 *Ibid.*, p. 289.
7 *Ibid.*, p. 293.
8 Lange, *Reines Deutschtum*, p. 19.
9 Woltmann, *op. cit.*, p. 245.
10 *Ibid.*, p. 321.
11 O. Ammon, *Die Gesellschaftsordnung und ihre natürlichen Grundlagen* (Jena, 1895), p. 82.
12 Woltmann, *op. cit.*, p. 307.
13 *Ibid.*, p. 325.
14 L. Kuhlenbeck, *Rasse und Volkstum* (Munich, 1905), pp. 24–5.
15 *Ibid.*, pp. 16–7.
16 F. Lange, *Deutsche Politik* (Berlin, 1894), p. 16.
17 Phelps, "Theodor Fritsch und der Antisemitismus," *Deutsche Rundschau*,

★ It has been suggested that Lanz von Liebenfels, whose writings coincided with Hitler's Vienna period, particularly influenced him. But there is no direct evidence that this ingredient was more important than any other in the porridge of Hitler's *Weltanschauung*.

Vol. LXXXVII, No. 5 (1961), p. 445.

18 Frymann, *Wenn ich der Kaiser wär*, pp. 63, 95–7; Fritsch, "Mittelstandspolitik" (1905), in *Neue Wege*, p. 163.

19 Lange, *op. cit.*, p. 7.

20 Ammon, *op. cit.*, p. 279.

21 *Ibid.*, p. 284.

22 Geiser, *Deutsches Reich und Volk*, p. 182.

23 Curtius, *Der politische Antisemitismus*, p. 116.

24 Lange, *Reines Deutschtum*, p. 358.

25 *Ibid.*, p. 135.

26 Stern, *The Politics of Cultural Despair*, p. 100.

27 *Ibid.*, p. 155.

28 See in particular Hughes, *Consciousness and Society*, p. 33 and ch. 2, *passim*; J. Barzun, *Darwin, Marx, Wagner. Critique of a Heritage* (London, 1942), pp. 110–37, and ch. 5, *passim*.

29 A. J. Langbehn, *Rembrandt als Erzieher* (38th ed., Leipzig, 1891), p. 70.

30 *Ibid.*, pp. 101, 311–12.

31 *Ibid.*, p. 312.

32 *Ibid.*, pp. 320, 138.

33 *Ibid.*, p. 157.

34 *Ibid.*, p. 38.

35 *Ibid.*, p. 125.

36 *Ibid.*, pp. 276, 281–5.

37 *Ibid.*, p. 43.

38 *Ibid.*, p. 292.

39 *Ibid.*, p. 293.

40 Stern, *op. cit.*, p. 142.

41 Anon. (i.e., A. J. Langbehn), *Der Rembrandtdeutsche. Von einem Wahrheitsfreund* (Dresden, 1892), p. 192.

42 *Ibid.*, p. 184.

43 B. M. Nissen, *Der Rembrandtdeutsche, Julius Langbehn* (Freiburg, 1926), p. 125.

44 Stern, *op. cit.*, p. 168.

45 Lange, *Reines Deutschtum*, pp. 39 40.

46 Nissen, *Der Rembrandtdeutsche*, p. 64.

47 Daim, *Der Mann, der Hitler die Ideen gab*, pp. 71–2.

48 A. Schuler, *Fragmente und Vorträge aus dem Nachlass* (ed. L. Klages), (Leipzig, 1940), p. 151.

49 G. von List, *Das Geheimnis der Runen* (Leipzig, 1908), *Die Ursprache der Ario-Germanen und ihre Mysteriensprache* (Leipzig, 1913). See G. L. Mosse, "The Mystical Origins of National Socialism," *Journal of the History of Ideas*, Vol. XXII, No. 1 (1961), p. 86.

50 *Ostara*, Nos. 72, 18. Quoted in Daim, *op. cit.*, pp. 114, 146.

51 *Ostara*, new series, No. 3. Quoted in *ibid.*, p. 156.

52 *Ostara*, new series, No. 9. Quoted in *ibid.*, p. 158.

26

The Intellectual Prestige of
Anti-Semitism

The cloak of academic respectability which was being thrown
over anti-Semitism helped to secure its growing acceptance
among *bien-pensants*. This was due, at least in part, to the
conscious effort on its behalf by recognized scholars. The earliest,
Rohling and Dühring, were altogether too extreme and dotty to
be in the main stream of academic anti-Semitism. (Not that high
standards of learning are necessary in order to succeed as an
anti-Semitic prophet; but the mountebank has had an easier time
in the twentieth century than the nineteenth.)

Far outweighing either of these in his standing as a public
figure and the adulation which he inspired as a teacher was
Heinrich von Treitschke, historian and political theorist. The
evolution of his thought, from Saxon Liberal to the high priest
of Prussianism, excellently illustrates the tragic cleavage which
entered between the German Liberal and national traditions after
1866 and which was to be observed nowhere more fully than in
German university life.★

The universities have always played a more important part in
politics on the European continent than in Anglo-Saxon countries, and more in Germany than in most European countries.

★ The historian Droysen provides a good example. "I have sent my friends an
election manifesto," he wrote to Treitschke (March 3, 1867), "which will have
thoroughly disappointed them if they believed that at the congress I was going
to side with the liberal opposition which, *ad vocem* the foundation of a German
power, wants to add a few loads of fundamental rights and other freedoms; I
am truly liberal at heart, but this German prodigality with liberties, side by side
with the most blameworthy political impotence, nauseates me" (Wucher,
Theodor Mommsen, p. 179).

Before the middle of the century, under a system of more or less general absolutism, and in the absence of any opinion-forming classes in society, it was inevitable that young men coming face to face with stimulating ideas and speculations should seize the leadership of such public opinion as there was.

Even later in the century, the fact that a university education was a condition of entry into any of the multifarious government services, whose tradition of bureaucratic omnipotence still gave them considerable influence under constitutional systems and the exaggerated respect with which the *Herr Doktor* is treated in Central Europe, gave student politics an importance quite unlike anything in Britain. The student of today was the teacher, official or country doctor of tomorrow, and student opinion of one decade could easily become the national opinion of the next.

Throughout the nineteenth century student opinion in Austria was predominantly nationalist; nationalist and Liberal before 1848, nationalist and illiberal after 1867. Student anti-Semitism, stronger in Austria than in Germany, was predominantly nationalist; indeed it vied with anti-clericalism for the dominant place in the students' political passions. Clericalism, especially in Austria, was associated with censorship, absolutism, and the Karlsbad decrees; the dominant mood of the universities was *freiheitlich*. Second, and this again applies mainly to Austria, the graduate, faced always with the dangers of sinking into an intellectual proletariat, especially in education-hungry countries where there tended to be an overproduction of graduates, was aware of Slav, Italian, and Rumanian competition, and of the desire of the minority nations to gain a share in the bureaucracy and the professions where there had hitherto been a German monopoly. When there were student riots at Prague, Graz, or Innsbruck, they were directed more often than not at Slav or Italian students, or Catholic students who tended to support non-German claims, rather than at Jews. Anti-Semitism was common enough at Prague and Graz, but only in Vienna did it have a clear lead.

Third, racialism had a greater intellectual appeal. It was a "theory,' which conservative, social anti-Semitism was not; and the more extreme it was, the more impressive the pseudo-intellectual apparatus with which it could be rationalized.

It was during the crucial decades of the 1870's and 1880's,

when the decisive shift in student sentiment was taking place, that Treitschke was at the height of his reputation and power, and that to attend his lectures at Berlin was an eagerly fought-for privilege. In 1879 and 1880 appeared the celebrated series of articles by him in *Preussische Jahrbücher,*[1] of which he was editor. In phrases which were perhaps among the most widely quoted in anti-Semitic politics he wrote:

> Year after year there pours over our Eastern frontier . . . from the inexhaustible Polish cradle, a host of ambitious, trouser-selling youths, whose children and children's children are one day to dominate Germany's stock exchanges and newspapers. . . . Right into the most educated circles, among men who would reject with disgust any thought of ecclesiastical intolerance or national pride, we can hear, as if from one mouth, 'The Jews are our misfortune.'[2]

Two months later, he returned to the attack with arguments which were all the more effective for their familiarity and unoriginality:

> Our indifference and clumsiness could learn much from the economic virtues of the Jewish race. Instead, we have been only too receptive to the weaknesses and diseases of Jewish life. Our cosmopolitanism met the Jewish half way, our censorious spirit delighted in the inflammatory speeches of the Jewish scandal press.
>
> A nation with firm national pride would never have tolerated the slanders of Börne's *epigoni;* a nation well impregnated with morality would have defended its language more strongly from the coarse incursions of Jewish humorous papers. Above all, however, the unhappy confusion of our Church life, the materialism and love of mockery of so many Christians have cultivated Jewish arrogance.
>
> In the frivolous, unbelieving circles of Jewry it is firmly held that the great majority of educated Germans have long ago broken with Christianity. The time will come, and is perhaps not so far off, when necessity will teach us once more to pray. . . . The German Jewish Question will not come to rest . . . before our Hebrew fellow-citizens have become convinced, by our attitude, that we are a Christian people and want to remain one.[3]

Treitschke later denied that he was an anti-Semitic propagandist and even agreed to contribute to Schrattenholz' *Antisemiten-Hammer* (an anthology with the aim of refuting anti-Semitism).[4] Yet there is no doubt that his example gave moral encouragement to Stöcker's agitation and to the anti-Semitic petition then circulating among students.[5] Heinrich Class claims that it was Treitschke who converted him to anti-Semitism.[6] Though his excursuses brought him embarrassing demonstrations of loyalty from his students,[7] they involved him in much public controversy, particularly with Theodor Mommsen. The two men exchanged open letters[8] and Mommsen published in reply to Treitschke's articles his pamphlet *Auch ein Wort über unser Judentum*.[9] A number of Germany's most eminent public figures, including Mommsen, Droysen, Virchow, and Siemens were moved to issue a declaration* (the "Declaration of the Notables" as it came to be known), condemning those who:

> are undermining the legacy of Lessing, men who should be proclaiming from pulpits and lecturers' desks that our culture has overcome the isolation of that race which once gave to the world the worship of the one God.

But from one lecturer's desk German youth heard annually:

> Whenever he finds his life sullied by the filth of Judaism, the German must turn from it and learn to speak the truth boldly about it. The party of compromise must bear the blame for any unsavoury wave of anti-Semitism which may arise.[10]

Only a very small section of Treitschke's work is devoted to the Jews, and memories of his occasional utterance on the Jewish question are not likely to have been among the profoundest impressions carried away by his hearers. His main services to anti-Semitism were indirect: he helped very materially to spread the type of coarse, brassy, aggressive national pride which, in the German context, was part of the emotional complex with which anti-Semitism was associated.

Second in importance to Treitschke was Lagarde. In his critique of German education and culture he was admired by a great many sensitive men, such as Ernst Troeltsch, Hermann Bahr, Thomas Mann, and Thomas Masaryk, whatever reservations they might have had about some of his other tenets.[11] But as a prophet of anti-Semitic nationalism he was embraced by all the leaders of that school—Fritsch and Förster, Bartels and

* Appendix I.

Lange. Like Treitschke, he was a patron saint of the *Verein deutscher Studenten.*[12]

It was among students that, as an accompaniment to the newer, illiberal nationalism, anti-Semitism was making the greatest headway. In general, this was a new departure for them. There is little evidence of it in the earlier "heroic" period of their history. Jewish participation in the Wars of Liberation, in 1813 and 1814, had rendered opinion comparatively favorable to them. In the constitution of the Jena *Burschenschaft,* generally considered to be the earliest of these bodies, there is no mention of the Jewish question, although Jews had been admitted to the university since 1790.[13] The Heidelberg *Burschenschaft* of 1817 expressly opened membership to all students, irrespective of denomination.[14]

After the Wartburg Festival (1817) a more strongly exclusive nationalist note crept in; the *Burschenschaft* conference at Jena in 1818 discussed the resolution that

> to become a member, it is necessary to be an honest German *Bursche* and a Christian . . . but "German" means anyone who, through the German language, belongs to the German people, irrespective of whether his race has brought him the misfortune of foreign rule.*

The conference, in fact, left decisions on these matters to the individual *Burschenschaft* and the regulations at Berlin were probably typical:

> Foreigners as well as Jews can be accepted, provided it is made clear to them that the whole life of the *Burschenschaft* is Christian-German."[15]

After 1819, when the *Burschenschaften* were banned by Metternich, the position became less clear. Although the secret conference at Dresden in 1820 decided to exclude Jews,[16] this cannot have been rigorously enforced. Records show that Heine was a member of the *Burschenschaften* at Bonn and Göttingen, Stahl at Würzburg, Lassalle at Breslau, and Ludwig Bamberger at Heidelberg.[17]

---

* Scheuer, *op. cit.,* pp. 15–6. This was intended also for the benefit of members of the Czech and Polish educated classes, who were at that time assimilating themselves to German culture.

There was thus a tradition of general nationalism, but virtually none of specifically anti-Jewish sentiment, at German universities when anti-Semitism became a political force in the 1870's. In Germany there were few signs of student anti-Semitism until the 1860's. Even the 1886 constitution of the *Allgemeiner Deputierten Convent,* which included all *Burschenschaften* in Germany, made no mention of Jewish membership, but a certain amount of social discrimination did arise because Jews could not obtain reserve commissions.

In Austria, however, anti-Semitism—and extreme opinions generally—made more rapid advances. The most important student organization in Vienna, the *Leseverein der Deutschen Studenten* became openly nationalist in the mid-seventies. It was the first to invite Schönerer to become an honorary member—on the proposal of a Jewish student named E. Abeles.[18] While there was no unconditional acceptance of Schönerer's pan-German views, they tended to prevail over more moderate doctrines. The spirit of 1817 and 1848, with its message of national unity, still held sway. By 1885, eighteen *Burschenschaften* at Graz, Vienna and the German University of Prague specifically acknowledged Schönerian pan-Germanism on the basis of the Linz Programme.[19]

Here, as in Germany, there seemed to be encouragement from above. The *Leseverein* contained 135 lecturers on the eve of its dissolution in 1873.[20] Theodor Billroth, the eminent medical pioneer, had drawn attention to the dangers of Jewish predominance in medicine,[21] although he later withdrew from this position, became a member of the *Verein zur Abwehr des Antisemitismus,*[22] and founded an interdenominational nursing home, the *Rudolfinerhaus.* *

The first *Burschenschaft* to expel its Jewish members was the *Libertas* of Vienna which decreed in 1878 that:

> Jews cannot be regarded as Germans, and not even when they are baptised.[23]

---

* Cf. also his letter (July 3, 1883) to Czerny, regretting that the surgeon Wölfler had failed to secure an appointment: "But that crooked nose! Sad that the nose today determines the filling of chairs at German universities." (F. Kobler, *Juden und Judentum in deutschen Briefen aus drei Jahrhunderten,* Vienna, 1935, p. 348.)

By 1890 all the *Burschenschaften*** were anti-Semitic[24] and in 1886 the *Deutsche Lesehalle* at the Technical Academy had also pronounced itself anti-Semitic.[25] It was also from the universities, it will be remembered, that an attempt was made to impose an anti-Semitic policy on the *Deutscher Schulverein*. At the Bohemian and Moravian universities the German-Czech struggle took precedence over the German-Jewish, and there was for a long time a section of opinion which welcomed Jews as allies against the Czechs. The Prague *Teutonia* excluded Jews in 1879,[26] but others were slow to follow, as was the Technical Academy at Brno, which was permeated with the more liberal atmosphere of Moravia. By 1888, according to the Minister of Education, out of 235 student organizations at Austrian universities, eighty-one were German Nationalist,[27] and during the Badeni period extremism received a further fillip.

The touchstone of anti-Semitism among the *Burschenschaften* soon became the question of dueling. Again the lead came from Vienna where it was the *Libertas* which forbade its members in 1881 to accept duels with Jews.[28] The conference of the *Waidhofener Verband* in 1896, which included all dueling student organizations, accepted the motion proposed by an extremist member, Florian Albrecht:

> In full appreciation of the fact that there exists between Aryans and Jews such a deep moral and psychic difference, and that our qualities have suffered so much through Jewish mischief, in full consideration of the many proofs which the Jewish student has also given of his lack of honour and character and since he is completely void of honour according to our German concepts, today's conference . . . resolves: "No satisfaction is to be given to a Jew with any weapon, as he is unworthy of it."†

---

* It must be remembered that only those student bodies which "bore colours" and made compulsory dueling a condition of membership were called by this name.

† *UDW*, April 1, 1896. Albrecht, who volunteered for service with the Afrikaner armies during the South African War, was something of a philosopher on the subject of dueling. "While therefore," he wrote, "for the noble character, above all the German, with whose spirit it corresponds most closely, the duel is a moral action, deeply founded in the individual folk-outlook and situation, it becomes for the Jew a so-called 'conventional lie'" (*UDW*, March 1, 1896).

The next year Albrecht proposed the total exclusion of Jews from universities;[29] already in 1892 a meeting of German Nationalist students had demanded the introduction of a quota system for Jews.[30]

Nevertheless, as was frequently the case in Austria, the translation of high-sounding principles into action turned out to be not too easy. Prague lagged as usual and continued to duel with Jews; the only *Burschenschaft* to attempt to carry out the Waidhofen resolution suffered suspension.[31] Students who held reserve commissions could not easily decline a duel since, although dueling was illegal, refusal to accept a challenge could lead to the loss of a commission, by sentence of a "court of honor."

Anti-Jewish agitation, which in Austrian politics was dying down after Lueger's victory, continued to flourish with full force in the universities, leading to frequent riots with which the forces of the law were prevented, by academic privilege, from interfering.

At the German *Hochschultag* in Vienna in 1905, the *pro-Rektor* of Vienna University had to report that:

> The old enmity between Jewish and German students continues undiminished, the aversion between German National-ist and Catholic students . . . is once more increasing perceptibly, national passions may break out again with full violence at the slightest provocation.[32]

In Germany, where German-Jewish antagonism was not intensified by other national hatreds and where the Liberal tradition was stronger, anti-Semitism never became universal. Its beginnings we may see in the special students' petition, which circulated at the time of Bernhard Förster's Anti-Semitic Petition and prefaced the ordinary text with an explanatory paragraph in which "the German student body" acknowledged that "the continuation of the struggle for the maintenance of our national-ity will one day be placed in its hands to no small extent."[33] Nearly half the students at Berlin University signed it; there were 1000 signatures at Leipzig and 350 at Halle.[34] A special students' meeting at Göttingen preferred the petition to one condemning anti-Semitism by a large majority. However, there was little support for it in the South.[35]

It was the organizers of the petition who founded the first

It was the organizers of the petition who founded the first coherent anti-Semitic student movement. This was the *Verein deutscher Studenten*. Its first conference took place on the Kyffhäuser mountain in 1881, hence it was also known as the *Kyffhäuserverband*.[36] It did not restrict its ideology to anti-Semitism. Other incentives to its formation were "the growth of anti-patriotic Social Democracy, the revival of the old army dispute, the excesses of parliamentary power and the behaviour of the greater part of the daily press."[37] Its growth was slow; by 1914 it had 1500 student members and 10,000 old members, less than 5% of the academic population.[38] Only after 1918 did its influence become decisive. But parallel with it other anti-Semitic developments took place. An extraordinary conference of the *Allgemeiner Deputierten-Konvent* in 1893 decided religious affiliation should be indicated on membership cards.[39] The next term the *Konvent's* register showed only two Jews, in 1894 there was none,[40] and in 1896 it accepted a motion that:

> The *Burschenschaft* rests on the basis of German *Volkstum*, therefore only students of German descent can be accepted in it. Note: Jewish citizens of the *Reich* are not to be regarded as Germans.[41]

It was in the students' gymnastic clubs, imbued with the muscular nationalism of Jahn, that intolerance was most pronounced. The *Akademischer Turnerbund* was founded in 1883 on a consciously pan-German basis; recommended reading for members later included the works of Gobineau.[42] Its membership in 1904, representing twenty-two universities (including Graz) was 1161.[43] Gobineau, as well as Chamberlain, Naumann, Sombart, and Winterstetten (the author of *Berlin-Bagdad*) was also recommended to the *Verein deutscher Studenten*.[44]

Germany, moreover, had something which never existed in Austria, namely a national organization of students specifically opposed to anti-Semitism. This, the *Deutscher Allgemeiner Burschenbund*, was also opposed to dueling and extravagant living. Although some of its branches were *judenrein*, it proclaimed at its 1905 conference that:

> German nationality is not waived by descent which is not purely-German

and incorporated this principle in its new constitution in 1912.[45]

While anti-Semitic rowdyism among students could in the last resort be dismissed as immature high spirits, it was more serious when the graduate carried the spirit imbibed at the university into his professional life, especially teaching. We have already established that Hitler's schoolmasters held, and spread, such notions; in Germany the situation appeared to be similar. A notice in the official *Reichsanzeiger* of Kassel instructed inspectors of schools as follows:

> It has in recent times repeatedly happened that Jewish adults and children have been publicly insulted and jeered at in their capacity as Jews by Christian pupils. According to information received, individual teachers have not only neglected the appropriate punishment of the school-children, but have now and again, through their own uncautious attitude, given encouragement to an unChristian lack of charity, manifesting itself in such scenes, which we, as an educational authority, must from the pedagogic point of view, decidedly discountenance. Your Excellencies will therefore take the opportunity of drawing the attention of the teachers subordinate to you to these points at the next official teachers' conference, and of making it their duty always to offer determined opposition to such goings-on detrimental to school discipline and at the same time, through moderation and restraint in their public life, to give an example of Christian tolerance towards the holders of other beliefs among the school-children entrusted to them.[46]

and in 1903 the Prussian Ministry of Education had to circularize a warning to schools to avoid anything that might widen differences between pupils of different denominations.[47]

Why nationalism in general and anti-Semitic nationalism in particular should have made this strong appeal to the intelligentsia is discussed below. Almost alone of the historians of his generation, Mommsen recognized these political vices and deplored them. No stronger condemnation of his colleagues and fellow countrymen can be found than the codicil of his testament, not published until 1948:

> In my innermost being, and I mean with the best of what is in me, I have always been an *animal politicum* and wanted to be a citizen. That is not possible in our nation, where the individual, even the best, never gets beyond the stage of subordinate service

which I belong has determined me never to step personally, in so far as this is possible, before the German public, for which I lack all respect.[48]

He never forgave Treitschke his anti-Semitism. When, despite his opposition, Treitschke was elected to the Prussian Academy, he wrote to his wife, "My fate is like that of the Lord Mayor of Vienna, whom they have given an anti-Semite as deputy and who has now taken his leave. Treitschke has been proposed and will without doubt be elected. Next to him I cannot remain."[49]

REFERENCES

1 *Preussiche Jahrbücher*, Nov. 1879, Dec., 1879, Jan. 1880, Dec., 1880, Jan, 1881, Vols. XLIV, pp. 572–6, 660–70; XLV, pp. 85–95; XLVI, pp. 661–3; XLVII, pp. 101–10.
2 *Ibid.*, Vol. XLIV, pp. 572–3, 575.
3 *Ibid.*, Vol. XLV, pp. 94–5.
4 J. Schrattenholz, *Antisemiten-Hammer. Eine Anthologie aus der Weltlitteratur* (Düsseldorf, 1894), p. 466.
5 Buchheim, *Geschichte der christlichen Parteien*, p. 255; Broszat, *Die antisemitische Bewegung*, p. 61.
6 Class, *Wider den Strom*, p. 16.
7 H. von Treitschke, *Deutsche Kämpfe* (Leipzig, 1896), pp. 119–22.
8 Mommsen in *National-Zeitung*, Nov. 20, 1880; Treitschke in *Die Post*, Nov. 21, 1880. See Treitschke, *Deutsche Kämpfe*, pp. 123–5.
9 Treitschke's articles had been published under the title *Ein Wort über unser Judentum*.
10 Treitschke, *Politics*, Vol. I, p. 302.
11 Stern, *The Politics of Cultural Despair*, pp. 85–6; R. W. Lougee, *Paul de Lagarde, 1827–1891. A Study of Radical Conservatism in Germany* (Cambridge, Mass., 1962), pp. 225, 280.
12 Stern, *op. cit.*, p. 91.
13 O. F. Scheuer, *Burschenschaft und Judenfrage. Der Rassenantisemitismus in der deutschen Studenschaft* (Berlin, 1927), p. 6.
14 *Ibid.*, p. 12.
15 *Ibid.*, p. 20.
16 *Ibid.*, p. 32.
17 *Ibid.*, pp. 27, 28, 36.
18 *Ibid.*, p. 46.
19 P. Molisch, *Politische Geschichte der deutschen Hochschulen in Österreich von 1848 bis 1918* (Vienna, 1939), pp. 88, 89, 95.
20 *Ibid.*, p. 92.
21 T. Billroth, *Über das Lehren und Lernen medizinischer Wissenschaften* (1875).
22 A. Fuchs, *Geistige Strömungen in Österreich, 1867–1918* (Vienna, 1949), p. 177.

The Intellectual Prestige of Anti-Semitism

23 Pichl, *Schönerer*, Vol. II, p. 319.
24 Molisch, *op. cit.*, p. 121.
25 *Ibid.*, p. 126.
26 *Ibid.*, p. 122.
27 *Ibid.*, p. 109.
28 Pichl, *op. cit.*, Vol. II, p. 320.
29 Molisch, *op. cit.*, p. 137.
30 *Ibid.*, p. 135.
31 Pichl, *op. cit.*, Vol. VI, p. 288.
32 Molisch, *op. cit.*, p. 216.
33 Anon., (i.e., L. Quidde), *Die Antisemitenagitation und die deutsche Studentenschaft* (Göttingen, 1881), pp. 13–4.
34 H. von Petersdorff, *Die Vereine deutscher Studenten. Neun Jahre akademischer Kämpfe* (Leipzig, 1891), p. 13.
35 Quidde, *op. cit.*, p. 17.
36 Petersdorff, *op. cit.*, p. 106.
37 *Ibid.*, p. 5.
38 Broszat, *op. cit.*, p. 142.
39 Scheuer, *op. cit.*, p. 41.
40 *Ibid.*
41 *Ibid.*, p. 42.
42 *ATB*, Vol. XV, No. 10, July, 1902, pp. 325–31.
43 *ATB*, Vol. XVII, No. 12, Sept., 1904, p. 447.
44 *Akademische Blätter*, Aug. 16, 1917.
45 Scheuer, *op. cit.*, pp. 44–5.
46 *Deutsche Antisemitenchronik*, p. 52.
47 *MVA*, Sept. 30, 1903, p. 318.
48 A. Wucher, *Theodor Mommsen, Geschichtsschreibung und Politik* (Göttingen, 1957), pp. 218–9.
49 March 15, 1895, *ibid.*, p. 195.

251

27

The Social Democrats

Despite certain points of superficial resemblance—the radical language, the popular method of campaigning, the rejection of Liberal economics—anti-Semites and Social Democrats were at opposite poles of the political world and their mutual enmity was deep and lasting. Whatever may have been its subsequent performance in practice, whatever totalitarianism may be read into its theory, in its moral appeal Marxian Socialism was clearly related to nineteenth-century Liberalism. It was inspired by a revulsion against tyranny and poverty, by optimism and a belief in progress, by the assumption that if a formula could be found to explain how society worked, spread by education and applied, the world's evils could be abolished. It was international in its appeal, its morality was universal. Against these factors, which Socialism had in common with Liberalism, anti-Semitism was concerned not with more emancipation but with less, with the interests of traditional, not of new classes, with the primacy of the national and the integral over the universal. In particular it could not fail to notice that many of the founders and leaders of international Socialism were Jews.

In effect, two questions are here involved—the relationship between the Social Democrats and Jews, and the attitude of the Social Democrats to anti-Semitism. The prominence of Jews in the Social Democratic leadership provided ammunition for both anti-Semitism and anti-Socialism; it is a little pointless to argue whether there would have been this mutual hostility between the two movements if international Socialism had been less Jewish, for Social Democratic ideology was determined to a considerable extent by Jewish influence.

A number of reasons could be suggested why Jews should

associate themselves with Socialism. Delbrück in the *Preussiche Jahrbücher* was brutally frank:

> In so far as there exists at present a coalition between Jews and Social Democrats, it rests on the fact that both feel themselves slighted by the bourgeois classes,[1]

and the *Neue Zürcher Zeitung* commented at the time of the 1912 election:

> If we ask who, in the bourgeois camp, is prepared to give electoral support to the Social Democrats, then an objective observer . . . will come to the conclusion that . . . it is in the main Jewish voters who wish to protest, by handing in a red ballot-paper, against the state in which they have indeed nominal equality, but in fact do not in any respect feel themselves to be legal equals.[2]

In addition, Jews ambitious for a career in politics found their opportunities more and more constricted outside the extreme Left. It was virtually impossible for a Jew to enter politics as a Conservative in either Germany or Austria.

In the period immediately after 1867 it was natural for a Jew to associate himself with Liberalism. Writing before the elections to the Prussian Diet in 1873, the Jewish *Allgemeine Zeitung* said:

> It would be a superfluous task . . . for us to remind our co-religionists everywhere to vote for the Liberal Party during the coming elections.[3]

Of the fourteen Jews elected to the Reichstag between 1871 and 1884, three were National Liberals, eight were Progressives, and three Social Democrats; the eight elected to the Prussian Diet between 1873 and 1885 divided into two National Liberals and six Progressives.[4]

After that the picture changed. How the Jews were gradually edged out of Austrian Liberalism has already been shown. After 1880, when Lasker and Bamberger left the National Liberals, no Jew was elected on that party's ticket and the Progressives elected none after 1890 until 1912, when two Jews again appeared in their ranks. The graded franchise in Prussia enabled the two Liberal parties to be a little bolder in presenting Jewish candidates,* but by and large any Jewish parliamentarian elected from 1890 onward tended to be a Social Democrat.†

The actions of those Jews who engaged in party leadership were not necessarily reflected by the Jewish electorate at large. In Germany the majority of Jewish voters probably continued to support Liberalism. In Austria the situation was complicated by the differing conditions of the various Jewish communities, and with the growth of Zionism a Jewish National Party was formed which, in 1907, elected five members. The number of Jews who, before 1914, deliberately voted Social Democrat solely because that party alone was uncompromising on the anti-Semitic issue cannot have been large, and the Social Democrats did not welcome them unreservedly.[5]

Nor must we generalize about Jewish predilections for radical politics from conditions peculiar to a certain time and place. In Britain, where assimilation had gone farther, there was much less Jewish involvement with the Left. In 1900 there were twelve Jewish members of Parliament, eight Conservative and four Liberal; in 1906, the year of the Liberal landslide twelve Liberals and four Conservatives, but candidates were divided seventeen to fifteen.[6] In Israel, where this, as so many other clichés, about the Jews has been dispelled, the Left-wing parties (Mapai, Mapam, Ahdut Avoda, and the Communists) tend to gain 50 to 55% of the votes at elections, a not abnormal percentage for a Westernized industrial country.‡

Yet there are two forces driving the Jew to the Left which, though they may vary in strength from place to place, merit consideration irrespective of context. It is in the main those Jews who attempted to cut themselves loose most completely from their environment who became the Socialist leaders, such as Adler and Bauer in Austria, Singer and Kurt Eisner in Germany, Rosa Luxemburg in Poland, and Trotsky and Zinoviev in

---

* No Jews were elected to the diet in 1893, but there were two Progressives in 1893, six in 1903, and seven each in 1908 and 1913. In 1913 there were also two National Liberals (*MVA*, Dec. 3, 1893, Nov. 18, 1903. A. Plate, *Handbuch für das preussische Abgerodnetenhaus*, Berlin, 1908, p. 354;*ibid.*, Berlin, 1914, p. 348).

† The number of Social Democrats is impossible to determine, since, in accordance with the Gotha Programme which declared religion to be *Privatsache*, the majority described themselves as "konfessionslos".

‡ True up to 1977, not since then.

Russia.* They were intellectuals who disavowed their own heritage and background and yet did not feel at home in the new tradition to which they tried to adapt themselves. It was not that they deliberately took up a revolutionary posture in defiance of some snub or indignity they had suffered, rather that they identified themselves emotionally with the ideology of protest that is natural to the uprooted intellectual, whether he is an "angry young man" or a bomb-throwing *narodnik*. Above all the ideologies of the Left, which promised to emancipate men from restrictive or divisive loyalties, also helped the Jew to reidentify himself with society.

The influence of the closed Jewish community, too, continued to haunt the *déraciné*, however much he might try to exorcise it. It endowed him, first, with an exaggeratedly intellectual and cerebral view of the world's problems, derived from the enforced, undilutedly urban culture of Jewish life and the Talmudic scholasticism which was the mainstay of ghetto education. (This gift also tended to make the Jew better at financial operations than industrial management and, with his international connections, to become the ideal "middleman.') Second, he was the heir to that legacy of the puritanical visionary, the Hebraic tradition, embodied by the Jew who does not feel comfortable unless the prophet's cloak is warming his shoulders, the living communicant of Judaism's greatest contribution to Western civilization. The intellectual trying to theorize about politics is in any circumstances likely to come to conclusions more or less critical of the *status quo*. If to this is added the prophetic impulse, it is easy to see why a Jew, quite apart from any given social or economic obstacles, should be driven to radical Liberalism in the middle of the nineteenth century and Socialism at the end. We can see, too, why more often than not, the Jew is likely to be associated with the extreme wing of his party.

The problem of reconciling the paradox that the Jews had invented both capitalism and the means of destroying it, was a comparatively trivial one for the anti-Semite. To the contention that the Jewish world political plot had been hatched in Paris in

* When asked whether he considered himself a Russian or a Jew, Trotsky replied, "Neither, I am a Socialist."

the 1840's by a trio comprising Heinrich Heine, James Rothschild, and Karl Marx* we may, perhaps, reply with Horace, *"Credat Judaeus Apella";* but most of the other arguments were little less extravagant and little more plausible. The basic quarrel anti-Semites have with Marxists is in their attitude to capitalism. The anti-Semites extolled "honest" industrial capital, regarding financial capitalism—the banks, stock exchanges, mortgage societies—as the villain; Marxists attacked industrial capitalism and ignored the rest as an incidental excrescence of the system. Thus by diverting the workers' attention from the real sources of economic evil, the Marxists were playing the Jews' game. The Marxist doctrine, Alexander Berg argued, that the forces of production, and the classes owning these, dominate the politics and thought of a society is naturally welcome to the Jewish bourgeoisie.[7]

Marxists argued that capitalism was "objectively progressive"; in destroying "petty burghers, guildworkers and small traders declining into ruin," it was helping Austria and Germany forward.[8] It was therefore the duty of the proletariat to further the process of capitalist development, a doctrine calculated to endear the bourgeoisie to the proletariat as the indirect contributor to its liberation, and at the same time to strengthen the position of Jewry by diverting the proletariat's attention from the possibility of short-term improvements.[9] To attack capital but not the Stock Exchange, said Frantz, was to defer reform *ad calendas graecas.*[10] Lassalle's plan to finance producers' cooperatives with state loans was a "genuinely Jewish idea" *("echter Judengedanke"),* in reducing social reform to a matter of credit business.[11] To the more old-fashioned kind of Conservative anti-Semitism, the fundamental similarities shared by Liberals and Socialists in any case loomed large—their humanism, positivism, internationalism, and the revolutionary origins of their theories all seemed to come out of the same stable.

The hostility with which Social Democracy replied to these anti-Semitic attacks was dictated by a mixture of idealism and

---

* Berg, *Judentum und Sozialdemokratie,* p. 15. The historian must acknowledge his debt to the anti-Semitic press for many superficially implausible facts which would otherwise have escaped him. But for the assiduity of *Das Schwarze Korps* (July 22, 1937), for instance, we should never have known that Cardinal Pacelli (later Pope Pius XII) was in league with the Kremlin.

expediency. Before the mid-eighties there was a good deal of anti-Semitism in the European Socialist movement. In the first half of the nineteenth century Jews could be easily identified not merely as rich men but, in their capacity as court bankers, as the very pillars of the old, illiberal order. In addition, a great deal of Socialism was simply a revulsion from industrialism; in Proudhon, Fourier, and above all the Bakuninists we see a "primitive," "idyllic" revulsion from sophisticated bourgeois society very similar to that of the extreme Right a generation or two later. In France this Left-wing anti-Semitism survived until the Dreyfus Case, especially among the anarchistically inclined group round the *Revue Socialiste,* such as Benoît Malon, Auguste Chirac and Gustave Rouanet.* In Germany anti-Semitism had crept into the Lassalleans' anti-Marxism before the Gotha reunification of 1875. Jews were much more numerous among the Marxists (then collaborating with the Liberals) and Schweitzer, Lassalle's successor, lampooned Jews rather unkindly in a novel, *Lucinde.*[12] Marx himself is often accused of anti-Semitism, not so much on the grounds of his early pamphlet, *Die Judenfrage,* but on the score of later remarks in conversation, correspondence, and newspaper articles.[13]

With the general triumph of the "scientific" school of Socialism, this anti-Semitic undercurrent disappeared. Social Democrats were long tempted to ignore its resurgence on the Right, preferring to regard it as a dogfight among sections of the bourgeoisie,† but were forced to pay attention to it when it appeared as a dangerous rival for political support. This was particularly grave in Vienna in the 1880's, where the Socialist movement was weak and divided and anti-Semitism threatened to seize a monopoly of radical politics. Kautsky, who was in Zürich at the time and in touch with Vienna, wrote to Engels:

> We are having great trouble in stopping our people from fraternising with the anti-Semites. The anti-Semites are now our most dangerous opponents, much more dangerous than in

---

* Malon even received the accolade of Drumont (*La Fin d'un Monde,* pp. 122–5).

† As an outstanding example see Jules Guesde's original attitude to the Dreyfus Affair (G. Chapman, *The Dreyfus Case,* London, 1955, p. 182). For a fuller discussion see A. Norland, *The Founding of the French Socialist Party,* 1893–1905 (Cambridge, Mass., 1956), pp. 61–84.

Germany, because their appearance is oppositional and demo-cratic, thus appeal to the workers' instincts.[14]

Six months later he wrote of the "enormous proportions" assumed by

> anti-Semitism here, which has recruited a good part of the petty bourgeois—including some very "radical"—elements who had hitherto been with us.[15]

In Germany the question became an issue when the party was faced with Böckel's success, and at the 1890 conference, the first held after the lapsing of the Anti-Socialist Act, the Marburg delegation proposed a resolution:

> that in consideration of the advances made by the anti-Semitic movement and of the objectionable fighting methods which the anti-Semites use, especially against The Social Democrats, the party and the party members be assisted in some way, so that a strong counter-agitation may be developed in the hot-bed of anti-Semitism.[16]

The motion was, however, referred to the executive and the subject was not discussed until three years later.

Meanwhile at the International Socialist Congress at Brussels, the American Jewish delegation had proposed a resolution condemning anti-Semitism, but it was opposed by Singer and Adler;[17] instead a more neutrally worded resolution, the terms of which laid down the orthodox Socialist line for the future, was accepted:

> The Congress, considering that the Socialist and workers' parties of all lands have always maintained that there could not be for them any antagonism or struggle of race or nationality, but only the struggle between proletarians of all races and capitalists of all races, . . . while condemning anti-Semitic and philo-Semitic agitation as one of the manoeuvres by which the capitalist class and reactionary governments try to make the Socialist movement deviate and to divide the workers, decides that there is no need to discuss the question raised by the delegation of American Socialist groups of Jewish language and passes to the order of the day.[18]

However embarrassing the subject might be, discussion could not be shelved forever, and at the 1893 Congress of the German Social Democratic Party, a platform resolution, proposed by

Bebel, was adopted, though not before one of the Berlin delegates had suggested that as anti-Semitism contained many revolutionary elements, the party had no reason to set itself up in opposition to it.[19]

Bebel's analysis of anti-Semitism became the classic text for the party. The origins of the movement were economic—the 1873 crash, the unwelcome competition of industry for artisans, the widespread dependence of peasants on Jews in all trade matters, the indebtedness of underpaid officers and civil servants, and of aristocrats. In the long run, however, anti-Semitism would benefit the Social Democrats, because the classes whose discontent was being exploited by the anti-Semites would eventually realize where their true salvation lay.[20] The resolution passed by the conference summarized Bebel's speech and remained the permanent policy of the party.*

Already in its election manifesto the previous spring, the party had come out unequivocally against anti-Semitism, because "Social Democracy defends general equality before the law."[21]

In their dialectical view of anti-Semitism lay the strength and weakness of the Social Democrats' estimate of it. Viewed in the light of the evolution of economic classes, it was the death agony of doomed and moribund forces of production:

> nothing else than the reaction of mediaeval, declining social strata against modern society which consists mainly of capitalists and wage-labourers.[22]
>
> Its origin compels anti-Semitism to make demands which are as much in contradiction with the laws of economic and political development of capitalism as they are hostile to progress.[23]

Anti-Semitism, therefore, whatever its evils and whatever its nuisance value as a diversionary tactic, was not a permanent problem; the symptom would die when the organism of which it was an excrescence had expired. This was in fact a more subtle and serious assessment than had so far been produced by the Liberals. the Social Democrats saw the root of the matter in the social and economic structure and drew conclusions that were at any rate plausible and logical; the Liberals had mainly expressed distress and disgust at the irrationality and coarseness of anti-Semitism and taken refuge in the hope that such periodic waves

* See Appendix V.

of darkness would recede as they had advanced.* They were not complacent and above the struggle about anti-Semitism as the Social Democrats sometimes were, but they felt more helpless in face of it and knew no weapon except exhortation with which to kill it.

If the Social Democrats secured a better insight into the causes of anti-Semitism, they were misled sadly about its future.

They argued first that the Jews as a separate community were bound to disappear in the course of economic progress. Anti-Semitism was aimed at the Jews as a class, for they were not a nation, only a community united by religion and a common economic fate—a view which, though contested by individual Jewish Socialists like Moses Hess, is to be found in Marxist writing from Marx himself to Kautsky. The advance of capitalism deprived Jews of their characteristic economic function; like their greatest enemies they were being inexorably driven into one or other of the only two classes that now mattered. The solution of the Jewish question, like that of all other problems, would be provided by the coming of Socialism, which would not only remove the economic basis of anti-Semitism but do away with the separate identity of the Jews. Hence all forms of Jewish Nationalism and Zionism were denounced as reactionary romanticism, hence the refusal of the Austrian party to admit a specifically Jewish section, and the perennial difficulties of the *Bund*,† hence the great reluctance with which the Yiddish language was accepted as a proper means of agitation even as a temporary expedient.

The class nature of anti-Semitism also meant that it was necessary, in accordance with the Brussels resolution, to condemn "philo-Semitism" equally with anti-Semitism.

* After the debate in the Prussian Diet two typical comments of the Viennese Liberal press were (*Wiener Allgemeine Zeitung*, Nov. 22, 1880) "There is something infinitely lamentable that one must even concern oneself with these matters that the whole of public life is filled with a quarrel about things which it would not have occurred to an educated and thinking man to question for the past hundred years," and (*Neues Wiener Tagblatt*, Sept. 18, 1895) "The anti-Semitism of our day will doubtless once find a place in the textbooks of mental epidemics and enable the psychiatrist to produce not uninteresting material. . . ."
† In 1912 the Russian Social Democrats did finally accord cultural autonomy to Jewish groups.

Liberals often sought to protect Jews against attack

> because the assault on Jewish property tows in its wake the assault
> on the neighbouring Christian property. It is dangerous to fight
> with weapons of that kind . . . .[24]

In so far as anti-Semitism was anti-capitalist, the Socialist argument ran, it represented a "step forward in historico-political development,"[25] and to use the excesses of an Ahlwardt or a Böckel to defend capitalism was unacceptable.

On the occasion of a by-election at Kassel, in Hesse, when the anti-Semites were supporting the Progressive against the Social Democrat, *Neue Zeit,* wrote:

> Philo-Semitism is no whit better than anti-Semitism. If the
> one claims to be fighting capitalism by persecuting the Jews, then
> the other claims to protect the Jews by defending capitalism
> through thick and thin. . . . . As opposed to the brutalities
> committed by anti-Semitism, more in word than deed, against
> the Jews, we must not forget the brutalities committed by
> philo-Semitism, more in deeds than words, against all, be they
> Jews or Turks, Christians or heathen, who oppose capitalism.[26]

There was, second, the determination to believe that

> [anti-Semitism], despite its reactionary character and against its
> will, ultimately acts in a revolutionary way, because the . . . strata
> stirred up against the Jewish capitalist must come to realise that
> not only the Jewish capitalist but the capitalist class generally is
> their enemy, and that only the realisation of Socialism can free
> them from their misery.[27]

and Viktor Adler observed, "They are doing the Social Democrats' business."[28]

It was never explained, however, on what compulsion those who had been awoken from political apathy by anti-Semitism "must" eventually turn to Socialism. The assumption sprang, in fact, not from any logical grounds but from the basic optimism and belief in the power of reason which the nineteenth-century Marxists shared with their Liberal contemporaries. They could not, any more than the Liberals, bear the thought that a doctrine like anti-Semitism was capable of prospering.

As it turned out, the two main groups adversely affected by capitalism—the proletariat, and the artisans and peasants—did not join forces but diverged from each other. The proletariat was a new class, created by conditions which, it was convinced, would ultimately work in its favor. It could therefore accept a political ideal which, while also appealing to its economic interest, was inspired by hope and by such notions as universal brotherhood which involved fairly heavy moral responsibility. For declining classes, anxious to hold what they daily see slipping, such ideals would be less attractive. Hence we have their predilection for doctrines of despair, their intolerance, and their rejection of universal moral values. Both had visions of a golden age, the workers in the future, the artisans in the past. Because the Merrie Germanie of *Die Meistersinger* never existed, because the workers' utopia might never come, these dreams must not be dismissed as idle. What men dream becomes the facts of politics.

It is a strange comment on the pre-1914 world that even revolutionary Marxists felt secure in its stability and reasonableness. They consoled themselves with repeating the *mot,* often attributed to Bebel,★ that anti-Semitism was "the Socialism of the dolt" *("der Sozialismus des dummen Kerls")*. So convinced were they, and the signs were indeed pointing that way, that anti-Semitism and the classes supporting it were on the way out, that Bebel could comment, in a 1906 reprint of his 1893 speech, that anti-Semitism had no prospect of ever exerting a decisive influence on German politics.[29]

REFERENCES

1 *Preussiche Jahrbücher,* Vol. CXXXI, Jan. 26, 1908, p. 376.
2 Quoted by A. Grimpen, *Judentum und Sozialdemokratie in ihren Beziehungen beleuchtet* (2nd ed., Hamburg, 1914), pp. 26–7.
3 *AZJ,* Oct. 14, 1873.
4 *AZJ,* Oct., 1871, Nov., 1873, Jan., 1874, Jan., 1877, Oct. 1877, Aug., 1878, Oct., 1879, Nov. 1881, Nov., 1882, Nov. 1884, Nov. 1885.
5 *Verhandlungen des 6. österreichischen Sozialdemokratischen Parteitages abgehalten zu Wien* (Vienna, 1897), pp. 91–2.
6 E. Halévy, *A History of the English People in the Nineteenth Century,* Vol. VI (2nd ed., 1952), p. 65.
7 A. Berg, *Judentum und Sozialdemokratie* (Berlin, 1891), p. 38.
8 F. Engels in *AZ,* May 9, 1890.

★ Its origin was probably with Ferdinand Kronawetter,, the full expression being *"der Sozialismus des dummen Kerls von Wien"*.

9 Berg, *op. cit.*, pp. 33, 43, 56.
10 Frantz, *Der Untergang der alten Parteien*, p. 58.
11 *Ibid.*
12 For a detailed discussion of anti-Semitism in European Socialist parties, see the articles by E. Silberner in *Historia Judaica*, Vol. XIII, No.2, Vol. XIV, No. 1, Vol. XIV, No. 1 (1951–1954). His *Sozialisten zur Judenfrage* (Berlin, 1962) was published too late to be used by me.
13 E. Silberner, "Was Marx an Anti-Semite?" *Historia Judaica*, Vol. XI, No. 1 (1949).
14 June 23, 1884. Kautsky, *Aus der Frühzeit des Marxismus*, p. 122.
15 Dec. 22, 1884. *Ibid.*, p. 160.
16 *Protokoll über die Verhandlungen des Parteitages der Sozialdemokratischen Partei Deutschland in Halle* (Berlin, 1890), pp. 270–2.
17 Silberner, "Austrian Social Democracy and the Jewish Question", *Historia Judaica*, Vol. XIII, No. 2 (1951), p. 122.
18 J. Joll, *The Second International* (London, 1955), p. 68.
19 *Protokoll über die Verhandlungen des Parteitages der Sozialdemokratischen Partei Deutschlands, abgehalten zu Köln am Rhein* (Berlin, 1893), p. 104.
20 *Ibid.*, pp. 224–40.
21 *Die Tatigkeit des Deutschen Reichstages, 1890–93*, quoted in *MVA*, July 13, 1893.
22 Engels, *AZ*, May 9, 1890.
23 Resolution of 1893 SPD congress, *Protokoll*, p. 223.
24 Speech by Ritter von Gniezow, Feb. 13, 1890. *StPA*, X. Sess., 364. Sitz., p. 13405.
25 *Neue Zeit*, June 21, 1893, Vol. XI, Pt. 2, p. 389.
26 *Ibid.*, July 27, 1891, Vol. IX, Pt. 2, pp. 586–7.
27 Resolution of 1893 SPD congress, *Protokoll*, p. 224.
28 *Gleichheit*, May 8, 1887. Quoted by Silberner, *Austrian Social Democracy*, p. 136.
29 A. Bebel, *Sozialdemokratie und Antisemitismus* (Berlin, 1906), p. 38.

The Catholic and Protestant Churches

One of the most striking features of German anti-Semitism was the way its fortunes in Catholic regions contrasted with those among Protestants, or indeed among Austrian Catholics.

A brief discussion of these puzzling topics cannot be very satisfactory, but it ought not to be omitted altogether. The question of Protestant anti-Semitism in Germany is part of the strange and, it would seem, uncharacteristic role played by Protestantism in German politics. Why did the "Protestant political ideal" fail so signally in Germany? It is a little superficial to claim that it is only Calvinism or Anglo-Saxon sectarianism which, by liberating the conscience of the individual, paved the way for modern Liberalism, while Lutheranism, by enjoining obedience to the ruler, perpetuated a theocratic concept of the state.[1] Gerhard Ritter is nearer the mark when he suggests:

> It is from Lutheranism that the German derives (at least in part) the tendency not to demand all that much political "liberty" once he is in possession of spiritual freedom, but to confide unquestioningly in his secular superiors and to rely on the "conscientiousness" of the governors rather than politically organised control by the governed. The aversion of the German educated classes from too close a contact with politics, their well-known trait of unworldliness, is essentially Lutheran. Because the German churches never had to fight for political influence (as did the Calvinist ones of Western Europe), and because the political life of their particular states was in the main sunk in static inactivity, they lacked the natural desire to participate in politics; thence, *and from the narrowness of life in the German petty principalities—not, however, from Lutheranism as such—the notorious political passivity of German Lutheranism is derived.*[2]

The special place of the Lutheran Church in the Prussian state structure is thus seen to be a symptom rather than a cause. It was the German context which insured that the pattern imposed by the Great Elector should survive, while, for instance, the militant Protestant authoritarianism of Gustavus Adolphus in Sweden did not.

·Because the political conditions which characterized Luther's Germany survived, in their essentials, until the nineteenth century, the Protestant-Catholic struggle could, during periods of enthusiasm, become a nationalist one, with ultramontanism as the enemy of national unity. This entanglement of the national struggle with the religious can be followed even more clearly in Austria. There German Nationalism ranged from the ordinarily anti-clerical to the active idealization of Protestantism by the Schönerer fringe. Austrian Catholic anti-Semitism was of the reactionary Romantic school, and during the 1870's German Catholism did not keep aloof from it. The difference came when Nationalist anti-Semitism superseded it. In Germany it was able to identify itself with Protestantism, and German Catholics gained an interest in opposing both. In Austria the Church was playing for different stakes and found anti-Semitism necessary for taking the wind out of Nationalist sails.

The chaotic state of German politics in the seventeenth and eighteenth centuries made men prize order above justice and put in the firm establishment of a social hierarchy the trust they could not put in princes; while disgust with the world put a premium on withdrawal from it. The most significant development in German religious thought in these centuries was Pietism, and even the German Enlightenment seems a little half-hearted in contrast with that of other countries. Germany produced her Leibniz and her Kant—but no Diderot or Voltaire, no Locke or Hume.

The main contents of Pietism were emotionalism, enthusiasm, and mysticism. It was anti-rational and anti-intellectual, both essential qualities (as we have seen) in the nationalist and anti-Semitic reaction against the cosmopolitan Enlightenment and rationalist Liberalism. Protestantism, and Pietism in particular, profoundly influenced every aspect of German Romantic thought. Herder, Schleiermacher, and Naumann were pastors; Hegel, Fichte, and Paul de Lagarde were educated for the

Church; and Nietzsche and Hermann Hesse were sons of clergymen. The families of Schleiermacher and Hardenberg (Novalis) belonged to the Moravian sect.*

The Church directly played a prominent part in anti-Semitic politics. Apart from Stöcker, four other pastors sat in the Reichstag as anti-Semites (Burckhardt, Iskraut, Mumm, and the egregious Krösell, who barnstormed through Pomerania with tales of ritual murder) and another (Schall) was a member of the Prussian Diet.

The contrast with the German Catholics could not have been greater. True, there were the *Germania* articles, and Rohling had won his spurs in Germany. At the time of the *Kulturkampf* and the brief omnipotence of Liberalism the "Jewish" press was naturally anti-clerical; so were Jewish politicians, since they were without exception Liberals or Social Democrats, although they generally thought of themselves as thoroughly assimilated and not as Jews. Specifically Jewish opinion, too, was anti-clerical and anti-Catholic,[3] and even a very moderate Jewish historian could later write of this episode:

> When Bismarck's government began the *Kulturkampf* against Catholicism, the Jews could regard it only as a historical retribution against that power which had once oppressed those who professed Judaism, and inhibited progress.[4]

During the *Kulturkampf* the mood of the Centre Party was to beat Bismarckian Liberalism with the anti-Semitic stick, nor did anti-Semitism die out altogether once Bismarck had "gone to Canossa." At the time of the anti-Semitic petition, pressure in the party to support it and the Stöcker movement was strong; only Windthorst's threat to resign from the leadership prevented it from prevailing.[5] When the petition was debated in the Prussian Diet, all Centre speakers opposed the Liberals' censure of it.[6] A number of Centre politicians, especially on the Right of the

---

* K. S. Pinson has suggested that Pietism made a direct contribution to German nationalism: "In appealing to the lower classes it gave them a feeling of self-respect and prestige, and thus helped to cement the widely separated classes into a unified national whole. This appeal to the lower classes involved, in turn, a more intense cultivations of the language of the lower classes, German, as opposed to the learned Latin and the aristocratic French" (*Pietism as a Factor in German Nationalism*, New York, 1934, pp. 25–6).

party, continued to be actively anti-Semitic. Freiherr von Loë, an agrarian reformer, was a contributor to the *Eisenbahnzeitung* and a collaborator of Vogelsang;[7] and Count Ballestrem could not overcome the genuine Conservative's dislike of the *Reformjude* in the Prussian education debate of 1892.[8] The sometimes demogagic leader of the Catholic Left, Erzberger, also made anti-Semitic speeches, principally directed against the Social Democratic trade union leaders.[9]

Anti-Semitic articles in the Catholic press were in general restricted to provincial Bavarian papers,[10] though the *Kölnische Volkszeitung,* one of the party's two leading organs, commented on the Böckel-Ahlwardt campaign:

> In our view, the Rhenish Centre party has paid far too little attention to these events. It should long ago have declared its attitude towards the anti-Semitic movement at its public meetings. This attitude is obviously: decisive rejection of "pure" anti-Semitism which works with inflammatory slogans, energetic action against genuinely existing Jewish excesses, particularly in commercial life, but only on the basis of common law.[11]

But these were exceptions, however significant, to the general policy. From the 1880's onward, the Centre not only refused to embrace anti-Semitism, but also went out of its way to denounce it. A prophetic evaluation of anti-Semitism was made by Windthorst's successor, Lieber:

> As a minority in the Reich, we have not forgotten how we were treated and for this reason alone, not to speak of higher considerations and deeper motives, we shall never lend a hand to forge weapons to be used today against the Jews, tomorrow against the Poles, the day after against the Catholics . . . . Do not expect our support in making it possible for you to exult, "We have got rid of the Jews. Now *bon voyage* to the Catholics."[12]

Several explanations may be offered for this changed attitude. First, having itself been the victim of discriminatory legislation, it was on weak ground when proposing it against others. Thus the great majority of Centre deputies were throughout its duration opposed to the Anti-Socialist Act★ at a time when Papal

---

★ The Social Democrats returned the compliment by voting for the partial repeal of the anti-Jesuit law in 1904.

denunciations of Marxism must have been ringing in every Catholic's ear.

Second, once the *Kulturkampf* had been called off and the power of Liberalism broken, the Centre had no further need to pursue a policy of unconditional opposition. From now on it could argue from a position of strength: it was always in a pivotal position in the Reichstag.*

Third, the center of gravity of German Catholicism was the Rhineland and, along this centuries-old artery of European trade and culture, it assumed a character rather different from that in some remote Bavarian or Styrian valley or muddy Galician hamlet. This openness to the world and receptiveness to enlightened ideas singled the Rhineland Catholics out from their European contemporaries—whether at the time of Görres, or Ketteler, or Windthorst.

Fourth, the German Catholics appreciated earlier than most other Churches that anti-Semitism was ultimately also anti-Christian, more in Germany than anywhere else through its connection with pagan mysticism and racialism.

All these, however, are no more than logical reasons why the Centre should abjure anti-Semitism, and logical reasons are seldom the sole guides to political action. Thus it is well known that minorities are not necessarily kind to each other; unable to vent their anger or aggressiveness against the real oppressor, they are apt to turn on weaker fellow sufferers. Moreover, the bulk of the Centre Party's electoral following came from the countryside and small towns, especially after it began losing some of its working-class support to the Social Democrats.† This occurred in precisely those sections of the community who in other parts of Germany had shown themselves most receptive to anti-Semitism.‡

* Only between 1887 and 1890, and 1907 and 1909 did Chancellors succeed in governing without the Centre.
† By 1914 the largest Catholic cities—Munich, Cologne, Düsseldorf—all had Social Democrat majorities, and the Centre vote was ebbing perceptibly in the most highly industrialized areas.
‡ Weber, in the course of elaborating his thesis on the connection between Protestantism and capitalism, claims that during this period German Catholics had a much lower *per capita* income than German Protestants. Basing himself on detailed statistics from Baden, he showed that Protestants were more heavily represented in modern economic processes, both as entrepreneurs and as skilled

The Centre might well, in the short run, have gained on balance by making mild anti-Semitism part of its program.

It is natural that the day-to-day policy of the Centre should have been dictated more by opportunism than by immutable principles. Anti-Semitism apart, there were certainly meeting points for the Christian-Social doctrines which were a force in both Catholic and Protestant conservatism. Drawing in its horns slightly in the 1912 elections, the Centre withdrew in eight constituencies in favor of the Christian-Socials, in ten in favor of the German-Socials, and in one case it withdrew in favor of the Reform Party, where its own chances were negligible. Altogether this brought these anti-Semitic parties about 70,000 votes.[13]

But there is no doubt that the Centre Party owed its devotion to constitutional liberties to a great degree to the influence of one man, Ludwig Windthorst, who taught his followers to oppose anti-Semitism even when it was not in their direct and immediate interest to do so.

The resistance of the Centre meant that political anti-Semitism stood little chance of gaining a foothold in Catholic regions, for the German Catholic population was remarkably faithful to its political party. Even at a time when every other party was becoming more and more closely associated with specific economic groups, the Centre succeeded in holding together its heterogeneous following, ranging from landowners to coalminers. In 1907 and 1912 there were 146 constituencies in which over 50% of the electorate was Catholic and 127 constituencies where over 60% was Catholic.[14] The following table shows the extent to which, even then, when the heat of the *Kulturkampf* had long subsided, Catholic voters returned candidates of Catholic parties.*

Thus where the old-established parties had difficulty in breaking in, the campaign of the anti-Semites was doubly arduous. No anti-Semite was ever elected for a Catholic constituency, and their polls were generally poor. In 1890, of thirty-one seats contested, three were Catholic, and these

laborers (*Gesammelte Aufsätze zur Religionssoziologie*, Tübingen, 1920, Vol. I, pp. 17–22).
* That is, Centre Polish, or Alsatian.

TABLE 10. REPRESENTATION OF GERMAN CATHOLIC CONSTITUENCIES

Party	1907 50% Catholic	1907 60% Catholic	1912 50% Catholic	1912 60% Catholic
Centre	101	93	90	87
Other Catholic parties	26	24	28	26
Conservatives	5	2	4	2
National Liberals	7	4	8	....
Progressives	1	1	2	2
Social Democrats	6	3	12	8
Bavarian Peasant	....	....	2	2
	146	127	146	127

accounted for 303 out of 47,536 votes.[15] In their biggest effort, in 1898, the anti-Semites put up 110 candidates; nineteen stood in Catholic constituencies polling 7314 votes out of a total of 284,000. Four of the candidates polled fewer than fifty votes.[16] In 1903 eight of the sixty-five candidatures were in Catholic constituencies; they gained 5838 votes out of the total of 244,000.

Of the anti-Semitic deputies Oswald Zimmermann was an Old Catholic. No other deputy and very few other candidates were Catholics. Cremer, as has already been mentioned, contested one of the Berlin seats in 1881. In 1887 Dr. Winkler of the *Westfälischer Courier*—Rohling's earliest ally—stood for the Prussian Diet under Böckel's aegis.[17] Conradt, a Silesian chimney-sweep and a functionary of the *Mittelstandsvereinigung*, became a member of the Prussian Diet.*

We cannot accept the statement of one modern Catholic writer—"In general I have encountered very few Catholic anti-Semites in my life"[18]—as according with universal experience, but it is characteristic that in the 1930's one of the voices of the German Church should have been that of Cardinal Faulhaber, while the Austrian spoke with that of Cardinal Innitzer.

---

* This is probably not an exhaustive list, but the full catalogue cannot be much more impressive.

REFERENCES

1 For this view see, for instance, Aris, *History of Political Thought in Germany*, pp. 296–7.

2 My italics. G. Ritter, "Die Ausprägung deutscher und westeuropäischer Geistesart im konfessionellen Zeitalter," *Historische Zeitschrift*, Vol. CXLIX, No. 2, (1934), pp. 247–8.

3 For example, July 2, 1872; April 22, 1873. But of the four Jewish members of the Reichstag, three voted against the anti-Jesuit law and the other abstained.

4 Dubnow, *Neueste Geschichte des jüdischen Volkes*, Vol. II, p. 333.

5 L. F. A. von Pastor, *August Reichensperger, 1808–95, Sein Leben und Wirken* (Freiburg, 1899), Vol. II, p. 191.

6 *StBPrA*, Sept. 20, 1880, Vol. CCLXXXVI, pp. 231 ff.

7 Gehlsen, *Aus dem Reiche Bismarcks*, p. 65; R. H. Bowen, *German Theories of the Corporate State* (New York, 1947), p. 108.

8 *KZ*, April 17, 1892.

9 K. Epstein, *Matthias Erzberger and the Dilemma of German Democracy* (Princeton, 1959), p. 402; *MVA*, Jan. 3, 1912, p. 3; May 22, 1912, p. 83.

10 *MVA*, March 19, 1893, p. 121; May 8, 1912, p. 79.

11 *Kölnische Volkszeitung*, Nov. 28, 1892.

12 Speech on March 6, 1895. *StBR*, IX. Leg., 53. Sess., pp. 1286–7.

13 *MVA*, Jan. 17, 1912, pp. 10–11.

14 Kürschner, *Der neue Reichstag*, 1907, 1912.

15 Fritsch, *Antisemiten-Katechismus*, pp. 337–8.

16 *StBR*, X. Leg., 1. Sess., *Anlage 77*, pp. 437–525.

17 Wawrzinek, *Die Entstehung der deutschen Antisemitenparteien*, p. 72.

18 R. Haglestange, "Metamorphosen des Antisemitismus," *Deutsche Rundschau*, Vol. LXXX, No. 12 (1954), p. 1256.

29

The Sociology of Anti-Semitic Movements

A great deal has already emerged in the preceding chapters about the social composition of the anti-Semitic movements in both countries; nevertheless a recapitulation and analysis would be useful here.

In general, anti-Semitism drew little strength from either the working class or the aristocracy. The industrial proletariat of Germany and Austria was well organized, well drilled, and politically conscious to a degree which was probably unequaled in any other country. The German party was the model child of the Second International and the Austrian party—or at least its German section—was its Siamese twin. Most of the worker's educational and cultural needs were met by party organizations, and he was proud of the understanding of history, economics, and politics he had gained from evening lectures, theoretical journals, and twenty-pfennig pamphlets. He knew that national and religious arguments were at best irrelevant to a solution of his problems and at worst a deliberate attempt to cloud his view of the "real issues."

Against such indoctrination by party educational machines, the Churches, Catholic and Protestant, could do little. As Bernanos puts it:

> It is merely comic for us to tremble with fervour and offer the encyclical *Rerum Novarum* to men who have read Marx and Lenin and have dreamt the great dream of proletarian revolution.[1]

In Germany, it is true, the Centre Party continued to hold the loyalty of a substantial, though diminishing, proportion of Catholic workers, but they supported it less out of sympathy with its social program (which was not in any way remarkable) than out of traditional feelings, strengthened by the hard-pressed minority position of the German Church. Similarly, the Nationalist labor movement claimed some working men in Bohemia. But these two examples are worth mentioning as the only major exceptions.

The economic reform programs of the anti-Semitic parties did not hold out much attraction for industrial workers. Although some sort of factory legislation was generally urged, there were few proposals to remedy the even worse conditions of employees and apprentices employed in artisan businesses,★ where union organization was much more difficult, and an extension of the guild system would have threatened what little chance for betterment was open to the average working man.

The workers did not see the Jews with the same eyes as the upper or middle classes. If they were exploited by a Jewish employer, they generally knew that conditions in Gentile establishments were no better; and the financier and broker seemed a less immediate enemy than the capitalist. They did not fail to notice that there were many Jews—including some who could have led comfortable middle class existences had they chosen to—who had taken up their cause. They had no particular reason either to hate or to love Jews as a group. Certainly at a time when the working class as a whole felt discriminated against and without a stake in the country, they were not going to concern themselves too much with discrimination against Jews, some of whom, at any rate, seemed not to be doing too badly.

Similarly, the aristocracy did not associate itself in large numbers with political anti-Semitism, a fact which the handful of well-known anti-Semitic aristocrats should not allow us to overlook. Certainly there were social barriers which made it difficult for the moneyed Jew to mix on equal terms with the aristocracy, but these existed for the Gentile *parvenu* also. For Jews to be admitted in Vienna or Potsdam as freely as were the Sassoons, Cassels, or Rothschilds at the court of King Edward

---

★ For a significant description of the exploitation of these apprentices at this time, see the autobiography of the Christian-Social trade union leader Leopold Kunschak. Conditions in carpentry, shoemaking, and tailoring "cried to heaven." (*Steinchen vom Wege*, Vienna, 1952, p. 29).

VII* would have been unthinkable, but there was a fair amount of intermarriage, a tendency which the more radical, anti-Junker type of anti-Semites made much play of. (One anti-Semitic publication, the *Semi-Gotha,* listed over 1000 families whom penury had driven into *Verjudung.*)

The more hard-pressed *Krautjunker* might subscribe to the anti-Jewish clauses of the Tivoli Program, but neither they nor the Agrarian League can be considered the driving force of the anti-Semitic movement. The days of the Free Corps, the *Stahlhelm,* and the *Heimwehr* were not yet; the same snobbery which kept the aristocrat aloof from the Jewish bourgeoisie kept him also from demagogic anti-Semitism.

We are therefore driven to seek the bulk of anti-Semitic support in the middle class and above all in a particular section of it—the middle and lower professional grades and the middle and small businessmen. The large industrialists in general were not interested. There were few Jewish rivals at that level. Krupp, Stinnes, Thyssen, and Stumm had little to fear from Jew or fellow Gentile. This is borne out by such detailed analysis as is possible of the membership of anti-Semitic organizations. As good an example as any, because it was a nation-wide body, is the Pan-German League which was half-inside, half-outside the anti-Semitic camp.

TABLE I I. MEMBERSHIP OF PAN-GERMAN LEAGUE
BY PROFESSIONS, 1901[2]

	In Germany	Outside Germany
Professors, University Lecturers	5,339	560
Small Businessmen	4,905	383
Artists, Officials, Teachers	3,760	262
Artisans, Workers	2,673	186
Others	1,507	221
Total	18,184	1,612

* Occasionally levées were arranged on Thursdays instead of Fridays to suit Lord Swaythling.

TABLE I2. PERCENTAGE OF TEACHING AND MEDICAL PROFESSIONS
AMONG LOCAL OFFICERS OF THE PAN–GERMAN LEAGUE[3]

	1896	1906	1914
Teaching Profession	25%	36%	24%
Medical Profession	8	10	8

The occupations of party leaders and members of parliament
are a less reliable guide, first because some professions, such as the
law and journalism, are prominent in the parliamentary representation of all parties, second because many deputies describe
themselves as "publicists" or "party secretaries," which gives no
clue to their social origins. Summarizing the biographical
information given about the German anti-Semitic deputies in the
Reichstagshandbücher, "which is neither complete nor too specific,"
Massing observes:

> In terms of social background, three major groups were not,
> or hardly, represented. None of the members came from the
> ranks of industrial labour. With the exception of two, Lieber-
> mann von Sonnenberg and Count Ludwig von Reventlow, the
> aristocracy was ostensibly missing . . . . Although the group
> contained men who declared themselves to be merchants and the
> sons of merchants, not one of them came from, or represented,
> big industry, trade or finance. Next to small industrial and
> agricultural enterpreneurs, artisans and small merchants, the
> group counted among its members teachers, lawyers, civil
> servants and [white collar] employees.
> The group's educational level was above the average. Of the
> forty-three men for whom educational data are available,
> nineteen had a university background and only thirteen did not
> have more formal education than high school; the remainder had
> gone to college or its equivalent in special art schools, trade
> schools, etc. The proportion of men with academic background
> and holding public office increased somewhat in later years.[4]

In Austria, as we have already noted, the German Nationalists
were chiefly representative of the professional *Mittelstand;* indeed
the *Volkspartei* came to be nicknamed *Professorenpartei.* Of its
founders, Steinwender was a schoolmaster and Strohal a professor of law. The Nationalists, representing the literate—and
therefore ultimately more dangerous—wing of anti-Semitism,

could hardly feel at ease with Christian-Social fundamentalists like Hermann Bielohlawek who called Tolstoi an *"alter Tepp,"* and whose reactions to the mention of a book* anticipated the more celebrated response of Baldur von Schirach on a similar topic.

The romantic nationalism imbibed during university days also influenced the politics of professional men in later life, again more decisively in Austria than in Germany, where the distinction between being "Christian" and "national" hardly existed. True, the wild enthusiasm of pan-German beer orgies gave way to the more staid and constitutional sentiments of, say, the *Volkspartei,* as the graduate began to taste Imperial patronage— and to take a pride in his part in the administration and maintenance of the Empire. Still, the nationalist sentiments of the older and younger generations sustained each other through the *Burschenschaften* where the *alte Herren* mixed with students; how decisively this cross-fertilization of ideas could act is shown by Professor Wandruszka[5] who points out that in the 1930's in Austria it was in the main the younger generation of "national" opinion who persuaded their fathers that Nazism was merely the logical application of the slogans they had been mouthing since their *Burschenschaft* days—as indeed it was.

More significant than the parliamentary representation of a party is the social composition of its rank-and-file and subaltern leadership. Two undated manuscript registers of the Viennese executive committee of Schönerer's party indicate the fairly narrow range which formed the hard core of the movement. The first[6] names forty professional and twenty-three businessmen: nine civil servants or clerks, seven lawyers, five doctors, five accountants, five property owners, and three students are among those named. On the second[7] there are twenty-three professional men, including seven officials, four lawyers, three teachers, three accountants, and two doctors; and fifteen businessmen, including a photographer, a dispensing chemist, and a coffee-roaster.

The pan-German movement, more active, as we have seen, outside the strictly political field than in it, also paid more attention to the economic needs of the *Mittelstand.* A party

* *"Wann i a Büachl sieh, dös hob' i schogfressen."*

employment exchange, the *Deutschvölkische Stellenvermittlung in Wien*, a "nonpolitical association," existed for the purpose of "assisting unemployed Germans (of Aryan descent) to a livelihood"[8] and in 1890 *Ostmark*, a co-operative society, savings bank, and low-interest loan institute for self-employed persons, was founded to shield prospective members "from the dangers of the international capitalist economy and exploitation by the ever-lusting workings of stock exchange speculation."[9] The foundation appeal had ninety-four signatories—thirteen officials, six doctors, five teachers, three accountants, two architects, and altogether forty-three businessmen, including a soap-boiler, a decorator, a baker, a coppersmith, a glazier, an innkeeper, a cheesemonger, and Herr Josef Schneider, *Personaleinkommensteuerschätzungscommissionsmitgliedersatzmann*.[10] Other economic organizations in Vienna included a Register of German Tradespeople (1899) and a *Deutschvölkischer Gehülfenverein*.

The German *Handlungsgehilfenverband* had already shown what a fruitful field for anti-Semitic recruitment this was. The new class of white-collar workers, a natural result of the concentration and bureaucratization of industry and the expansion of the distributive trades, was in fact growing numerically more than any other section of society. In the great cities the percentage of inhabitants in commercial employment rose from 6.5 to 12.7.[12]

TABLE 13. PERCENTAGE INCREASE OF EMPLOYERS, INDUSTRIAL WORKERS, AND WHITE-COLLAR WORKERS IN GERMANY[11]

	1882–1907	1895–1907
Employers	-7.9	-2.52
Industrial Employees	109.78	44.28
Commercial Employees	592.40	160.10

Economically, the members of the "new *Mittelstand*" as it was often called) were almost indistinguishable from the proletariat, since their essential function was to sell labor which was, at best, semi-skilled in exchange for wages. In social status, however, they were distinct from the working class and in a society as rigidly hierarchic as the German, they were strongly endowed with *Standesdünkel*, or "consciousness of class superiority." Their wages and conditions of work were generally far from good, and their aversion to cloth-cap methods like strikes and collective bargaining made their position even more precarious. They were therefore, despite the apparent increase of their economic importance, a classic example of a class constantly threatened with depression into the proletariat. Their two preoccupations were to keep their distance from those below and to secure from their employers—more likely to be Jewish in commerce than in industry—better conditions.

Some of the sources of political anti-Semitism, therefore, are self-evident. Among farmers and traders there was economic discontent; among aristocrats and climbers there was snobbery; among some of all classes there was religious prejudice, dating from a pre-Liberal, pre-capitalist era. But these did not provide the sole motivating force. The characteristic of twentieth-century politics has been the triumph of ideology over self-interest. The ideology which increasingly provided the impulse to political anti-Semitism toward the end of our period was common to both Germany and Austria—pan-Germanism. Wherein did its appeal to the professional classes, the intelligentsia, above all to students lie?

There was first the legacy of classical nationalism, derived from Rousseau and Herder. The object of this is widely assumed to have been the creation of nation-states, proclaiming the right of all those who spoke the same language to determine the boundaries of their polity. It very rarely worked out like that. The distinction between "states" and "peoples" came from Rousseau. It created no insoluble problems in the "West'—North-western Europe and North America—and was there able to accommodate itself as popular control of already existing (or simultaneously created) national states. Later it was transplanted to areas more backward in social and political development, where the concept of the nation was in contradiction with that of the existing state pattern. In Germany, and outside Western Europe generally, nationalism

> did not find its justification in a rational societal conception, it found it in the "natural" fact of a community held together, not by the will of its members, nor by any obligations of contract, but by traditional ties of kinship and status. German nationalism

278

substituted for the legal and rational concept of "citizenship" the infinitely vaguer concept of "folk."[13]

This means that the revolutionary intellectual becomes a rebel only against the particular authoritarianism which puts the claims of dynasties above those of "nations," not against authoritarianism as such.

The notion of the primacy of the nation over the state was reinforced by two other factors. The first is that east of the Rhine and north of the Alps no nation occupied a closed area. Each was burdened with mixed regions, enclaves, and irredenta. In particular, the Bismarckian Empire notoriously failed to solve the question of the unity of the German nation. The second is that the landlocked states of Central and Eastern Europe were handicapped in the late-nineteenth-century race to expand overseas. The victims of imperial domination would have to be "nonhistoric" neighbors or strangers within the gate. The base for this continental, as opposed to overseas, imperialism was not the existing state, but the folk community transcending boundaries. It differed from overseas imperialism in that it offered few material or economic advantages; it moved from abstract premises to speculative conclusions. As Hannah Arendt has pointed out:

> Continental imperialism . . . started with a much closer affinity to race concepts, enthusiastically absorbed the tradition of race-thinking, and relied very little on specific experiences. Its race concepts were completely ideological in basis, and developed much more quickly into a convenient political weapon than similar theories expressed by overseas imperialists which could always claim a certain basis in authentic experience . . . .
>
> Among [its] leaders, therefore, we find almost no businessmen and few adventurers, but many members of the free professions, teachers and civil servants.[14]

Pan-Germanism was not a policy, it was the expression of a mood; how this mood arose we have seen in the writings of Lagarde and Langbehn, in the facts of German and Austrian political development after 1867.

REFERENCES

1 G. Bernanos, *La Grande Peur des Bien-Pensants* (Paris, 1931), p. 441.
2 From data given by Wertheimer, *The Pan-German League*, p. 65. See also, L. Werner, "Der Alldeutsche Verband, 1890–1918," *Historische Studien* 278 (Berlin 1935), pp. 64–6.
3 Wertheimer, *op. cit.*, p. 66.
4 Massing, *Rehearsal for Destruction*, pp. 236–7.
5 H. Benedikt (ed.), *Geschichte der Republik Österreich* (Munich, 1954), pp. 402, 405–6.
6 *NP, ÖVA*, Box 37, fol. 2.
7 *NP, ÖVA*, Box 37, fol. 1.
8 *NP, ÖVA*, Box 37, fol. 3.
9 *NP, ÖVA*, Box 40.
10 *NP, ÖVA*, Box 40.
11 E. Lederer and J. Marschak, "Der neue Mittelstand," *Grundriss der Sozial-ökonomik*, Vol. IX, No. 1 (Tübingen, 1926), pp. 127–8.
12 *Ibid.*
13 H. Kohn, *The Idea of Nationalism* (New York, 1946), p. 331.
14 Arendt, *Origins of Totalitarianism*, pp. 224, 225.

30

The Position in 1914

Many are still hesitating to attach themselves openly to the movement . . . . [the *Österreichischer Volksfreund* complained 1882]. The main cause is concern at being considered intolerant, unenlightened, reactionary if they attach themselves to anti-Semitism, and this argument is being exploited with great cleverness and habitual shamelessness by the Jewish press.[1]

In those days, under the all-pervading influence of Liberal broadmindedness, anti-Semitism was felt to be one of the vestiges of the Middle Ages finally overhauled by progress. A generation later anti-Semitic propagandists were able to claim victory:

For a number of years [according to Kuhlenbeck] there has been a remarkable swing in the *Weltanschauung* of at least the educated circles, away from the cosmopolitan or universalist points of view which, in particular, clung as a matter of principle to the equal worth of all human beings, without difference of race, in its estimate of their fitness for culture and political life.[2]

Lange was even blunter:

I assert that the attitude of educated Germans towards Judaism has become totally different from what it was only a few years ago . . . . The Jewish Question is today no longer a question of "whether"? but only one of "how"?[3]

Even members of royal houses were less concerned with keeping aloof from anti-Semitism than the generation of William I or Francis Joseph had been. William II annotated Count Münster's dispatches on the Panama Affair with *"Juden-moral"*[4] and his son, the Crown Prince, attended conferences of the *Verein deutscher Studenten* in the company of anti-Semitic deputies.[5] In Austria there were complaints of public anti-Semitic utterances by the Archdukes Frederick and Francis Ferdinand.[6]

Insofar as they had impregnated wide sections of the population with anti-Semitic ideas, the anti-Semitic parties had not only succeeded in their object but also worked themselves out of a job. On the other hand, they had failed to secure the adoption of any of their legislative proposals, and the fact that most of their electoral followers seemed content with rhetoric, slogans and gestures made the achievement of this seem all the more remote.

Some originally anti-Semitic bodies were adopting a studied vagueness in their attitude to the Jewish Question. One Christian-Social candidate (Linz) in the German elections of 1907 felt obliged to

> point out that in the fifteen years in which I have been active in public life, no unfriendly, let alone harsh, word about our Israelite fellow-citizens has ever passed my lips.[7]

and the *Kreuzzeitung* complained that at Kolmar (Pomerania) in the same election:

> Nobody has heard so much as a word against the Jews from the anti-Semitic agitators.[8]

The gap between the fanatically and specifically anti-Semitic bodies and those pursuing primarily economic or nationalist aims was therefore widening. Indeed, we can, by 1914, distinguish between two categories: those which needed to reinforce their initial anti-Semitic appeal with an economic and social program and those whose economic and social program remained a bait for anti-Semitic recruitment. For instance, the *Deutsche Mittelstandsvereinigung* was never, as we have already seen, fully committed to anti-Semitism,* and was even less reliable on this matter after it had split in 1908 on the protection issue.[9] A new, protectionist, nominally apolitical organization was set up in the *Reichsdeutscher Mittelstandsbund* in 1911; like all protectionist bodies, such as the *Bund der Handwerker,* it necessarily became a satellite of the Agrarian League, a fact which it frankly acknowledged.[10]

* See pp. 188–9.

The electoral record of the anti-Semitic parties showed the same tendencies at work. In 1903 at Marburg Hellmut von Gerlach, of Naumann's National Social Party, defeated Böckel, only to be himself beaten by the anti-Semites in 1907. Throughout this period the Naumannite and anti-Semitic votes were virtually interchangeable. Again, at a by-election in 1913, Naumann himself won the nearby seat of Waldeck from the anti-Semites. Notwithstanding the great number of anti-Semitic candidatures, the Jewish Question itself was hardly an issue in the 1912 election. It was essentially a battle between the urban, constitutional, free-trading elements, represented by the Progressives and the Social Democrats and the "blue-black" *bloc* of Centre and Conservatives, resulting in a massive victory for the Left. The Agrarian League was speaking for a small minority when it concluded that

> this electoral battle has shown itself as the assault by Judaism, or more broadly, the Jewish spirit, on the foundations of our national and popular life, the like of which in intensity and openness, has never been seen in Germany.[11]

But this minority, the "national opposition" as it was called in retrospect, took the defeat with deadly seriousness. Heinrich Class' *Wenn ich der Kaiser wär,* which appeared some months later, was one rallying point; another was the "masonic" *Germanen-Orden.* * Rather less secretive was the "Association against Jewish Arrogance," but it was significant that its leading lights came from the para-political organizations—the Pan-German League, the Commercial Employees' Union, gymnasts, and student bodies.[12] Fritsch, who had always regarded electoral politics as useless, lamented, "It is bitterly true: the anti-Semitic movement has lost a campaign."[13]

But, for reasons he could not possibly have foreseen, there was a most dramatic reversal of fortunes within a few years.

REFERENCES

1 *ÖV,* July 2, 1882.
2 Kuhlenbeck, *Rasse und Volkstum,* pp. 1–2.
3 Lange, *Reines Deutschtum,* pp. 90–1.

* See pp. 225–6.

4 W. Frank, *Nationalismus und Demokratie im Frankreich der 3. Republik, 1871 bis 1918* (Hamburg, 1933), p. 294.
5 *MIU*, Jan., 1905, p. 19.
6 *MIU*, Aug., 1904, p. 25.
7 Curtius, *Der politische Antisemitismus*, p. 8.
8 *Ibid.*, p. 21.
9 Bürger, *Die deutsche Mittelstandsbewegung*, p. 28.
10 Kiesenwetter, *Fünfundzwanzig Jahre wirtschaftspolitischen Kampfes*, p. 169.
11 *Deutsche Tageszeitung*, Jan. 25, 1912.
12 Buch, *50 Jahre antisemitische Bewegung*, p. 27.
13 Fritsch, *Neue Wege*, pp. 287–8.

EPILOGUE: 1914–1938

Anti-Semitism, either systematically pursued for its own sake or as an integral part of a wider political ideology, flourishes only in particular economic and social conditions. It is a product of the post-liberal age; an age which has experienced the impact of industrialization, scientific thought, and democratic ideals.

In Anglo-Saxon countries, and in Western Europe generally, the "industrial revolution" was both slow and thorough. It gave to the industrial nations a bourgeois character that ranged wider than the class which created the changes: the doctrine "may the best man win" was—and is—widely accepted. As long as the ideology of the open society flourishes, organized political anti-Semitism will find it difficult to strike political roots. As we travel further east and south across Europe, the less capitalism had developed by 1914, the less successfully had Liberal ideas and institutions been grafted on to the societies concerned. Only a fraction of the industrialization could be ascribed to autochthonous entrepreneurs; the state played a large part (Prussian coal mines, Russian railways), as did foreign investors (Rumanian railways, Viennese gas services). Where the money for industrialization was raised domestically, it came generally from banks and credit institutes and was thus a matter for a small and closed group. After the "finger-burning" of 1873, the general public of Germany and Austria had no further desire to speculate in equities. The more the balance of power favored financial capital over industrial, the greater was the share of the Jew in determining the course of the economy.

Reasons have already been suggested why Jews inclined more to financial operations than to industrial empire building. In Germany heavy industry was a predominantly Gentile business and banking partly, but by no means entirely, Jewish; in cisleithan Austria, finance was almost entirely in Jewish hands, as were certain sections of industry (textiles, paper milling, some

285

coal mines); further east still, where social immobility was even greater and the terms "bourgeois" and "Jew" for a long time almost synonymous, manufacturers as well as bankers were overwhelmingly Jewish. Where, therefore, the growth of capitalism was a process with which the majority of the population could not identify itself and where it failed thoroughly to stir the class pot, those feelings of pessimistic anger and pseudo-revolutionary conservatism, which we have seen are to be associated with anti-Semitism, were bound to assert themselves. Where the financial-capitalist community was not only easily identifiable but already burdened with centuries of religious hatred, all prerequisite factors were present.

Moreover, as far as Germany and Austria were concerned, the experience of earlier "industrial revolutions" had, by the time industrialization spread to these countries, helped to evolve a coherent theory of Socialism; this was imported ready-made—the North German Parliament of 1867 already contained two Social Democrats—and the lower social mobility enabled it to spread much faster than in the earlier industrial powers (Great Britain, France, United States). Thus Liberalism was even less capable of seizing the imagination of the majority and quickly became the creed only of a minority class with a stake in capitalism. It even alienated large sections of the middle class who had been Liberals from the 1840's to the 1860's, and anti-Semitism was able to take advantage of their political homelessness.

Second, the new ways of thought introduced by the scientific revolution were influential. This may seem surprising and is certainly paradoxical. Anti-Semitism may be irrational, anti-intellectual, and often superstitious; in general it treats with suspicion the findings of science and the respect for fact and logic which characterize the modern scholar. It has, nevertheless, tried to build an anti-science of its own, drawing with bewildering eclecticism on biology, anthropology, theology and psychology to construct a theory of "race." Indeed, it is instructive to follow the changing anti-Semitic attitude to Darwin. Early Christian-conservative anti-Semites not only rejected Darwinism on biblical grounds, but disliked any attempt to justify a competitive economy with Darwinian analogies. But from the turn of the century onward the theory of "the survival of the fittest" became increasingly attractive to the political anthropologists and increasingly useful to doctrines of racial superiority. Parallel to this change there evolved a revised attitude toward religion. Whereas the generation of the 1860's and 1870's had in the main been orthodox Christians, the more democratically inclined anti-Semites were often "liberal" in religious outlook and anti-clerical. The great majority of racialists have either been overtly hostile to orthodox Christianity or at best lukewarm toward it. They disliked its links with Judaism, is universality, and its gospel of compassion. Under the impact of nineteenth-century thought they regarded religion as a social or national characteristic, devoid of universal moral validity.

Third, this anti-Semitism is unthinkable without democracy. This, too, may seem paradoxical; and anti-Semitism is certainly incompatible with parliamentary government and the civil rights which this implies; but, aimed as it is at the "small man" and the *Lumpenproletariat,* it must recognize the right of the masses to take part in the political process. Modern anti-Semitism, even in its earliest beginnings with Stöcker and Schönerer, has been demagogic. It has, from its beginnings, made a populistic appeal to grass roots—anti-élitist, anti-individualist, anti-intellectual. Its democracy was plebiscitary, presaging that "tyranny of the majority" which Liberals from Aristotle onward have feared as the outcome if the masses entered politics; but it could flourish only in a century already familiarized by Liberalism with the principle of popular participation in government.

It is to be identified in particular with that important byproduct of Rousseau-ian democracy, nationalism. Based on the principle of self-determination, nationalism also claims to be derived from Liberal doctrine. Unfortunately, experience shows that in the pursuit of that one object it quickly loses sight of all other tenets of Liberalism and of the moral obligations which Liberalism imposes, and assumes a single, infallible, general will.

Nationalism degenerates, like the larger Romantic movement of which it was a part, first into irresponsibility, then into nihilism. The literary representatives of its last phase are Barrès, d'Annunzio or Roy Campbell, combining *le culte du moi* with swashbuckling military enterprises. Though often inspired in its first stage by the urge to emancipate, it finds its logical conclusion in a paroxysm of destructiveness. Realizing this, we can understand Hitler's threat—so nearly carried out—that if the Thousand-Year *Reich* collapsed it would drag the world with it; we can understand also the terrorism which so frequently accompanies nationalist agitation.

An important factor in the violence of anti-Semitic politics was the feeling of powerlessness which was common to anti-Semites. Throughout the nineteenth century some or all Jews in Western or Central Europe appeared to occupy a privileged position. Before emancipation this applied to the court bankers, afterward to all those who took advantage of the Liberal, capitalist order that seemed tailor-made to serve their peculiar ambitions, and to all those who succeeded in circumventing barriers which seemed insurmountable for Gentiles constricted within a rigid social system. In Austria-Hungary this attitude to the "privileged" Jew was complicated by the conflict of nationalities. To the nonhistoric nations the Jew appeared as an accomplice of the dominant, historic nations; to the lower middle class among the historic nations as a member of the wealthy oligarchy; to pan-Germans or pan-Slavs who wished to destroy the Monarchy as one of the supranational, centripetal forces, helping the Habsburg domains to cohere.

The despair of ever being able to defeat the Jew in an equal fight is common to all anti-Semitic writers, for his triumph is merely a sympton of universal rottenness. Vogelsang opposed Jewish emancipation because it leads directly to Jewish domination;[1] Lagarde echoed him, "because I know the Germans, I cannot wish that Jews should be allowed to mingle with them;"[2] Langbehn began his book with the words:

> It has gradually become an open secret that the spiritual life of the German people is at the present time in a state of slow—some would even say, rapid—decay.[3]

The lesser pamphleteers spoke in the same vein:

> We Germans completed in the year 1848 our abdication in favour of the Jews . . . . Life and the future belong to Judaism, death and the past to Germandom

wrote Marr;[4] Ahlwardt wrote of the Aryans' "desperate struggle" and Glagau lamented, "How quickly has all the glory, recently won, paled and waned!"[5]

After 1918 this pessimism became even more acute, but the change was quantitative, not qualitative. Social psychologists working in the 1940's and 1950's report findings very similar to the evidence of the earlier period. Bettelheim and Janowitz, investigating United States war veterans, note that many more anti-Semites than others thought that army service had set them back in some way, or that they had a "bad break" during their time in the forces,[6] although there was no noteworthy discrepancy between the two groups in the type of army experience. The authors comment:

> A man's evaluation of his army career in retrospect was largely independent of the actual deprivations experienced and depended mainly on his emotional attitude towards this experience in particular and, one may add, life in general.[7]

Robb, working in Bethnal Green, London, describes the typical extreme anti-Semites as

> display[ing] a marked degree of pessimism and lack of confidence in themselves and in the groups to which they belong, but the weaknesses implied in these attitudes are justified by reference to the power of external forces. These are sometimes located in other groups (e.g., the Jews), but even more frequently seen as impersonal and vague, e.g., the action of fate. The world as a whole is seen as threatening and bad.[8]
> One outstanding trait of these individuals is that they manage to imply both strength and weakness at the same time. They are strong, good, hard-working and altogether worthy, and the people like themselves . . . with whom they identify, are similarly outstanding. But at the same time circumstances are too much for them. Fate, traitors, outsiders, the force of events, are against them and somehow just cannot be overcome.[9]

On the other hand not everyone who is down on his luck or facing poor prospects hates the Jews:

> Tolerant persons [says Robb] seem to be not so much lacking in conflicts as more aware of the nature of the conflicts, even though they may be little more successful in dealing with them.[10]

As political despair and collective paranoia grow, as nationalism becomes more debased, so the attitude to Jews changes. We can trace this from generation to generation: the Liberals of 1848 who embraced them as fellow Germans; Treitschke who was one of the first to draw the distinction between "acceptable" occidental Jews and Polish Jews with whom Germans had nothing in common;[11] and the racial mystics to whom the Jews were the most pernicious non-Germans.

There lies the fundamental antinomy of anti-Semitism and Liberalism, the fundamental assault by anti-Semitism on those Western values on whose survival the Jew more than anybody else depended. Not for nothing did one Nazi historian conclude:

> It was clear that the German Jewish community signified a kind of prolongation of the Western world, born of the French Revolution, towards the East.[12]

In contrast, surprising as it may once have seemed, Liberalism has reconciled itself with a fair amount of economic collectivism in most advanced states. The reason, as we have had cause to notice before, is that the moral inspiration (as opposed to the economic theories) of both Liberalism and Social Democracy sprang from the same sources, and modern Social Democracy has taken over from—or shares with—Liberalism many of its traditional attitudes and favorite causes.

With anti-Semitism, on the other hand, there has always been a total failure of communication, in a way which underlines the humaneness of Liberal thought and its underestimate of human capacity for wickedness.

> Anti-Semitism [wrote Lucien Wolf in the *Encyclopaedia Britannica*] has left no permanent mark of a constructive kind on the social and political evolution of Europe . . . . It has spent itself in intrigues of transparent dishonesty . . . while its political activity has revealed the vulgarity and ignorance which constitute its main sources of strength.[13]

For most Liberals this would have been an adequate discussion of the topic; indeed they sometimes replied with mere impatience to any argument of its case. Of Treitschke's articles the *Neue Freie Presse* wrote:

> With its leading thought we see him place himself on a standpoint which absolves any liberal-minded and educated person in future from concerning himself with him,[14]

and Mommsen, pressed to make yet another appeal for reason and tolerance, wearily declined:

> You are mistaken if you believe that I could achieve anything in this matter. You are mistaken if you believe that anything at all could be achieved by reason. In years past I thought so myself and kept protesting against the monstrous infamy that is anti-Semitism. But it is useless, completely useless. Whatever I or anybody else could tell you are in the last analysis reasons, logical and ethical arguments which no anti-Semite will listen to. They listen only to their own envy and hatred, to the meanest instincts. Nothing else counts for them. They are deaf to reason, right, morals. One cannot influence them. What is there really to tell someone who follows the *Rektor* of all Germans? Such a man is hopeless. There is no protection against the mob, be it the mob of the streets or of the parlours. *Canaille* remains *canaille*. It is a horrible epidemic, like cholera—one can neither explain nor cure it. One must patiently wait until the poison has consumed itself and lost its virulence.*

But, when all is said and done (it may be argued), the movements and ideologies described in these pages could show only the most negligible results by 1918. Emancipation was untouched. The statute books remaned unamended. The parties and their leaders were without influence. This is to miss the point. Thirty years of incessant propaganda had been more effective than men thought at the time; anti-Semitism was no longer disgraceful in wide social and academic circles; the vulgarities of men like Bielohlawek and Ernst Schneider in representative assemblies† permanently lowered the tone of public debate. Above all, it is a fact sometimes forgotten in the history of ideas that all the movements most fashionable in the 1920's and 1930's—artistic and literary as well as political—had their intellectual roots in the pre-war years. The great prophets of violence, irrationalism, and pessimism belong to that period.‡

---

* Massing, *op. cit.*, p. 168. Even Social Democrats sometimes relied on mere invective as a weapon of rebuttal. Liebknecht reserved for anti-Semitism the worst insult in the German vocabulary: it represented *Anti-Kultur* (Speech in Reichstag, November 30, 1893. *StBr*, IX. Leg., 2. Sess., p. 180).
† For examples of continuous insinuations against Jewish doctors see Kolmer, *op. cit.*, Vol. V, pp. 236–7, Vol. VI, p. 145, Vol. VII, pp. 246, 256–7.
‡ See p. 234.

The arsenal was fully assembled in 1918. It was merely a question of waiting for the order to fire.

The main difference between the political anti-Semitism of the post- and pre-war periods lies not in its content, but in its success. There were some changes in emphasis, a general increase in virulence of tone and unscrupulousness, and a growing acceptance of physical violence; but one would have to go a very long way through the anti-Semitic literature of the 1920's or early 1930's to discover a point or argument which had not already been used before 1914. The generation of Alfred Rosenberg appears as mere *epigoni*. What we need to know, therefore, is what changed in the political and social environment that turned the ravings of obscure sects into major prophecies.

Even here we have to be careful, and note the undercurrents of continuity beneath the surface of revolutionary changes. The victories of the Social Democratic parties in Germany and Austria did not bring victory for Socialism; on the contrary they liberalized society and the state still further, completing the process begun by the legislation of the years after 1867 — democratization, secularization, social atomization. The Socialist parties used the military defeat of the old order to exact from it concessions whose context was essentially the pre-1914 world — that world whose end was signalized by the end of the war. The societies of post-1918 Central Europe were therefore characterized by greater social mobility, more blatant capitalism, an even bigger influence exercised by the metropolis; they were, more than before, *parvenu* societies.

That is to say, whatever the extreme Right had found objectionable in pre-war society they now found more objectionable still, even though it took some time for this strengthened opposition to emerge in organized form. In Germany this opposition was initially, and primariy, represented by the Nationalist Party (DNVP) which was not the lineal successor of any pre-war body. Indeed, to understand its position and the whole pattern of Weimar politics, we have to go back to Spring, 1917, when a majority of the Reichstag, led by Erzberger and consisting of the Social Democrats, the Centre, and the Progressives, passed a motion in favor of a negotiated peace, as opposed to a "peace by victory" which was the aim of official policy. In response to this "defeatism" the *Vaterlandspartei* was formed by men of the traditional Right, but including also some National Liberals and a number of others from further to the Left who had succumbed to the call of patriotism. It was the parties of the Reichstag majority which secured, in the last week of the war, the reform of the franchise and the establishment of responsible cabinet government; it was they who were basically responsible for the elaboration of the Republican constitution and who became known as the "Weimar coalition."

The groups included in the *Vaterlandspartei* coalesced in the DNVP. It was composed of the two old Conservative parties, the Christian-Socials and the *Deutschvölkische Partei*, comprising all that remained of the pre-war radical anti-Semites, recruits from the Agrarian League, and the Pan-Germans, of whom Hugenberg was the most important, and many non-Conservatives who had been drawn to the Right by the war, such as ex-Pastor Gottfried Traub and the economist Karl Helfferich. For the moment, the need to avert revolution concealed the fact that this was an uneasy coalition of two quite distinct tendencies, which might be called the "conservative" and the "*völkisch.*"

The origin of this split was in the Wilhelmine period when, as we have noticed, the Right opposition had been united by a rejection of the positivist and materialistic ideas of progress and human happiness, but divided by the extent of its rejection. On the one hand there were reformers like Stöcker and his Austrian opposite number, Lueger, who were not alienated from the ruling groups but wished to influence them. They worked within existing conservative parties or in close contact with them.

There were others, prophets of opposition and self-confessed outsiders, who rejected the brassy, plutocratic establishment *in toto*. Their chief mentor was Nietzsche, though his hatred of modern vulgarity made him also hate anti-Semitism and racialism.* Lagarde and Langbehn were the leading anti-Semites of that school and the Youth Movement the main offspring of their neo-Romanticism. They shared with the *völkisch* school of

---

* Nietzsche's weakness on this point caused the racialists some embarrassment. The official historian of the Pan-German League attributed it to his "Sarmatian" ancestry (Bonhard, *Geschichte des Alldeutschen Verbandes*, p. 187).

both Germany and Austria a complete lack of interest in that typical artefact of nineteenth-century Liberalism, the territorial nation-state. Occupying a halfway stage between these two tendencies was the Pan-German League. It belonged, in part, to the official Imperialism and *Weltmacht* ideology of the Wilhelmine period; but the circle round Class and Schemann, with its admiration of Chamberlain and Gobineau, belonged to the racialist school, less interested in short-term power-politics. It is evident that Germany's disappearance as a great power, the heady emotional experience of the war—the *Fronterlebnis*—and the disillusionment with a "Revolution" which did nothing to reform society, would enormously strengthen the radical, revolutionary Right at the expense of the smug or cautious wings, concerned only with restoring the frontiers and the social order of 1914.

It was both these horses that the DNVP tried to ride; the discredit of orthodox conservatism and its association with the pre-war leadership gave the racialists and social reformers in the party, such as the Commercial Employees' Union, their chance. They helped considerably to extend its influence in Western Germany and the big cities, so that it became the nation-wide party it had never been in the Empire.[15] Nevertheless, the Stöckerian element remained strong, the more so as the majority of the party's votes came from women.[16]

Anti-Semitism was not restricted to the far Right, however much the other parties might officially disavow it. This was particularly true of the German People's Party, the successor of the National Liberals, which was a close electoral competitor with the Democrats among whom the middle-class Jewish element was strong. It also cropped up in the Centre Party, especially during the revolutionary turmoils,* but virtually disappeared once the reactionary Bavarian wing had seceded. The Communists, too, were prepared to outbid the Right in nationalist fervor in this as in other respects; at the time of the Silesian plebiscite *Rote Fahne* denounced the Jewish coal owners and Ruth Fischer found it necessary to warn the students of Berlin against "Jewish capitalism" during the French occupation of the Ruhr.[17]

* "In Germany, too, we may note . . . that the Jews in general harbour a decided inclination towards Spartacist agitations" (*Germania*, July 1, 1919).

Nevertheless none of these episodes adds up to very much; anti-Semitism not only had its home in the Right but was more than ever an essential part of it. A number of DNVP leaders were opposed to it, such as von Posadowsky and von Oppeln-Bronikowski, and anti-Semitism made no appearance in the party's initial manifesto. But it was widespread in the DNVP's election campaign for the Constituent Assembly (except in Silesia and Poznania, where there were too many Jewish voters).[18] How far, in the chaotic conditions of those days, there was an official initiative is impossible to ascertain. By 1920 both leadership and rank-and-file were convinced that anti-Semitism was indispensable to the party's survival and it fought the first Reichstag elections against

> every decomposing, un-German spirit, . . . against the Jewish predominance in government and public life, which has come to the fore more and more fatefully since the Revolution.[19]

The anti-Semitism had not only come to stay, but in its indiscriminate ferocity the propaganda of the DNVP was quite indistinguishable from that of other specifically racialist groups or the Nazi Party. Nothing illustrated better the difficulty of switching it off once it had been switched on than Karl Helfferich's naive remark after polling day, "Anti-Semitism stopped on June 6th at 6 P.M." Nor ought it to be assumed that the Conservative element was behind-hand compared with the *völkisch*. Count Westarp, and Walter Lambach of the DHV, who both broke with the Nationalists in 1930 in order to rally to the support of Brüning, were among the most ardent of the party's anti-Semites, whereas Hugenberg was far too obsessed with "Marxism" to bother with the Jews.*

The bias toward the *völkisch* ideology among the Right was further helped by two developments. The first was the evolution, from the war and the upheaval that followed it, of a new political force, "Right-wing Radicalism." It was common to many European states, and it tasted almost immediate political success in Hungary with the "white terror" that followed the overthrow of the Soviet Republic, and in Italy with the March

---

* He appears to have been indifferent to this issue, never making anti-Semitic speeches himself, but never stopping his supporters from making them.

on Rome. The "Right Radicals" were recruited from persons whose social and economic position was either ruined or threatened with ruin: ex-servicemen, particularly ex-officers unable to adjust themselves to civilian routine, axed officials of Empires no longer on the map, debt-ridden peasants, and the academic classes, particularly students, whose addiction to racial doctrines we have already noted—one and all, "wanderers in the void," as Radek christened Leo Schlageter, a Free Corps saboteur shot by the French in 1923 who became a folk hero among both extreme Left and extreme Right. On the one hand these classes had no stake in the capitalist process of production and did not identify themselves with either of the main power groups within it; on the other hand they had a fear of proletarianization, and contempt for the notion of class solidarity. They hated the capitalists with their "work or die" gospel; they hated the proletariat as Caliban did his image in the glass. They were therefore accessible to slogans of social revolution and even "Socialism," provided these did not take a traditional liberal-humanist form. They were a spontaneous and autonomous category; although established conservative forces—industry, landowners, or the Church—often supported them organization-ally or financially, these forces could never "create them" and generally continued to harvest cynicism or distrust in return for their generosity.

The other factor was simply the inability of Conservative counterrevolutionaries to meet the needs of the day. This was demonstrated by the Kapp *putsch* of 1920. Although the infantry for this enterprise was provided by the freebooters of the Erhardt brigade, this was essentially an enterprise on behalf of pre-1914 monarchism and failed dismally. Its old-fashioned character was illustrated by the absence of anti-Semitism in its program. All Kapp wanted to do was expel Eastern European Jews who had immigrated since the war.

A similar evolution toward an uncompromisingly *völkisch* position took place within the Pan-German League. Paragraph nine of its new constitution (the "Bamberg Declaration") committed the League to combating "all those forces which inhibit, or detract from the *völkisch* development of the German people, particularly the xenomania (*Fremdsucht*) and Jewish predominance to be found in almost all departments of state, the economy and culture."[20] The League sponsored vehemently anti-Semtic publications, such as Paul Bang's *Judas Schuldbuch* ("Judah's register of crimes") and Otto Bonhard's *Vom Ghetto zur Macht* and *Deutschlands Schuld und Sühne* ("From the ghetto to power," "Germany's guilt and expiation"). More than most bodies devoted to the overthrow of the Republic it had a clear notion of what the new *Reich* would be like. The rigorous exclusion of Jews from commercial, professional, and political life, and the need specifically to brand any Jewish enterprise as such, were demanded in Freiherr von Vietinghoff-Scheel's *Grundzüge des völkischen Staatsgedankens*. Though they closely anticipated the Nuremberg Decrees, these proposals merely echoed what Class had already written in 1912.* In 1931 Class told the League:

> We Pan-Germans have an objective that goes beyond the breakthrough of the nationalist opposition and the transformation of our present system of government . . . . The very special obligation of the Pan-German League [is] the creation of a *völkisch* German state, the first in history to perform the basic duty of concern for the spiritual and physical well-being of its people.[21]

But the League remained what it had been before the war, an élite group, though, in its connections with the DNVP, the plebiscite against the Young Plan and the Harzburg Front, an influential one. It touched the masses and the Right-radical movement through a daughter-organization, the *Deutsch-völkischer Schutz- und Trutzbund,* of which the general secretary was Alfred Roth of the DHV and the president General von Gebsattel, Class's deputy in the League. Within a few months it had a membership of 300,000; when, after the murder of Rathenau, it was banned by the authorities, its members were advised to join the Nazi Party.[22] *The Schutz- und Trutzbund* was indeed a vanguard of Nazism, flaunting not only its contempt for established law and authority, but doing so specifically for the racialist and anti-Semitic cause. It thus had an ideological cohesion which the Free Corps never had, and it provided a much better cross section of Right-radical opinion than the

* According to Class, anyone whose religion or ancestors' religion was Jewish on January 18, 1871 was to be considered a Jew (*Wenn ich der Kaiser wär*, p. 75).

DNVP, combining pre-war racial ideologues like Fritsch and Bartels, the pan-German publisher Lehmann, and leaders of the Agrarian League, such as von Bodelschwingh and von Thüngen.

The assassination of Rathenau, though neither the first political murder in the Republic nor the first act of violence against a Jew, was of especial importance, firstly because of the distinguished position of its victim, secondly because his only crime was to be a Jew. He had been pursued by a wave of hate propaganda from the day of his appointment.

> Now we have it [wrote the *Alldeutsche Blätter*]. Germany has a Jewish Foreign Minister . . . . His appointment is an absolutely unheard-of provocation of the people, an even more unheard-of provocation of the *völkisch*-thinking part of the people.[23]

And Right-wing gangs, heartened by their assassination of Erzberger, sang:

> *Knallt ab den Walter Rathenau,*
> *Die gottverdammte Judensau.**

The Commercial Employees' Union, with its contacts in the DNVP and the Pan-German League, was another important link with the pre-war world. Its membership continued to rise: it numbered over 400,000 members by the end of the twenties and was supported by the major part of the white-collar workers.† Its publishing activities continued to be important. In 1921 it bought up the *Hanseatische Verlagsanstalt* and thus became the sponsor of Wilhelm Stapel's *Deutsches Volkstum,* one of the most widely read of neo-Conservative periodicals.

But it was among youth that alienation from the official Liberal values of the Republic made the most rapid advances. Among students the Jewish question had to be faced as soon as the war was over, with the formation—for the first time—of a general body to speak for all students, in conformity with the general trend toward representative institutions. This, the *Deutsche Studentenschaft,* was *völkisch* in at least one respect, that it

---

* "Mow down Walter Rathenau,
  The god-damned Jewish swine."
† In the social security elections of 1927, the union's list got 42% of the vote, the Socialist list 28%, and the Liberal list 25% (W. Lambach in M. Weiss [ed.] *Der nationale Wille,* p. 226).

included students from German universities outside the boundaries of the Republic, that is from Austria, Czechoslovakia, and Danzig. The desire to exclude Jews was strong among many delegates, and the greatest pressure came, as was to be expected, from those of the former Habsburg lands. "Think German, think *völkisch,*" Dr. Oberegger of Graz appealed to the opening conference.[24] Constitutional considerations, however, made it difficult to accept this advice, for the German government would refuse to recognize as representative any body that practiced discrimination, while the Austrian and Sudeten sections stoutly refused to admit any Jewish members.

It was only in 1922 that a compromise statute was agreed on: the *Studentenschaft* of Germany was to consist of all students who were German citizens, or noncitizens who were Germans by "language, history, or culture"; the Austrian and Sudeten *Studentenschaften* were restricted to members "of German descent and mother tongue."[25] Radical, racial anti-Semitism among Austrian students was almost universal, and beatings-up of Jewish students at Vienna were regular. In this they enjoyed the sympathy of many of the teaching staff who joined them in demanding a quota system on the model of Hungary and Poland. Indeed, only the intervention of the law courts prevented the implementation of new statutes drawn up on these lines in 1929.

In Germany, too, the ultranationalist traditions of the *Verein deutscher Studenten* and the corporations predominated. The racialist students, dissatisfied with the tolerant precepts imposed on them, formed their own organization, the *Hochschulring deutscher Art,* which had close links with the DNVP and quickly became the strongest party within the *Studentenschaft.* By 1921 in the Berlin student elections 4005 out of 6231 votes were cast for anti-Semitic lists.[26] As the nationalist tide rose again in the late 1920's, riots against Jewish students and professors and demands for a *numerus clausus* became more frequent.[27] In 1931 the Nazi list got an absolute majority in the *Studentenschaft* elections, at a time when that party had perhaps half that support in the country as a whole.

The same trends were at work at schools. Jewish pupils reported that support for Republican institutions was rare in the upper forms of high schools once the slump had begun and there were complaints about the bias of some teachers.[28] Nor did some of the approved textbooks help: *völkisch* and neo-romantic sentiments, praise for "true" Germans like Nietzsche, Lagarde, and Langbehn were not uncommon.[29]

The link among the teachers, the older schoolboys, and the students in this neo-romantic rejection of their materialistic environment was the Youth Movement. It was symptomatic in demonstrating the failure of communication between the official Republic and the most articulate and sensitive of the younger generation; in the very idea of putting forward the ideal of "youth," preferring impulse and enthusiasm to reason and experience; and in the basic irrationality of supposing that "youth," as a category, had claims that could be specifically formulated. The Youth Movement was perhaps the archetypal form of that "wandering in the void" that was so characteristic of the German middle class under Weimar. Youth organizations of one kind or another were widespread; in 1927 they had a membership of well over four millions; but the "Youth Movement" proper, the members of the *Bünde* (brotherhoods), numbered only about 55,000.[30] On the other hand much of the ideological content of the *Bünde* spilled over into the Church or party youth groups: the authoritarian, hierarchic leadership, the idealization of the provinces and the countryside, the convictions of the peculiarity and superiority of everything Germanic. In any other country the question of whether Jews might belong to hiking or folk-dancing clubs would be considered ludicrously irrelevant: in Germany it was necessarily central to the movement's soul searching.

Even before and during the war the Jewish question split the *Wandervogel*. The memoirs of early leaders show that not merely Langbehn and Lagarde but Houston Stewart Chamberlain, Friedrich Lange, and Paul Förster were the formative intellectual influences on them.[31] As early as 1914, 92% of the *Wandervogel* had no Jewish members, the great majority of them as a matter of principle.[32] That it *was* a matter of principle was neither hypocrisy nor mere rationalization. For the leaders and members of this movement, however unconscious they might be of their position on the party-political spectrum, belonged precisely to that radical Right opposition to whom Jewish influence and values symbolized everything that was wrong in Germany. After the war, then, the exclusion of Jews was almost universal in the "Youth Movement" proper, though aggressive or abusive anti-Semtism was restricted to a few extremist groups such as the "Beggars" (*Geusen*), "White Knights," or "Eagles and Falcons," which were fairly accurate anticipations of the S.S. The "Eagles and Falcons" had their main strength in Austria and the Sudetenland.

On the extreme Right of the movement the mystique of blood fused with the mystique of the soil; the belief that the only truly productive creative work was tilling the land, and that it was therefore the occupation of the ideal German. The country boarding schools, whose aim was to educate children in close contact with nature, were coeval with the Youth Movement and overlapped closely with it. The pioneer of these schools, Wilhelm Lietz, had closed his establishments to Jewish pupils as early as 1909 and in the Third Reich one of his assistants, Alfred Andreesen, became a leading educational administrator.[33] There was also a specific back-to-the-land movement, agricultural settlements were founded, devoted to the simple life—vegetarianism, temperance, mystical philosophies, and race consciousness. Most important of all were the *Artamanen*, a group of men and women devoted to saving German soil from Slav settlers, who hired themselves out to work on Junker estates, an experience which gave many of them a sharp jolt to the Left. Prominent members were Heinrich Himmler, Rudolf Hoess, later commandant of Auschwitz, and Walther Darré, Hitler's minister of agriculture and author of the Nazis' agrarian philosophy which made the peasant "the life-spring of the Nordic race." Revulsion from the city really was one of the basic ingredients of the whole of the "national opposition."

> Emphasis on the city, let alone the capital, has never been Germanic . . . . Germany's restoration to health will begin only when the cities have lost their over-valuation in the minds of the people.[34]

In contrast

> Semitic thinking has . . . on no occasion and in no period of world history shown any understanding for the value of the peasantry.[35]

The more Germany was covered with slag-heaps, slum tenements, and giant office blocks, the more tantalizing became her rivers and forests, her ruined castles and half-timbered townships. The more the average German was a slave to his wage or his mortgage, the more attracted he was to his mythical ancestor, the heroic warrior-peasant, loyal to his tribe, protector of his womenfolk, obedient to his chieftain. Max Hildebert Boehm, the disciple of Moeller van den Bruck, lamented that industrialism had killed the *volkhaft* elements of life.[36]

What, then, was the common ideological property of this heterogeneous multitude of clubs and sects in terms of actual or potential political forms? In the first place, rejection of the West. Initially the victory of the democracies over the monarchical Central Powers had raised the prestige of Western institutions in German eyes; but very soon admiration turned to hatred of "that foreign spirit . . . which was imported among us with the Weimar Constitution."[37] "Our formal democracy," wrote M. H. Boehm, "has capitulated not only to the material superiority of the enemy, but to the ideas of the West."[38] As after 1806 and 1849, nationalist Germany and particularly Young Germany sought the answers to its needs in the depths of the native past, and fiercely resisted any foreign idea that might threaten its tradition. "Versailles and Geneva are the symbols of the victory of 1789," wrote Edgar Jung, one of the most influential of the neo-Conservatives. "Versailles and Weimar are the guarantees of the Central European defeat and the Western European victory." "The Weimar Republic is . . . a belated break-through by the Enlightenment into the middle . . . of Europe."[39] What are the forces that will overcome this incursion of intellectualism and doctrine? They are tradition, blood, and historical spirit.[40] "The new European epoch will be opposed in every detail to the values and social forms of the world of 1789."[41]

It is not only the Allied armies who foisted an unwanted way of life on the Germans; it was also the foreigner within:

> The Jew needs merely to get hold of the party of enlightenment and individualism in order to undermine from within the structure of the German social framework. Thus he does not have to fawn his way to the peaks of society, instead he has forced on the

Germans a social theory which was bound to help the Jews up to the towering heights.[42]

As Class, and others before him, had already pointed out before the war, "The strongest weapon of Judaism is the democracy of the non-Jews."[43]

Equally abhorrent are the economic forms typical of the West. The "anti-capitalist yearning" of which Gregor Strasser spoke was genuinely widespread, and while it was reinforced by the experiences of the inflation and the Depression it also has a long history as part of German national sentiment. "Socialism" was a respectable word among men of the Right at least as far back as Rodbertus and Adolf Wagner:* the dirty word was "Marxism." Socialism of some kind, however idiosyncratic or subjective, was preached by almost every major Right-wing theoretician, from Moeller van den Bruck to Spengler, from Troeltsch to Rathenau, from Diederichs to Sombart.

Few people expected German capitalism to survive the deat of 1918 unscathed: paradoxically it was the Social Democrats' craving for respectability, their refusal to nationalize, that caused much of the disenchantment and disillusion with the Revolution, among the middle as well as the working class. And, as we have seen, the disassociation of the Right-radicals from any stable form of property made them equally accessible to slogans of revolution and Socialism. This Socialism was very different from that of Marxist or orthodox labor parties; it never implied social egalitarianism, rather anti-individualism, a form of national or racial solidarism, and its intellectual roots are in German idealism. Capitalism was an agent of proletarianization; it created the city with its mass of anonymous ants. In contrast with the Marxists, therefore, the "German" Socialists wished to fend off capitalism rather than conquer it. Even a party as closely identified with big business as the DNVP was immersed in this anti-capitalist ideology. In its anthology of great German Right-wing biographies there were plenty of poets, landowners, and generals, but only three captains of industry, Kardorff, Stumm, and Helfferich, and their connections with the world of capital were treated defensively and apologetically.[44]

Against this inner decomposition, against the enemy under-

* See pp. 44–5.

mining the fortress from within, the revival of *Volkstum*, of national peculiarity, was the surest defense. The question of *Volkstum* was now central to German-Jewish antagonisms. Here again we see not so much a revolutionary contrast with the pre-war period as an intensification of trends already noticeable then. The ideology of *Volkstum* was one of self-admiration: it consisted originally of two strands, an aggressive one which was expressed in policies of Imperialism, naval expansion or *Mitteleuropa*, and a defensive one, of withdrawal from foreign (particularly Western and Mediterranean) influences into the uniqueness of primitive Germanic virtue. The outcome of the war made the first impracticable; therefore the second became doubly influential. It nourished an "internal Imperialism" of which the nonconformist, in particular the racial nonconformist, became the chief victim. As Wilhelm Stapel, the editor of the widely read *Deutsches Volkstum*, put it, "It is the natural right of every people that it should want to have its destiny guided in accordance with its own instincts."[45]

By no means every advocate of *Volkstum* was a racialist; the influence of Lagarde, making Germanic qualities a matter not of heredity but of a state of mind (*Gemüt, nicht Geblüt*) was still strong.

> In truth [wrote Jung] *Volk* opposes *Volk* and spirit spirit. Whatever may be racially determined in the national antagonism has nothing to do with the alleged dichotomy between Aryans and Semites.[46]

Similarly those intellectuals who are vulgarly supposed to be the main precursors of National Socialism generally held themselves aloof in one form or another from full-blown anti-Semitism. Both Moeller van den Bruck and Oswald Spengler, however cloudy their own thought and imprecise their own concepts, rejected racialism as nonsense.[47] Moeller resorted to anti-Semitism only in his refutation of Marx, arguing that Marx, being a foreigner to Europe, could not understand the essence of European needs.[48] Spengler indeed, actually favored assimilation as the best solution to the Jewish Question,[49] a view held by almost nobody else on the Right after 1918. Similarly, when he demonstrates that capitalism is un-German, he denounces it not as Jewish but as English—another throw-back to the period before 1914 when anti-English propaganda on these lines was popular. Marx is in his view not an unregenerated Jew, but an assimilated Englishman in his estimate of capitalism;[50] the duty of Prussianism and Socialism is to fight jointly against that "internal England, that *Weltanschauung* which penetrates, paralyses and despiritualises the whole of our life as a people"[51] Moeller certainly played his part in undermining the frail structure that was German parliamentary democracy, and so did the other members of that literary coterie over which he presided, the *Juni-Klub*, with its periodical *Gewissen*. Its members had wide ramifications in German publishing, such as the *Deutsche Rundschau* and *Preussische Jahrbücher*. But Moeller's notion of a third *Reich* was far removed from the state Hitler created; it was not a polity but a realm metaphorically conceived, inspired by the mystical connotations of the triad that come so easily to the German idealist. *Gewissen*, like Moeller himself, was only rarely anti-Semitic, at any rate before Moeller's death in 1925.[52] After that, it changed, as did the *Herrenklub*, the lineal successor of the *Juni-Klub*, which was much more reactionary and under the aegis of Papen.

Nevertheless, for the majority of those seeking a proof of greatness and a justification of agression, now that the state was unworthy of loyalty and chauvinistic power-politics offered no scope, race was the only satisfactory one to hand. It was the only rationalization that provided foolproof cover for all fantasies and all ambitions. In any case, the subtle debates in literary journals on whether *Deutschtum* was a matter of culture or ethnology left stone-cold the majority of those who were groping for a new loyalty and hungering for someone to hate.

How obscure was the dividing line between the conservative and the *völkisch* attitudes to nationality is shown by the religious question. The Stöcker tradition was still strong and inspired many Lutheran clergymen to take part in anti-Semitic organizations such as the *Deutsch-evangelischer Volksbund für öffentliche Mission des Christentums*, but the general trend was toward a renunciation of orthodox Christianity, emancipating religious Germans from any residual affinity they might feel toward the people of the Old Testament. Its extreme form was the conscious and aggressive denunciation of Christianity by neopagans like the Ludendorffs. In the main, however, the attempt to provide a religion suitable for, and expressive of, the German people took the form of some marriage between Protestantism and racialism. This was not too difficult: the role of Protestantism in German nationalist mythology, as the Teutonic counterblast to Latin, internationalist Catholicism has already been noted. Movements like the *Deutschkirche* of the 1920's and the *Deutsche Christen* of the 1930's, which aimed at recruiting Lutheranism for the *völkisch* cause, brought serious difficulties and embarrassments into the Church. The leaders of such bodies were often ex-pastors, such as Gottfried Traub and Max Maurenbrecher, both of whom had broken with the Church in their young, Left-wing days and then turned to the extreme Right.

For many, an important aspect of "Germanizing" Christianity was to prove that Jesus Christ was an Aryan, a theory already fashionable before the war. Similarly, all those moral qualities, like love and compassion, which were associated with the historical Christ, had to be purged from the German Christ. Artur Dinter, the novelist and Nazi politician, wanted a "Heroic Messiah"; like many other "national Christians" (such as Lietz of the boarding schools) he wanted the Old Testament removed from religious teaching. In matters of religion, as in matters of nationality, we cannot help thinking that the racialists were desperately trying to neutralize some advantage the Jews had gained over them. Pan-Germanism, after all, making the *Volk* a community based only on ties of blood, and transcending the frontiers of states and nations, mirrored the image that the racialists had constructed of the Jews. So, too, "national' Christianity was to provide the God the Germans needed, as Jehovah had arisen out of Jewish national needs.

It is evident that in this groping for a new racial or religious truth, in the search for proofs of irrational or unverifiable assumptions, charlatanism could flourish. Already before 1914 the crudest dabblings in occult mumbo-jumbo had been frequent;* now they could luxuriate more than ever. A best-selling novel of the period was Artur Dinter's *The Sin against the Blood*, a piece of racialist pornogaphy which argued a Gresham's Law of racial degeneration. Dinter followed this with a spiritualist work, *The Sin against the Spirit*. Theories about the

* See pp. 65–6, 237–8.

origins and achievements of the Aryan race abounded. Paul Sentsius claimed that the Germans were one of the lost tribes of Israel; Karl Georg Zschaetsch that the Aryans originated on the lost continent of Atlantis; Franz von Wendrin that the Garden of Eden was in Mecklenburg with the river Jordan a tributary of the Elbe, and that the Jewish *thora* is derived from the great god Thor; Ernst Fuhrmann that all the Romance languages were Teutonic dialects; Max Bewer that Christ was not merely an Indo-European but of Westphalian descent;[53] and Guido von List that Buddha, Osiris, and Moses were all Saxons.[54] Interwoven with these paeans to Aryanism there came, from List and Liebenfels in Vienna, from Ludwig Klages and Herbert Reichstein in Germany, doctrines of spiritualism, "ariosophy," theosophy (with its renunciation of medical science, meat eating, and alcohol) and "theozoology." The most important link between these various interests was the publisher Eugen Diederichs. He was a mentor of the Youth Movement and, with Schuler's apostle, Klages, one of the organizers of its apocalyptic jamboree on the Hohe Meissner mountain in October, 1913.* He founded the *Sera* circle, devoted to the mysticism of sun-worship and the Aryan life-spirit[55] and edited the influential journal *Die Tat*. This publication linked the Right-wing oppositions of the Republic and the Wilhelmine era: its issue commemorating the emperor's silver jubilee bitterly attacked the culture and politics of the era. After 1918 the journal attracted many of the best minds among the neo-Conservatives, preaching the need for a socially conscious élite to regenerate the nation.

To this world of fantasy and fabrication belonged the one addition made after 1918 to the arsenal of anti-Semitic arguments, the Protocols of the Elders of Zion. This work was assembled in 1905 by Serge Nilus on behalf of the Russian political police and was, in the 1920's, conclusively proved to be a forgery. It was almost unknown in the West until introduced by White Russian refugees. In Germany its chief publicists were the Baltic exiles of Hitler's entourage, Max-Erwin Scheubner-Richter and Alfred Rosenberg.[56] In the Protocols we again see the racialists' fantasies about themselves mirrored. The Aryans' mystic powers were to be summoned to meet those of others.

* On the centenary of the "peoples' battle" of Leipzig.

Guido von List's secret nature-wisdom, the symbolic truths enshrined in runes, sun wheels, and swastikas were Aryan substitutes for the supposed Zionist protocols or Masonic rites. Hitler, with his dietetic and medical fads and his admiration for the clairvoyant Hanussen, and Himmler's attitude to horoscopes fit perfectly into this intellectual underworld.

Enough has been said to indicate the enormous proliferation of extreme Right-wing bodies which arose in Germany after 1918 in an attempt to purge Germany of the defeat and to bring down the Republic. Some were openly and primarily anti-Semitic; others tolerated anti-Semitism or coquetted with it; some were reticent, but accepted the doctrines of *Volkstum* and authoritarianism which undoubtedly endangered Jewish civil rights. Their total number will probably never be established; one historian of the period has accounted for 430.[57] Their memberships overlapped; at the same time they were divided, often deeply, on questions of theory, tactics or personalities. At any rate, the enormous growth of the movement, out of the tiny nucleus of the Right-wing opposition before 1914, indicates the profound political change the war and the Republic brought.

Austria, too, went through a war and a democratic revolution; there, too, the effect was to accentuate those tendencies that anti-Semites and anti-Liberals had objected to before 1914. Like their German counterparts they felt that "behind the mask called popular sovereignty and republican constitution . . . we will find the invisible, but real, ruler of our miserable *Judenrepublik*."[58] But because the organization of anti-Semitic movements and the penetration of anti-Semitism into social life had gone much further than in Germany by 1914, there was, on the surface, a less spectacular expansion after the war. The political partes saw no reason to change their attitudes. The Christian-Social Party's manifesto, published on Christmas Eve, 1918, read:

> The corruption and power-mania of Jewish circles, evident in the new state, forces the Christian-Social Party to call on the German-Austrian people for most severe defensive struggle against the Jewish peril. Recognised as a separate nation, the Jews shall be granted self-determination; they shall never be the masters of the German people.[59]

The various German nationalist groups combined into a *Gross-deutsche Volkspartei* whose program, in addition to demanding political union with Germany, proclaimed "the idea of the folk-community" which implied "the combating of red and black internationalism and the ruinous influence of Judaism."

> The party . . . is in favour of a campaign of enlightenment about the corrupting influence of the Jewish spirit and the racial anti-Semitism necessitated thereby. It will combat Jewish influence in all areas of public and private life.[60]

The old Liberal Party, dependent on a minority of the Jewish voters in Vienna now that Bohemia and Moravia had been detached from Austria, disintegrated altogether. The result was that the Social Democrats became more of a "Jewish" party than ever before.

In one respect the collapse of the Monarchy enabled the bourgeois parties to draw closer together. There were no significant minorities in the new Austria, and the Jews could not any longer be said to be a cohesive force in it; paradoxically, therefore, the end of the nationalist struggles made politics more uncompromisingly nationalist than before, and enabled the Christian-Social Party to compete with the Pan-Germans on their own ground. Nor were they insincere in this. Catholic reactionaries were as deeply imbued as nationalist ones with the theories of the "organic" state, the corporate society, and the folk community which had always been stronger in Austria than in Germany. Moreover with the end of the multinational empire, the Catholic Greater German tradition, linguistic and cultural and deriving from the Romanticism of a hundred years earlier, was revived. Both camps were attracted by the corporatist theories of Othmar Spann, Professor of Sociology at the University of Vienna, and bodies like Richard von Kralik's *Gralbund* which combined Catholicism with pan-Germanism. They differed, of course, on the role of religion in this ideally integrated state, and on the question of political union with Germany. Most Christian-Social leaders disliked the idea of an *Anschluss*, whether by the "red" Republic or by the "brown" dictatorship. Nevertheless, when they did formulate their opposition to Jews, they did so increasingly in national, not religious or economic terms, rejecting even baptism as a solution to the antagonism. Emmerich Czermak, the party's president, laid down:

> We Germans gladly encounter the Jewish people and its national religion with full respect; we wish to see them protected, but also to protect ourselves . . . .
>
> In future [the Jews] will have to leave us to ourselves in our own concerns . . . in our national culture they will not be allowed to have their say say except as guests . . . .
>
> The religious German must decisively reject baptism as an "entrance ticket" for the Jews.[61]

This does not mean that the Christian-Social Party's anti-Semitism had become less ambiguous or opportunistic than before the war. On the one hand there were licensed tub-thumpers like the trade-union leader Leopold Kunschak, whose anti-capitalism was no doubt sincere; on the other there was the relative restraint of the party's leader, Mgr. Ignaz Seipel, who never descended to abuse himself and dismissed it—in the true tradition of Lueger—as *"für die Gasse"* ("for the street corner"). Most of the party did not bother their heads about questions of detail. For them, anti-Semitism was an emotional and electoral necessity. They neither did, nor could, decide whether they hated the Jew as a capitalist or a Socialist, as the member of a false religion or of a foreign race.

Anti-Semitism naturally drew the two parties together, too: the *Antisemitenbund* was presided over jointly by the Christian-Social Anton Jerzabek and the pan-German Robert Körber. But the intensification of anti-Semitic propaganda brought little in the way of anti-Semitic action. A Christian-Social proposal in 1919 to bar any but German-Austrians from the state service foundered on administrative difficulties, and a Pan-German attempt, in 1921, to legislate against the immi-gration of Eastern European Jews fared no better. The reason for this general ineffectiveness is not far to seek. The real object of hatred was the Jewish intellectual: in that respect nothing had changed. The Jewish intelligentsia were prominent in the Social Democratic Party and its administration of Vienna; the Jewish bourgeoisie—bankers like Rudolf Sieghart, industrialists like Fritz Mandl—had every reason to welcome, and subsidize, the anti-Socialist coalition governments of Christian-

Socials and Pan-Germans which ruled from 1920 to 1932.

Real anti-Semitism, violent anti-Semitism came only from the Right-radicals. In Austria these were to be found in the *Heimatschutz* or *Heimwehr,* a loosely organized para-military formation whose origins were similar to those of the Free Corps. It had been formed to defend the frontiers against Hungarian, Slovene, and Italian invaders after the end of the war; later to defend the countryside against marauding groups of workers from the towns in search of food. It was therefore restricted to the provinces; until the late twenties its place in Vienna was taken by a number of organizations, such as the *Frontkämpferverein-igung* (which was certainly not restricted to war veterans).

The Austrian social revolution had been less extensive than in Germany; the radical Right was therefore less numerous and its leadership and membership were almost entirely aristocratic and bourgeois. Of its principal leaders, Pfrimer and Steidle were lawyers and Prince Starhemberg came from an old land-owning family; of the provincial commanders many were titled ex-officers. Starhemberg was a veteran of the Silesian Free Corps and of the Hitler-Ludendorff *putsch.* Its chief military organizer, Waldemar Pabst, a former officer of the German Army, was a veteran of the *Oberland* Free Corps, the Kapp *putsch,* and the Luxemburg-Liebknecht murder. What united these men was hatred of the Republic, of democracy, and of "red" Vienna Their real rival was the Social Democratic militia, the *Repub-likanischer Schutzbund.* Unlike the regular political parties they believed in violence as the only effective weapon.

Their anti-Semitism was an integral part of their anti-Marxism and anti-liberalism. Characteristically, Starhemberg's *bête noire* was Hugo Breitner, the author of the punitive prop-erty taxes which financed the Viennese social services, proclaim-ing that "the head of that Asiatic would have to roll in the dust." (Equally characteristically, he retracted the statement the next day, claiming he had not wished to hurt anyone's feelings.)[62] It was the Right-radicals, and their main contingent, the students, who were responsible for the occasional outbreaks of public anti-Semitic violence in Vienna, of which the most serious were the riots at the time of the World Zionist Congress in 1925.

After the general strike of 1927, in protest against the acquittal of some Right-wingers accused of killing by-standers at a

Socialist demonstration, still more after the Great Depression, the Christian-Social Party formed an open alliance with the *Heimwehr* in order to destroy parliamentary institutions. The success of this campaign culminated in the proclamation of the new, corporative constitution in 1934, which stressed the "Christian-German" character of the state, although guaranteeing the rights of equal citizenship to Jews. Nevertheless it was ominous that Christian-Social leaders had on numerous occasions declared a genteel form of *apartheid* to be their chosen solution for the Jewish question, and that in January 1933, nine days before Hitler's seizure of power, the Bishop of Linz issued a pastoral letter on it. After blaming "degenerate Judaism" and "world free-masonry" for "mammonistic capitalism" and Bolshevism, he went on:

> It is not only the undisputed right, but the strict and conscientious duty of every devout Christian to fight against this harmful influence of Judaism, and it is much to be desired that these dangers and damages arising out of the Jewish spirit should be . . . ever more strongly combated by the Aryan and Christian side.[63]

As before, the bark was worse than the bite. New school regulations in Vienna and Burgenland, aimed at religious segregation in the classroom, were only haphazardly carried out. Discrimination in the public service was not much more systematic and was, with some notable exceptions, directed against Social Democrats rather than Jews. With the artisan Josef Kresse as deputy mayor under the new régime, the petty jobbery of Lueger's golden days seemed to have returned. All in all, the only consistent characteristic of official anti-Semitism under the Republic and the Dolluss-Schuschnigg régime was *Schlamperei*.

It has been possible so far to relate the fortunes and ramifications of the inter-war anti-Semitic movement without once mentioning the National Socialist Party. This is not remarkable, for Nazism was, until 1929, of little interest or significance, and even thereafter it was a beneficiary rather than an innovator. And though Nazism was quintessentially a phenomenon of the twenties and thirties it had significant organizational links with pre-war fringe movements.

The *Deutsche Arbeiterpartei* was founded at the end of the war in Munich by Anton Drexler, a locksmith who had graduated from the *Vaterlandspartei*, and Gottfried Feder, an engineer who wanted a vehicle for his populist economics. Hitler joined the party seven months later. Both Feder and Dietrich Eckart, another prominent early member, belonged to the *Thule-Gesellschaft*, an offspring of the pre-war *Germanen- und Wälsungsorden*.[64] At almost the same time the *Deutschsozialistische Partei* was founded in Hanover by other members of *Thule*, under the aegis of another populist engineer, Alfred Brunner, "free from Jews and without capital."[65] There was a good deal of overlap in membership, but the main link came through the Nuremberg branch of the DSP of which Julius Streicher had gained control. When the DAP absorbed Streicher's branch, as well as Otto Dickel's "Occidental Working Comumnity" in Augsburg, the DSP in Northern Germany did not survive for long.[66] The main strength of all these groups lay in Bavaria, where the revolutionary turmoils of 1919 had engendered a strong reaction and where the Right-wing administration was much more hospitable than the Left-dominated governments further north. But there was also the proximity to the irredenta of Austria and the Sudetenland, and the fact that Munich had become the center of racialist activity in Germany even before 1914.*

The National Socialist German Workers' Party (NSDAP), as the DAP renamed itself in 1920, maintained contact with the National Socialist parties of Austria and Czechoslovakia. the successor organizations of Riehl's *Deutsche Arbeiterpartei*,† and a number of international conferences were held. The Austrian party was the first to use the swastika as its emblem.

The NSDAP's program (the "Twenty-Five Points") was drawn up by Feder. It had a tone of strong social radicalism: emancipation from "interest slavery," the confiscation of war profits, the socialization of private trusts and department stores, industrial profit sharing and land reform.[67] Jews were excluded from membership of the nation. But even in its revulsion from capitalist practices (and Roman law) this party was no more advanced than most of the intellectuals of the neo-Conservative movement. In its membership, too, it differed little from the

* See pp. 225–6, 283.
† See pp. 205–6.

innumerable other Right-radical movements. It collected the socially displaced and the intellectually uprooted, though their moral character was probably even lower than that of rival bodies—depraved voluptuaries like Röhm, Heines and Esser; drunkards and drug addicts like Eckart and Goering; brawlers and jailbirds like Maurice, Weber, and Graf; and psychopaths like Streicher. Hitler himself did not care for the Socialist overtones of the program—indeed he did not care much for any program—being almost exclusively interested in questions of race and foreign policy. It is noteworthy that those party members who were closest to Hitler—Hess, Goebbels, Rosenberg, and Goering—all came from the better-off *strata* and were conservative in their social outlook. A good many members continued to take the party's "Socialism" seriously, particularly the Strasser brothers, though Drexler himself was soon edged out and disappeared from the political scene; but whether the demand for a "second revolution" from Röhm's storm troopers was anything more than a nihilistic desire to dispossess the respectable is impossible to establish.

Hitler's first major incursion into politics was in October, 1923, when he attempted to persuade von Kahr and von Lossow, the Prime Minister and Army commander of Bavaria, to seize power and depose the Berlin régime. It was a time of great confusion in Germany, with the country only just recovering from the inflation and the French occupation of the Ruhr, and goverments containing Communists only recently overthrown in Saxony and Thuringia. But Kahr and Lossow refused, Hitler went ahead on his own, aided by the storm troopers (S.A.) —mainly ex-Free Corpsmen—and Field-Marshal Ludendorff. Hitler was arrested, tried, imprisoned and wrote *Mein Kampf.*

The encounter with Ludendorff enabled the party to widen the basis of its support in preparation for its second incursion (one to which Hitler himself was opposed). Ludendorff was a leading light in the *Deutsch-völkische Freiheitspartei* which had been founded in 1922 by a number of politicians who considered the DNVP too tame on the racial issue. Other members included Count Ernst Reventlow, an old Pan-German and publisher of *Der Reichswart* and Theodor Fritsch, who had always dismissed the DNVP as useless and founded his own *Deutsche Erneuerungsgemeinde.* The Ludendorffs, with their assiduity in publishing such periodicals as *Judentum und Freimaurerei* and *Am heiligen Quell deutscher Kraft* were regarded as decidedly quaint even within the lunatic fringe. The NSDAP and the *Freiheitspartei* joined forces for the Reichstag elections of May 1924, and gained thirty-two seats out of 472. But the ultra-nationalist wave evoked after the tribulations of 1923 soon subsided under Stresemann's firm leadership; by December the Nazis' seats were down to fourteen, in the 1928 elections they gained only twelve. In the presidential election of 1925 Ludendorff polled less than 1%. In 1927 the *Freiheitspartei* dissolved itself.

For the first ten years of its life, then, the NSDAP made no net impact on politics. Its program was in no way remarkable, and it made no contribution to the ideology of the *völkisch* Right. (The one major work of theory produced by a party member, Alfred Rosenberg's *The Myth of the Twentieth Century*, appeared in 1930, too late to have any influence on public opinion.) Its views on the Jewish question were not distinctive. Gregor Strasser formulated them for the 1930 elections.

> We desire no persecution of the Jews, but we demand the exclusion of the Jew from German life. We demand German leadership without Jewish spirit, without Jewish wire-pulling and the interests of Jewish capital, to which almost the whole world of party has today succumbed. We demand protection of our cultural goods against Jewish arrogance and aggression.[68]

No orthodox Right-winger would have batted an eyelid at such a policy.†

What, then, was special about the Nazis? To put it bluntly, they had the courage of their convictions. This was particularly true of violence. Violence was common enough as a weapon of the extreme Right, and sadism has, as we have seen, always been an important element in anti-Semitic propaganda. But the violence of the Free Corps and the murder organizations was that of the self-appointed outlaw, something they regarded as their

---

* "At the sacred fount of German might."
† It is sometimes suggested that the "Socialists" in the party, because they had a positive program, needed anti-Semitism less than the Right-wingers, who had nothing else to agitate with. But it was Strasser and Feder who introduced a bill in the Reichstag to expropriate Eastern Jews without compensation, and were forced to withdraw it on Hitler's orders.

special privilege and were unwilling to share with others; and the sadism of the classical anti-Semitic writer was largely cerebral and verbal. Whenever an actual pogrom took place after an anti-Semitic meeting before 1914, the anti-Semitic parties were careful to disclaim responsibility—the tribute that they paid to virtue—and even the DNVP could be embarrassed by Chancellor Wirth's tirade after the murder of Rathenau. Hitler would not have been embarrassed. He would have gloried in the crime, as Mussolini gloried in the murder of Matteotti,* and his *squadristi* publicly proclaimed their belief in rubber truncheons and castor oil. For the Nazis, systematic violence was an essential method, both for the attraction that it exerted on some and the fear and uncertainty it instilled in others.[69] In this they represented the true decadence of European politics. Some of their exploits became famous, such as the riots which led to the withdrawal of the film *All Quiet on the Western Front,* or the progrom in Berlin at the time of the Jewish New Year, 1931, in which over a thousand S.A. men took part. In the nine years from 1923 to 1931 there were 106 desecrations of Jewish cemeteries and forty of synagogues; the great majority of those caught turned out to be connected with Nazi organizations.[70]

> *Erst müssen Juden bluten*
> *Erst dann sind wir befreit.*†

The other exceptional gift that the Nazis had, and it arose directly out of their total lack of scruples, was that of rousing the masses. The chief object of their rabble-rousing was the dispossessed and disillusioned middle class. But the Nazis also succeeded in breaching the barrier between the older Right-radical movements and the working class. It was for this reason that Hugenberg after he had gained control of the DNVP, decided to enlist the support of Hitler, even at the cost of splitting his own party, and for this reason that Thyssen and Stinnes decided to subsidize him. Schemann, in his critical biography of Kapp, remarked:

* Indicative of the half-way house that Italian Fascism occupied between ordinary strong-arm politics and degenerate totalitarianism, Mussolini at first denied responsibility for the murder and only later boasted of it.
† "First Jews will have to bleed
Only then will we be liberated." (S.A. song)

The attitude of our leading spirits to the great economic powers is indicative of our German ways. Unmistakably our greatest and truly creative statesmen have been inspired by something like love for agriculture and no more than respect for industry.[71]

The Nazis, as we have seen, had their share of agrarian romanticism, but they were the only Right-radical party also to build up a system of factory cells, and in 1932 at least a quarter of their votes must have come from the proletariat. Hitler, after all, had learnt his politics in Vienna, where the leaders of anti-Semitism had succeeded in conquering the masses, an objective in which all their German contemporaries had failed.

It was in Austria, too, that the Nazis alone succeeded in breaching this barrier. Austrian politics were even more rigidly ideological and class bound than German. The Nazis therefore made much slower progress initially. By 1932 they had conquered almost all the pan-German and Right-radical camp, but this amounted to only about 20% of the total. It was only after the establishment of the clerical-corporate régime that they made spectacular headway. The failure of the 1934 Social Democrat rising discredited the Jewish leaders of that party; the undoubted unpopularity of the régime and the apparent economic dynamism of the Third Reich, with its rapidly declining unemployment, did the rest. Austrian Nazism was oppositional, anti-clerical, pro-annexation, and called itself a "workers' " party. This enabled it to penetrate deep into all classes of society.

Nazism, therefore, was the most advanced form of the Right-radicalism widespread in post-war Germany and Austria, which gained power in a political and economic crisis uniquely favorable to it. It was a *völkisch* movement; its anti-Semitism was the driving force of its anti-capitalism in which many of its followers believed. Whether the Nazi "opposition" that was eliminated in June, 1934 would also have tried physically to destroy the Jews if they had won we can never know. The Strassers never talked in those terms and even Ludendorff had wished merely to consign the Jews to a vast Eastern European ghetto. Hitler was extreme as a racialist even by Nazi standards: "There are no revolutions except racial revolutions: there cannot be a political, economic or social revolution," he declared in 1930.[72]

Even if Hitler had not triumphed, the position of the Jews would have been seriously endangered. This is evident from the repeated declarations of bodies like the DNVP or the Pan-German League in Germany, the Christian-Socials in Austria, and the statements of almost all "neo-Conservative" and "national-revolutionary" intellectuals in both countries. The Jew could flourish only in the sort of classical Liberal society that existed in Western Europe and that the late nineteenth century had introduced to Central Europe. There this brief period was evidently drawing to a close: as Czermak, of the Austrian Christian-Socials wrote:

> In our times . . . of the total collapse of the Liberal world of ideas, the liquidation of democratic institutions . . . the times of the intellectual reorientation of the European nations, the re-establishment of internally consolidated communities and an authoritarian order, the Jewish Question cannot be by-passed.[73]

Moreover, the ideology of anti-Semitism became much more systematic after 1918. Economic fear and social envy continued to play an important, but no longer the decisive, part in it.

> It emerged that the Jewish Question was neither one of beliefs nor of economics, but one of races and *Volkstümer* [wrote H. F. K. Günther, one of Hitler's racial experts]. Opposition to the Jews was a racial-psychic group phenomenon of occidental history.[74]

Due allowance must be made for party jargon; it nevertheless remains true that hatred of the Jew was a result as much as a cause of the increased urge to *völkisch* solidarity. The nationalist anti-Semites of the nineteenth century attacked the Jew for retaining his separate identity: they wanted him to be assimilated. The racialists of the twentieth century frantically tried to prove that the Jew must always remain different. What offended them was his all-too-successful assimilation. The much-vaunted increase in Jewish influence in public life was more than ever a rationalization, not an originator, of the heightened anti-Semitism of the Right. In Germany in particular the charge of "Jewish preponderance" will hardly bear serious examination. Jewish politicians were predominant immediately after the armistice, but after that hardly at all. In the whole history of the Republic only five Jews held cabinet office.* Industry was almost entirely in Gentile hands, and there was plenty of Gentile competition even in banking and newspaper ownership (e.g., Hugenberg's publishing and film combine). More significant, no doubt, was that Jews were able for the first time to penetrate into the administration and the judiciary. In Austria, where the native bourgeoisie was less well developed, the Jewish community was correspondingly more influential. This had two divergent consequences. It meant that official bourgeois anti-Semitism was in a much weaker executive position *vis-à-vis* the Jews. When in power after 1934, it did remarkably little; less, probably than the German Right would have done, precisely because the Jewish "problem" in Germany was much smaller. On the other hand, mob anti-Semitism was much stronger in Austria than anywhere in Germany, as the street scenes in Vienna after the *Anschluss* were to show.

What the post-war period did bring was an increase of urban preponderance in politics, of the *avant-garde* in the arts, of mobility in the social structure. In the survival, or at least toleration, of these, the Jewish community had a vital interest; and, like any other emanation of modernity they were anathema to the Right. The attack against them was carried out on a broad front. The attack was continuous and consistent, and before 1929 its extent hardly varied with the ups and downs of economic and political life. Moeller van den Bruck denounced Liberalism as "the grave-digger of cultures, the annihilator of religions, the destroyer of fatherlands and the solvent of mankind"; [75] Ernst Jünger proclaimed "the absolute bankruptcy of humanitarian thinking"; [76] Oswald Spengler prophesied the imminence of "the time when the fully formed powers of the blood, displaced by the rationalism of the big cities, are re-awakening in the depths";[77] for Edgar Jung nations were equal "only metaphysically";[78] and *Die Tat* gloated in 1929, "We must, in the meantime, expectantly approve the necessity of the process of disintegration."[79] It would show a misunderstanding of historical causality to lump these men together as "precursors of Nazism"; it was by no means evident when they wrote who would be the beneficiary of

* They were Preuss, Rathenau, Gradnauer, Landauer, and Hilferding.

of chaos. If most of them later resisted, or suffered under Nazism, they greeted the "national revolution" enthusiast ically at the moment when it hovered on the razor's edge between success or failure.

> Many Conservatives who had become spiritually homeless [wrote one of them] found their way into the ranks of National Socialism, from the very best of motives and in perfect good faith. They certainly did not do so for the sake of its programme, which was all too plainly a mixture of inconsistencies and simple nonsense. They joined it for its resoluteness and "moral energy"....
> Our toleration, even temporarily, even with suspended judgment, of invasions of right and humanity and of the inviolability of the person . . . created the atmosphere in which persons of the highest character succumbed to the temptations of the system and sank to the level of the Catalinarians.[80]

The branch on the tree of civilization which these men occupied fell because they themselves sawed it off; unfortunately a great many other innocent persons were on it, too.

Ernst Niekisch's often-quoted epigram that "Hitler is the retribution for Königgrätz" is true at many levels. It summarized, above all, the victory of the South German *völkisch* ideology over the classical nationalism and chauvinism of Prussia and the North. It was the self-appointed task of this ideology to destroy every vestige of the Liberal civilization painstakingly and uncertainly built in Central Europe in the previous hundred years.

This Liberal civilization had not been slow to recognize an enemy in anti-Semitism. But it was slower to recognize that anti-Semitism flourished through its own failure to respond to human needs. It was these failures, some traceable to sins of commission and omission, others traceable to larger and older political factors, which, combined with the particular situation of the Jews in Germany and German Austria, form the background to the events related here. Not all political movements of the kind associated with German anti-Semitism become necessarily anti-Semitic: Italian Fascism did not. And a large and prosperous Jewish commercial community does not inevitably produce anti-Semitism: Holland would disprove such a contention. But German-speaking Central Europe provided that correct "conjunction of facts and ideas" which we have seen to be essential if a political movement is to prosper.

320

To that extent, therefore, anti-Semitism was a "spontaneous" product, arising out of a particular situation, not a creed foisted on the public from above by an unscrupulous ruling class. Once its possibilities were apparent, however, it undoubtedly was exploited, and with the catastrophic success which we all know. Perhaps those who exploited it in its early days thought they would be able to master the force they had released. Perhaps they did not even consider the problem. But they would have done well to ponder the medieval Papal warning to those who commune with dark spirits: *Ipse simulat se captum, ut te capiat; a te inclusum, te finaliter concludat.**

REFERENCES

1 Klopp, *Die sozialen Lehren*, p. 189.
2 Lagarde, "Über die gegenwärtigen Aufgaben der deutschen Politik," *Schriften*, Vol. I, p. 41.
3 Langbehn, *Rembrandt*, p. 1.
4 Marr, *Der Sieg des Judentums*, pp. 27, 44.
5 Glagau, *Der Börsen- und Gründungsschwindel in Deutschland*, p. xvii.
6 B. Bettelheim and M. Janowitz, *Dynamics of Prejudice. A Psychological and Sociological Study of Veterans* (New York, 1950), pp. 220–31.
7 *Ibid.*, p. 68.
8 J. H. Robb, *Working-Class Anti-Semite. A Psychological Study in a London Borough* (London, 1954), pp. 165–6.
9 *Ibid.*, p. 146.
10 *Ibid.*, p. 167.
11 *Preussische Jahrbücher*, Vol. XLIV, pp. 662–3, Vol. XLV, p. 88.
12 Frank, *Hofprediger Adolf Stöcker*, p. 73.
13 "Anti-Semitism," *Encyclopaedia Britannica*, 11th ed.
14 *NFP*, Jan. 22, 1880.
15 W. Liebe, *Die deutschnationale Volkspartei, 1918–1924* (Düsseldorf, 1956), p. 8; L. Hertzmann, "The Founding of the German National People's Party (DNVP) Nov. 1918–Jan. 1919," *Journal of Modern History*, Vol. XXX, No. 1 (1958), pp. 31–2.
16 G. Bremme, *Die politische Rolle der Frau in Deutschland* (Göttingen, 1956), pp. 70–1, 76.
17 *MVA*, , Vol. XXXI, No. 10, May 25, 1921, p. 76; O. K. Flechtheim, *Die Kommunistische Partei Deutschlands in der Weimarer Republik* (Offenbach, 1948), p. 89.
18 Hertzmann, *loc. cit.*
19 F. Salomon, *Die deutschen Parteiprogramme*, Vol. III (Berlin, 1930), p. 137.

* He feigns surrender in order to capture you; contained by you, he finally overcomes you.

20 Kruck, *Geschichte des Alldeutschen Verbandes*, p. 130.
21 *Ibid.*, pp. 180–1.
22 *Ibid.*, pp. 132–3.
23 *ADB*, Feb. 11, 1923.
24 H. Volkmann, *Die deutsche Studentenschaft in ihrer Entwicklung seit 1919* (Leipzig, 1925), pp. 16–17.
25 *Ibid.*, pp. 245, 249.
26 *MVA*, Vol. XXXI, No. 4, Nov. 24, 1921, p. 35.
27 *CV-Zeitung*, March 13, 1931.
28 *Ibid.*, Jan. 2, 1931; Oct. 1, 1931; Oct. 4, 1932.
29 For example, W. Gehl's *Geschichte für höhere Schulen*; A. Meyer's *Die neue Zeit*; E. Willmann's *Deutsche Geschichte*.
30 K. von Klemperer, *Germany's New Conservatism* (Princeton, 1957), p. 97.
31 Laqueur, *Young Germany*, pp. 74–5 and ch. 9 passim.
32 L. Fick, *Die deutsche Jugendbewegung* (Jena, 1939), p. 65.
33 G. L. Mosse, *The Mystical Origins of National Socialism*, p. 96.
34 H. F. K. Günther, *Die Verstädterung. Ihre Gefahren für Volk und Staat* (Leipzig, 1934), p. 49.
35 R. W. Darré, *Das Bauerntum als Lebensquell der nordischen Rasse* (2nd ed., Hamburg, 1933), pp. 58–9.
36 M. H. Boehm *Das eigenständige Volk* (Göttingen, 1932), p. 26.
37 F. Everling in M. Weiss (ed.,) *Der nationale Wille. Werden und Wirken der deutschnationalen Volkspartei* (Essen 1928), p. 155.
38 M. H. Boehm, *Ruf der Jungen* (3rd ed., Freiburg, 1933), p. 52.
39 E. J. Jung, *Die Sinndeutung der deutschen Revolution* (Oldenburg, 1933), pp. 42, 43, 46.
40 *Ibid.*, p. 78.
41 Quoted by K. Sontheimer, *Antidemokratisches Denken in der Weimarer Republik* (Munich, 1962), p. 151.
42 Jung, *Die Herrschaft der Minderwertigen*, p. 124.
43 Frymann, *Wenn ich der Kaiser wär*, p. 215.
44 H. von Arnim and G. von Below, *Deutscher Aufstieg. Bilder aus der Vergangenheit und Gegenwart rechtsstehender Parteien* (Berlin, 1925), pp. 274, 286, 381–2.
45 Quoted by Jung, *Die Herrschaft der Minderwertigen*, p. 123.
46 *Ibid.*, p. 69.
47 K. von Klemperer, *op. cit.*, p. 196; H. J. Schwierskott, *Arthur Moeller van den Bruck und der revolutionäre Nationalismus in der Weimarer Republik* (Göttingen, 1962), pp. 99–103.
48 Moeller van den Bruck, *Das dritte Reich* (3rd ed., Hamburg, 1931), pp. 38–9.
49 O. Spengler, *Der Untergang des Abendlandes* (Munich, 1920–22), Vol. I, p. 392.
50 O. Spengler, *Preussentum und Sozialismus* (Munich, 1920), p. 75.
51 *Ibid.*, p. 98.
52 Stern, *The Politics of Cultural Despair*, p. 229.
53 P. Sentsius, *Die Stämme der Israeliten und Germanen* (Leipzig, 1931); K. G. Zschaetsch, *Atlantis, die Urheimat der Arier* (Berlin, 1932); F. von Wendrin,

Die Entdeckung des Paradieses (Brunswick, 1924); E. Fuhrmann, *Die französische Sprache ein deutscher Dialekt* (Hagen, 1923); M. Bewer, *Der deutsche Christus* (1923). See in this connection A. Mohler, *Die Konservative Revolution in Deutschland, 1918–32* (Stuttgart, 1950), pp. 168–71.

54 Mosse, *op. cit.*, p. 92.

55 *Ibid.*, pp. 84, 87.

56 W. Z. Laqueur, "Hitler and Russia, 1919–1923," *Survey 44/45* (London, 1962), pp. 101, 110–11.

57 Mohler, *op. cit.*, p. 94.

58 Anton Orel, quoted by A. Diamant, *Austrian Catholics and the First Republic. Democracy, Capitalism and the Social Order* (Princeton, 1960), p. 144.

59 *Reichspost*, Dec. 24, 1918.

60 Pichl, *Schönerer*, Vol. V, p. 290.

61 E. Czermak and O. Karbach, *Ordnung in der Judenfrage* (Vienna, 1933), pp. 44, 47, 66.

62 Gulick, *Austria from Habsburg to Hitler*, Vol. II, p. 906.

63 Czermak and Karbach, *op. cit.*, pp. 138–9.

64 G. Franz-Willing, *Die Hitler-Bewegung*, Vol. I; *Der Ursprung, 1919–1922* (Hamburg, 1962), pp. 127, 129.

65 *Ibid.*, p. 88.

66 *Ibid.*, p. 91; M. Rühl, *Der Stürmer und sein Herausgeber, Versuch einer politischen Analyse* (unpublished dissertation, Nuremberg, 1960), pp. 43–4, 47.

67 Oakeshott, *The Social and Political Doctrines of Contemporary Europe*, p. 191.

68 Salomon, *op. cit.*, Vol. III, p. 30.

69 Hitler, *Mein Kampf*, p. 406.

70 *MVA (Abwehr-Blätter)*, Vol. XLII, No. 4, p. 50.

71 L. Schemann, *Wolfgang Kapp und das März-Unternehmen vom Jahre 1920* (Munich, 1937), pp. 196–7.

72 A. Bullock, *Hitler, A Study in Tyranny* (4th imp., London, 1959), p. 141.

73 Czermak and Karbach, *op. cit.*, p. 1.

74 H. F. K. Günther, *Die Rassenkunde des jüdischen Volkes* (Munich, 1930), pp. 318, 323.

75 Moeller van den Bruck, *Das dritte Reich*, p. 84.

76 E. Jünger (ed.,), *Krieg und Krieger* (Berlin, 1930), p. 65.

77 Spengler, *Untergang des Westens*, Vol. II, p. 583.

78 Jung, *Die Sinndeutung*, p. 78.

79 Quoted by K. Sontheimer, "Der Tat-Kreis," *Vierteljahreshefte für Zeitgeschichte*, Vol. VII, No. 3 (1959), p. 234.

80 H. Rauschning, *The Revolution of Nihilism* (London, 1939), pp. 119–20.

APPENDICES

I The Declaration of the Notables*

Fierce battles have unified our fatherland into an Empire of mighty aspirations. This unity has been achieved by the victory which the feeling of essential community has gained in the popular conscience of the Germans over the distinctions of descent and creed, which have cleft our nation like no other. To let individual citizens atone for such differences is neither just nor noble, and hits above all those which are honestly and seriously attempting to throw aside their peculiarities and to march loyally together with the nation and with those whom they know to be striving towards the same objectives. Such action merely hinders what remains the common aim: the ironing-out within the German nation of all differences still operating. Now, in an unexpected and deeply shameful way, racial hatred and the fanaticism of the Middle Ages are being resurrected in various places, notably in the major cities of the Empire, and directed against our Jewish fellow-citizens. How many of these have, through hard work and talent, brought profit and honour to the fatherland, in trade and industry, in science and the arts—that is forgotten; the precept of law and the behests of honour that all Germans are equal in rights and duties—these are ignored. The carrying-out of this equality is not merely the province of the tribunals, but of the conscience of every single citizen. The revival of an ancient folly is threatening, like a contagious pestilence, to poison the relations which Christians and Jews have proclaimed on the basis of tolerance in state and parish, in society and the family. If at present envy and malice are preached by the leaders of this movement only in the abstract, the crowd will not delay to draw the practical conclusions from such vague speech-making.

Men who should be proclaiming from the pulpits and the seats of learning that our culture has overcome the isolation of that race which once gave to the world the worship of the one God, are undermining the legacy of Lessing. Already we can hear the cry for discriminatory legislation and the exclusion of Jews from this or that trade or profession, honour or position of confidence. How long will it be before the herd clamours for this too? There is yet time to step against

* *National-Zeitung*, Berlin, Nov. 14, 1880.

326

Appendix I

confusion and to avert national disgrace; the artificially inflamed passions of the multitude can yet be broken by the resistance of determined men. Our call goes out to Christians of all parties to whom religion is the tidings of peace; our call is addressed to all Germans to whose hearts the ideal inheritance of their great princes, poets and thinkers lies close. Defend by public declarations and with calm expositions the fundamentals of our common life: respect for every belief, equal rights, equal favours in competition, equal recognition of capability and enterprise for Christians and Jews.

SIGNED BY DROYSEN, GNEIST, MOMMSEN, VIRCHOW, SIEMENS, FORCKENBECK, ET AL.

II Erfurt Programme of Böckel's Anti-Semitic People's Party

1. The Anti-Semite Party is faithful to Emperor and *Reich*, Prince and fatherland. It aims at the repeal, by legal means, of Jewish emancipation, the placing of Jews under an Aliens' Law, and the creations of healthy social legislation.

2. It is in favour of maintaining the military strength of the nation, resting on the Germanic principle of general liability for service, and is prepared to make the necessary sacrifices for the protection and defence of our fatherland.

3. Wise economy in the budget is demanded in the interests of the welfare and independence of the Reich.

4. The collection of the financial means necessary for the state shall be carried out with consideration for the economic position of the lower classes of the people and heavier demands on big business. In particular the party supports:

   (a) The introduction of progressive tax on incomes, dividends and legacies, with the creation of proper regulations against false declarations and property.

   (b) The rational reconstruction of the Stock Exchange tax, as well as a tax on foreign issues and securities.

   (c) The extension of indirect taxes to imported articles of luxury and refined taste.

5. International regulation of Stock Exchanges, especially prohibition of speculations endangering peace and of instalment trading with the necessities of the life of the people.

6. Institution of a really national *Reichsbank*, for the support and fertility of institutes serving artisans, agriculture and petty industry, with abolition of privileges of note-issue by private banks.

7. Protection of agriculture against foreign competition, against usury and expropriation. Homestead laws, reduction of all taxes and duties concerning agriculture.

8. Support for the artisan class by removing unrestricted freedom of enterprise and the competition of prison labour; introduction of

328

reduced limitations [i.e., of estates]; promotion of artisans' organizations and extension of their rights.

9. Honest business transactions are to be protected against unfair competition by revising the regulations on insolvency proceedings, by further restriction on door-to-door selling, and by prohibition of bazaars, knock-down sales, itinerant markets, as well as the evil of advertising.

10. The social condition of the workers is to be improved by legislation for the protection of labour on the basis of international agreements, by introducing maximum hours of work, according to the individual industry, legal restriction of Sunday labour to the minimum, by increasing the number of factory inspectors; by better control of homework, as well as speedy abolition of female and child labour.

11. A parliamentary commission is to enquire into the conditions of the middle and lower ranges of officials and those classes of officials whose situation is in need of improvement are to be granted one forthwith.

12. Reform of the entire legal code, including civil laws, based on German principles of law and the thorough displacement of Roman concepts of law. Lowering of court and lawyers' fees, abolition of compulsory legal representation; introduction of a new law on mortgages and dispossession.

13. Only Christian German men (of non-Jewish extraction) are to be elected into legislative bodies and to be employed in state or municipal offices.

14. Every religious community is to be accorded freedom for the practice of its ceremonies, in so far as its customs do not clash with the laws of the state or provoke public annoyance.

15. Promotion of a genuinely national education of youth.

16. Maintenance of universal, direct, secret suffrage, which is to be extended to the parliamentary bodies within the individual states, and payment of members of the Reichstag.

17. Freedom of speech and publication, freedom of assembly and association.

18. Creation of a German citizenship law to prevent immigration harmful to the common good.

III Lueger's First Anti-Semitic Speech*

For my part, I like to ignore the small differences which might exist between one or other of the parties about the method of the struggle; I have very little regard for words and names, and much more for the cause. Whether Democrat or anti-Semite, the matter really comes to one and the same thing. The Democrats in their struggle against corruption come up against the Jews at every step, and the anti-Semites, if they want to carry out their economic programme, have to overcome not only the bad Jews but the bad Christians also. . . .

All my party comrades share my opinion that it is the first duty of a Democrat to take the side of the poor oppressed people and to take up the fight with all determination against the unjustified and even harmful domination of a small fraction of the population. To be sure, the Manchester-Liberal papers have the habit of describing a Democrat in somewhat different terms. They claim, for instance, that it would be the duty of such a Democrat to come forward as an enemy of the Christian religion, to mock and ridicule its believers and priests. But we know that the motive of such a manoeuvre is solely to mislead the people, which we may deduce from the remarkable fact that were anybody to come forward against the Jewish religion and ridicule its doctrines and believers he would be branded by the same organs as a reactionary obscurantist. However, this strange conception can be seen even more clearly in an economic question. Quite shamelessly the Liberal organs threaten the confiscation of the property of the Church and claim that the goods of the "dead hand" are harmful. By this means an attempt is made to divert the attention of the people from the property of the "living hand" which, in my view, harms the people in a most grievous way. But what a yell of rage would go up from the Liberal press if one were to substitute the slogan "confiscation of Church property" with the slogan "confiscation of the goods of the conscious, living hand!" He who would dare this would risk at once being portrayed as injuring the sacred rights of property, as an anarchist, a communist who wanted to subvert the social order and destroy all existing things. And now I ask: is the title of property of the

* ÖV, Oct. 2, 1887.

conscious, living hand stronger or more sacred than the title to the property of the Church? Surely not. And so it is more than extraordinary if one were to confiscate the property of the comparatively poor priests and through this help the rich of another denomination to increase their wealth!

IV The Original "Los-von-Rom" Manifesto*

"Break with Rome!"

Motto: "O Germany, unhappy of her own free will, unable to see with open eyes, unable to understand with plain reason!"

(ULRICH VON HUTTEN)

Ever more clearly and plainly we may see that Slav insolence and Roman lust for power have closely allied themselves in the old German East-mark in order to annihilate Germandom in this Empire which has been built up on German foundations.

Clerical spirit of intrigue is influencing the whole of public life in Austria more than ever before, with dangerous effects on the free exercise of the German people's national powers in a way which is justly causing anxiety to every German.

In view of the steadily growing peril which is threatening us from Rome and Prague, in view of the clerical agitation, asserting itself more insolently from day to day and disposing of the most powerful means, the final target of which is the undermining of the mighty imperial structure created by Bismarck and which needs as an implement to this end an Austria totally given over to Slavism, the genuine German patriot must consider the timely application of an appropriately potent antidote.

The struggle against the anti-German power of Rome can be carried only under the general battle-cry:

"Break with Rome"

in the hope of the final victory of Germandom over the un-German, quarrelsome, Roman Church.

For long enough now there has been talk of going over to Protestantism or Old Catholicism. In view of the rising danger, determined deed shall at last follow the spoken word!

Therefore, away with the shackles which bind us to an anti-German Church!

Not Jesuit, but Germanic spirit shall rule and command in German lands.

Krems, Nebelung [November] 1898/2011 n.N.

With unfeigned German greeting,

GEORG SCHÖNERER   REICHSRAT DEPUTY

* *UDW*, Nov. 16, 1898.

V Resolution Passed at Berlin Congress of Social Democratic Party

Anti-Semitism springs from the discontent of certain bourgeois strata, who find themselves adversely affected by the development of capitalism and are in part destined to decline through this development, but who, mistaking the actual cause of their situation, direct their struggle not against the capitalist economic system, but against a symptom appearing in it which becomes inconvenient to them in the competitive struggle against Jewish exploitation.

Thus its origin compels anti-Semitism to make demands which are as much in contradiction with the laws of economic and political development of capitalism as they are hostile to progress. Hence also the support which anti-Semitism finds among Junkers and clerics.

The one-sided fight of anti-Semitism against Jewish exploitation must necessarily be without success, because the exploitation of man by man is not a specifically Jewish form of livelihood but one peculiar to bourgeois society, which will end only with the decline of bourgeois society.

Since Social Democracy is the most determined enemy of capitalism—irrespective of whether Jews or Gentiles are its agents—and since its aim is the removal of bourgeois society by bringing about its transformation into a Socialist society, whereby an end will be made of all domination of man over man, as well as all exploitation of man by man, Social Democracy declines to divide its forces in the struggle against the existing state and social order through false and thereby ineffectual struggles against a symptom which stands and falls with bourgeois society.

Social Democracy fights anti-Semitism as a movement directed against the natural development of society, which, however, despite its reactionary character and against its will, ultimately acts in a revolutionary way, because the petty bourgeois and peasant strata stirred up against the Jewish capitalists must come to recognize that not only the Jewish capitalist but also the capitalist class generally is their enemy and that only the realization of Socialism can free them from their misery.

333

VI The Urbanization of Central
European Jews

(A) GERMANY

	1871		1910		1925	
	Number of Jews	As % of Total Population	Number of Jews	As% of Total Population	Number of Jews	As % of Total Population
Berlin	36,015	4.4	144,007	3.7	172,672	4.3
Frankfurt	10,009	11.0	26,228	6.3	29,385	6.3
Breslau	13,916	6.2	20,212	3.9	23,240	4.2
Hamburg	13,796	4.1	19,472	1.9	19,794	1.8
Cologne	4,523*	3.1	12,393	2.1	16,093	2.3
Munich	2,097	1.2	11,083	1.9	10,086	1.4
Leipzig	1,739	1.6	9,434	1.6	12,954	1.9
Poznán	7,325	13.0	5,611	3.6		

Sources: Vierteljahrsheft zur Statistik des Deutschen Reiches, Vol. I, No. 2 (1873); *Vierteljahreshefte des Kaiserlichen Statistischen Amtes*, 1911, No. 3 and 1912, Nos. 2–4; *Statistik des Deutschen Reiches*, Vol. 240 (1915); J. Kreppel, *Juden und Judentum von Heute*.

In general, the growth of Jewish populations kept pace with the general trend. Where old-established Jewish communities existed, notably in Frankfurt, Hamburg, and Poznán, the rate of growth was somewhat slower; medium towns like Mannheim, Mainz, and Fürth show the same tendency. Where Jewish settlement is new, however, the rate of increase is faster than the general, e.g., Munich and Leipzig. Since the Jewish population of Germany rose more slowly than the total, Jewish urbanization is due almost entirely to migration, not to natural increase. In predominantly rural provinces the Jewish share of the population fell sharply between 1871 and 1914. West Prussia showed a

* Figures for 1880.

decline from 2.0 to 0.8%, Pomerania from 0.9 to 0.5%, the Bavarian Palatinate from 2.0 to 0.9%, Swabia from 0.8 to 0.4%, and the Grand Duchy of Hesse from 3.0 to 1.9%.

(B) AUSTRIA–HUNGARY AND SUCCESSION STATES

	1869		1910		1923	
	Number of Jews	As % of Total Population	Number of Jews	As% of Total Population	Number of Jews	As % of Total Population
Vienna	40,277	6.1	175,294	8.6	201,510	10.08
Czernowitz	9,552	28.2	28,613	32.8	74,716*	40.0

					1930	
Budapest	44,890	16.6	203,687	23.1	204,370	20.03
Bratislava	4,552	9.8	8,207	10.5	14,882	12.0
Prague	13,056	8.2	18,041	8.1	35,425*	4.2
Brno	4,505	6.1	8,947	7.1	11,003*	4.2

					1921	
Lvov	26,694	30.6	57,387	27.8	76,783	35.0
Cracow	17,670	35.5	32,321	21.3	45,401	33.4
Tarnopol	10,808	53.9	13,997	41.3		
Kolomea	9,119	53.2	18,930	44.4		
Brody	15,138	80.9	12,150	67.5		

Sources: *Statistische Monatsschrift, Vol. VII* (Vienna, 1880); *Österreich-isches Städtebuch,* Vol. XIV (1913); *Annuaire Statistique Hongrois,* Vols. I, XIX; *Statistiches Jahrbuch der Haupt- und Residenzstadt Budapest,* Vol. IV (1902); J. Kreppel, *Juden und Judentum von Heute;* M. Moskovitz, "The Jewish Situation in the Protectorate of Bohemia and Moravia," *Jewish Social Studies,* Vol. IV (1942).

The strength of Vienna as a magnet throughout the period is consistent and undiminished. In the metropolitan areas of Hungary and Bohemia-Moravia Jewish increase exceeds total increase until the turn of the century; thereafter the curve flattens out, partly because of the lure of Vienna as a second-stage metropolis. Changes in municipal boundaries distort the

★ Boundaries changed.

significance of percentages to some extent. In Galicia cities with large pre-emancipation communities tend to lose Jews not only relatively but—e.g. Brody—absolutely.

BIBLIOGRAPHICAL NOTE

1. Books dealing with political anti-Semitism in Germany and Austria fall into two broad categories: older works, often dating from the time of the events they record, at least some of which remain standard works of reference; and articles, monographs and general histories, published in the last ten or fifteen years and illustrating the explosion of interest in this subject. Only the principal works can be dealt with here. Two institutions must be singled out for their contributions. The Wiener Library's catalogues are virtually exhaustive up to the date of their publication. Volume 3 (London, 1958), supplemented by Volume 6 (London, 1978), deals with *German Jewry* and Volume 5 (London, 1971) with *Prejudice: Racist–Religious–Nationalist*. The *Year Books* of the Leo Baeck Institute in London (1956–) as well as being a storehouse of scholarly monographs, also contain comprehensive bibliographies, as do the Institute's various symposium volumes. Three of these, edited by Werner E. Mosse and Arnold Paucker, deal with periods central to our study, *Juden im Wilhelminischen Deutschland 1890–1914* (Tübingen: J. C. B. Mohr, 1976), *Deutsches Judentum in Krieg und Revolution 1916–1923* (Tübingen: J. C. B. Mohr, 1971) and *Entscheidungsjahr 1932: Zur Judenfrage in der Endphase der Weimarer Republik* (Tübingen: J. C. B. Mohr, 1965). Each contains extensive sections on anti-Semitism, by Werner Jochmann in the first two and George L. Mosse in the third, and on Jews in public life by Peter Pulzer, Werner T. Angress and E. G. Lowenthal respectively. Two other of the Institute's symposium volumes are also relevant, *Revolution and Evolution: 1848 in Jewish History* (Tübingen: J. C. B. Mohr, 1981), edited by Werner E. Mosse, Arnold Paucker and Reinhard Rürup, with sections on emancipation by Rürup and Mosse, and *The Jews in Nazi Germany, 1933–1945* (Tübingen: J. C. B. Mohr, 1986), edited by Arnold Paucker and Barbara Suchy, with sections by Peter Pulzer and Reinhard Rürup on the impact of anti-Semitism and Werner E. Mosse on Weimar Jewry.

2. On the social and political history of German and Austrian Jewry a number of older works remain indispensable: Martin Philippson, *Neueste Geschichte des jüdischen Volkes* (2nd edn., Frankfurt: Kauffmann, 1922–30); S. M. Dubnow, *Die neueste Geschichte des jüdischen Volkes* (Berlin: Jüdischer Verlag, 1920–1923 — English translation, *A History of the Jews* (5 vols., Cranbury NJ: Cornwall Books, 1967–73); Salo W. Baron, *Social and Religious History of the Jews* (New York: Columbia University Press, 1937) and Artur Ruppin, *Die Soziologie der Juden* (Berlin, 1930–31). *The Jews: Their History, Culture and Religion,* edited by Louis Finkelstein (New York: Harper and Brothers, 1960) covers a wide range. Calvin Goldscheider and Alan S. Zuckerman, *The Transformation of the Jews* (Chicago: University of Chicago Press, 1984) is an ambitious and stimulating essay on the political and social impact of modernization on Jewish existence. The most important recent works are Jakob Toury, *Soziale und politische Geschichte der Juden in Deutschland 1847–1871: Zwischen Revolution, Reaktion und Emanzipation* (Düsseldorf: Droste, 1977); Jacob Katz, *Out of the Ghetto: The Social Background of Jewish Emancipation, 1770–1870* (Cambridge: Harvard University Press, 1973); David Bronsen (ed.) *Jews and Germans from 1860 to 1933: The Problematic Symbiosis* (Heidelberg: Carl Winter, 1979), which includes contributions on Austria, and Donald L. Niewyk, *The Jews in Weimar Germany* (Baton Rouge: Louisiana State University Press, 1980). Paul R. Mendes-Flohr and Jehuda Reinharz (eds.) *The Jew in the Modern World: A Documentary History* (Oxford: Oxford University Press, 1980) covers a wide span. Particularly good for Germany are the three volumes edited, with scholarly introductions, by Monika Richarz, *Jüdisches Leben in Deutschland, Selbstzeugnisse zur Sozialgeschichte* (Stuttgart: Deutsche Verlags-Anstalt, 1976–82); and Jehuda Reinharz and Walter Schatzberg (ed.), *The Jewish Response to German Culture* (Hanover, NH: New England University Press, 1986). Wanda Kampmann, *Deutsche und Juden: Geschichte der Juden in Deutschland vom Mittelalter bis zum Beginn des ersten Weltkrieges* (Heidelberg: Lambert Schneider, 1963, reprinted as Fischer Taschenbuch, Frankfurt, 1979), is a useful introduction. *Jewish Assimilation in Modern Times,* edited by Bela Vago (Boulder: University of Colorado Press, 1981), has contributions on Germany by L. Yahil and on Hungary by W. O. McCagg.

3. On Jews in politics and public life, in addition to the Leo
Baeck Institute's symposia, (para. 1) there are Jakob Toury, *Die
politischen Orientierungen der Juden in Deutschland. Von Jena bis
Weimar* (Tübingen: J. C. B. Mohr, 1966) and Ernest Hamburger's
exemplary *Juden im öffentlichen Leben Deutschlands. Regierungsmitglieder, Beamte und Parlamentarier in der monarchischen Zeit,
1848–1918* (Tübingen: J. C. B. Mohr, 1968.) Hamburger was
unfortunately unable to complete his projected companion
volume on the Weimar period. An edited part of his draft has
appeared as Ernest Hamburger and Peter Pulzer, "Jews as Voters
in the Weimar Republic", *Leo Baeck Year Book* XXX (1985).
Juden in der Weimarer Republik, edited by Walter Grab and Julius
H. Schoeps (Stuttgart: Burg Verlag, 1986), contains valuable
biographical monographs. Of books on prominent individual
Jews pride of place must go to Fritz Stern, *Gold and Iron.
Bismarck, Bleichröder and the Building of the German Empire* (New
York: Knopf, 1977). In addition: Peter Gay, *Freud, Jews and other
Germans* (Oxford: Oxford University Press, 1978); Stanley S.
Zucker, *Ludwig Bamberger. German Liberal Politician and Social
Critic, 1823–99* (Pittsburgh: University of Pittsburgh Press, 1975);
Lamar Cecil, *Albert Ballin. Business and Politics in Imperial
Germany, 1888–1918* (Princeton: Princeton University Press,
1967); James F. Harris, A *Study in the Theory and Practice of German
Liberalism. Eduard Lasker, 1829–1884* (Lanham, MD: University
Press of America, 1984); E. Rosenbaum and A. J. Sherman, *M. M.
Warburg & Co. 1798–1938. Merchant Bankers of Hamburg* (London:
C. Hurst, 1979); Ernst Schulin, "Die Rathenaus—Zwei Gene-
rationen jüdischen Anteils an der industriellen Entwicklung
Deutschlands" in *Juden im Wilhelminischen Deutschland;* and Ernst
G. Lowenthal, *Juden in Preussen. Ein biographisches Verzeichnis*
(Berlin: Bildarchiv Preussischer Kulturbesitz, 1981). *Historia
Judaica* and *Jewish Social Studies* contain numerous relevant
articles, as does the *Encyclopaedia Judaica* (Jerusalem-New York:
Macmillan, 1971–72). The first systematic study of the role of
Jews in the economy was Kurt Zielenzieger, *Juden in der deutschen
Wirtschaft* (Berlin: Heine Bund, 1930). Modern works include
Simon Kuznets, "Economic Structure and Life of the Jews" in
Finkelstein's *The Jews* (para.2); David Landes, "The Jewish
Merchant: Typology and Stereotypology in Germany" in *Leo
Baeck Year Book* XIX (1973); and, most recently, Werner E.

Mosse, *Jews in the German Economy. The German- Jewish Economic Elite, 1820–1935* (Oxford, Oxford University Press 1987). On the place of Jews in cultural life, see Sigmund Kaznelson (ed.) *Juden im deutschen Kulturbereich. Ein Sammelwerk* (Berlin:Jüdischer Verlag, 1959) and Walter Grab (ed.) *Juden in der deutschen Wissenschaft* (Tel-Aviv: Institut für deutsche Geschichte, 1985). Two important recent books on Eastern Jews in Germany are Steven Aschheim, *Brothers and Strangers. The Eastern German Jews in German and German Jewish Consciousness* (Madison: University of Wisconsin Press, 1982), cultural and ideological in emphasis, and Jack Wertheimer, *Unwelcome Strangers. East European Jews in Imperial Germany* (New York: Oxford University Press, 1987), which emphasises administrative measures and social structure.

4. On anti-Semitism itself most of the older books are now superseded, though some, like Bernard-Lazare, *L'Antisémitisme, son Histoire et ses Causes* (Paris: Léon Chailley, 1894) are still of interest. General surveys include Alex Bein, *Die Judenfrage. Biographie eines Weltproblems* (Stuttgart: Deutsche Verlags-Anstalt, 1980) which contains an extensive scholarly apparatus; Léon Poliakov, *History of Antisemitism,* (Vols I-III, London: Routledge & Kegan Paul, 1974–75, Vol. IV, Oxford: Oxford University Press, 1984): the third volume covers the nineteenth century, the fourth goes up to 1933; Rainer Erb and Michael Schmidt (ed.) *Antisemitismus und jüdische Geschichte. Studien zu Ehren von Herbert A. Strauss* (Berlin: Wissenschaftlicher Autoren-Verlag, 1987); and Jacob Katz, *From Prejudice to Destruction: Anti-Semitism 1700–1933* (Cambridge: Harvard University Press, 1980) which deals with France as well as Germany and Austria. The scholarly treatment of modern German political anti-Semitism begins with Kurt Wawrzinek, *Die Entstehung der deutschen Antisemitenparteien* (Historische Studien 168, Berlin: Ebering, 1927), Koppel S. Pinson (ed.), *Essays on Anti-Semitism* (New York: Conference on Jewish Relations, 1946) and Paul W. Massing, *Rehearsal for Destruction. A Study of Political Anti-Semitism in Imperial Germany* (New York: Harper and Brothers, 1949). The early nineteenth century is covered by Eleanore Sterling, *Judenhass. Die Anfänge des politischen Antisemitismus in Deutschland (1815–1850)* (Frankfurt: Europäische Verlags-Anstalt, 1969). Other important recent works include, in addition to Jochmann's essays (para. 1), Hans Martin Klinkenberg, "Zwischen

Liberalismus und Nationalismus" in Konrad Schilling, *Monumenta Judaica. 2000 Jahre Geschichte und Kultur der Juden am Rhein* (Cologne: Stadt Köln, 1963); Hermann Greive, *Geschichte des modernen Antisemitismus in Deutschland* (Darmstadt: Wissenschaftliche Buchgesellschaft, 1983); Richard A. Levy, *The Downfall of the Anti-Semitic Political Parties in Imperial Germany* (New Haven: Yale University Press, 1975); Reinhard Rürup, *Emanzipation und Antisemitismus. Studien zur "Judenfrage" in der bürgerlichen Gesellschaft* (Göttingen: Vandenhoek & Rupprecht, 1975); Egmont Zechlin, *Die deutsche Politik und die Juden im ersten Weltkrieg* (Göttingen: Vandenhoek & Rupprecht, 1969); and Sarah Ann Gordon, *Hitler, Germans and the "Jewish Question"* (Princeton: Princeton University Press, 1984). Walter Mohrmann, *Antisemitismus. Ideologie und Geschichte im Kaiserreich und in der Weimarer Republik* (Berlin (East): Deutscher Verlag der Wissenschaften, 1972) provides an East German perspective. The best regional study is David Peal's Columbia University Ph.D. thesis, *Anti-Semitism and Rural Transformation in Kurhessen. The Rise and Fall of the Bockel Movement* (1985). Walter Boehlich (ed.), *Der Berliner Antisemitismusstreit* (Frankfurt: Insel Verlag, 1965) deals with the Treitschke-Mommsen controversy. On Treitschke, see also Andreas Dorpalen, *Heinrich von Treitschke* (New Haven: Yale University Press, 1957).

There are numerous valuable studies of *völkisch* and racialist ideology and of anti-Semitic propagandists. Fritz Stern, *The Politics of Cultural Despair* (Berkeley—Los Angeles: University of California Press, 1961) deals with Paul de Lagarde, Julius Langbehn and Moeller van den Bruck. George L. Mosse, *The Crisis of German Ideology* (New York: Grosset & Dunlap, 1964) deals with neo-Romanticism more generally. Constantin Frantz is dealt with by Louis Sauzin in the UNESCO volume *The Third Reich* (London: Weidenfeld and Nicolson, 1955). For his correspondence see *Constantin Frantz. Briefe,* edited by Udo Sautter and Hans Elmar Onnau (Wiesbaden: Steiner, 1974). To the older standard work on Adolf Stoecker, Walther Frank, *Hofprediger Adolf Stoecker und die christlichsoziale Bewegung* (2nd edn., Hamburg: Hanseatische Verlagsanstalt, 1935) we can now add Günther Brakelmann, Martin Gerschat and Werner Jochmann, *Protestantismus und Politik. Werk und Wirkung Adolf Stöckers* (Hamburg: Christians, 1982) and a scholarly treatment of

Wilhelm Marr in Moshe Zimmermann, *Wilhelm Marr. The Patriarch of Antisemitism* (New York: Oxford University Press, 1986). Wilfried Daim, *Der Mann der Hitler die Ideen gab. Von den religiösen Verirrungen eines Sektierers zum Rassenwahn eines Diktators* (Munich: Isar Verlag, 1958), an informative but not very reliable work on Jörg Lanz von Liebenfels and the "Ariosophists", should now be supplemented with Nicholas Goodrick-Clarke, *The Occult Roots of Nazism. The Ariosophists of Austria and Germany, 1900–1935* (Wellingborough: The Aquarian Press, 1985); Léon Poliakov, *The Aryan Myth. A History of Racist and Nationalist Ideas in Europe* (New York: Basic Books 1971); George L. Mosse, *Towards the Final Solution. A History of European Racism* (New York: 1979). Norman Cohn, *Warrant for Genocide. The Myth of the Jewish World-Conspiracy and the "Protocols of the Elders of Zion"* (London: Eyre and Spottiswoode, 1967) is a masterpiece of detective-work and interpretation. Johannes Rogalla von Bieberstein, *Die These von der Verschwörung. Philosophen, Freimaurer, Juden, Liberale und Sozialisten als Verschwörer gegen die Sozialordnung* (Frankfurt: Lang, 1978) deals with conspiracy theories in a wider context. Two works that have become classics are Eva G. Reichmann's sociological interpretation, *Hostages of Civilisation. The *Social Sources of National Socialist Anti-Semitism* (London: Gollancz, 1949) and Hannah Arendt's brilliant if idiosyncratic *The Origins of Totalitarianism* (3rd edn. London: Allen and Unwin, 1968), which links anti-Semitism to the rise of imperialism and the general pathology of modern political forms. The most important books on individual racialist ideologues are Robert Cecil, *The Myth of the Master Race. Alfred Rosenberg and Nazi Ideology* (London: Batsford, 1972) and Geoffrey G. Field, *Evangelist of Race. The Germanic Vision of Houston Stewart Chamberlain* (New York: Columbia University Press, 1981).

5. The vast and highly uneven literature on Nazi genocide policy contains some works with valuable discussions of anti-Semitism, e.g. Raul Hilberg, *The Destruction of the European Jews* (2nd edn., New York: Holmes & Meier, 1985); Lucy Dawidowicz, *The War Against the Jews, 1933–45* (New York: Holt, Rinehart & Winston, 1975) and Helmut Krausnick et al., *Anatomy of the SS-State* (London: Collins, 1968). Léon Poliakov's trilogy, *Das Dritte Reich und die Juden, Das Dritte Reich und seine Diener, Das Dritte*

Reich und seine Denker (Berlin: Arani, 1955–60) constitutes an excellent documentation.

6. On the general question of Jewish-German relations and Jewish defence measures: Alfred D. Low, *Jews in the Eyes of Germans* (Philadelphia: Institute for the Study of Human Issues, 1980); Sanford Ragins, *Jewish Responses to Anti-Semitism in Germany* (Cincinatti: Hebrew Union College Press, 1981); Ismar Schorsch, *Jewish Reactions to German Anti-Semitism, 1870–1914* (New York: Columbia University Press, 1972); Hans Liebeschütz, *Das Judentum im deutschen Geschichtsbild von Hegel bis Max Weber* (Tübingen: J. C. B. Mohr, 1967), very scholarly and rather charitable; Marjorie Lamberti, *Jewish Activism in Imperial Germany and the Struggle for Civil Equality* (New Haven: Yale University Press, 1978); Evyatar Friesel, "The Political and Ideological Development of the Centralverein before 1914", *Leo Baeck Year Book* XXXI (1986); Arnold Paucker, *Der jüdische Abwehrkampf gegen Antisemitismus und Nationalsozialismus in den letzten Jahren der Weimarer Republik* (Hamburg: Leibniz, 1967); Barbara Suchy, "The Verein zur Abwehr des Antisemitismus", *Leo Baeck Year Books* XXVIII (1983) and XXX (1985) and Udo Beer, *Die Juden, das Recht und die Republik. Verbandswesen und Rechtsschutz, 1919–1933* (Frankfurt: Lang, 1986). On particular political factions in the Jewish community, see George L. Mosse, *German Jews Beyond Judaism* (Bloomington: Indiana University Press, 1985). Jehuda Reinharz, *Fatherland or Promised Land. The Dilemma of the German Jew, 1893–1914* (Ann Arbor: University of Michigan Press, 1975); Ulrich Dunker, *Der Reichsbund jüdischer Frontsoldaten, 1919–1938. Geschichte eines jüdischen Abwehrvereins* (Düsseldorf: Droste, 1977); Carl J. Rheins, "The Verband deutschnationaler Juden, 1921–1933", *Leo Baeck Year Book* XXV (London, 1980); Marion A. Kaplan, *The Jewish Feminist Movement in Germany. The Campaigns of the Jüdischer Frauenbund, 1904–1938* (Westport, CN: Greenwood Press, 1979); Jehuda Reinharz (ed.) *Living With Anti-Semitism. Modern Jewish Responses* (Hanover, NH: University Press of New England, 1987). See also para. 10 on the Left and the Jews.

7. On the connection between political parties, interest organizations and anti-Semitism there are some useful works of reference: Wolfgang Treue, *Deutsche Parteiprogramme seit 1861* (4th edn., Göttingen: Musterschmidt, 1968); Felix Salomon, *Die deutschen*

Parteiprogramme (Leipzig: Teubner, 1907–30); Dieter Fricke (ed.) *Lexikon der Parteiengeschichte. Die bürgerlichen und kleinbürgerlichen Parteien und Verbände in Deutschland (1789–1945)*, 4 vols. (Leipzig: Bibliographisches Institut, 1983 ff.). The most valuable monographs are: Hans Booms, *Die Deutsch- Konservative Partei* (Düsseldorf: Droste, 1954); Karl Buchheim, *Geschichte der Christlichen Parteien in Deutschland* (Munich: Kösel, 1963); Geoff Eley, "Some Thoughts on the Nationalist Pressure Groups in Imperial Germany" and David Blackbourn, "Roman Catholics, the Centre Party and Anti-Semitism in Imperial Germany", both in Paul Kennedy and Anthony Nicholls (eds.) *Nationalist and Racialist Movements in Britain and Germany Before 1914* (London: Macmillan, 1981).

On economic and social groups: Hans-Jürgen Puhle, *Agrarische Interessenpolitik und preussischer Konservatismus im Wilhelminischen Reich, 1893–1914* (2nd edn., Bonn: Neue Gesellschaft, 1975); ibid., *Von der Agrarkrise zum Präfaschismus. Thesen zum Stellenwert der agrarischen Interessenverbände in der deutschen Politik am Ende des 19. Jahrhunderts* (Wiesbaden, 1972). Shulamit Volkov, *The Rise of Popular Antimodernism in Germany. The Case of the Urban Master Artisans, 1873–1896* (Princeton: Princeton University Press, 1978); Robert Gellately, *The Politics of Economic Despair. Shopkeepers and German Politics, 1890–1914* (London: Sage, 1974); Siegfried Mielke, *Der Hansa-Bund für Gewerbe, Handel und Industrie, 1909–1914* (Göttingen: Vandenhoek & Rupprecht, 1976); Heinrich August Winkler, "Der rückversicherte Mittelstand: Die Interessenverbände von Handwerk und Kleinhandel im deutschen Kaiserreich" in W. Rüegg & O. Neuloh (eds.) *Zur soziologischen Theorie und Analyse des 19. Jahrhunderts* (Göttingen: Vandenhoek & Rupprecht, 1971); ibid., *Mittelstand, Demokratie und Nationalsozialismus. Die politische Entwicklung von Handwerk und Kleinhandel in der Weimarer Republik* (Cologne: Kiepenheuer & Wietsch, 1972); William W. Hagen, *Germans, Poles and Jews. The Nationality Conflict in the Prussian East, 1772–1914* (Chicago: Chicago University Press, 1980); Iris Hamel, *Völkischer Verband und nationale Gewerkschaft. Der deutschnationale Handlungsgehilfen-Verband* (Frankfurt: Europäische Verlagsanstalt, 1967); Uwe Lohalm, *Völkischer Radikalismus. Die Geschichte des deutschvölkischen Schutz- und Trutzbundes, 1919–1923* (Hamburg: Leibniz, 1870); Hartmut Becker, *Antisemitismus in der*

344

deutschen Turnerschaft (St. Augustin: H. Richarz, 1980); Gary D. Stark, *Entrepreneurs of Ideology. Neo-Conservative Publishers in Germany, 1890–1933* (Chapel Hill: University Press of North Carolina, 1981).

On Jews and the armed forces see Karl Demeter, *The German Officer Corps in State and Society, 1650–1945* (London: Weidenfeld & Nicolson, 1965); Herbert Rumschöttel, *Das bayerische Offizierkorps, 1866–1914* (Berlin: Duncker & Humblot, 1967); and two articles by Werner T. Angress, "Prussia's Army and the Jewish Reserve Officer Controversy before World War I" and "The German Army's 'Judenzählung': Genesis, Consequences, Significance" in *Leo Baeck Year Books* XVII (1972) and XXIII (1978) respectively. On Jews and anti-Semitism in higher education: Monika Richarz, *Der Eintritt der Juden in die akademischen Berufe. Jüdische Studenten und Akademiker in Deutschland, 1678–1848* (Tübingen: J. C. B. Mohr, 1974); Fritz K. Ringer, *The Decline of the German Mandarins. The German Academic Community, 1890–1933* (Cambridge: Harvard University Press, 1969); Konrad Jarausch, *Students, Society and Politics in Imperial Germany. The Rise of Academic Illiberalism* (Princeton: Princeton University Press, 1982); Norbert Kampe, *Studenten und "Judenfrage" im Deutschen Kaiserreich* (Göttingen, Vandenhoeck & Rupprecht, 1988); Michael H. Kater, *Studentenschaft und Rechtsradikalismus 1918 bis 1933. Eine sozialgeschichtliche Studie zur Bildungskrise in der Weimarer Republik* (Hamburg: Hoffmann & Kampe, 1975); Michael S. Steinberg, *Sabers and Brown Shirts. The German Students' Path to National Socialism, 1918–1935* (Chicago: Chicago University Press, 1977); Gabrielle Michalski, *Der Antisemitismus im deutschen akademischen Leben in der Zeit nach dem ersten Weltkrieg* (Frankfurt: Lang, 1980).

On parties and political movements in the Weimar period the most important relevant literature is: Armin Mohler, *Die konservative Revolution in Deutschland, 1919–1932. Ein Handbuch* (2nd ed., Darmstadt: Wissenschaftliche Buchgesellschaft, 1972); Klemens von Klemperer, *Germany's New Conservatism. Its History and Dilemma in the Twentieth Century* (Princeton: Princeton University Press, 1973); Kurt Sontheimer, *Antidemokratisches Denken in der Weimarer Republik. Die politischen Gedanken des deutschen Nationalismus zwischen 1918 und 1933* (Munich: Nymphenburger Verlag, 1962); Martin Broszat, "Die völkische Idee und

der Nationalsozialismus", *Deutsche Rundschau,* 1958; Robert H. Phelps, "Before Hitler Came": Thule Society and Germanen-Orden", *Journal of Modern History,* 1963; Lewis Hertzmann, *DNVP. Right-Wing Opposition in the Weimar Republic* (Lincoln: Nebraska University Press, 1963); Jan Striesow, *Die Deutsch-nationale Volkspartei und die Völkisch-Radikalen, 1918–1922* (Frankfurt: Haag & Herchen, 1981); Bruce B. Frye, *Liberal Democrats and the Weimar Republic. The History of the German Democratic Party and the German State Party* (Carbondale and Edmondsville: Illinois University Press, 1985); George L. Mosse, *Germans and Jews. The Right, the Left and the Search for a "Third Force" in Pre-Nazi Germany* (New York: Orbach & Chambers, 1970). See also, Hamburger and Pulzer, para.3. The best studies of the rise of the Nazi party are regional, e.g. William S. Allen, *The Nazi Seizure of Power. The Experience of a Single German Town* (Chicago: Chicago University Press, 1965); Jeremy Noakes, *The Nazi Party in Lower Saxony, 1921–1933* (Oxford: Oxford University Press, 1971); Geoffrey Pridham, *Hitler's Rise to Power. The Nazi Movement in Bavaria, 1923–1933* (London: Hart-Davis & MacGibbon, 1973); Richard Bessel, *Political Violence and the Rise of Nazism* (New Haven: Yale University Press, 1984).
8. On the attitude of the churches to Jews and anti-Semitism there are now numerous scholarly accounts: Karl Heinrich Rengstorff and Siegfried von Kortzfleisch (eds.) *Kirche und Synagoge. Handbuch zur Geschichte von Christen und Juden* (Stuttgart: Klett, 1968–70), in particular for the contributions by Rudolf Lill, "Die deutschen Katholiken und die Juden in der Zeit von 1860 bis zur Machtübernahme Hitlers" and Erika Weinzierl, "Katholizismus in Österreich"; Uriel Tal, *Christians and Jews in Germany. Religion, Politics and Ideology in the Second Reich, 1870–1914* (Ithaca: Cornell University Press, 1975); Ernst Heinen, "Antisemitische Strömungen im politischen Katholizismus während des Kulturkampfes" in Ernst Heinen and Hans-Joachim Schoeps (eds.) *Geschichte in der Gegenwart. Festschrift für Kurt Kluxen zu seinem 60. Geburtstag* (Paderborn: Schöningh, 1972); Hermann Greive, *Theologie und Ideologie. Katholizismus und Judentum in Deutschland und Österreich* (Heidelberg: Lambert Schneider, 1969); Richard Gutteridge, *Open Thy Mouth for the Dumb. The German Evangelical Church and the Jews, 1879–1950* (Oxford: Basil Blackwell, 1976); J. R. C. Wright, *"Above*

Parties". *The Political Attitudes of the German Church Leadership,*
1918–1933 (Oxford: Oxford University Press, 1974). Stefan Lehr,
*Antisemitismus—religiöse Motive im sozialen Vorurteil. Aus der
Frühgeschichte des Antisemitismus in Deutschland 1870–1914* (Munich,
1974).
9. The literature on Austria is growing, but is still a fraction of
that on Germany. *Studia Judaica Austriaca* (Eisenstadt, 1974–) has
numerous interesting articles, but mainly on earlier periods. Two
of the most significant works are unpublished, Dirk van Arkel,
Antisemitism in Austria (Proefschrift, Leiden, 1966) and J. C. P.
Warren, *The Political Career and Influence of Georg Ritter von
Schönerer* (Ph.D. dissertation, London, 1963). Nicholaus Vielmetti
(ed.) *Das österreichische Judentum. Voraussetzungen und Geschichte*
(Vienna: Verlag Jugend und Volk, 1974) and Joseph Fraenkel
(ed.) *The Jews of Austria. Essays on their Life, History and
Destruction* (London: Valentine, Mitchell, 1967) both contain
relevant contributions. Older books on the situation of the Jews
include Hans Tietze, *Die Juden Wiens* (Leipzig: Tal, 1933) and
Joseph Bloch, *Erinerrungen aus meinem Leben* (Vienna: Löwitt,
1922) are valuable.
   Among the flood of recent books, Marsha L. Rozenblit, *The
Jews of Vienna 1867–1914. Assimilation and Identity* (Albany: State
University of New York Press, 1985), Steven Beller, *Vienna and
the Jews, 1867–1938. A Cultural History* (Cambridge: Cambridge
University Press, 1988) and Ivar Oxaal, Michael Pollak and
Gerhard Botz (eds.) *Jews, Antisemitism and Culture in Vienna*
(London: Routledge & Kegan Paul, 1987), with chapters on the
pre-1918, inter-war and post-1945 periods, are outstanding. See
also Ivar Oxaal & Walter R. Waitzmann, "The Jews in Pre-1914
Vienna: An Exploration of Basic Sociological Dimensions", *Leo
Baeck Year Book XXX* (1985) and relevant contributions by
Brigitte Hamann and Peter Pulzer in Peter Berner (ed.) *Wien um
1900. Aufbruch in die Moderne* (Vienna: Verlag für Geschichte und
Politik, 1986).
   On the Christian Social movement there is now John W.
Boyer, *Political Radicalism in Late Imperial Vienna. Origins of the
Christian Social Movement, 1848–1897* (Chicago: Chicago Univer-
sity Press, 1981), of which a second volume is promised, and ibid.,
"Karl Lueger and the Viennese Jews" in *Leo Baeck Year Book
XXVI* (1981); Richard S. Geehr (ed.) *"I decide who is a Jew!"*

The Papers of Dr. Karl Lueger (Washington, DC: University Press of America, 1982)—not very revelatory; Isaak Arie Hellwing, *Der konfessionelle Antisemitismus im 19. Jahrhundert in Österreich* (Vienna-Freiburg, 1972). Older books containing important material are Wiard Klopp, *Leben und Wirken des Sozialpolitikers Karl Freiherr von Vogelsang* (Vienna: Typographische Anstalt, 1930), Rudolf Kuppe, *Karl Lueger und seine Zeit* (Vienna: Österreichische Volksschriften, 1923) and Friedrich Funder's memoirs, *Vom Gestern ins Heute* (2nd edn., Vienna: Herold, 1953).

On the German-nationalist movement Andrew G. Whiteside, *The Socialism of Fools. Georg von Schönerer and Austrian Pan-Germanism* (Berkeley–Los Angeles: University of California Press, 1975) and ibid., *Austrian National Socialism before 1918* (The Hague: Martinus Nijhoff, 1962) are exemplary. Also Bruce F. Pauley, *Hitler and the Forgotten Nazis. A History of Austrian National Socialism* (Chapel Hill: North Carolina University Press, 1981). Older important books are Paul Molisch, *Geschichte der deutschnationalen Bewegung Österreichs* (Jena: Georg Fischer, 1926) and Eduard Pichl's turgid but detailed *Georg Schönerer und die Entwicklung des Alldeutschtums in Österreich* (2nd edn., Munich: Oldenburg, 1938).

On the general political and intellectual atmosphere in pre-1918 Austria, Albert Fuchs, *Geistige Strömungen in Österreich, 1867–1918* (Vienna, 1949, reprinted: Vienna: Löcker, 1984); William J. McGrath, *Dionysian Art and Populist Politics in Austria* (New Haven: Yale University Press, 1974) and Carl E. Schorske, *Fin-de-Siècle Vienna. Politics and Culture* (New York: Knopf, 1980).

On the inter-war period: Alfred Diamant, *Austrian Catholics and the First Republic* (Princeton: Princeton University Press, 1960); F.L. Carsten, *Fascist Movements in Austria. From Schönerer to Hitler* (London: Sage, 1977) and the rather more idiosyncratic study by Martin Kitchen, *The Coming of Austrian Fascism* (London: Croom Helm, 1980); Clifton E. Edmondson, *The Heimwehr and Austrian Politics, 1918–1936* (Athens: University of Georgia Press, 1978); Walter Wiltschegg, *Die Heimwehr. Eine unwiderstehliche Volksbewegung?* (Munich: Oldenburg, 1985); S. Maderegger, *Die Juden im österreichischen Ständestaat 1934–1938* (Vienna: Geyer, 1973); Anton Pelinka, *Stand oder Klasse? Die*

Christliche Arbeiterbewegung Österreichs 1933–1938 (Vienna: Europa-Verlag, 1972). John Haag, "The Spann Circle and the Jewish Question", *Leo Baeck Year Book* XVIII (1973).

For Hungary, Randolph L. Braham (ed.) *Hungarian-Jewish Studies* (New York: World Federation of Hungarian Jews, 1966); Wolfdieter Bihl, *Das Judentum Ungarns, 1780–1914*, Studia Judaica Austriaca III (Eisenstadt, 1977); Nathaniel Katzburg, *Hungary and the Jews, Policy and Legislation, 1920–1943* (Ramat Gan: Bar Ilan University Press, 1981); Andrew Handler, *Blood Libel at Tiszaeszlar* (New York: Columbia University Press, 1980).

On the Czech crown-lands, Hillel J. Kieval, *The Making of Czech Jewry. Conflict and Jewish Society in Bohemia, 1870–1918* (New York: Oxford University Press, 1987); Gary B. Cohen, *The Politics of Ethnic Survival. Germans in Prague, 1861–1918* (Princeton: Princeton University Press, 1981) is also useful; as is Ferdinand Seibt (ed.) *Die Juden in den böhmischen Ländern* (Munich: Oldenbourg, 1983), which includes essays on assimilation, economic life and the First Republic.

On Galicia see Wolfgang Häusler, *Das Galizische Judentum in der Habsburger Monarchie* (Munich: Oldenbourg 1979) and Frank Golczewski, "Rural anti-Semitism in Galicia before World War I" in Chimen Abramsky et al. (eds.) *The Jews in Poland* (Oxford: Basil Blackwell, 1986).

10. The relationship between the Socialist movement and Jews and anti-Semitism continues to stimulate research and controversy. See Robert S. Wistrich, *Socialism and the Jews. The Dilemmas of Assimilation in Germany and Austria–Hungary* (London: Associated University Press, 1982), learned and comprehensive; Edmund Silberner, *Sozialisten zur Judenfrage* (Berlin: Colloquium Verlag, 1962) and *Kommunisten zur Judenfrage. Zur Geschichte von Theorie und Praxis des Kommunismus* (Opladen: Westdeutscher Verlag, 1983), informative but schematic. The best recent surveys on the pre-World War I period are: Walter Grab (ed.) *Juden und jüdische Aspekte in der deutschen Arbeiterbewegung 1848–1918* (Tel-Aviv: Tel-Aviv University, 1977); Rosemarie Leuschen-Seppel, *Sozialdemokratie und Antisemitismus im Kaiserreich. Die Auseinandersetzungen der Partei mit den konservativen und völkischen Strömungen des Antisemitismus, 1871–1914* (Bonn: Neue Gesellschaft, 1978); Shlomo Avineri, "Marx and Jewish Emancipation", *Journal of the History of Ideas* (July, 1964);

Arno Herzig, "The Role of Antisemitism in the Early Years of the Workers' Movement", *Leo Baeck Year Book* XXVI (1981); Robert S. Wistrich, "Anti-Capitalism or Antisemitism? The Case of Franz Mehring", *Leo Baeck Year Book* XXII (1977); ibid., "Victor Adler: A Viennese Socialist against Philosemitism", *The Wiener Library Bulletin*, n.s. 32 (1974); ibid., "Austrian Social Democracy and Anti-semitism, 1890–1914", *Jewish Social Studies,* Summer–Fall, 1975. Avraham Barkai, "The Austrian Social Democrats and the Jews", *The Wiener Library Bulletin*, n.s. 18–19, (1970), and the chapter by John Bunzl in Gerhard Botz et al, (eds.), *Bewegung und Klasse. Studien zur österreichischen Arbeitergeschichte* (Vienna: 1978).

The most important studies on Jews active in the Socialist movement are: Robert S. Wistrich, *Revolutionary Jews from Marx to Trotsky* (London: Harrap, 1976); Shlomo Na'aman, *Ferdinand Lassalle* (Hanover: Verlag für Literatur und Zeitgeschehen, 1970); J. P. Nettl, *Rosa Luxemburg* (Oxford: Oxford University Press, 1966); Franz Schade, *Kurt Eisner und die bayerische Sozialdemokratie* (Hanover: Verlag für Literatur und Zeitgeschehen, 1961); Kenneth R. Calkins, *Hugo Haase. Democrat and Revolutionary* (Chapel Hill, University Press of North Carolina, 1979); Werner T. Angress, "'Between Baden and Luxemburg'—Jewish Socialists on the Eve of World War I", *Leo Baeck Year Book* XXII (1977); Charlotte Beradt, *Paul Levi. Ein demokratischer Sozialist in der Weimarer Republik* (Frankfurt: Europäische Verlagsanstalt, 1969); see also the works in para. 2.

On the inter-war period: Donald L. Niewyk, *Socialist, Anti-Semite and Jew. Social Democracy Confronts the Problem of Anti-Semitism, 1918–1933* (Baton Rouge: Louisiana State University Press, 1971); Hans-Helmut Knütter, *Die Juden und die deutsche Linke in der Weimarer Republik, 1918–1933* (Düsseldorf: Droste, 1971); George L. Mosse, "German Socialists and the Jews in the Weimar Republic", *Leo Baeck Year Book* XVI (1971). For analyses of Jewish intellectuals and the Left, see above all Istvan Deak, *Weimar Germany's Intellectuals* (Berkeley & Los Angeles: University of California Press, 1968); Peter Gay, *Weimar Culture. The Outsider as Insider* (New York: Harper & Row, 1968) and Martin Jay, *The Dialectical Imagination. A History of the Frankfurt School and the Institute of Social Research* (Boston: Little, Brown, 1973).

INDEX

Index

356